Facets
Non-Violent, Non-Sexist
Children's Video Guide

Compiled by Virginia A. Boyle

Facets Multimedia, Inc./Academy Chicago Publishers
Chicago

© 1996 Facets Multimedia, Inc.

Published by: Facets Multimedia, Inc.
                                      1517 W. Fullerton Avenue
                                      Chicago, IL 60614

Printed and bound in the U.S.A.

Distributed to the trade by: Academy Chicago Publishers
                                     363 W. Erie Street
                                     Chicago, IL 60610

Library of Congress Cataloging-in-Publication Data

Facets non-violent, non-sexist children's video guide / compiled by Virginia A.
Boyle.
    p. cm.
    Includes bibliographical references and indexes.
    ISBN 0-89733-420-5
    1. Video recordings for children — Catalogs.   I. Boyle, Virginia A.,
1952 -
PN1992.945.F23   1996   95-43580
011'.37--dc20   CIP

Contents

Upfront...i

The Facets Non-Violent, Non-Sexist Children's Video Guide............................1

Title Index..167

Age Index 179

Listing of Subject Areas 195

Subject Index 197

Author Index...227

Resources 231

Acknowledgments

This book was edited by Laurie Chapkin, Nicole Dreiske, Catherine Foley, Pamela Masco, Hope Anne Nathan and Milos Stehlik. Special thanks to Anita and Jordan Miller of Academy Chicago Publishers, to Dr. Judith Arcana and Dr. Minnie Bruce Pratt of the Union Institute, and to those who helped evaluate the videos for this guide: Susana Aguilar of Project Heal, Ed Pino of Orozco School, Michael Wilson, Martha Leaf, and Claire Oxtoby of the University of Chicago Lab School, Juanita Saucedo of Kanoon Magnet School, Myrna Alvarez of the Casa Aztlan After School Program, Ed and Kailin Husayko, David Hernandez, Batya, Hannah and Jeff Goldman, Helen Gramates, Natasha and Nika Maurody, Cynthia Gallaher, Carlos and Julian Cumpian.

Our thanks to the many distributors, producers, video publishers and individuals who provided stills and illustrations and who are individually identified in the captions, and to Sara Downey of Academy Chicago Publishers and to Streamline Studios for cover design.

Upfront

"What's particularly exciting about video is that it enables us to provide choices for our children. We have to help parents find what's available so they can lobby libraries and video stores to carry it." — Peggy Charren, former president of Action for Children's Television.

Facets Non-Violent, Non-Sexist Children's Video Guide is written for everyone who cares about what children watch and how it affects them.

For twenty years, Facets has shown great films and videos to children through The Chicago International Children's Film Festival, and the Chicago Children's Film Center. During that time, hundreds of parents asked us, "How can I find *on video* the kinds of children's films you show here?" This book is the answer to their call for help.

Navigating through the thousands of children's videos that flood the supermarkets, video stores and fast food chains has become a near-impossible challenge for parents. The sheer volume of video products means that adults could spend hours each day just trying to orient themselves to the market. Yet amid all the cartoons, new releases and action-adventures are hidden gems that may not be obvious from their packages.

We decided to make the world of children's video a little easier for every adult who wants to find the very best in non-sexist, non-violent video programs.

Every video in this book has passed "child safe" criteria for violence, sexism and racial, ethnic and religious stereotyping. Facets focused on finding videos that:
- promote positive images of boys and girls
- offer models for alternative dispute resolution
- show positive ways to manage, face and overcome violence and sexism in life.

You may be surprised: many award-winning videos and timeless classics failed the "child safe" test.

In May 1993, the American Academy of Pediatrics (AAP) warned, "For parents, the only two alternatives that now exist are either to allow their children to watch television and be exposed to violence, or to turn the television off...."

There is an alternative — with home video, parents can choose videos that offer positive images of the richness and diversity of life. Careful selection by parents can help children distinguish between desirable and undesirable traits and actions. For example: positive, televised programs can promote positive social behavior, such as helping, sharing, cooperation, self-control and tolerance for frustration and delay.

The AAP has recommended that families participate in the selection of programs children watch. As often as possible, watch television and video *with* children.

Actively entering the world of your child's television and video viewing buffers the impact of what they see and helps children to develop articulation skills and storytelling abilities. *Discussing* videos with children can also help them verbalize feelings, and boost their self esteem.

Video can expand children's horizons, increase their awareness of the outside world and provide them with positive role-models outside the family. It can become a vehicle for improving parent/child communication.

We have deliberately searched for and included videos that inform children about people and cultures who are under represented on television. By choosing carefully, adults can provide children with positive media images of many people from diverse races, religions and economic backgrounds.

This *Guide* has been created to help parents use video as a positive force in children's lives. Each title includes a description of the video, an age-range recommendation, the running time and current purchase price.

SIMPLE STEPS FOR SELECTING THE BEST:

- This guide is organized **alphabetically by title** with several indices.
- A good way to start is to look for videos that have been recommended for the **age range** of your child.
- You can use the **subject index** to help you find good titles on themes of particular interest to you or your child.
- Look at the subject heading called **"Book-Based"** to find videos based on children's literature.

YOU MAY WANT TO KNOW:

- In certain descriptions, we recommend that an adult watch a particular video *with* the childen. This may be because the theme is scary, or the plot or characters need some explanation.
- We have also pointed out scenes which may be upsetting to children and which occur in some popular, well-known videos such as *The Maurice Sendak Library*, and *The Amazing Bone & Other Stories.*
- A number of recommended tapes are packaged with violent commercials preceeding the start-up of the feature. It's best to cue-up tapes to the start of the feature.

If you want to keep up with what is happening in children's video, check the "Recommended Resources" section of this *Guide*. It includes the names of publications which review children's video. You can also join the growing national and international network of people involved in children's media issues. We've listed a wide range of organizations that offer children's media services and programs. If you are one of the millions of parents who care about what your children watch, find out what these organizations do, and get involved!

Many of the videos included in this *Guide* will be available at your local video store, but if you can't find a video we've listed, call us at 1-800-331-6197. All of these videos are currently available for sale from Facets Video and many of them are available for rent-by-mail.

Videos originally created for an educational market have typically charged a higher price than mass market videos created for home entertainment. This is reflected in the higher-than-normal prices indicated for some of the videos listed in the *Guide*. As the distinctions between education and entertainment disappear, video pricing is changing dramatically. Like any other product, video prices can be expected to change over time and titles do go out of print.

Videos that are available with Public Performance Rights are so listed and described.

AGE RECOMMENDATIONS INDEX:

Age recommendations have more to do with which age group will best *appreciate* a video. The age recommendations included in the *Guide* are general guidelines based on our observations of children watching each video. Unless specifically noted in the video description, all videos in the book are considered "child-safe" and acceptable for children under age 12.

TODDLERS / Videos suitable for birth through age 3

STARTING SCHOOL / Videos suitable for ages 4-5

PRIMARY GRADES 1-3 / Videos suitable for ages 6-9

INTERMEDIATE GRADES 4-6 / Videos suitable for ages 10-12

Each year, enormous numbers of videos are produced for the children's market. We hope that this *Guide* will make it easier for parents, teachers and caregivers to select the best for their children. As you use this book, please know that we welcome your suggestions, experiences and insights.

Facets Non-Violent, Non-Sexist Children's Video Guide

Abuela's Weave

Esperanza's grandmother is a traditional Mayan weaver. Because the grandmother is afraid that the birthmark on her face may frighten off buyers, the girl goes out to sell the tapestries by herself. Based on the story by Omar S. Casteneda. 12 minutes. Age Recommendation: S (Starting school, starting to read, starting pre-school, starting kindergarten; Ages 4-5); P (Primary grades, grades 1-3; Ages 6-9); I (Intermediate grades, grades 4-6; Ages 10-12).

VHS: S21884. $44.95.

African Story Magic

Brock Peters narrates the tale about a young child's odyssey from urban life to discover the power and wonder of ancient African folklore and ritual. 27 minutes. Age Recommendation: S (Starting school, starting to read, starting pre-school, starting kindergarten; Ages 4-5); P (Primary grades, grades 1-3; Ages 6-9).

VHS: S17765. $12.98.

Afro-Classic Folk Tales

This collection of folk tales promotes positive self-affirming values among all children.

Afro-Classic Folk Tales, Volume 1
Storyteller Sybil Destu tells two traditional folk tales about Anansi the spider and Tiger. Animated. 30 minutes. Age Recommendation: T (Toddler; Ages Birth-3 years); S (Starting school, starting to read, starting pre-school, starting kindergarten; Ages 4-5); P (Primary grades, grades 1-3; Ages 6-9).
VHS: S20620. $29.95.

Afro-Classic Folk Tales, Volume 2
This second installment of *Afro-Classic Folk Tales* includes animated stories of Brer Rabbit and Woodpecker, as well as an old African tale told with puppets. 30 minutes. Age Recommendation: T (Toddler; Ages Birth-3 years); S (Starting school, starting to read, starting pre-school, starting kindergarten; Ages 4-5); P (Primary grades, grades 1-3; Ages 6-9).
VHS: S20621. $29.95.

Alejandro's Gift

Based on the book by Richard E. Albert. Alejandro is an old man living alone in the desert. He plants a garden and is visited by desert animals searching for water. He digs a well as a gift to all the desert animals. 8 minutes. Age Recommendation: S (Starting school, starting to read, starting pre-school, starting kindergarten; Ages 4-5); P (Primary grades, grades 1-3; Ages 6-9).
VHS: S22345. $39.95.

Alexander and the Terrible, Horrible, No Good, Very Bad Day

Based on the best-selling book by Judith Viorst about Alexander's bad day. With one disaster after the next, Alexander comes to see that some days are just like that. With music by Charles Strouse. 30 minutes. Age Recommendation: S (Starting school, starting to read, starting pre-school, starting kindergarten; Ages 4-5); P (Primary grades, grades 1-3; Ages 6-9).
VHS: S23276. $12.95.

Alice Walker (1944-Present) — Author

From *The Black Americans of Achievement Series, Set II*. This video is based upon the acclaimed book by Jack Rummel, drawing from the expertise of a brilliant group of consultants and experts. Alice Walker is well known for her

Pulitzer Prize-winning novel, *The Color Purple*. This is the story of her life, including her involvement in Civil Rights demonstrations in Atlanta in the 1960's. This video also touches on the subject of women's equality and deals with historical violence in a positive manner. 30 minutes. Age Recommendation: I (Intermediate grades, grades 4-6; Ages 10-12).

VHS: S24103. $39.95.

All About ABC's

Children have fun visiting Alphabet Land with Letter Lizard and Magic Man. 30 minutes. Age Recommendation: T (Toddler; Ages Birth-3 years); S (Starting school, starting to read, starting pre-school, starting kindergarten; Ages 4-5).

VHS: S24359. $6.99.

Alphabet Library

A child's home and world become a library where things familiar to children are presented in an alphabetical review. Each volume of this series is 30 minutes. Age Recommendation: T (Toddler; Ages Birth-3 years); S (Starting school, starting to read, starting pre-school, starting kindergarten; Ages 4-5).

Alphabet City.
VHS: S10319. $29.95.

Alphabet House.
VHS: S10321. $29.95.

Alphabet Zoo.
VHS: S10322. $29.95.

Amazing Bone and Other Stories, The

Based on the book by William Steig. The adventures of various humans and animals are shown in this collection of four award-winning animated films based on favorite children's literature. The title piece, narrated by John Lithgow, is about a young pig who spends her time with a talking bone. Warning — though the end is happy, the section where the wolf leads the little girl pig to her death is frightening and morbid. 30 minutes. Age Recommendation: P (Primary grades, grades 1-3; Ages 6-9).

VHS: S11226. $14.95.

Amazing Things

Dr. Misterio is a magician and a prankster. He encourages children to participate in the creative process by turning household objects into toys and performing feats of magic. Interactive, make-it-yourself magic, perfect for parties and rainy afternoons. Age Recommendation: P (Primary grades, grades 1-3; Ages 6-9); I (Intermediate grades, grades 4-6; Ages 10-12).

Amazing Things, Volume 1.
56 minutes.
VHS: S13070. $9.98.

Amazing Things, Volume 2.
55 minutes.
VHS: S13071. $9.98.

American Women of Achievement Video Collection

This is a ten-part video series celebrating the lives and accomplishments of outstanding women. Spanning a two-hundred year period, the series explores the thoughts, hopes and accomplishments of women who were and are the best in their fields, leaders of their generation. Each program includes archival film footage, still photographs, letters and poems. Historians and women's studies experts act as guides. These biographies were designed for classroom use. 30 minutes each video. Age Recommendation: I (Intermediate grades, grades 4-6; Ages 10-12).

Abigail Adams (1744-1818) — Women's Rights Advocate
She was the first woman to live in the White House and witnessed first hand many important events that shaped the early years of the U.S. Her letters to her husband, President John Adams, offered counsel and support during the turbulent times before and during the American Revolution.
VHS: S24436. $39.95.

Jane Addams (1860-1935) — Social Worker
Born into prosperity, Jane Addams dedicated her life to the millions who crowded the 19th century slums of the U.S. Her social programs lifted families out of poverty and gave them tools to improve their own lives. She worked for peace, reform of child-labor laws, women's rights and the protection of civil liberties.
VHS: S24437. $39.95.

Marian Anderson (1902-1993) — Singer
Her great voice toppled barriers of racial prejudice, and she became an internationally renowned singer. She blazed a trail for other African

American artists. She established a scholarship program for vocalists of all races and served as a member of the U.S. delegation to the United Nations.
VHS: S24438. $39.95.

Susan B. Anthony (1820-1906) — Woman Suffragist
In addition to her work for women's suffrage, Susan B. Anthony fought against slavery and for civil rights. She worked as a school teacher who was willing to go to jail for her beliefs and she is remembered as a pioneering U.S. feminist.
VHS: S24439. $39.95.

Clara Barton (1821-1912) — Founder, American Red Cross
Called "the angel of the battlefield," Clara Barton claimed a place in history by going into battlefields to nurse wounded soldiers during the Civil War. She dedicated her life to founding the American Red Cross.
VHS: S24440. $39.95.

Emily Dickinson (1830-1890) — Poet
Considered one of the great U.S. poets, Emily Dickinson lived a sheltered, reclusive life. While only a few of her poems were published during her lifetime, thousands were discovered after her death. Her poetry reflects her despair and explores images of faith.
VHS: S24441. $39.95.

Amelia Earhart (1897-Disappeared in 1937) — Aviator
She remains one of the most famous female aviators in history. Amelia Earhart was the first to fly solo across the Atlantic Ocean. Her accomplishments in the field of aviation opened doors previously closed to women.
VHS: S24442. $39.95.

Helen Keller (1880-1968) — Humanitarian
As an infant, a severe illness left Helen Keller blind and deaf, but she refused to let these disabilities prevent her from making her mark. Her success as a scholar and lecturer inspired many. She proved to the world that strength, determination and patience can overcome many obstacles.
VHS: S24443. $39.95.

Sandra Day O'Connor (1930-Present) — Supreme Court Justice
Sandra Day O'Connor grew up milking cows, riding horses and driving tractors. She began reading at age four and her studies brought her to careers in law and politics. She became the first woman to sit on the U.S. Supreme Court.
VHS: S24444. $39.95.

Wilma Rudolph (1940-Present) — Champion Athlete
This great athlete was born the twentieth of 22 children to a poor family in the segregated South. Though she was partially paralyzed by polio, her

determination helped her to walk. Later, she went on to win three Olympic gold medals in track and field.

VHS: S24445. $39.95.

American Women of Achievement 10 Volume Set.
VHS: S24446. $399.50.

Anansi (Rabbit Ears)

Reggae hit-makers UB40 and Oscar-winner Denzel Washington unite to recount the Jamaican/African tale of Anansi the spider, who outwits a prideful snake and wins all stories for himself. In the end, Anansi gets caught in his own web of lies and loses his hair in the process. 30 minutes. Age Recommendation: P (Primary grades, grades 1-3; Ages 6-9); I (Intermediate grades, grades 4-6; Ages 10-12).

VHS: S14454. $9.95.

Anansi
(Illustrated by Steve Guarnaccia/Rabbit Ears Productions)

Anansi Goes Fishing

In Eric A. Kimmel's story, illustrated by Janet Stevens, the spider Anansi accepts Turtle's invitation for a fishing trip. At first, Anansi thinks that Turtle will do all the work, but Anansi quickly learns otherwise. In the process, Anansi discovers how to fish and build nets. 11 minutes. Age Recommendation: S (Starting school, starting to read, starting pre-school, starting kindergarten; Ages 4-5); P (Primary grades, grades 1-3; Ages 6-9).

VHS: S20045. $36.95.

And the Children Shall Lead

A product of the Rainbow Television Workshop, this is the story of a young African American girl growing up during the Civil Rights movement. Set in Mississippi, the focus of the video is the role of children in the movement. This video deals with historical violence and inequality in a positive way. Featured actors include Danny Glover and Denise Nichols. From the Wonder-Works series. USA. 1984. 58 minutes. Age Recommendation: P (Primary grades, grades 1-3; Ages 6-9); I (Intermediate grades, grades 4-6; Ages 10-12).

VHS: S12404. $29.95.

Angela's Airplane (plus The Fire Station)

Angela wanders onto a huge empty plane, pushes some buttons and winds up flying it. Also included is the short story *The Fire Station*. Animated stories by Robert Munsch. 25 minutes. Age Recommendation: T (Toddler; Ages Birth-3 years); S (Starting school, starting to read, starting pre-school, starting kindergarten; Ages 4-5).

VHS: S24985. $12.95.

Animal Alphabet

This unique program takes kids around the globe. The video combines live-action animal photography with colorful animated letters. 30 minutes. Age Recommendation: T (Toddler; Ages Birth-3 years); S (Starting school, starting to read, starting pre-school, starting kindergarten; Ages 4-5).

VHS: S04134. $14.95.

Animal Babies in the Wild

Stories, songs and baby animal bloopers. 30 minutes. Age Recommendation: T (Toddler; Ages Birth-3 years); S (Starting school, starting to read, starting pre-school, starting kindergarten; Ages 4-5).

VHS: S04135. $14.95.

Animal Stories

A program of three animated stories: *Petunia, the Silly Goose, Andy and the Lion* and *Why Mosquitoes Buzz in People's Ears*, a story of how a tale is passed from animal to animal. Morton Schindel, USA, 1986. 35 minutes. Age Recommendation: S (Starting school, starting to read, starting pre-school, starting kindergarten; Ages 4-5); P (Primary grades, grades 1-3; Ages 6-9).

VHS: S00056. Currently out of print. May be available for rental in some video stores.

Animals Are Beautiful People

A program which looks at the creatures living in Africa. This documentary will fascinate and educate children with its magnificent footage. Filmmaker Jamie Uys, who also directed *The Gods Must Be Crazy*, spent four years filming African animals. 92 minutes. Age Recommendation: P (Primary grades, grades 1-3; Ages 6-9); I (Intermediate grades, grades 4-6; Ages 10-12).
VHS: S03886. $19.98.

Anna Maria's Blanket

Based on the book by Joanne Berken, Anna Maria explains to her blanket that she's starting nursery school, and the sad blanket can't join her. A sweet story about starting pre-school. 11 minutes. Age Recommendation: T (Toddler; Ages Birth-3 years); S (Starting school, starting to read, starting pre-school, starting kindergarten; Ages 4-5).
VHS: S22358. $39.95.

Anne of Green Gables

Based on the book by L.M. Montgomery. Canadian actress Megan Follows, Tony Award-winner Colleen Dewhurst and Richard Farnsworth are featured in this award-winning epic that follows the provocative life drama of Anne Shirley, an endearing orphan, from her struggles as an adolescent and her budding romantic interest, to the death of her adopted father and her triumphs as a young woman. Canada. 1986. 204 minutes. Age Recommendation: I (Intermediate grades, grades 4-6; Ages 10-12).
VHS: S05376. $59.95.

Annie Oakley (Rabbit Ears)

Keith Carradine reprises his prize-winning stage role of American humorist Will Rogers to narrate this spirited, wonderfully textured tale of Annie Oakley, the sharpshooter whose extraordinary skills made her the international star of Buffalo Bill's Famous Wild West Show, as well as one of the most famous women of her time. This excellent tale of the American West actively challenges stereotypes, presenting a very strong, positive female role model. The plight of Native Americans is well represented. The video shows sharpshooting as a non-violent sport. With a musical score by Los Lobos. 30 minutes. Age Recommendation: S (Starting school, starting to read, starting pre-school, starting kindergarten; Ages 4-5); P (Primary grades, grades 1-3; Ages 6-9); I (Intermediate grades, grades 4-6; Ages 10-12).
VHS: S17025. $9.95.

Are You My Mother?

Three wonderful, well-known stories by P.D. Eastman: *Are You My Mother?*, in which the little bird asks everyone the title question; the ever-popular *Go, Dog, Dog, Go!*, centered on the concepts of color and direction; and *The Best Nest*, in which Mr. and Mrs. Bird try out several strange homes. 25 minutes. Age Recommendation: T (Toddler; Ages Birth-3 years); S (Starting school, starting to read, starting pre-school, starting kindergarten; Ages 4-5).

English Version. VHS: S22016. $14.95.

Spanish Version: Eres Tu Mi Mama? VHS: S22015. $14.95.

Art Lessons for Children

Art teacher Donna Hugh demonstrates how easy it is to produce beautiful art projects using simple, inexpensive materials. Each volume includes several complete lessons. Age Recommendation: P (Primary grades, grades 1-3; Ages 6-9); I (Intermediate grades, grades 4-6; Ages 10-12).

Volume 1: Easy Watercolor Techniques
All you need is a box of watercolor paints, a brush, construction paper, a black crayon and a black felt-tipped pen for these four great lessons: *Watercolor Flowers*, *Watercolor Discovery*, *Desert Scene* and *Opaque Watercolors*. 50 minutes.
VHS: S16155. $29.95.

Volume 2: Easy Art Projects
These three lessons use a limited number of readily available materials to open the creative minds of children everywhere: *Working with Oil, Pastel, Foil Art* and *Printmaking*. 50 minutes.
VHS: S16156. $29.95.

Volume 3: More Fun with Watercolors
Four lessons in watercolors, using simple, commonplace materials. 53 minutes.
VHS: S17843. $29.95.

Volume 4: Felt Pen Fun
Four more lessons from art teacher Donna Hugh. 58 minutes.
VHS: S17844. $29.95.

Volume 5: Animals of the Rain Forest
The creatures who inhabit one of the earth's most fascinating environments provide the inspiration for this exploration of art techniques. 58 minutes.
VHS: S22089. $29.95.

Volume 6: Plants of the Rain Forest
In this tape, the first thing children do is see how plants grow in the rain forest. Then, art teacher Donna Hugh demonstrates techniques which can make beautiful artwork depicting these interesting and unusual plants. 48 minutes.
VHS: S21250. $29.95.

Astronomy 101: A Family Adventure

Subtitled *A Beginner's Guide to the Night Sky*, this video features Michelle and her mother as they explore the night sky together. Astronomy proves to be a fascinating family activity. It is refreshing to see the mother/daughter team as the focus of the activity. 25 minutes. Age Recommendation: P (Primary grades, grades 1-3; Ages 6-9); I (Intermediate grades, grades 4-6; Ages 10-12).
VHS: S24358. $19.95.

At Home in the Coral Reef

Based on the book by Katy Muzik. Kids look at the tropical coral reef and learn about the creatures who live there, including flashlight fish, feather duster worms and sea squirts. Viewers also find out how the coral reef fits in with the larger ocean environment. 12 minutes. Age Recommendation: P (Primary grades, grades 1-3; Ages 6-9); I (Intermediate grades, grades 4-6; Ages 10-12).
English Version. VHS: S22362. $39.95.
Spanish Version. VHS: S22363. $39.95.

At the Zoo

Viewers join a group of kids on their visit to the zoo. With charming songs. 30 minutes. Age Recommendation: T (Toddler; Ages Birth-3 years); S (Starting school, starting to read, starting pre-school, starting kindergarten; Ages 4-5).

VHS: S24595. $14.95.

Attic-in-the-Blue

An imaginative animated work about an ancient whaler who embarks on a dangerous mission to the Attic-in-the-Blue to find his lost love. He is helped by his octopus-like companion. Winner of 1992 Best Animated Film, Chicago International Children's Film Festival. 27 minutes. Age Recommendation: S (Starting school, starting to read, starting pre-school, starting kindergarten; Ages 4-5); P (Primary grades, grades 1-3; Ages 6-9).

VHS: S18930. $14.95.

Public Performance Rights. VHS: S18406. $39.95.

Baby Animal Fun

B

Live footage of baby animals interacting with kids. 30 minutes. USA, 1989. Age Recommendation: T (Toddler; Ages Birth-3 years); S (Starting school, starting to read, starting pre-school, starting kindergarten; Ages 4-5); P (Primary grades, grades 1-3; Ages 6-9).

VHS: S24596. $29.95.

Baby Animals Just Want to Have Fun

Peter Puppy, Raindance the Pony and other favorite baby animals romp around in five humorous adventure stories. Enchanting songs and live photography in this video will make children love baby animals even more. With music and dialogue. 30 minutes. Age Recommendation: T (Toddler; Ages Birth-3 years); S (Starting school, starting to read, starting pre-school, starting kindergarten; Ages 4-5).

VHS: S02996. $14.95.

Baby Goes...Songs to Take Along

Ten toe-tapping tunes celebrate and explore the joys of a child's everyday world. This live-action video follows a variety of children, ages one to six, as they practice counting, dress themselves, pack their toys on moving day, get ready for bed and more. A variety of musical styles — reggae, rock, rap, swing and lullaby — accompany the activities of the children. 30 minutes. Age Recommendation: T (Toddler; Ages Birth-3 years); S (Starting school, starting to read, starting pre-school, starting kindergarten; Ages 4-5).

VHS: S23943. $12.95.

Baby Songs Series

A very good series of live-action music videos for pre-schoolers. 30 minutes each. Age Recommendation: T (Toddler; Ages Birth-3 years); S (Starting school, starting to read, starting pre-school, starting kindergarten; Ages 4-5).

Baby Songs 1
Ten sing-alongs with singer/songwriter Hap Palmer including "Share," "Piggy Toes," and "Security." USA, 1987, 30 minutes.
VHS: S03520. $12.95.

Baby Songs 2: More Baby Songs
Hap Palmer returns! This video is geared toward the youngest viewers, showing how much fun the simplest activities can be.
VHS: S24337. $12.98.

Baby Songs: Even More Baby Songs
Ten charming songs by Hap Palmer that reach into a child's everyday life for their subject matter.
VHS: S24338. $12.98.

Baby Songs Christmas
Puppets and pageants bring these interesting multicultural Christmas sing-alongs to life.
VHS: S24597. $14.95.

Baby Songs Presents: Follow Along Songs with Hap Palmer
Children are encouraged to enact the lyrics to songs which include "The Mice Go Marching," "Parade of Sticks," and "Homemade Band." The songs also help kids learn colors, the alphabet and how to make musical instruments.
VHS: S24772. $12.98.

Baby Songs Presents: John Lithgow's Kid-Size Concert
Acoustic guitar, a wonderful actor and a chance to sing along. With "I Can Put My Clothes on By Myself," "Getting Up Time " and "What A Miracle I Am." A songbook is included with the video. 1990.
VHS: S24341. $12.98.

Baby Songs: Sing Together
Nine sing-alongs feature rhymes and melodies for musical playtime. 1992.
VHS: S24598. $14.95.

Baby Songs: Super Baby Songs
More great sing-along tunes with Hap Palmer.
VHS: S24340. $12.98.

Baby Vision

Produced in New Zealand, this is a fascinating series of films for very young children. Each volume is 45 minutes. Age Recommendation: T (Toddler; Ages Birth-3 years).

Baby Vision Volume 1
Volume 1 centers on soft images, a bit of narration and music related to toys and animals.
VHS: S24342. $14.95.

Baby Vision Volume 2
Volume 2 centers on soft images, a bit of narration and music related to motion, plants and liquids, such as waterfalls and juice being poured.
VHS: S24343. $14.95.

Baby's Bedtime

Folk singer Judy Collins invites young viewers on a gentle journey into dreamland with this new collection of best-loved lullabies. Tuck in a child to the beautiful animation and memorable melodies of "Hush Little Baby," "The Land of Nod," "Lullaby and Good Night" and other classics. Parents' Choice Award. 26 minutes. Age Recommendation: T (Toddler; Ages Birth-3 years); S (Starting school, starting to read, starting pre-school, starting kindergarten; Ages 4-5).
VHS: S11417. $12.98.
Public Performance Rights. VHS: S17148. $50.00.

Baby's Morningtime

Greet the day with a song and a smile as Judy Collins sings the works of Robert Browning, Emily Dickinson, Gertrude Stein and others. Enhanced by Ernest Troost's winsome score and Sesame Street's Daniel Ivanick's animation. 25 minutes. Age Recommendation: T (Toddler; Ages Birth-3 years); S (Starting school, starting to read, starting pre-school, starting kindergarten; Ages 4-5).

VHS: S17136. $12.98.

Public Performance Rights. VHS: S17149. $50.00.

Baby's Nursery Rhymes

Mother Goose gets a refreshing update in this animated version of Kay Chorao's *The Baby's Lap Book*, sung by Phylicia Rashad, star of *The Cosby Show*. Set to the sparkling contemporary music of Jason Miles. Honors include the California Book & Video Award, Parents' Choice Award, *TV Guide* Top 10 List for Children's Home Video, and Oppenheim Toy Portfolio Award. 26 minutes. Age Recommendation: T (Toddler; Ages Birth-3 years); S (Starting school, starting to read, starting pre-school, starting kindergarten; Ages 4-5).

VHS: S17137. $12.98.

Public Performance Rights. VHS: S17150. $50.00.

Baby-Sitters Club Videos

Based on the popular Scholastic books, these stories center on seven diverse girls who start a business and find that together they can solve any problem. Live-action. USA. 30 minutes. Age Recommendation: P (Primary grades, grades 1-3; Ages 6-9); I (Intermediate grades, grades 4-6; Ages 10-12).

The Baby-Sitters Club: The Baby-Sitters and the Boy Sitters
The boys start their own baby-sitting club!
VHS: S24345. $14.95.

The Baby-Sitters Club: The Baby-Sitters Remember
This video looks back, reviewing some of the best and funniest adventures of the Baby-Sitters.
VHS: S24349. $14.95.

The Baby-Sitters Club: Christmas Special (1991)
In this moving Christmas story, the girls go to a Christmas party at a hospital. After eating too many cookies, Stacey, one of the Baby-Sitters (who is also diabetic) has to enter the hospital herself.
VHS: S24356. $14.95.

The Baby-Sitters Club: Claudia and the Missing Jewels
The mystery unfolds when Claudia launches a jewelry-making business and a pair of earrings are stolen.
VHS: S24354. $14.95.

The Baby-Sitters Club: Claudia and the Mystery of the Secret Passage
Claudia follows the clues from a note found in a secret passage, as the Baby-Sitters hope to settle an ancient feud.
VHS: S24344. $14.95.

The Baby-Sitters Club: Dawn and the Dream Boy
In this story about dating, two sisters work through their discovery of plans to go to a teen dance with the same boy.
VHS: S24355. $14.95.

The Baby-Sitters Club: Dawn and the Haunted House
Dawn thinks Claudia is spending too much time with the neighborhood "witch" in this story about appreciating differences.
VHS: S24351. $14.95.

The Baby-Sitters Club: Dawn Saves the Trees
When the city plans to build a road through the local park, Dawn leads the Baby-Sitters in a fight to save the trees. The story also touches on responses to issues of recycling and conservation.
VHS: S24346. $14.95.

The Baby-Sitters Club: Jessi and the Mystery of the Stolen Secrets
The Baby-Sitters go undercover to find out who is stealing club secrets.
VHS: S24347. $14.95.

The Baby-Sitters Club: Kristy and the Great Campaign
A third-graders' bid for class president yields a look at self-concept and gender stereotypes.
VHS: S24353. $14.95.

The Baby-Sitters Club: Mary Ann and the Brunettes (1990)
Two girls' clubs find a rational way to work out their differences. The story also concerns two teenage girls working out the fact that they want to date the same boy.
VHS: S24350. $14.95.

The Baby-Sitters Club: Stacey Takes a Stand
The Baby-Sitters help Stacey figure out what to do when she is torn between her divorced mom and dad.
VHS: S24348. $14.95.

The Baby-Sitters Club: Stacey's Big Break
Stacey has a chance at fashion modeling. A dialogue ensues concerning priorities and anorexia.
VHS: S24352. $14.95.

Bach and Broccoli

Winner of the Best Film prize at the 1987 Chicago International Children's Film Festival, a truly wonderful film for children from Andre Melancon, the director of *The Dog Who Stopped the War*. In *Bach and Broccoli*, 11-year-old Fanny meets her uncle Jonathan for the first time when she comes to live with him. They are strong-willed, independent people who are worlds apart. Fanny's best friend, Broccoli, her pet skunk, adds to the hilarity in this tale of the odd couple as they learn to love and need each other. Full of smart girls, the film shows cooperation and conflict resolution between friends, children and adults. Produced by Rock Demers. Directed by Andre Melancon, Canada, 1987. 96 minutes. Age Recommendation: P (Primary grades, grades 1-3; Ages 6-9); I (Intermediate grades, grades 4-6; Ages 10-12).
VHS: S06616. $14.95.

Ballet Shoes

Refusing to let a money crunch hinder their ballet careers, three young girls decide to pursue their dreams. The possibilities and realities of fame and fortune are creatively displayed in this live-action film based on the Noel Streatfield children's novel of the same name. 120 minutes. Age Recommendation: P (Primary grades, grades 1-3; Ages 6-9); I (Intermediate grades, grades 4-6; Ages 10-12).
VHS: S12636. $29.95.

Barney and the Backyard Gang

Our evaluators found the Barney series to be appealing to children, while promoting positive messages. Made with a focus on quality, the videos combine favorite traditional songs and rhymes, live-action and animation. Actress Sandy Duncan plays Mom to kids Michael and Amy. The children and their neighborhood friends have a special pal, Barney the dinosaur, who magically comes to life to lead the Backyard Gang through various activities. Age Recommendation: T (Toddler; Ages Birth-3 years); S (Starting school, starting to read, starting pre-school, starting kindergarten; Ages 4-5).

Barney Goes to School
Barney and pals enjoy fingerpainting, creative learning and the search for Zippity the hamster. 1990. 30 minutes.
VHS: S24599. $14.95.

Barney in Concert
Barney and the 2 year-old Baby Bop perform fun songs which encourage interaction. 1991. 45 minutes.
VHS: S24600. $14.95.

Barney's Best Manners
Barney goes on a picnic which features songs and games that teach manners, including "Does Your Chewing Gum Lose Its Flavor," "Please and Thank You," and "Snackin' on Healthy Food." 30 minutes.
VHS: S24601. $14.95.

Barney's Birthday
Birthday songs and birthday customs from around the world. 1993. 30 minutes.
VHS: S24602. $14.95.

Barney's Campfire Sing-Along
Fun with camping, animals, stars and forest safety. 40 minutes.
VHS: S24603. $14.95.

Barney's Home Sweet Homes
Discover the variety of homes — homes for animals and homes for people — around the world and under the sea. 30 minutes.
VHS: S24604. $14.95.

Barney's Imagination Island
Fun with songs, rhymes and problem solving. Barney helps his friends go sailing and they discover a toy inventor who learns about sharing from the visitors. 1994. 48 minutes.
VHS: S24940. $19.99.

Barney's Magical Musical Adventure
When the Backyard Gang builds a sand castle, Barney takes them to a real castle. 1992. 48 minutes.
VHS: S24605. $14.95.

Barney's Safety Video
Kids join BJ, Barney and firefighter Frank to learn about important safety issues such as crossing the street and safety at home. 48 minutes.
VHS: S24942. $14.95.

Rock with Barney
Barney sings some of his favorite songs. 30 minutes.
VHS: S24606. $14.95.

Waiting for Santa
Barney and the Gang travel to the North Pole to learn the true meaning of Christmas. 1991. 30 minutes.
VHS: S24607. $14.95.

Barry's Scrapbook: A Window into Art

Join Barry Louis, a singer and writer of children's songs, as he visits an art museum and meets a collage artist, an illustrator and a sculptor. He sings about art and recyclables. 42 minutes. Age Recommendation: S (Starting school, starting to read, starting pre-school, starting kindergarten; Ages 4-5); P (Primary grades, grades 1-3; Ages 6-9); I (Intermediate grades, grades 4-6; Ages 10-12).
VHS: S22130. $26.95.

Basil Hears a Noise

A vigorous and heartwarming Muppets musical tale starring Basil and his friends. When they are trapped inside an enchanted forest, they must find the inner courage to overcome their fear and conquer their personal demons. Special appearance by Elmo, the furry red monster. 28 minutes. Age Recommendation: T (Toddler; Ages Birth-3 years); S (Starting school, starting to read, starting pre-school, starting kindergarten; Ages 4-5).
VHS: S19159. $12.98.

Beady Bear

Based on the book by Don Freeman; a stuffed bear realizes he needs more than just a cave — he needs love! 8 minutes. Age Recommendation: S (Starting school, starting to read, starting pre-school, starting kindergarten; Ages 4-5); P (Primary grades, grades 1-3; Ages 6-9).
VHS: S24508. $37.95.

Bear Who Slept Through Christmas, The

Little Ted E. Bear wants to discover the meaning of Christmas, while the rest of the town sleeps. 30 minutes. Age Recommendation: T (Toddler; Ages Birth-3 years); S (Starting school, starting to read, starting pre-school, starting kindergarten; Ages 4-5).
VHS: S24360. $12.98.

Beethoven Lives Upstairs

It is 1820's Vienna, and Ludwig Van Beethoven is desperately trying to compose his Ninth Symphony. As he struggles to balance his musical obsession with the reality of his increasing deafness, Beethoven rents the upstairs flat in the depressed household of ten-year-old Christoph. Beethoven swiftly turns Christoph's house into chaos. Live-action with brilliant music. David Devine, USA, 1990. 51 minutes. Age Recommendation: P (Primary grades, grades 1-3; Ages 6-9); I (Intermediate grades, grades 4-6; Ages 10-12). VHS: S16706. $19.98.

Berenstain Bears Videos

Based on the best-selling books by Jan and Stan Berenstain, these videos feature a charming bear family which works out problems in a thoughtful and entertaining manner. Animated. Each video is 20-30 minutes. Age Recommendation: S (Starting school, starting to read, starting pre-school, starting kindergarten; Ages 4-5); P (Primary grades, grades 1-3; Ages 6-9).

Berenstain Bears and the Messy Room
Brother and Sister's room is a mess. Mama is about to toss everything out when Papa Bear offers a neat solution.
VHS: S07716. $14.95.

Berenstain Bears and the Trouble with Friends
The new girl cub in the neighborhood is the same age as Sister Bear — and just as bossy. Mama Bear helps both cubs learn that you can't always have your own way if you want to be friends. In *The Coughing Catfish*, the Bears find a way to help their friend who lives in polluted waters. A good introduction to the concept of doing something about pollution.
VHS: S09230. $14.95.

Berenstain Bears and the Truth
Brother and Sister Bear learn that breaking Mama Bear's trust in them is worse than breaking her lamp.
VHS: S07715. $14.95.

Berenstain Bears and Too Much Birthday and To the Rescue
Is there such a thing as too much birthday? Sister doesn't think so, but she learns the hard way when she coaxes Mama and Papa to throw a big bash for her sixth birthday. *To the Rescue* features Papa helping the Bear Scouts.
VHS: S09229. $14.95.

Berenstain Bears Christmas Tree
Papa Bear realizes that Christmas trees are also animals' homes.
VHS: S24509. $9.98.

Berenstain Bears Easter Surprise
A nice little Easter story in Bear Country, where Papa helps the Easter Bunny.
VHS: S24510. $9.98.

Berenstain Bears Get in a Fight
Brother and Sister Bear turn a minor disagreement into a major war, and it's up to Mama Bear to call a truce.
VHS: S07713. $14.95.

Berenstain Bears in the Dark
When Brother reads Sister a scary story, she can't fall asleep in the dark. Papa Bear helps Sister conquer her fear.
VHS: S09231. $14.95.

Berenstain Bears Learn About Strangers
When Papa Bear tells the cubs they should never talk to strangers, Sister thinks all strangers are ominous. It's up to Mama to bring some common sense to the problem.
VHS: S07714. $14.95.

Berenstain Bears: No Girls Allowed and the Missing Dinosaur Bone
When Sister Bear wins several important games, Brother Bear and his friends create a mysterious clubhouse strictly off-limits to Sister Bear and her friends. This video focuses on the issue of differences between boys and girls. In *Berenstain Bears and the Missing Dinosaur Bone*, the Bear Detectives pursue the trail of a rare dinosaur bone stolen from Actual Factual's Museum.
VHS: S18614. $14.95.

Best Friends

Videos for children with or without pets, this series of animated stories demonstrates how to act responsibly toward our animal friends and the environment.

Best Friends Part I
A mouse, dog, turtle, rabbit and frog talk about what they want to receive from a human friend in the first part of this engaging series. 25 minutes. Age Recommendation: S (Starting school, starting to read, starting preschool, starting kindergarten; Ages 4-5); P (Primary grades, grades 1-3; Ages 6-9).
VHS: S14990. $14.95.

Best Friends Part II

A fish, cat, guinea pig, pony and bird take their turns telling entertaining animated stories which show children how to respect and care for our best pet friends. 25 minutes. Age Recommendation: S (Starting school, starting to read, starting pre-school, starting kindergarten; Ages 4-5); P (Primary grades, grades 1-3; Ages 6-9).

VHS: S15240. $19.95.

Best Friends
(Interama, Inc.)

Best of Beakman's World, The

A collection of highlights from the acclaimed cable series. The quirky scientist Beakman takes his viewers on an intellectual odyssey as he provokes children into asking important and fundamental questions about life, art, science, nature and their existence. Beakman finds an accessible means of conveying scientific information, using wit, visual shocks and surprise as he issues challenges, offers facts, solves problems and demonstrates experiments that can be accomplished at home. 60 minutes. Age Recommendation: P (Primary grades, grades 1-3; Ages 6-9); I (Intermediate grades, grades 4-6; Ages 10-12).

VHS: S19160. $14.95.

Bethie's Really Silly Clubhouse

Learn about animals while joining singer Bethie's hilarious club. 45 minutes. Age Recommendation: T (Toddler; Ages Birth-3 years); S (Starting school, starting to read, starting pre-school, starting kindergarten; Ages 4-5).

VHS: S24512. $14.98.

Big Bird's Favorite Party Games

Big Bird's having a party and everyone's invited. There's music, participation games, and even a game of "Oscar Says." 30 minutes. Age Recommendation: T (Toddler; Ages Birth-3 years); S (Starting school, starting to read, starting pre-school, starting kindergarten; Ages 4-5).

VHS: S07710. $9.98.

Biggest Bears!, The

This nature video provides information about grizzly bears and other wild animals and birds in Alaska. 30 minutes. Age Recommendation: S (Starting school, starting to read, starting pre-school, starting kindergarten; Ages 4-5); P (Primary grades, grades 1-3; Ages 6-9).

VHS: S22160. $14.95.

The Biggest Bears!
(©Richard Visser/Bullfrog Films, Inc.)

Bill Cosby's Picturepages

This series has been recommended by the National Education Association. The videos feature Bill Cosby as an entertaining and gentle teacher. The tapes include activity books with follow-up ideas for adults and children. Each tape is 30 minutes. Age Recommendation: S (Starting school, starting to read, starting pre-school, starting kindergarten; Ages 4-5).

What Goes Where?
Matching games and connect-the-dots.
VHS: S22132. $9.95.

What's Different?
Matching, differences and correlation.
VHS: S22133. $9.95.

What's That Shape?
VHS: S22952. $9.95.

What's Missing?
VHS: S22134. $9.95.

Who's Counting?
VHS: S22131. $9.95.

Bill Nye the Science Guy

The popular science show stars wacky Bill Nye, full of jokes, puns and fun. Find out how and why "SCIENCE RULES!" Each show has a theme, and features science tricks, profiles of scientists, demonstrations and experiments which can be done by children at home. Each tape is approximately 47 minutes. Age Recommendation: I (Intermediate grades, grades 4-6; Ages 10-12).

Bill Nye: Dinosaurs/Those Big Boneheads
VHS: S22337. $12.99.

Bill Nye: The Human Body/The Inside Scoop
VHS: S22338. $12.99.

Bill Nye: Outer Space/Way Out There
VHS: S22336. $12.99.

Birthday Dragon

The story of a girl and her dragon friend. 30 minutes. Age Recommendation: S (Starting school, starting to read, starting pre-school, starting kindergarten; Ages 4-5).
VHS: S24513. $9.98.

Birthday! Party/Professor Iris

Part of the *Ready, Set, Learn* series with Professor Iris, this birthday video is both entertaining and educational. The series is recommended by the

National Educational Association and the PTA. Also, see listings for *Creepy Critters/Professor Iris*, *Let's Do It!/Professor Iris*, *Music Mania/Professor Iris* and *Space Cadets/Professor Iris*. 40 minutes. Age Recommendation: T (Toddler; Ages Birth-3 years); S (Starting school, starting to read, starting pre-school, starting kindergarten; Ages 4-5).

VHS: S23018. $19.95.

Boy Who Loved Trolls, The

12-year-old Paul wishes that all the wonderful stories he reads about trolls and mermaids and far away kingdoms could be real. Imagine his amazement when one day a loveable old troll named Ofoeti appears and transports him to a fabulous fantasy world! Based on the play *Ofoeti* by John Wheatcroft, the video features actors Sam Waterston and Susan Anton. 58 minutes. Age Recommendation: P (Primary grades, grades 1-3; Ages 6-9); I (Intermediate grades, grades 4-6; Ages 10-12).

VHS: S14481. $29.95.

Brave Little Toaster, The

Five electrical appliances in a country cottage suddenly feel dumped when their young owner mysteriously disappears. Together they set out for the big city in search of their beloved master. Their quest becomes an unforgettable journey. "A family film in the truest sense of the term; one that adults can enjoy as well as children!" (*Los Angeles Times*). USA, 1988. 90 minutes. Age Recommendation: S (Starting school, starting to read, starting pre-school, starting kindergarten; Ages 4-5); P (Primary grades, grades 1-3; Ages 6-9); I (Intermediate grades, grades 4-6; Ages 10-12).

VHS: S14257. $19.99.

Brer Rabbit and the Wonderful Tar Baby (Rabbit Ears)

The comic adventures of that original American trickster, Brer Rabbit. This story is the classic and hilarious tale of how he outsmarts his wily nemesis, Brer Fox, with a clever contraption he calls a "tar baby." Read by Danny Glover, with music by Taj Mahal. 30 minutes. Age Recommendation: S (Starting school, starting to read, starting pre-school, starting kindergarten; Ages 4-5); P (Primary grades, grades 1-3; Ages 6-9); I (Intermediate grades, grades 4-6; Ages 10-12).

VHS: S12475. $9.95.

Bubbe's Boarding House Series

These charming videos help young children understand the Jewish holidays. Age Recommendation: S (Starting school, starting to read, starting pre-school, starting kindergarten; Ages 4-5); P (Primary grades, grades 1-3; Ages 6-9); I (Intermediate grades, grades 4-6; Ages 10-12).

Chanuka at Bubbe's
Delightful Muppet-like characters create an irresistible cast in this program explaining the traditions and significance of Chanuka. Great family entertainment with wide appeal for people of any background. USA. 60 minutes. Age Recommendation: S (Starting school, starting to read, starting pre-school, starting kindergarten; Ages 4-5); P (Primary grades, grades 1-3; Ages 6-9); I (Intermediate grades, grades 4-6; Ages 10-12).
VHS: S14949. $19.95.

Passover at Bubbe's
This program explains the traditions and significance of the Passover holiday. The video was made to include people of all faiths. The wonderful jokes are very appealing. 60 minutes. Age Recommendation: S (Starting school, starting to read, starting pre-school, starting kindergarten; Ages 4-5); P (Primary grades, grades 1-3; Ages 6-9); I (Intermediate grades, grades 4-6; Ages 10-12).
VHS: S14950. $19.95.

Bugs Don't Bug Us

One of the award-winning Bo Peep Productions. Kids learn about real bugs and other creepy crawlers: worms, snails, grasshoppers, bees, beetles, spiders, caterpillars, butterflies — all in their natural settings. In this live-action video, children see the transformations through which some of these creatures go. Presents a diverse cast of boys and girls. 35 minutes. Age Recommendation: T (Toddler; Ages Birth-3 years); S (Starting school, starting to read, starting pre-school, starting kindergarten; Ages 4-5).
VHS: S22381. $19.95.

Bump — My First Video

An evocative adaptation of six stories detailing the whimsical adventures of the precocious elephant Bump and his peculiar friend Birdie. Narrated by Simon Cadell. 30 minutes. Age Recommendation: S (Starting school, starting to read, starting pre-school, starting kindergarten; Ages 4-5).
VHS: S19423. $12.98.

C Can I Be Good?

A puppy tries to be good, but he can't help being a puppy. Finally he becomes an indispensable member of the family that loves him just as he is. Children see themselves as a golden retriever sees them in this enjoyable read-along video. 11 minutes. Age Recommendation: S (Starting school, starting to read, starting pre-school, starting kindergarten; Ages 4-5).

VHS: S22359. $39.95.

Candles, Snow and Mistletoe

This original music fantasy unfolds as Sharon, Lois and Bram take a trip home for the holidays. On the way, they meet an assortment of eccentric fellow passengers, including a charming elephant. Together they take the ride of their lives and rediscover the true meaning of the holiday season. 50 minutes. Age Recommendation: S (Starting school, starting to read, starting pre-school, starting kindergarten; Ages 4-5).

VHS: S22224. $9.98.

Caribbean Kids

Stories about real kids of Latin American and Caribbean backgrounds who live and learn in today's world. Includes original entertaining music. 55 minutes. Age Recommendation: S (Starting school, starting to read, starting pre-school, starting kindergarten; Ages 4-5); P (Primary grades, grades 1-3; Ages 6-9); I (Intermediate grades, grades 4-6; Ages 10-12).

English Version. VHS: S06729. $29.95.

Spanish Version. VHS: S06730. $29.95.

Carlitos, Dani y Luis Alfredo

Three puppets and their human companion use song, movement and dialogue to teach basic Spanish language and social interactions. Four different segments cover colors, shapes, health, conservation and healthy eating. The video is accompanied by a parent/teacher guide with vocabulary, language exercises and follow-up activities. In Spanish and English. 30 minutes. Age Recommendation: S (Starting school, starting to read, starting pre-school, starting kindergarten; Ages 4-5); P (Primary grades, grades 1-3; Ages 6-9).

VHS: S19775. $39.95.

Caterpillar's Wish, A

Written and illustrated by first graders in Washington, D.C., this inventive tale concerns the shifting moods of two friends. Chad Caterpillar longs for wings, like the kind his friend Janet Ladybug sprouts. Fortunately Chad is eventually transformed into a yellow butterfly. 6 minutes. Age Recommendation: T (Toddler; Ages Birth-3 years).

VHS: S19603. $39.00.

Chanter Pour S'Amuser

This Canadian series involves song, dance and movement to make an impression on young students of French. Each program introduces vocabulary through movements and songs that children will find quite engaging. Each video is 50 minutes. Age Recommendation: S (Starting school, starting to read, starting pre-school, starting kindergarten; Ages 4-5); P (Primary grades, grades 1-3; Ages 6-9); I (Intermediate grades, grades 4-6; Ages 10-12).

L'Album de Marie-Soleil
Concentrates on parts of the body, animals and prepositions.
VHS: S19784. $35.00.

Une Journée Avec Marie-Soleil
Deals with the alphabet, numbers and adjectives.
VHS: S19785. $35.00.

Chanter Pour S'Amuser Set
Set of two videos.
VHS: S19786. $62.00.

Charles the Clown

Watch Charles Kraus as he becomes a clown right before your eyes. This live-action video gives a fascinating look at the fine art of clowning. 30 minutes. Age Recommendation: S (Starting school, starting to read, starting pre-school, starting kindergarten; Ages 4-5); P (Primary grades, grades 1-3; Ages 6-9).

VHS: S24515. $9.98.

Cherries and Cherry Pits

Based on the award-winning book by Vera B. Williams, this is the story of a girl named Bidemmi, who draws pictures with colorful markers. One day, she draws pictures of herself buying a bag of cherries, eating the cherries, saving the pits for....just guess! 15 minutes. Age Recommendation: S (Starting school, starting to read, starting pre-school, starting kindergarten; Ages 4-5); P (Primary grades, grades 1-3; Ages 6-9).

VHS: S16339. $44.95.

Chicken Sunday

A story by Patricia Polacco about loss, acceptance and assimilation. A young Russian-American girl is initiated into a neighbor's family following the death of her grandmother. She must stake out a series of new relationships and friendships and learns about trust, love and family bonds. 14 minutes. Age Recommendation: P (Primary grades, grades 1-3; Ages 6-9); I (Intermediate grades, grades 4-6; Ages 10-12).

VHS: S19999. $44.95.

Child of Mine:
The Lullaby Video

Thirteen different female artists perform an eclectic and touching collection of lullabies that acknowledge the special bonds between mother and child. The artists include Mary Chapin Carpenter, Roseanne Cash, Gloria Estefan, Dionne Warwick and Carole King. 52 minutes. Age Recommendation: T (Toddler; Ages Birth-3 years); S (Starting school, starting to read, starting pre-school, starting kindergarten; Ages 4-5).

VHS: S20300. $19.98.

Child's Christmas in Wales, A

A wonderful adaptation of Dylan Thomas' memories of Christmas in Wales circa 1910, reliving childhood in one magical evening. Live-action, directed by Don McBrearty, Canada, 1987. 55 minutes. Age Recommendation: P (Primary grades, grades 1-3; Ages 6-9); I (Intermediate grades, grades 4-6; Ages 10-12).

VHS: S07446. $9.98.

Classroom Holidays

Created by Miriam Cohen and illustrated by Lillian Hoban, the stories of Jim and his first-grade classmates highlight issues of trust, warmth, independence, humor and compassion. Age Recommendation: S (Starting school, starting to read, starting pre-school, starting kindergarten; Ages 4-5); P (Primary grades, grades 1-3; Ages 6-9).

Bee My Valentine: A Valentine's Day Story
Little George is hurt when he receives fewer valentines than his peers. He hides out in a coat room until Jim devises a music fest that uplifts George's spirits. 8 minutes.
VHS: S20060. $44.95.

Don't Eat Too Much Turkey: A Thanksgiving Story
When Anna Maria writes a Thanksgiving play, she believes that it entitles her to cast and direct the work, which upsets her classmates. The teacher intervenes and settles the dispute by getting the entire class involved in the production. 8 minutes.
VHS: S20058. $44.95.

Liar, Liar, Pants on Fire: A Christmas/Chanukah Story
Alex has a hard time adjusting to his new first grade and tells lies to impress his classmates, but nobody believes him. Finally, at the class' holiday party, he summons up enough strength to tell the truth. 7 minutes.
VHS: S20059. $44.95.

Starring First Grade: An Anytime Celebration
Jim is upset when he is forced to play a tree rather than a troll in the school play. The kids have to deal with adjustments and problem-solving in arguing over roles. 8 minutes.
VHS: S20061. $44.95.

Classroom Holidays Set
A set of all four programs on the joys and confusion of first grade. 31 minutes.
VHS: S20062. $159.95.

Clean Your Room, Harvey Moon!

Based on the book by Pat Cummings. Harvey Moon's room is a mess! Socks, marbles, trains and even a map of the brain are crowding it. His mother won't let him watch cartoons until his room is spotless. This Saturday morning cleaning spree is told in upbeat verse with true-to-life humor. Pat Cummings won the Coretta Scott King Award for illustration. 6 minutes. Age Recommendation: S (Starting school, starting to read, starting pre-school, starting kindergarten; Ages 4-5); P (Primary grades, grades 1-3; Ages 6-9).
VHS: S16341. $44.95.

Clifford's Fun With....Series

Clifford the Big Red Dog and his owner Emily Elizabeth are the stars of these Scholastic Learning Library videos, based on the best-selling books by Norman Bridwell and developed by early childhood specialists. Each video is 30 minutes. Age Recommendation: S (Starting school, starting to read, starting pre-school, starting kindergarten; Ages 4-5).

Clifford's Fun with Letters
Join Clifford and his friends as they learn and play with the alphabet.
VHS: S13733. $12.95.

Clifford's Fun with Numbers
Clifford and his friends lead children through fun and games with numbers.
VHS: S13732. $12.95.

Clifford's Fun with Opposites
Clifford shows kids about things that are different.
VHS: S24517. $12.95.

Clifford's Fun with Rhymes
Clifford and Emily Elizabeth want to join the Rhyme Cats, but must solve these rhyming riddles. Engaging.
VHS: S24516. $12.95.

Clifford's Fun with Shapes and Colors
Join the scavenger hunt and search for shapes and colors. Full of fun songs.
VHS: S24518. $12.95.

Clifford's Fun with Sounds
Clifford teaches children about sounds.
VHS: S24519. $12.95.

Clifford's Sing-a-Long Adventure
Clifford and his friends lead children at home in a musical adventure that gets them to sing, dance, clap and compose their own songs. Features old and new musical classics, live-action and video animation.
VHS: S04154. $14.95.

Cloudy with a Chance of Meatballs

Adaptation of Judy Barrett's fantasy about the land of Chewandswallow and the day the skies stopped raining their sensible, square meals three times a day. 15 minutes. Age Recommendation: S (Starting school, starting to read, starting pre-school, starting kindergarten; Ages 4-5); P (Primary grades, grades 1-3; Ages 6-9).
VHS: S08408. $36.95.

Corduroy Bear

Three bear stories! In *Corduroy Bear*, a loveable stuffed bear goes searching for a missing button and finds a new home with an African American girl; *Blueberries for Sal* is about the adventures of a little girl and a baby bear; *Panama* is about Little Bear and Little Tiger searching for a wonderful smell. Gary Templeton, USA, 1986. 38 minutes. Age Recommendation: S (Starting school, starting to read, starting pre-school, starting kindergarten; Ages 4-5); P (Primary grades, grades 1-3; Ages 6-9).
VHS: S00270. $14.95.

Creative Dance for Preschoolers

Imparts the fun of movement while teaching important basic principles of dance. 60 minutes. Age Recommendation: S (Starting school, starting to read, starting pre-school, starting kindergarten; Ages 4-5).
VHS: S24608. $42.95.

Creative Movement: A Step Towards Intelligence

Melissa Lowe's instruction is designed to help children develop self-awareness, confidence and expressive capabilities. The program shows children having fun singing, clapping, moving to music, and learning motor skills and coordination. 80 minutes. Age Recommendation: S (Starting school, starting to read, starting pre-school, starting kindergarten; Ages 4-5); P (Primary grades, grades 1-3; Ages 6-9); I (Intermediate grades, grades 4-6; Ages 10-12).
VHS: S19687. $19.95.

Creepy Critters/Professor Iris

Professor Iris introduces kids to snakes, bats, bugs and bees in this entertaining and educational pre-science lesson. This video is part of the *Ready, Set, Learn* series which first aired on The Learning Channel, and which has been recommended by the National Educational Association and the PTA. Also, see listings for: *Birthday! Party/Professor Iris*, *Let's Do It!/Professor Iris*, *Music Mania/Professor Iris* and *Space Cadets/Professor Iris*. 40 minutes. Age Recommendation: T (Toddler; Ages Birth-3 years); S (Starting school, starting to read, starting pre-school, starting kindergarten; Ages 4-5).
VHS: S24520. $12.95.

Cri-Cri: El Grillito Cantor

This is a tribute to the most important composer and singer of Latin American children's music, Francisco Gabilondo Soler. Featured are songs that three generations have enjoyed, beautifully animated by Walt Disney: "La Patita," "El Chorrito," "El Rey Bombon," "El Ropero" and "Los Cochinitos Dormilones." Enter the world of Cri-Cri, the Singing Cricket. 90 minutes. Age Recommendation: S (Starting school, starting to read, starting pre-school, starting kindergarten; Ages 4-5); P (Primary grades, grades 1-3; Ages 6-9); I (Intermediate grades, grades 4-6; Ages 10-12). In Spanish.
VHS: S16366. $39.95.

Curious George Videos

Based on the books by Margaret and H.A. Rey, these videos feature the adventures of the mischievous little monkey George. Age Recommendation: T (Toddler; Ages Birth-3 years); S (Starting school, starting to read, starting pre-school, starting kindergarten; Ages 4-5).

Curious George
A puppet animation version of the story of George's arrival from Africa and how his curiosity leads him to the city zoo. 1986. 30 minutes.
VHS: S24771. $12.95.

Curious George Goes to Town
Join George at the airport, at the library, at a wedding and in an ice cream shop. 20 minutes.
VHS: S24610. $14.95.

Curious George: Fun in the Sun
Join George in an amusement park, painting billboards, playing with elephants, and more. 20 minutes.
VHS: S24609. $14.95.

Corduroy Bear
(© Weston Woods/Children's Circle Home Video)

Daisy-Head Mayzie

D

A newly found treasure by Dr. Seuss! No longer lost after many a year — *Daisy-Head Mayzie* is finally here! This animated version of Dr. Seuss' last book includes *The Making of Daisy-Head Mayzie*. 40 minutes. Age Recommendation: S (Starting school, starting to read, starting pre-school, starting kindergarten; Ages 4-5); P (Primary grades, grades 1-3; Ages 6-9); I (Intermediate grades, grades 4-6; Ages 10-12).

VHS: S24805. $9.98.

Dan Crow's Oops!

Dan Crow is respected as an educator, a songwriter and a performer of songs and stories for children. This concert video is guaranteed to keep Dan's old fans happy, and gain him lots of new ones. 30 minutes. Age Recommendation: S (Starting school, starting to read, starting pre-school, starting kindergarten; Ages 4-5); P (Primary grades, grades 1-3; Ages 6-9); I (Intermediate grades, grades 4-6; Ages 10-12).

VHS: S15307. $14.98.

Dancing with the Indians

Based on the book by Angela Shelf Medearis. This award-winning video tells the fascinating story of a young African American girl and her family's annual visit to participate in the ceremonies of the Seminole tribe. During the Civil War, some seventy years earlier, the Seminole had given sanctuary to the girl's grandfather, who had escaped slavery. 8 minutes. Age Recommendation: P (Primary grades, grades 1-3; Ages 6-9); I (Intermediate grades, grades 4-6; Ages 10-12).

VHS: S24521. $37.95.

Danny and the Dinosaur and Other Stories

Based on the book by Syd Hoff. Danny's friend for the day is the very dinosaur that he had just been admiring in the Museum. What child wouldn't want to ride, go for a swim and play hide-and-seek with a real, live dinosaur? The video also includes the charming *Camel Who Took a Walk* (written by Roger Duvoisin), the runaway *Happy Lion*, and *The Island of Skog* (written by Steven Kellog), an allegory about persecuted mice who later become victimizers. 35 minutes. Age Recommendation: S (Starting school, starting to read, starting pre-school, starting kindergarten; Ages 4-5); P (Primary grades, grades 1-3; Ages 6-9).

VHS: S14494. $14.95.

Dancing with the Indians
(Live Oak Media)

Discovery Stories

Imaginative situations are presented through beautifully illustrated stories which make children aware of the world in which they live. The video highlights the need to protect the Earth and to find positive ways in which to live. 25 minutes. Age Recommendation: S (Starting school, starting to read, starting pre-school, starting kindergarten; Ages 4-5); P (Primary grades, grades 1-3; Ages 6-9).

VHS: S10316. $29.95.

Divorce Can Happen to the Nicest People

A video specially designed for kids who ask the toughest questions. In a half hour of animation, the video employs love, honesty and a sense of humor to explain some of life's toughest questions. Helps to take the mystery and pain out of this difficult time. USA, 1987. 30 minutes. Age Recommendation: P (Primary grades, grades 1-3; Ages 6-9); I (Intermediate grades, grades 4-6; Ages 10-12).

VHS: S04762. $19.95.

Doctor De Soto and Other Stories

Doctor De Soto (written by William Steig) is the Academy Award-winning short film about a mouse dentist who finds a way to treat a crafty fox with a sore tooth. This tape also features the stories *Curious George Rides a*

Bike, based on the books by Margaret and H.A. Rey, in which George the monkey sets off on a bike to rescue a baby bear, *The Hat*, based on the book by Tomi Ungerer, featuring an adventuresome hat, and *Patrick*, a story by Quentin Blake which features upbeat violin music. 30 minutes. Age Recommendation: S (Starting school, starting to read, starting pre-school, starting kindergarten; Ages 4-5); P (Primary grades, grades 1-3; Ages 6-9).

VHS: S00353. $14.98.

Dog Who Had Kittens, The

Based on the book by Polly M. Robertus. Baxter the Basset Hound adopts Eloise the cat's kittens. 14 minutes. Age Recommendation: S (Starting school, starting to read, starting pre-school, starting kindergarten; Ages 4-5); P (Primary grades, grades 1-3; Ages 6-9).

VHS: S24522. $37.95.

Dog Who Stopped the War, The

A huge international success from the director of the award-winning *Bach and Broccoli*. Luke declares the Great Snowball War and launches his army of friends against a rival group commanded by Mark. The objective of this entertaining feature is to teach the peaceful resolution of conflicts. Andre Melancon, Canada, 1985. 95 minutes. Age Recommendation: P (Primary grades, grades 1-3; Ages 6-9); I (Intermediate grades, grades 4-6; Ages 10-12).

VHS: S01775. Currently out of print. May be available for rental in some video stores.

Doing Things: Eating, Washing, in Motion

One of the award-winning Bo Peep Productions, this video includes children from a variety of ethnic and racial backgrounds. Live-action footage shows kids and farm animals doing all sorts of interesting things like playing, eating and romping. The music provides a nice backdrop for a non-verbal soundscape which includes the real sounds of kids and animals. 27 minutes. Age Recommendation: T (Toddler; Ages Birth-3 years); S (Starting school, starting to read, starting pre-school, starting kindergarten; Ages 4-5).

VHS: S22378. $19.95.

Don Cooper: Mother Nature's Songs

Entertainer Don Cooper encourages imaginations to blossom as children see, hear and imitate nature in this sing-along video featuring "The Not Ready for Bedtime Players." USA. 30 minutes. Age Recommendation: S (Starting school, starting to read, starting pre-school, starting kindergarten; Ages 4-5). VHS: S15321. $19.95.

Dozen Dizzy Dogs, A

Count up to twelve and back again with a lively, entertaining crew. Checkered dogs, dogs with stripes, dogs with spots and dogs with funny hats populate this zany counting adventure. The story is told twice — once to familiarize children with the characters and story; the second time with words printed on-screen so children can easily follow along. 30 minutes. Age Recommendation: S (Starting school, starting to read, starting pre-school, starting kindergarten; Ages 4-5); P (Primary grades, grades 1-3; Ages 6-9). VHS: S13528. $14.99.

Dr. Seuss Videos

These videos, based on the books by Dr. Seuss, are loved by adults and kids alike, who often find in them a special life-affirming message important today. The stories are wildly imaginative, often focusing on a positive theme, presenting male and female characters in multi-dimensional ways. The videos also stimulate an interest in reading the books on which they are based.

Dr. Seuss Video Festival
These two Dr. Seuss favorites focus on the lives of the "Whos down in Whoville." *Horton Hears a Who* is the story of the dedicated elephant who protects invisible "Whos" and *How the Grinch Stole Christmas* reveals how the nasty Grinch discovers the true meaning of Christmas. 48 minutes. Age Recommendation: S (Starting school, starting to read, starting pre-school, starting kindergarten; Ages 4-5); P (Primary grades, grades 1-3; Ages 6-9); I (Intermediate grades, grades 4-6; Ages 10-12). VHS: S01700. $29.95.

Dr. Seuss: The Butter Battle Book
On the last day of summer, ten hours before fall, representatives from the Yooks and Zooks wonder about destroying the world once and for all. Charles Durning narrates this allegorical children's tale about a common people foolishly divided over whether to consume their bread butter-side up or butter-side down. 30 minutes. Age Recommendation: S (Starting school, starting to read, starting pre-school, starting kindergarten; Ages 4-5); P (Primary grades, grades 1-3; Ages 6-9); I (Intermediate grades, grades 4-6; Ages 10-12). VHS: S12843. $9.95.

Dr. Seuss: The Cat in the Hat Comes Back
Three Dr. Seuss stories: *The Cat in the Hat Comes Back* (this time with bunches of little cats), *Fox in Socks*, the amazing rhyming tongue twister, and *There's A Wocket in My Pocket*. 30 minutes. Age Recommendation: S (Starting school, starting to read, starting pre-school, starting kindergarten; Ages 4-5); P (Primary grades, grades 1-3; Ages 6-9); I (Intermediate grades, grades 4-6; Ages 10-12).
VHS: S24524. $14.98.

Dr. Seuss: Green Eggs and Ham
The character Sam I Am presents the challenge to try something new. The video is brilliantly whimsical and highly entertaining. 28 minutes. Age Recommendation: S (Starting school, starting to read, starting pre-school, starting kindergarten; Ages 4-5); P (Primary grades, grades 1-3; Ages 6-9); I (Intermediate grades, grades 4-6; Ages 10-12).
VHS: S21536. $14.98.

Dr. Seuss: Hoober-Bloob Highway
An exotic story about a ribbon of light that leads from the sky to a floating island below. In this wonderfully animated piece, a scientist, after exploration of various options, sends a "baby" down to earth to begin its life. The viewers are just not sure what type of baby it will be. 1975. 24 minutes. Age Recommendation: S (Starting school, starting to read, starting pre-school, starting kindergarten; Ages 4-5); P (Primary grades, grades 1-3; Ages 6-9); I (Intermediate grades, grades 4-6; Ages 10-12).
VHS: S10093. $14.98.

Dr. Seuss: Hop on Pop
Three Dr. Seuss stories for the youngest readers. *Hop on Pop* is simple rhyming fun, *Oh Say Can You Say?* tells a story in tongue twisters kids love, and *Marvin K. Mooney, Will You Please Go Now!* completes the wonderful set. Age Recommendation: S (Starting school, starting to read, starting pre-school, starting kindergarten; Ages 4-5).
VHS: S24525. $14.98.

Dr. Seuss: Horton Hatches the Egg
Horton the Elephant helps out Mayzie the lazy bird by sitting on her egg while she goes on vacation. 30 minutes. Age Recommendation: S (Starting school, starting to read, starting pre-school, starting kindergarten; Ages 4-5); P (Primary grades, grades 1-3; Ages 6-9); I (Intermediate grades, grades 4-6; Ages 10-12).
VHS: S24811. $9.95.

Dr. Seuss: Horton Hears a Who
Dr. Seuss teams-up with Chuck Jones to bring Horton, the lovable elephant, and his wild and woolly friends to life. Filled with songs and tongue-twisting verse. "A person's a person. No matter how small." The video also includes *Thidwick the Big-Hearted Moose*. Chuck Jones, USA, 1970. 26 minutes. Age

Recommendation: S (Starting school, starting to read, starting pre-school, starting kindergarten; Ages 4-5); P (Primary grades, grades 1-3; Ages 6-9); I (Intermediate grades, grades 4-6; Ages 10-12).

VHS: S24810. $9.95.

Dr. Seuss: How the Grinch Stole Christmas

This timeless Dr. Seuss classic features the crotchety Grinch who tries to eliminate Christmas for the "Whos down in Whoville," only to discover the true meaning of Christmas. Narrated by the great Boris Karloff. 26 minutes. Age Recommendation: S (Starting school, starting to read, starting pre-school, starting kindergarten; Ages 4-5); P (Primary grades, grades 1-3; Ages 6-9); I (Intermediate grades, grades 4-6; Ages 10-12).

VHS: S03534. $14.95.

Dr. Seuss: 1 am NOT Going to Get Up Today!

A little boy claims that he will not get out of bed. The tape also includes *The Shape of Me and Other Stuff, Great Day for Up* and *In a People House*. 25 minutes. Age Recommendation: T (Toddler; Ages Birth-3 years); S (Starting school, starting to read, starting pre-school, starting kindergarten; Ages 4-5).

VHS: S24812. $9.95.

How the Grinch Stole Christmas

(©1966 Turner Entertainment Co. ©™ Dr. Seuss Enterprises, L.P. 1995. All rights reserved. From "How the Grinch Stole Christmas" courtesy of MGM/UA Home Video.)

Dr. Seuss: The Lorax
The well-known Dr. Seuss book that warns against uncontrolled progress is adapted by the author into an equally poignant animated film. The loveable Lorax, a "voice for the voiceless" speaks for the trees when they are threatened by the profit-greedy Once-ler and shares a contemporary message about concern for ecology. Note: this is a good video to watch *with* kids, as the message can be disturbing. 30 minutes. Age Recommendation: S (Starting school, starting to read, starting pre-school, starting kindergarten; Ages 4-5); P (Primary grades, grades 1-3; Ages 6-9); I (Intermediate grades, grades 4-6; Ages 10-12).
VHS: S10092. $14.98.

Dr. Seuss: One Fish Two Fish Red Fish Blue Fish
Another hit for the youngest readers, this video strengthens language concepts in a wonderfully fun, imaginative manner. In addition to the popular title story about numbers and colors, the video includes *Oh, The Thinks You Can Think*, about making up words, and *The Foot Book*. 30 minutes. Age Recommendation: T (Toddler; Ages Birth-3 years); S (Starting school, starting to read, starting pre-school, starting kindergarten; Ages 4-5).
English Version. VHS: S22018. $14.95.
Spanish Version. Un Pez Dos Peces Pez Rojo Pez Azul. VHS: S22017. $14.95.

Dr. Seuss: Pontoffel Pock
After the timid Pock gets a piano that magically takes him anywhere, the young man understands how to appreciate himself. Adapted by Dr. Seuss, this radiantly animated film contains the confidence-building lessons and simple fun found in the beloved books. 30 minutes. Age Recommendation: S (Starting school, starting to read, starting pre-school, starting kindergarten; Ages 4-5); P (Primary grades, grades 1-3; Ages 6-9); I (Intermediate grades, grades 4-6; Ages 10-12).
VHS: S10094. $14.98.

Dr. Seuss' ABC
Dr. Seuss' ABC is full of ABC fun. This tape also includes *I Can Read with My Eyes Shut*, featuring the Cat in the Hat, and *Mr. Brown Can Moo — Can You?*, which is full of interactive fun. Ages. 30 minutes. Age Recommendation: T (Toddler; Ages Birth-3 years); S (Starting school, starting to read, starting pre-school, starting kindergarten; Ages 4-5).
VHS: S24523. $14.95.

Dr. Seuss' Cat in the Hat
The all-time kids' favorite turns the house upside down with the zany Cat and his buddies, Thing 1 and Thing 2. 30 minutes. Age Recommendation: S (Starting school, starting to read, starting pre-school, starting kindergarten; Ages 4-5); P (Primary grades, grades 1-3; Ages 6-9); I (Intermediate grades, grades 4-6; Ages 10-12).
VHS: S10096. $14.98.

Dr. Seuss' Sleep Book
An epic poem recreates the classic book, with narration by Madeline Kahn. The story follows some crazy Seuss creatures as they prepare to sleep. 30 minutes. Age Recommendation: T (Toddler; Ages Birth-3 years); S (Starting school, starting to read, starting pre-school, starting kindergarten; Ages 4-5). VHS: S24813. $9.95.

Dreadlocks and the Three Bears

The classic tale is transformed into an essay about identity, heritage and roots. Director Alile Sharon Larkin draws on the works of collage artists Leo Lionni, Romare Bearden and Varnette Honeywood to tell the story of Dreadlocks, who finds herself in the home of the Three Bears in Teddy Bear Forest, while visiting her aunt. Written and illustrated by Larkin. 13 minutes. Age Recommendation: S (Starting school, starting to read, starting pre-school, starting kindergarten; Ages 4-5); P (Primary grades, grades 1-3; Ages 6-9). VHS: S18327. $14.95.

Drug Free Kids

This instructional program is designed to aid parents in recognizing and dealing with childhood drug abuse. Familiar faces who advise that kids say "no" to drugs include Ken Howard, Jane Alexander, Ned Beatty, Marla Gibbs and Melissa Gilbert. USA, 1987. 70 minutes. Age Recommendation: I (Intermediate grades, grades 4-6; Ages 10-12). VHS: S03641. $19.95.

E Eco, You, and Simon, Too!

This unique music video uses computer graphics to teach young children important lessons about friendship, nutrition and the preservation of the environment. Eco is a smart, energetic sea otter puppet and Simon is his intuitive, curious human friend. Singing, rhyming, fun. 40 minutes. Age Recommendation: S (Starting school, starting to read, starting pre-school, starting kindergarten; Ages 4-5); P (Primary grades, grades 1-3; Ages 6-9). VHS: S17110. $14.95.

Eight Super Stories from Sesame Street

A video twin-pack featuring Oscar the Grouch, Big Bird, Cookie Monster, Grover and the rest of the gang. 30 minutes. Age Recommendation: T (Toddler; Ages Birth-3 years); S (Starting school, starting to read, starting pre-school, starting kindergarten; Ages 4-5).

VHS: S24993. $12.95.

Ella Jenkins Live! At the Smithsonian

Ella encourages the audience to participate when she performs in this concert at the national museum. Twelve original and traditional songs. 30 minutes. Age Recommendation: S (Starting school, starting to read, starting pre-school, starting kindergarten; Ages 4-5); P (Primary grades, grades 1-3; Ages 6-9).

VHS: S15497. $14.95.

Ella Jenkins: For the Family

Ella Jenkins, a recognized national treasure, sings eleven favorite children's songs. 30 minutes. Age Recommendation: S (Starting school, starting to read, starting pre-school, starting kindergarten; Ages 4-5); P (Primary grades, grades 1-3; Ages 6-9).

VHS: S25036. $14.95.

The Emperor and the Nightingale
(Illustrated by Robert Van Nutt/Rabbit Ears Productions)

Emperor and Nightingale (Rabbit Ears)

Glenn Close narrates the famous Hans Christian Andersen story about the Emperor who is given a gift of a mechanical singing bird only to learn that the genuine song of the real nightingale is truly the best of all. With music by Mark Isham and illustrations by Robert Van Nutt. 40 minutes. Age Recommendation: P (Primary grades, grades 1-3; Ages 6-9); I (Intermediate grades, grades 4-6; Ages 10-12).

VHS: S04904. $14.95.

Emperor's New Clothes (Rabbit Ears)

When two swindlers cleverly announce that the magical garments they are weaving for the Emperor are invisible to anyone lacking intelligence, who has the courage to speak the truth? Sir John Gielgud tells the Hans Christian Andersen fairytale. 30 minutes. Age Recommendation: P (Primary grades, grades 1-3; Ages 6-9); I (Intermediate grades, grades 4-6; Ages 10-12).

VHS: S12474. $14.95.

Empty Pot, The

Based on a tale by Demi, *The Empty Pot* focuses on the efforts of Ping, an excellent gardener, to win the Emperor's unusual test in selecting an heir — the one who is able to raise flowers from a seed furnished by the Emperor. Ping is frustrated when his seed won't sprout. The detailed visual illustrations provide a picture of ancient China. 7 minutes. Age Recommendation: P (Primary grades, grades 1-3; Ages 6-9).

VHS: S20000. $44.95.

Ezra Jack Keats Library

These animated adaptations of stories by the acclaimed children's author include *The Snowy Day, Whistle for Willie, Peter's Chair, A Letter to Amy, Pet Show!* and *The Trip.* The video also includes a short documentary, *Getting to Know Ezra Jack Keats.* 45 minutes. Age Recommendation: S (Starting school, starting to read, starting pre-school, starting kindergarten; Ages 4-5); P (Primary grades, grades 1-3; Ages 6-9).

VHS: S22161. $14.95.

Family Farm

F

In this story by Thomas Locker, a brother and sister design a plan to save their family farm. This animated film shows contemporary rural life, including some of the realistic problems of small farmers. Fun, toe-tapping bluegrass music encourages children to follow the story. 12 minutes. Age Recommendation: P (Primary grades, grades 1-3; Ages 6-9); I (Intermediate grades, grades 4-6; Ages 10-12).

VHS: S14197. $44.95.

Farmer's Huge Carrot, The

Written and illustrated by kindergarten children in West Columbia, Texas, this engaging story details the efforts of a farmer and his wife to grow a vegetable garden in the midst of a summer drought. When a fire truck waters the garden, a carrot grows bigger than a tree, leading to all kinds of magical and funny surprises. 4 minutes. Age Recommendation: S (Starting school, starting to read, starting pre-school, starting kindergarten; Ages 4-5); P (Primary grades, grades 1-3; Ages 6-9).

VHS: S19602. $39.00.

50 Below Zero (plus Thomas' Snowsuit)

Follow the antics of Jason's sleepwalking father. The video includes the story *Thomas' Snow Suit*, in which Thomas is forced to wear his plain, ugly, brown snowsuit. Animated stories by acclaimed author Robert Munsch. 25 minutes. Age Recommendation: T (Toddler; Ages Birth-3 years); S (Starting school, starting to read, starting pre-school, starting kindergarten; Ages 4-5).

VHS: S24984. $12.95.

Fingermouse, Yoffy and Friends

Children will be intrigued by the stories of discovery as told by Yoffy, Fingermouse and other finger-puppet friends in this 3-tape series from the BBC which includes music and sound effects. With educational lessons accompanying each story, the series has been hailed as a "combination of imaginative play and substantive story." Three 60 minute tapes (180 minutes). Age Recommendation: S (Starting school, starting to read, starting pre-school, starting kindergarten; Ages 4-5); P (Primary grades, grades 1-3; Ages 6-9); I (Intermediate grades, grades 4-6; Ages 10-12).

VHS: S15539. $100.00.

Finn McCoul (Rabbit Ears)

The real hero seems to be Uno, Finn McCoul's clever wife, as the pair work together to defeat the famous giant Cuchulain in this modern re-telling of an Irish folk tale about out-foxing a bully. Narrated by comedienne Catherine O'Hara, this animated video contains music performed by the Irish quintet Boys of the Lough. 30 minutes. Age Recommendation: P (Primary grades, grades 1-3; Ages 6-9); I (Intermediate grades, grades 4-6; Ages 10-12). VHS: S16996. $9.95.

Fire and Rescue

Fact-filled and exciting, this video takes kids into a fire station and shares the facts of the job of firefighting. The video shows men and women of diverse backgrounds. 30 minutes. Age Recommendation: S (Starting school, starting to read, starting pre-school, starting kindergarten; Ages 4-5); P (Primary grades, grades 1-3; Ages 6-9); I (Intermediate grades, grades 4-6; Ages 10-12). VHS: S25040. $29.95.

Fireman Sam: The Hero Next Door

This British production focuses on friendship and helping. Fireman Sam is the hero of Pontypandy Town. 30 minutes. Age Recommendation: S (Starting school, starting to read, starting pre-school, starting kindergarten; Ages 4-5). VHS: S24611. $9.98.

First and Second Grade Feelings

The wonder, excitement and pain of children is beautifully evoked in these prize-winning tales by Miriam Cohen, illustrated by Lillian Hoban, that deal with friendship, independence, self-realization and honesty. "A multi-ethnic classroom, a loving teacher...amusing antics of Jim and the other children, natural sounding dialogue: who could ask for anything more?" (*Bulletin of the Center for Children's Books*). Originally designed for classroom use, parents can now watch these with kids at home. Age Recommendation: S (Starting school, starting to read, starting pre-school, starting kindergarten; Ages 4-5); P (Primary grades, grades 1-3; Ages 6-9).

Jim's Dog, Muffins
Based on the book by Miriam Cohen. Following the death of his dog, Jim is withdrawn and pensive and refuses to speak to his first-grade classmates. As his friends try to understand Jim's reaction to death, Paul helps him deal with his sorrow and loss. This video is noted for acknowledging the depth of children's feelings in response to the death of a pet. 7 minutes. VHS: S20041. $44.95.

The Real-Skin Rubber Monster Mask
Jim is excited about wearing his real-skin rubber monster mask until he sees his reflection on Halloween and fears that he's being transformed into a monster. Willy comes to his aid. 11 minutes.

VHS: S20043. $44.95.

See You in Second Grade!
Jim, Paul, Danny, George and Anna Maria celebrate at the end-of-the-year picnic on the beach. The teacher helps them recall the fantastic experiences of first grade and they eagerly await the forthcoming year in second grade. 7 minutes.

VHS: S20044. $44.95.

So What?
Jim feels ostracized because he is smaller than everybody else in the first grade. He tries to start a club, but people abandon him. Then a sympathetic girl from Chicago helps him overcome his insecurity and teaches him valuable lessons in independence. 8 minutes.

VHS: S20042. $44.95.

First and Second Grade Feelings Set
A collection all four titles. 33 minutes.

VHS: S18696. $159.95.

Five Lionni Classics

The power of imagination is shown in this visually exceptional collection of five animated pieces based upon Leo Lionni's popular animal fables. Characters Frederick, Cornelius and Swimmy are presented in adaptations by Lionni himself, who collaborated with animator Giulio Gianini to bring new dimensions to the author's picture books. Giulio Gianini, Italy, 1986. 30 minutes. Age Recommendation: T (Toddler; Ages Birth-3 years); S (Starting school, starting to read, starting pre-school, starting kindergarten; Ages 4-5).

VHS: S02846. $19.95.

Five Sesame Street Stories

In this collection are five exciting adventures, including *Super-Grover* and *Big Bird Brings Spring to Sesame Street*. 30 minutes. Age Recommendation: T (Toddler; Ages Birth-3 years); S (Starting school, starting to read, starting pre-school, starting kindergarten; Ages 4-5).

VHS: S24992. $5.95.

Five Stories for the Very Young

The five stories are *Changes* (based on the book *Changes, Changes* by Pat Hutchins), about the adventures of two wooden dolls, *Harold's Fairy Tale* (written by Crockett Johnson), which reveals how the title character employs purple crayons to create stories, *Whistle for Willie* (written by Ezra Jack Keats), which teaches Peter how to whistle, *Drummer Hoff* (written by Barbara & Ed Emberly); and the well known story, *Caps for Sale* (written by Esphyr Sbbodkina), in which a peddler can't get his hats back. Gene Deitch, USA, 1986. 30 minutes. Age Recommendation: T (Toddler; Ages Birth-3 years); S (Starting school, starting to read, starting pre-school, starting kindergarten; Ages 4-5).

VHS: S00447. $14.95.

Folk Games

This program features fun from a variety of countries, including the competitive broom stick-kick that's a favorite of Les Enfants du Morvan of France and the Crocodile masquerade that's popular in several Caribbean countries. You'll enjoy this program which also shows new twists to some old favorites in different cultural settings. Games are played by groups from Russia, China, France, England, Turkey and other countries. 60 minutes. Age Recommendation: P (Primary grades, grades 1-3; Ages 6-9); I (Intermediate grades, grades 4-6; Ages 10-12).

VHS: S10411. Currently out of print. May be available for rental in some video stores.

Five Stories for the Very Young
(© Weston Woods/Children's Circle Home Video)

Follow That Bunny!

This hoppin' claymation musical shows the adventures of some energetic bunnies who jump into action when Spring almost doesn't come one year. 27 minutes. Age Recommendation: S (Starting school, starting to read, starting pre-school, starting kindergarten; Ages 4-5); P (Primary grades, grades 1-3; Ages 6-9).

VHS: S18023. $12.98.

Follow the Drinking Gourd (Rabbit Ears)

Subtitled *A Story of the Underground Railroad*. Morgan Freeman narrates this absorbing and moving tale, adapted from the folksong, about one family's bid for freedom, achieved through the Underground Railroad. Note that the video deals with the violence of slavery, while focusing on a positive response. The authentic blues score is by Taj Mahal. 30 minutes. Age Recommendation: P (Primary grades, grades 1-3; Ages 6-9); I (Intermediate grades, grades 4-6; Ages 10-12).

VHS: S17888. $9.95.

Free to Be...You and Me

Marlo Thomas, Alan Alda, Harry Belafonte, Dick Cavett, Mel Brooks, Dustin Hoffman, Roberta Flash, Kris Kristofferson and many others join in this celebration of song, story and poetry, dedicated to helping children feel free to be who they are and who they want to be. The program actively promotes equality between the sexes; shows marriage as a partnership; addresses girl *and* boy gender stereotypes; even gives a liberated perspective on a "who will be her husband" fairy tale. From the 1970's, this may seem stylistically outdated to today's kids, but it still works well in the 90's. Marlo Thomas, USA, 1974. 44 minutes. Age Recommendation: S (Starting school, starting to read, starting pre-school, starting kindergarten; Ages 4-5); P (Primary grades, grades 1-3; Ages 6-9).

VHS: S00464. Currently out of print. May be available for rental in some video stores.

Frog and Toad Are Friends

Five short stories of the two best friends by Arnold Lobel. This tape also includes *Spring, The Story, A Lost Button, A Swim,* and *The Letter*. Amazing animation by director John Matthews. 18 minutes. Age Recommendation: S (Starting school, starting to read, starting pre-school, starting kindergarten; Ages 4-5); P (Primary grades, grades 1-3; Ages 6-9).

VHS: S24765. $12.95.

Frog and Toad Together

Easy-going Frog and excitable Toad share several amusing adventures and make some important discoveries. Based on Arnold Lobel's stories. Also included is the story *Dragons and Giants*, which could be a bit frightening. This multiple award-winner, directed by John Matthews, is presented in stop-action animation. 30 minutes. Age Recommendation: S (Starting school, starting to read, starting pre-school, starting kindergarten; Ages 4-5); P (Primary grades, grades 1-3; Ages 6-9).

VHS: S24988. $12.95.

Fun in a Box

These carefully crafted collections of award-winning animated and live-action films promote positive values and offer ideas for fun and games. Based on popular children's literature, these artfully executed shorts appeal to adults as well as children. Age Recommendation: S (Starting school, starting to read, starting pre-school, starting kindergarten; Ages 4-5); P (Primary grades, grades 1-3; Ages 6-9).

Fun in a Box Volume 1: Ben's Dream
From acclaimed author Chris Van Allsburg, the story of young Ben's travels around the world — in his house! The video also includes *Fish*, a "detective" story, and *Your Feets Too Big*, with animals dancing to Fats Waller's song. 1990. 30 minutes. Age Recommendation: S (Starting school, starting to read, starting pre-school, starting kindergarten; Ages 4-5); P (Primary grades, grades 1-3; Ages 6-9).

VHS: S16309. $14.95.

Fun in a Box Volume 2: New Friends and Other Stories
Howard, by James Stevenson, is the highlight story, about a duck who spends the winter in New York City. This program also includes *Metal Dogs of India* and *Why Cats Eat First*. 1990. 30 minutes. Age Recommendation: S (Starting school, starting to read, starting pre-school, starting kindergarten; Ages 4-5); P (Primary grades, grades 1-3; Ages 6-9).

VHS: S16308. $14.95.

Fun in a Box Volume 3: The Birthday Movie
This tape is full of interactive birthday fun and games. Most exciting is the multicultural fun with birthday traditions around the world. An interactive video hosted by The Birthday Spirit. 30 minutes. Age Recommendation: P (Primary grades, grades 1-3; Ages 6-9); I (Intermediate grades, grades 4-6; Ages 10-12).

VHS: S16307. $14.95.

Gateway to the Mind

G

A wonderful, animated excursion through the world of the five senses with Dr. Frank Baxter. Discover that grasshoppers can hear with their stomachs, fish can taste with their bodies, and sometimes the things we think we see aren't what they appear to be. Written and directed by master animator Chuck Jones. 58 minutes. Age Recommendation: P (Primary grades, grades 1-3; Ages 6-9); I (Intermediate grades, grades 4-6; Ages 10-12).

VHS: S14226. $19.98.

Get Ready for School

Young Brewster's first day of nursery school finds him overcoming his fears and having a great time learning things and making friends. Based on Richard Scarry's popular characters. 30 minutes. Age Recommendation: T (Toddler; Ages Birth-3 years).

VHS: S25034. $9.95.

Gift of Amazing Grace, The

Tempest Bledsoe is the only member of her gospel singing family who can't sing, but the former *Cosby Show* star is able to bring her family back together when things go wrong. USA. 48 minutes. Age Recommendation: P (Primary grades, grades 1-3; Ages 6-9); I (Intermediate grades, grades 4-6; Ages 10-12).

VHS: S16581. $9.98.

Gift of the Whales

A young Native American boy learns about whales from his grandfather and a visiting scientist. Since this deals with an endangered species, you may want to see this video *with* your children, to help them gain perspective. 30 minutes. Age Recommendation: P (Primary grades, grades 1-3; Ages 6-9); I (Intermediate grades, grades 4-6; Ages 10-12).

VHS: S10961. $29.95.

Gingerbread Christmas, A (Rabbit Ears)

Susan Saint James narrates this effervescent tale about the Prince and Princess of Gingerbread who are called into action to save the town of Gloomsbury, where Christmas has been cancelled. Music by Van Dyke

Parks. 30 minutes. Age Recommendation: S (Starting school, starting to read, starting pre-school, starting kindergarten; Ages 4-5); P (Primary grades, grades 1-3; Ages 6-9); I (Intermediate grades, grades 4-6; Ages 10-12).

VHS: S17773. $9.95.

Gingham Dog and the Calico Cat, The (Rabbit Ears)

The Gingham Dog and the Calico Cat are two Christmas presents who just don't get along — until Christmas Eve, when they fall out of Santa's sleigh and get lost in a great forest. This story is so good, don't wait until Christmas to see it! Narrated by Amy Grant, music by Chet Atkins. 30 minutes. Age Recommendation: S (Starting school, starting to read, starting pre-school, starting kindergarten; Ages 4-5); P (Primary grades, grades 1-3; Ages 6-9); I (Intermediate grades, grades 4-6; Ages 10-12).

VHS: S14679. $9.95.

Good Morning, Good Night: A Day on The Farm

One of the award-winning Bo Peep Productions. In this video, kids see close-up how animals (and children) eat, sleep and play. No real dialogue, just ooh's and moo's. Folk songs and music encourage kids to hop, skip and imitate animals. 17 minutes. Age Recommendation: T (Toddler; Ages Birth-3 years); S (Starting school, starting to read, starting pre-school, starting kindergarten; Ages 4-5).

VHS: S22379. $19.95.

Good Morning Miss Toliver

Acclaimed teacher Kay Toliver takes us to her New York City school, where we glimpse her incredible combination of math, art, acting and fun. This entertaining video was first seen on PBS. 26 minutes. Age Recommendation: P (Primary grades, grades 1-3; Ages 6-9); I (Intermediate grades, grades 4-6; Ages 10-12).

VHS: S24981. $19.95.

Good Morning Sunshine

Songs for a full day of wonder by Patti Dallas and Laura Baron. Filmed in a rich variety of outdoor settings, this video features fascinating instrumentation with dulcimers and recorders. Real kids dance and play. 30 minutes. Age Recommendation: T (Toddler; Ages Birth-3 years); S (Starting school, starting to read, starting pre-school, starting kindergarten; Ages 4-5).
VHS: S24895. $14.95.

Granpa

This beautifully animated video about exploring the imaginary worlds of past and future is based on John Burningham's prize-winning book and was created by the same team responsible for the perennial best-seller *The Snowman*. Narrated by Peter Ustinov. 30 minutes. Age Recommendation: S (Starting school, starting to read, starting pre-school, starting kindergarten; Ages 4-5); P (Primary grades, grades 1-3; Ages 6-9).
VHS: S15305. $14.98.

Gryphon

With a little bit of magic, a substitute teacher in a city school changes the life of a Latino boy. This film is based on a Charles Baxter short story. Themes concern not judging on appearance and not dismissing people who care about you. 58 minutes. Age Recommendation: P (Primary grades, grades 1-3; Ages 6-9); I (Intermediate grades, grades 4-6; Ages 10-12).
VHS: S13525. $14.95.

Good Morning Miss Toliver
(photo: Sherman Bryce/FASE Productions)

H Happy Birdy

In this birthday video, a bird hosts the party. Combining animation and puppetry, the words to songs are spelled out on the screen, encouraging viewers to sing along. 30 minutes. Age Recommendation: S (Starting school, starting to read, starting pre-school, starting kindergarten; Ages 4-5); P (Primary grades, grades 1-3; Ages 6-9). VHS: S25033. $9.98.

Harold and The Purple Crayon

Based on the stories of Crockett Johnson, this tape features *Harold's Fairy Tale* and *A Picture for Harold's Room*, in addition to the title story. The video includes *Animating Harold*, a documentary about the making of the Harold videos. 30 minutes. Age Recommendation: S (Starting school, starting to read, starting pre-school, starting kindergarten; Ages 4-5); P (Primary grades, grades 1-3; Ages 6-9). VHS: S22166. $14.95.

Harriet Tubman (1820- 1913) — Anti-Slavery Activist

From *The Black Americans of Achievement Series*. This video is based upon the acclaimed book by M. W. Taylor, drawing from the expertise of a brilliant group of consultants and experts. Courageous and fearless, even as a child, Harriet Tubman emerged from a life of slavery to become a major figure in the anti-slavery movement, a driving force in the Underground Railroad, and an effective spy for the Union against the Confederacy during the Civil War. Directly responsible for the freedom of more than 1,100 people, Harriet Tubman became a legend in her own time. The video deals with powerful, positive responses to violent situations, and frames historical events well. 30 minutes. Age Recommendation: P (Primary grades, grades 1-3; Ages 6-9); I (Intermediate grades, grades 4-6; Ages 10-12). VHS: S17388. $39.95.

Hawk, I'm Your Brother

From the series *Will Rogers, Jr. Presents: Stories of American Indian Culture*. Will Rogers, Jr. narrates this story of Native American culture based on the book by Byrd Baylor. Young Rudy Soto wants to fly into the wild blue yonder without the expense of taking an airplane. He seeks advice from a captured red-tailed hawk for natural flying tips. This children's story was winner of a Peace Pipe Award. USA. 25 minutes. Age Recommendation: P (Primary grades, grades 1-3; Ages 6-9); I (Intermediate grades, grades 4-6; Ages 10-12).

VHS: S13294. $14.99.

Here We Go

An informative show that captures children's fascinations with some of the most exciting vehicles ever made. Full of fantastic experiment and adventure. Narrated by Lynn Redgrave. Parents' Choice Award. 33 minutes each tape. Age Recommendation: T (Toddler; Ages Birth-3 years); S (Starting school, starting to read, starting pre-school, starting kindergarten; Ages 4-5).

Here We Go — Volume 1
Volume 1 features zeppelins, hover crafts, fire engines and ocean liners. 1985.

VHS: S04996. $12.95.

Here We Go — Volume 2
Sequences include land, sea and air, featuring helicopters, bulldozers, dump trucks and even a tramway. 1985.

VHS: S04997. Currently out of print. May be available for rental in some video stores.

Here We Go Again
Featuring 14 thrilling sequences from around the world. Lynn Redgrave provides valuable information and excitement at each intriguing location. Kids will get to ride on a San Francisco cable car, a farm tractor, in a police car, and in a propeller airplane, among other vehicles. (Note that there is a different video, one made in 1942 and featuring Fibber McGee, with the same title.) 60 minutes. 1987.

VHS: S16759. $12.95.

Hey, What About Me?

A warm, straight-forward attempt to talk to pre-schoolers about adjusting to new siblings. Pre-schoolers talk to pre-schoolers! This video also teaches games, lullabies and bouncing rhymes which the new siblings can play together. Winner of the American Film Institute Video Award and noted on the American Academy of Pediatrics suggested media list. 25 minutes. Age Recommendation: T (Toddler; Ages Birth-3 years); S (Starting school, starting to read, starting pre-school, starting kindergarten; Ages 4-5).

VHS: S10149. $14.95.

Hideaways, The

Based on the popular Newberry Award-winning book *From the Mixed-Up Files of Mrs. Basil E. Frankweiler* by E.L. Konigsburg. The legendary Ingrid Bergman headlines this wondrous tale of two children who run away to a secret hideout brimming with intrigue and excitement — New York's Metropolitan Museum of Art. This video shows how 12-year-old Claudia's fantasy is squelched by her responsibilities as the eldest girl in the family. The film depicts a positive relationship between an older woman (a recluse) and the girl, and teaches excellent lessons on dealing with society's stereotypes of girls. Featuring Richard Mulligan and Madeline Kahn. Fiedler Cook, USA, 1973. 105 minutes. Age Recommendation: P (Primary grades, grades 1-3; Ages 6-9); I (Intermediate grades, grades 4-6; Ages 10-12).

VHS: S02715. $19.98.

Hip Hop Animal Rock Workout

This "workout" tape features kids and animated animals in an enchanted rain forest. 30 minutes. Age Recommendation: P (Primary grades, grades 1-3; Ages 6-9).

VHS; S24531. $9.98.

Hoboken Chicken Emergency

When the Bobowicz family asked their son Arthur to pick up a turkey for Thanksgiving, they weren't expecting him to bring home a 266-pound live chicken named Henrietta. Neither was Hoboken. This wild comedy was based on the book by D. Manus Pinkwater, and produced by a multiple Emmy Award-winning production team. With Gabe Kaplan, Dick Van Patten and Peter Billingsley. 60 minutes. Age Recommendation: P (Primary grades, grades 1-3; Ages 6-9); I (Intermediate grades, grades 4-6; Ages 10-12).

VHS: S12403. $14.95.

Holidays for Children Video Series

This series explores the symbols, customs, rituals and folklore underlying some of the major traditional holidays. The programs combine traditional music, illustrated folk tales, animation, arts and crafts with informational segments about the meaning and significance of these celebrations. Live segments include guest performers.

Children learn about seasons, activities, animals and other symbols associated with each holiday. The videos aim to develop an appreciation of one's own heritage and foster understanding of the customs of others. Created by an impressive group of educators. Designed for classroom use. Highly recommended by *Video Librarian*. 30 minutes each video. Age

Recommendation: S (Starting school, starting to read, starting pre-school, starting kindergarten; Ages 4-5); P (Primary grades, grades 1-3; Ages 6-9).

Arbor Day
VHS: S24460. $29.95.

Chinese New Year
VHS: S24461. $29.95.

Christmas
VHS: S24462. $29.95.

Cinco De Mayo
VHS: S24463. $29.95.

Easter
VHS: S24464. $29.95.

Halloween
VHS: S24465. $29.95.

Hanukkah/Passover
VHS: S24466. $29.95.

Independence Day
VHS: S24467. $29.95.

Kwanzaa
VHS: S24468. $29.95.

Rosh Hashanah/Yom Kippur
VHS: S24469. $29.95.

Thanksgiving
VHS: S24470. $29.95.

Valentine's Day
VHS: S24471. $29.95.

Holidays for Children/Set of 12 Videos
VHS: S24472. $359.40.

How Come?

From the *Learn About Living Series* designed to help children sort out the challenges of growing up. Through the use of live-action and animation,

Windjammer Way becomes a fantasy playground for young minds to explore. Other titles in the series include *Mine and Yours*, *Never Talk to Strangers* and *Who Will Be My Friend?*. 30 minutes. Age Recommendation: S (Starting school, starting to read, starting pre-school, starting kindergarten; Ages 4-5). VHS: S24995. $9.95.

How the Leopard Got His Spots (Rabbit Ears)

In this marvelous African folk tale, a leopard discovers the value of protective coloration. Narrated by Danny Glover, with music by the South African group Ladysmith Black Mambazo. 30 minutes. Age Recommendation: S (Starting school, starting to read, starting pre-school, starting kindergarten; Ages 4-5); P (Primary grades, grades 1-3; Ages 6-9); I (Intermediate grades, grades 4-6; Ages 10-12). VHS: S09506. $14.95.

How to Hide Stories

Ruth Heller has composed six beautiful tales involving birds, amphibians and reptiles engaged in clever games of hide-and-seek with Mother Nature. With striking illustrations and a rhyming text, the stories deal with transformation and how animals camouflage in nature. Each video is 5-6 minutes. Age Recommendation: S (Starting school, starting to read, starting pre-school, starting kindergarten; Ages 4-5); P (Primary grades, grades 1-3; Ages 6-9).

How to Hide a Butterfly and Other Insects
VHS: S20020. $44.95.

How to Hide a Crocodile and Other Reptiles
VHS: S20015. $44.95.

How to Hide a Gray Treefrog and Other Amphibians
VHS: S20019. $44.95.

How to Hide a Polar Bear and Other Mammals
VHS: S20016. $44.95.

How to Hide a Whip-Poor-Will and Other Birds
VHS: S20017. $44.95.

How to Hide an Octopus and Other Sea Creatures
VHS: S20018. $44.95.

How to Hide Stories Set
Set of six videos. 32 minutes.
VHS: S20021. $239.95.

Human Race Club Series

This fully animated children's series emphasizes values and includes tips on growing up. Created by Joy Berry, the best-selling author of self-help books for children. Each video is 60 minutes. Age Recommendation: P (Primary grades, grades 1-3; Ages 6-9); I (Intermediate grades, grades 4-6; Ages 10-12).

Human Race Club: A Story About Fights between Brothers and Sisters
Sibling rivalry and handling uncomfortable feelings are the topics in this volume. Stories include *Casey's Revenge* and *The Lean Mean Machine*.
VHS: S10990. $29.95.

Human Race Club: A Story About Making Friends, A Story About Prejudice and Discrimination
Children learn about discrimination, prejudice and friendship in the animated stories *The Fair Weather Friend* and *Unforgettable Pen Pal*.
VHS: S10989. $29.95.

Human Race Club: A Story About Self-Esteem
This volume deals with self-esteem and earning money in stories entitled *The Letter on Light Blue Stationery* and *A High Price to Pay*.
VHS: S10988. $29.95.

I Can Build

A real family works together to build a two-story playhouse. The family cooperation of a big sister, younger brother, mom and dad presents a good role-model. The step-by-step process is shown, from shopping to sawing and hammering. With combined live-action, computer animation and time-lapse sequences, it is easy to see the construction process. 25 minutes. Age Recommendation: T (Toddler; Ages Birth-3 years); S (Starting school, starting to read, starting pre-school, starting kindergarten; Ages 4-5).
VHS: S24547. $14.95.

I Dig Fossils

An award-winning look at a young boy and his father going on a hunt for fossils that are older than dinosaur fossils. Includes useful science tips and advice on how to organize activities like "digs" with children. 25 minutes.

Age Recommendation: S (Starting school, starting to read, starting pre-school, starting kindergarten; Ages 4-5); P (Primary grades, grades 1-3; Ages 6-9); I (Intermediate grades, grades 4-6; Ages 10-12).

VHS: S23856. $19.95.

I Have a Friend

A small boy tells of his very special friend who keeps his dreams secret and safe. At night his friend disappears, but will be waiting for him with the sun. The friend is the boy's shadow. 7 minutes. Age Recommendation: T (Toddler; Ages Birth-3 years); S (Starting school, starting to read, starting pre-school, starting kindergarten; Ages 4-5).

VHS: S12261. $62.00.

I Need a Hug!

In this rhyme, a sad, lonely bug who longs for love and acceptance wants a hug, but the other bugs are too busy to notice his pain. Finally, he finds a soulmate. The story was composed and illustrated by first-grade students at Clara Barton Elementary in Bordertown, New Jersey. 6 minutes. Age Recommendation: S (Starting school, starting to read, starting pre-school, starting kindergarten; Ages 4-5); P (Primary grades, grades 1-3; Ages 6-9).

VHS: S19600. $39.00.

I Want to Be an Artist When I Grow Up

This video provides an overview of various careers in the arts. 15 minutes. Age Recommendation: S (Starting school, starting to read, starting pre-school, starting kindergarten; Ages 4-5); P (Primary grades, grades 1-3; Ages 6-9); I (Intermediate grades, grades 4-6; Ages 10-12).

VHS: S19929. $28.99.

I'm Not Oscar's Friend
Anymore and Other Stories

Four book-based stories which focus on friendship. In addition to the title story (written by Marjorie Weinman Sharmat), the video includes *Creole*, featuring a bird whose appearance frightens the other animals, *Hug Me* (written by Patti Stren), starring a porcupine desperate for a hug, and *Birds of a Feather*, a story about differences. 30 minutes. Age Recommendation: S (Starting school, starting to read, starting pre-school, starting kindergarten; Ages 4-5); P (Primary grades, grades 1-3; Ages 6-9).

VHS: S24533. $9.95.

Imaginaria: A Computer Animation Music Video for Children

Thirteen imaginative segments of creative color, music, stories, vignettes and flights of fancy. This video highlights trains, jugglers, world music, ducks, bluebirds, gadgets, and views through windshields. 40 minutes. Age Recommendation: S (Starting school, starting to read, starting pre-school, starting kindergarten; Ages 4-5); P (Primary grades, grades 1-3; Ages 6-9); I (Intermediate grades, grades 4-6; Ages 10-12).

VHS: S20649. $14.98.

Imagine That!

A touching video about a young boy adjusting to pre-school, which will help kids in (or preparing to go to) pre-school. 30 minutes. Age Recommendation: S (Starting school, starting to read, starting pre-school, starting kindergarten; Ages 4-5).

VHS: S24534. $9.95.

In the Company of Whales

Kids join a company of whales in the ocean, and find out more about the fascinating lives and habits of these mammals. 90 minutes. Age Recommendation: P (Primary grades, grades 1-3; Ages 6-9); I (Intermediate grades, grades 4-6; Ages 10-12).

VHS: S17011. $24.95.

In the Tall, Tall Grass

If you were a fuzzy caterpillar crawling through the tall, tall grass on a sunny afternoon, what would you see? You'd see ants, bees, birds — and hip-hopping bunnies, too! You'd even hear the sounds they make! This backyard tour, created with bold, colorful paintings and large simple words, is one children will enjoy. 6 minutes. Age Recommendation: S (Starting school, starting to read, starting pre-school, starting kindergarten; Ages 4-5); P (Primary grades, grades 1-3; Ages 6-9).

VHS: S16348. $44.95.

Indoor Fun

Contains four individual chapters, each of them an informative and interactive segment meant to be viewed while using simple household materials. The titles featured are *Body Talk*, *Making Faces*, *A Close Look at*

Volcanoes, and *A Short Journey into Space.* 30 minutes. Age Recommendation: P (Primary grades, grades 1-3; Ages 6-9); I (Intermediate grades, grades 4-6; Ages 10-12).

VHS: S08106. $29.95.

Introducing: The Flying Fruit Fly Circus

A documentary on the Flying Fruit Fly Circus, an Australian-based, youth performing arts company which was founded in 1979. The program offers thrilling spectacle, as the 40-member troupe — entirely made up of children — performs various tumbling acts. 50 minutes. Age Recommendation: P (Primary grades, grades 1-3; Ages 6-9); I (Intermediate grades, grades 4-6; Ages 10-12).

VHS: S19642. $24.95.

Ira Says Goodbye
(Live Oak Media)

Ira Says Goodbye

Ira is upset when his best friend Reggie has to move away. Based on the story by Bernard Waber. 1989. 18 minutes. Age Recommendation: S (Starting school, starting to read, starting pre-school, starting kindergarten; Ages 4-5); P (Primary grades, grades 1-3; Ages 6-9).

VHS: S24532. $37.95.

Ira Sleeps Over

Michael Sporn's lovingly crafted, whimsical animation is based on Bernard Waber's children's story about the fears experienced by Ira on his first night away from home when he sleeps over at Reggie's house. Should he bring his teddy bear? He discovers that Reggie has the same problem. 27 minutes. Age Recommendation: S (Starting school, starting to read, starting pre-school, starting kindergarten; Ages 4-5); P (Primary grades, grades 1-3; Ages 6-9).

VHS: S19546. $12.98.

It Zwibble: Earthday Birthday

Join a dinosaur family that wants to protect the Earth. After a journey on which the family sees the beauty as well as the destruction of the Earth, we learn that even small gestures can help our planet. Directed by Michael Sporn. 30 minutes. Age Recommendation: S (Starting school, starting to read, starting pre-school, starting kindergarten; Ages 4-5); P (Primary grades, grades 1-3; Ages 6-9).

VHS: S24514. $9.98.

It's Not Always Easy Being a Kid

The puppets at The Judy Theatre help children acquire skills for living. In this video, young Charlie comes to grips with his failure at school by working with a tutor. Also included are a fable and song which examine the temptation to smoke cigarettes and help find an alternative for feeling good about oneself. 30 minutes. Age Recommendation: P (Primary grades, grades 1-3; Ages 6-9); I (Intermediate grades, grades 4-6; Ages 10-12).

VHS: S24713. $19.95.

It's Not Easy Being Green

The Muppets sing 13 crowd-pleasers, accompanied by Kermit on his ukulele. Includes "Bein' Green," "Somewhere Over the Rainbow" and "In a Cabin in the Woods." 37 minutes. Age Recommendation: T (Toddler; Ages Birth-3 years); S (Starting school, starting to read, starting pre-school, starting kindergarten; Ages 4-5).

VHS: S24941. $12.99

It's the Muppets! Series

Highlights of the long-running and acclaimed *Muppet Show*. The video includes pig-latin musicals, episodes of "Pigs in Space," Kermit's famous song "It's Not Easy Being Green" and more! Each tape is 38 minutes. Age Recommendation: S (Starting school, starting to read, starting pre-school, starting kindergarten; Ages 4-5); P (Primary grades, grades 1-3; Ages 6-9).

Meet the Muppets!
VHS: S24711. $12.99.

More Muppets!
VHS: S24712. $12.99.

J

Jack and The Beanstalk (Faerie Tale Theatre)

Based on the book by Joseph Jacobs. Produced by Shelley Duvall, this is a very unusual but absolutely fascinating live-action realization of the tale. Dennis Christopher, Elliott Gould and Jean Stapleton star in this off-beat version of the well known story. 1982. 60 minutes. Age Recommendation: P (Primary grades, grades 1-3; Ages 6-9); I (Intermediate grades, grades 4-6; Ages 10-12).

VHS: S02884. Currently out of print. May be available for rental in some video stores.

Jack and the Beanstalk (Rabbit Ears)

Based on the book by Joseph Jacobs. Monty Python's Michael Palin returns this classic tale about Jack and an ogre to its decidedly English origins. Contemporary music by Dave Stewart, formerly of Eurythmics. 27 minutes. Age Recommendation: S (Starting school, starting to read, starting pre-school, starting kindergarten; Ages 4-5); P (Primary grades, grades 1-3; Ages 6-9); I (Intermediate grades, grades 4-6; Ages 10-12).

VHS: S14102. $9.95.

Jacob Have I Loved (Amanda Plummer)

Amanda Plummer plays Louise in this adaptation of Katherine Paterson's Newberry Award-winning novel about a young girl growing up on a tiny, isolated Chesapeake island and her relationship with her twin sister. 55 minutes. Age Recommendation: I (Intermediate grades, grades 4-6; Ages 10-12).

VHS: S07697. $119.00.

Jacob Have I Loved (Bridget Fonda)

Bridget Fonda stars in this thoughtful study in sibling rivalry, based on the popular novel by Katherine Paterson. Sixteen-year-old Louise (Fonda) has always felt that her sister was the favored child and so sets out to find her own special place in her small world. Produced by KCET-TV. 60 minutes. Age Recommendation: I (Intermediate grades, grades 4-6; Ages 10-12).

VHS: S12396. $29.95.

Janey Junkfood's Fresh Adventure

This Emmy award-winning TV special is a wildly funny program, which aims to excite and educate children (and families) about healthy food. 30

minutes. Age Recommendation: S (Starting school, starting to read, starting pre-school, starting kindergarten; Ages 4-5); P (Primary grades, grades 1-3; Ages 6-9); I (Intermediate grades, grades 4-6; Ages 10-12).
VHS: S24768. $99.00.

Jay Jay the Jet Plane and His Flying Friends Series

Model planes come to life in the storybook land where not even the sky is the limit. With joyful lessons about life, family, friends and things that really matter. Yes, some of the planes are female! Each video is 30 minutes. Age Recommendation: T (Toddler; Ages Birth-3 years); S (Starting school, starting to read, starting pre-school, starting kindergarten; Ages 4-5).

Volume 1. Jay Jay's First Flight and Three Other Stories
English Version. VHS: S22941. $12.95.

Volume 1. Tito Turbinitas Y Sus Amigos Voladores
Spanish Version. VHS: S24584. $12.95.

Volume 2. Old Oscar Leads the Parade and Three Other Stories
VHS: S24575. $12.95.

Jay O'Callahan: Herman & Marguerite

A tale of an insecure worm and a frightened caterpillar (later a butterfly) who learn to look at themselves and each other with love and respect as they help bring Spring to the Earth. A discussion guide accompanies the tape. Told by master storyteller Jay O'Callahan. 28 minutes. Age Recommendation: S (Starting school, starting to read, starting pre-school, starting kindergarten; Ages 4-5); P (Primary grades, grades 1-3; Ages 6-9); I (Intermediate grades, grades 4-6; Ages 10-12). Public performance rights included.
VHS: S09268. $19.95.

Jay O'Callahan: A Master Class in Storytelling

Storytelling sparks imagination. In *Master Class*, Jay O'Callahan shows what makes a story work and how characters can be brought to life. "Jay O'Callahan is a one-man cultural renaissance. These tapes should be required viewing for all between the ages of five and ninety-five" (*Video Librarian*). With workshop guide. 33 minutes. Age Recommendation: P (Primary grades, grades 1-3; Ages 6-9); I (Intermediate grades, grades 4-6; Ages 10-12). Public performance rights included.
VHS: S09265. $59.95.

Jay O'Callahan: Six Stories About Little Heroes

Jay O'Callahan's original tales on the universal themes of courage, friendship and truth are examples of how all of us can draw upon the power of the imagination to create our own stories. In *Six Stories*, the subjects include O'Callahan's creations of a king, various children and assorted frogs and bees. 38 minutes. Age Recommendation: P (Primary grades, grades 1-3; Ages 6-9); I (Intermediate grades, grades 4-6; Ages 10-12). Public performance rights included.

VHS: S09267. $19.95.

Jazz Time Tale

The animated story of a young girl's transformation following her encounter with the legendary piano player Fats Waller. Narrated by Ruby Dee. Directed by Michael Sporn. 29 minutes. Age Recommendation: P (Primary grades, grades 1-3; Ages 6-9); I (Intermediate grades, grades 4-6; Ages 10-12).

VHS: S17764. $9.98.

Jessi Sings Songs from Around the World

Jessi Colter performs 25 international children's songs, including such favorites as "La Cucaracha," "This Land Is Your Land," "Funiculi, Funicula," "London Bridge," "Too Ra Loo Ra Loo Ra," and "Aloha Oe." 57 minutes. Age Recommendation: S (Starting school, starting to read, starting pre-school, starting kindergarten; Ages 4-5); P (Primary grades, grades 1-3; Ages 6-9); I (Intermediate grades, grades 4-6; Ages 10-12).

VHS: S21875. $14.98.

Joan Baez (1941-Present) — Mexican American Folksinger

From *The Hispanics of Achievement Video Collection*. Includes music, photographs and commentary on the life of the pioneering folk singer and activist. This biography was designed for classroom use. 30 minutes. Age Recommendation: I (Intermediate grades, grades 4-6; Ages 10-12).

English Version. VHS: S24447. $39.95.

Spanish Version. VHS: S24943. $39.95.

Joe Scruggs First Video

A blend of animation, live-action and enchanting songs creates a musical masterpiece in a class by itself. Recommended by the American Library Association and Video Librarian, and a recipient of the Parents' Choice Award. 30 minutes. Age Recommendation: S (Starting school, starting to read, starting pre-school, starting kindergarten; Ages 4-5); P (Primary grades, grades 1-3; Ages 6-9).

VHS: S17139. $14.95.

Joe Scruggs in Concert

This tape features children's music videos for the whole family. Highlighted on this tape are Joe, his guitar, puppets and giant props. Even the audience is fascinating to watch as they sing along, clap along and sign along in Sign Language. 51 minutes. Age Recommendation: S (Starting school, starting to read, starting pre-school, starting kindergarten; Ages 4-5); P (Primary grades, grades 1-3; Ages 6-9).

VHS: S24536. $14.95.

John Henry (Rabbit Ears)

Denzel Washington narrates this poetic, dreamy and mythic tale. John Henry, an African American railroader, defeats a steam drill in a steel driving competition. Legendary blues performer B.B. King provides a richly textured score. 30 minutes. Age Recommendation: S (Starting school, starting to read, starting pre-school, starting kindergarten; Ages 4-5); P (Primary grades, grades 1-3; Ages 6-9); I (Intermediate grades, grades 4-6; Ages 10-12).

VHS: S17887. $9.95.

Johnny Appleseed (Rabbit Ears)

The tall tale which explains how apples came to be so prevalent in the young United States. Narrated by Garrison Keillor, author and radio personality. Music by Mark O'Connor. 24 minutes. Age Recommendation: S (Starting school, starting to read, starting pre-school, starting kindergarten; Ages 4-5); P (Primary grades, grades 1-3; Ages 6-9); I (Intermediate grades, grades 4-6; Ages 10-12).

VHS: S24040. $9.98.

Josephine's Imagination

Our evaluators give this video a special mention as one of the best. Based on Arnold Dobrin's story and illustrations, the story is about a young Haitian girl

and her mother who earns her living selling at the market. Josephine makes little dolls from the throw-away bits of things from the market. Soon she has her own little business going. Even the boys like her dolls! This is a very warm, gentle film, which shows Haitian culture at its best. 14 minutes. Age Recommendation: S (Starting school, starting to read, starting pre-school, starting kindergarten; Ages 4-5); P (Primary grades, grades 1-3; Ages 6-9).
VHS: S24537. $69.95.

Joshua's Masai Mask

Based on the book by Dakari Hru. Joshua loves playing his kalimba, a traditional African musical instrument, but his classmates like rap music. Joshua talks with Uncle Zambezi, who gives him a magical Masai mask, which grants wishes. 12 minutes. Age Recommendation: S (Starting school, starting to read, starting pre-school, starting kindergarten; Ages 4-5); P (Primary grades, grades 1-3; Ages 6-9); I (Intermediate grades; grades 4-6; Ages 10-12).
VHS: S22353. $39.95.

John Henry
(Illustrated by Barry Jackson/Rabbit Ears Productions)

Juggle Time

Learn confidence while learning to juggle in this fun-filled program designed to teach juggling in slow motion by using scarves (we tried it — it works!). Three colorful scarves are included in the package. Winner of the Questar/Mercom Gold Award and the National Educational Film and Video Festival Award. 30 minutes. Age Recommendation: P (Primary grades, grades 1-3; Ages 6-9); I (Intermediate grades, grades 4-6; Ages 10-12).

VHS: S17138. $14.95.

Jumanji

Fantasy and reality combine in this adaptation of Chris Van Allsburg's award-winning story about two bored children who find a mysterious game which brings a jungle into their living room. 13 minutes. Age Recommendation: P (Primary grades, grades 1-3; Ages 6-9); I (Intermediate grades, grades 4-6; Ages 10-12).

VHS: S08163. $65.00.

Junglies: First Day at School

A vivid collection of vignettes which dramatize individual situations of young children caught up in the awe and wonder of childhood. 30 minutes. Age Recommendation: S (Starting school, starting to read, starting pre-school, starting kindergarten; Ages 4-5).

VHS: S19433. $14.99.

Just Grandma and Me

One of Mercer Mayer's best-loved stories comes to life in this 1995 release. 30 minutes. Age Recommendation: S (Starting school, starting to read, starting pre-school, starting kindergarten; Ages 4-5); P (Primary grades, grades 1-3; Ages 6-9).

VHS: S25000. $12.95.

Just Me and My Dad

Mercer Mayer's ever-popular "Little Critter" is off to the woods for his first camp-out with Dad. Based on the book of the same title. 30 minutes. Age Recommendation: S (Starting school, starting to read, starting pre-school, starting kindergarten; Ages 4-5); P (Primary grades, grades 1-3; Ages 6-9).

VHS: S24999. $12.95.

Kids Get Cooking: The Egg

This celebration of food and cooking will thrill kids as they learn recipes, experiments, crafts and more. Puppets Herb and Bea add comedy to the cooking and songs. Endorsed by the National Education Association. 30 minutes. Age Recommendation: S (Starting school, starting to read, starting pre-school, starting kindergarten; Ages 4-5); P (Primary grades, grades 1-3; Ages 6-9); I (Intermediate grades, grades 4-6; Ages 10-12).

VHS: S10148. $14.95.

Public Performance Rights. VHS: S17152. $34.90.

Koi and the Kola Nuts
(Illustrated by Reynold Ruffins/Rabbit Ears Productions)

Kids Kitchen: Making Good Eating Great Fun for Kids!

Join the juggling nutrition magician and her diverse group of kids as they learn to create delicious, nutritious snacks without cooking. 45 minutes. Age Recommendation: S (Starting school, starting to read, starting pre-school, starting kindergarten; Ages 4-5); P (Primary grades, grades 1-3; Ages 6-9); I (Intermediate grades, grades 4-6; Ages 10-12).

VHS: S24769. $99.00.

Kidsongs Music Video Stories

A series of sing-a-long music videos featuring performances by the Kidsongs Kids, a group of multiracial, multiethnic, multitalented boys and girls. Based on the PBS series, the videos include themes and concepts which are developmentally important. The content is geared toward 2-6 year olds, but also interests older kids, as the subplots involve the older children who produce the show. We see children doing interviews, using cameras, and more. Each tape is 25 minutes. Age Recommendation: T (Toddler; Ages Birth-3 years); S (Starting school, starting to read, starting pre-school, starting kindergarten; Ages 4-5); P (Primary grades, grades 1-3; Ages 6-9).

Boppin' with Biggles
VHS: S24722. $14.95.

Cars, Boats, Trains and Planes
VHS: S06641. $14.98.

Country Sing-Along
VHS: S24723. $14.95.

A Day at Camp
VHS: S24538. $14.95.

A Day at Old MacDonald's Farm
VHS: S06639. $14.98.

A Day at the Circus
VHS: S06647. $14.98.

A Day with the Animals
VHS: S06640. $14.98.

Good Night, Sleep Tight
VHS: S06642. $14.98.

I'd Like to Teach the World to Sing
VHS: S06643. $14.98.

If We Could Talk to the Animals
VHS: S24539. $14.95.

Let's Play Ball!
VHS: S24540. $14.95.

Ride the Roller Coaster
VHS: S24541. $14.95.

Sing Out, America!
VHS: S06644. $14.98.

Very Silly Songs
VHS: S24542. $14.95.

We Wish You a Merry Christmas
VHS: S24784. $12.95.

What I Want to Be!
VHS: S06646. $14.98.

The Wonderful World of Sports
VHS: S06645. $14.98.

King Midas and the Golden Touch (Rabbit Ears)

Narrator Michael Caine adds a regal touch to the classic Greek tale of King Midas, in which a misguided monarch learns that there are some things in life more precious than gold. Music by Ellis Marsalis and Yo-Yo Ma. 30 minutes. Age Recommendation: P (Primary grades, grades 1-3; Ages 6-9); I (Intermediate grades, grades 4-6; Ages 10-12).
VHS: S14681. $9.95.

Kitten Companions

This program examines the friendships between children and kittens, as kids see the actions and behavior of kittens and learn how to respond to them. 30 minutes. Age Recommendation: S (Starting school, starting to read, starting pre-school, starting kindergarten; Ages 4-5); P (Primary grades, grades 1-3; Ages 6-9).
VHS: S18225. $14.95.

Knots on a Counting Rope

Based on the book by Bill Martin Jr. and John Archambault, illustrated by Ted Rand. In this award-winning story, a Native American boy and his grandfather sit around a campfire telling stories as the grandfather ties knots in the counting rope. A moving story of love, hope and courage as the boy faces the greatest challenge of his life — his blindness. 14 minutes. Age Recommendation: S (Starting school, starting to read, starting pre-school, starting kindergarten; Ages 4-5); P (Primary grades, grades 1-3; Ages 6-9); I (Intermediate grades; grades 4-6; Ages 10-12).
VHS: S14198. $44.95.

Koi and the Kola Nuts (Rabbit Ears)

Oscar-winner Whoopi Goldberg humorously retells this African folktale about the proud son of a chief who sets out to find his rightful place in the world. Grammy and Oscar-winning composer Herbie Hancock provides the inimitable score. 30 minutes. Age Recommendation: P (Primary grades, grades 1-3; Ages 6-9); I (Intermediate grades, grades 4-6; Ages 10-12).

VHS: S16549. $9.95.

Land of Pleasant Dreams, The

L

This is a series of animated videos in which chidren fall off to sleep and enter a lovely dreamland where their experience helps them know what to do in real life. 1987. Each video is 30 minutes. Age Recommendation: T (Toddler; Ages Birth-3 years); S (Starting school, starting to read, starting pre-school, starting kinder-garten; Ages 4-5).

Bearly There At All
Threads The Bear wants to feel special. The video includes the story *A Girl with The Pop-Up Garden*.

VHS: S24545. $14.95.

Fence Too High, A
Lacey, the quilted lamb, is convinced she can't win the fence-jumping contest. Peter helps her give it a try. The video includes the story *A Tailor-Made Friendship*.

VHS: S24543. $14.95.

Is It Soup Yet?
Join Ric Rac The Rabbit as he discovers that too many cooks can spoil the broth. The video includes the story *The Biggest Little Girl*.

VHS: S24544. $14.95.

Land of Sweet Taps, The

This is a fun-filled adventure for children who want to learn tap dancing. In addition to the fundamental sounds, rhythms and steps, there are shuffles and digs. The lyrics are fun and memorable, helping children remember the timing of the music. 57 minutes. Age Recommendation: S (Starting school, starting to read, starting pre-school, starting kindergarten; Ages 4-5); P (Primary grades, grades 1-3; Ages 6-9).

VHS: S21701. $19.95.

Language Primer

A blend of animation, music and sound effects is used to relate wordless stories about Max, a mouse. The program is designed to encourage children to take an active role in the learning process. The video instructs children on basic language skills: sequencing, recognizing a main idea, recalling details, storywriting and storytelling. The programming is "very effective," (*Video Rating Guide for Libraries*). Designed for classroom use, parents can use these videos at home to help boost kids' writing skills. Age Recommendation: S (Starting school, starting to read, starting pre-school, starting kindergarten; Ages 4-5); P (Primary grades, grades 1-3; Ages 6-9).

Adventuresome Max: Discovering the World
In eight vignettes, Max establishes friendships with an army of ants, an outcast snail and an alien from another world, and in the process, learns valuable information about himself and the outside world. 18 minutes.
VHS: S19960. $49.95.

Max in Motion: Developing Language Skills
Eight stories are expressed without words, each focusing on Max, an eccentric mouse with an innovative flair for problem solving. 18 minutes.
VHS: S19959. $49.95.

Max's Library: Beginning to Write
With the aid of puppets and animation, children learn how to create a short story — from conception through execution. They develop their story by learning to define a beginning, a middle and an end. 16 minutes.
VHS: S19961. $49.95.

Language Primer Set
The set of three programs. 52 minutes.
VHS: S19962. $129.00.

Language Stories

A collection of educational videos about language, thought and action. The works concentrate on sentence structure, parts of speech and appropriate usage. Age Recommendation: P (Primary grades, grades 1-3; Ages 6-9); I (Intermediate grades, grades 4-6; Ages 10-12).

A Cache of Jewels and Other Collective Nouns
The text is created from collective nouns and enlivened by bright, beautifully colored drawings. 11 minutes.
VHS: S20068. $44.95.

Kites Sail High

This video breaks down verbs in musical verses. "The verses are accompanied by bold, gaily colored graphics that are especially striking for their skillful use of pattern and design" (*Publisher's Weekly*). 11 minutes.

VHS: S20070. $44.95.

Many Luscious Lollipops

This video, subtitled *A Book About Adjectives*, points out how "adjectives are terrific when you want to be specific." 8 minutes.

VHS: S20069. $44.95.

Merry-Go-Round

This video about nouns highlights the different functions nouns serve. 16 minutes.

VHS: S20071. $44.95.

Language Stories Set

The collection of four programs. 46 minutes.

VHS: S20072. $159.95.

Learning About Me

In this educational series, an eccentric witch and a giant green dragon join forces to instruct children on the need for honesty, forgiveness, responsibility, developing self-worth and respect, and having the capacity to listen and communicate with their peers. "A lively, up-to-date program for the primary grades, designed to help children explore their own individuality in ways that will develop their capacity for making responsible choices" (*Booklist*). Age Recommendation: S (Starting school, starting to read, starting pre-school, starting kindergarten; Ages 4-5); P (Primary grades, grades 1-3; Ages 6-9).

A Is for Autonomy

Children learn how to unlock the mysteries of their own identities by solving intricate riddles. A special game called "Hidden Treasure" enables them to discover what is unique and special about their lives. 16 minutes.

VHS: S19943. $37.95.

B Is for Belonging

Children learn to make friendships as they tell frightening stories around a campfire and share personal experiences. 18 minutes.

VHS: S19944. $37.95.

Ipsilwhich Adventures

Inability to communicate is about to destroy an important cookout when Lollipop Dragon and Apple Blossom intervene and teach the children how to get along. 23 minutes.

VHS: S19942. $37.95.

Learning About Me Set

The set of three programs. 55 minutes.

VHS: S19945. $99.00.

Let's Create Art Activities

Teacher Ann Felice does exciting projects with real kids. This tape promotes positive values and features great music. 51 minutes. Age Recommendation: S (Starting school, starting to read, starting pre-school, starting kindergarten; Ages 4-5); P (Primary grades, grades 1-3; Ages 6-9); I (Intermediate grades, grades 4-6; Ages 10-12).

VHS: S18645. $29.95.

Let's Create Art Activities
(© Eric Capstick/Let's Create Productions)

Let's Create for Pre-Schoolers

Kids learn about colors and shapes in these six art projects accompanied by music. 51 minutes. Age Recommendation: T (Toddler; Ages Birth-3 years); S (Starting school, starting to read, starting pre-school, starting kindergarten; Ages 4-5).

VHS: S24546. $24.95.

Let's Do It!/Professor Iris

Professor Iris shares games, dancing and sports in this video developed for pre-schoolers. This video is part of the *Ready, Set, Learn* series which first aired on The Learning Channel, and which has been recommended by the National Educational Association and the PTA. See listings for *Birthday!*

Party/Professor Iris, Creepy Critters/Professor Iris, Music Mania/Professor Iris and for *Space Cadets/Professor Iris*. 40 minutes. Age Recommendation: T (Toddler; Ages Birth-3 years); S (Starting school, starting to read, starting pre-school, starting kindergarten; Ages 4-5).

VHS: S23017. $19.95.

Let's Get a Move On!

Millions of families move each year. Learn how to survive the impact of changing places, saying goodbye, and adjusting to new people, new situations and new spaces. Winner of the American Film Festival Award and the Parents' Choice Award. 25 minutes. Age Recommendation: S (Starting school, starting to read, starting pre-school, starting kindergarten; Ages 4-5); P (Primary grades, grades 1-3; Ages 6-9); I (Intermediate grades, grades 4-6; Ages 10-12).

VHS: S17140. $14.95.

Public Performance Rights. VHS: S17155. $34.90.

Let's Sing Along

Interactive music and sounds provide the inspiration for kids to play along with the child hosts on the video. 25 minutes. Age Recommendation: T (Toddler; Ages Birth-3 years); S (Starting school, starting to read, starting pre-school, starting kindergarten; Ages 4-5).

VHS: S25038. $14.95.

Lights: The Miracle of Chanukah

Narrated by Judd Hirsch and featuring the voices of Leonard Nimoy and Paul Michael Glaser, this film tells the story of Chanukah. Fully animated. 24 minutes. Age Recommendation: S (Starting school, starting to read, starting pre-school, starting kindergarten; Ages 4-5); P (Primary grades, grades 1-3; Ages 6-9); I (Intermediate grades, grades 4-6; Ages 10-12).

VHS: S22071. $16.95.

Linnea in Monet's Garden

The delightful best-selling children's book by Christina Bjork is now an animated feature. Linnea and her friend Bloom travel from Sweden to Monet's garden. While they are enjoying this magical and inspirational place, it comes to life. 30 minutes. Age Recommendation: P (Primary grades, grades 1-3; Ages 6-9); I (Intermediate grades, grades 4-6; Ages 10-12).

VHS: S22181. $19.95.

Lion and the Lamb, The (Rabbit Ears)

The animated Christmas story of a fierce lion who escapes from the circus and finds refuge with a meek lamb in a stable. Narrated by actor Christopher Reeve and singer Amy Grant. Music by Lyle Mays. 23 minutes. Age Recommendation: S (Starting school, starting to read, starting pre-school, starting kindergarten; Ages 4-5); P (Primary grades, grades 1-3; Ages 6-9); I (Intermediate grades, grades 4-6; Ages 10-12).
VHS: S24056. $9.98.

Lion, the Witch, and the Wardrobe, The (Animated)

A fascinating animated adaptation of the first book in C.S. Lewis' *The Chronicles of Narnia*. It's the story of four children (2 girls and 2 boys) hurled from a strange wardrobe closet into an expressive land of mythical creatures and talking animals. The children overcome the evil White Witch. In deciding whether to include this video, viewing children were divided over the "violence" and the stereotyped evil witch. The strong lead character, a girl, won the story its place in this book. Winner of the Emmy for Best Animated Special. 95 minutes. Age Recommendation: P (Primary grades, grades 1-3; Ages 6-9); I (Intermediate grades, grades 4-6; Ages 10-12).
VHS: S19158. $12.98.

Lion, the Witch, and the Wardrobe, The (WonderWorks)

Based on the first volume of C.S. Lewis's *The Chronicles of Narnia*. In a strange castle in the English countryside, four children open the door of an old wardrobe and find themselves transported to the magical kingdom of Narnia. The children discover that the evil White Witch has turned all of her enemies to stone, and they are the only ones capable of defeating her. Children who viewed this video recommended its inclusion in this book in spite of some violence, also pointing out that the girl character overcomes the evil witch. A WonderWorks/BBC co-production starring Barbara Kellerman, Richard Dempsey, and Sophie Cook. Great Britain. Two tapes; 169 minutes. Age Recommendation: P (Primary grades, grades 1-3; Ages 6-9); I (Intermediate grades, grades 4-6; Ages 10-12).
VHS: S14157. $29.95.

Little Crooked Christmas Tree, The

Christopher Plummer narrates this animated version of Michael Cutting's classic children's book. This is a warm tale about a Christmas tree farm and

the little bent tree that grew crooked to protect a dove and her nest. The Appleby Boys Choir perform Christmas carols. 30 minutes. Age Recommendation: S (Starting school, starting to read, starting pre-school, starting kindergarten; Ages 4-5); P (Primary grades, grades 1-3; Ages 6-9).
VHS: S22514. $14.98.

Little Duck Tale, A

This tender, heartwarming story portrays the true life adventures of Chibi and his duckling brothers and sisters as they struggle for survival in downtown Tokyo. Children and parents alike will find joy in this tale of determination and triumph. Recommended by Children's Video Report. 55 minutes. Age Recommendation: P (Primary grades, grades 1-3; Ages 6-9).
VHS: S17012. $14.95.

Little Engine That Could, The

Based on the book by Watty Piper. This is a classic tale of imagination, perseverance, hope and overcoming obstacles. A warm and evocative adaptation, with charismatic players and superb animation. 30 minutes. Age Recommendation: S (Starting school, starting to read, starting pre-school, starting kindergarten; Ages 4-5); P (Primary grades, grades 1-3; Ages 6-9).
English Narration. VHS: S18252. $12.98.
French Narration. VHS: S19812. $19.95.
Spanish Narration. VHS: S19813. $19.95.

Little Lou and His Strange Little Zoo

This tape chronicles the adventures of a young African American boy who lives in the city. Author and illustrator Mark Rubin offers children an interesting way to become involved in learning through engaging activities in subjects related to language arts, social studies and guidance, with a special emphasis on human relations and cooperation. 30 minutes. Age Recommendation: P (Primary grades, grades 1-3; Ages 6-9).
VHS: S06726. $29.95.

Little People Videos

There is a movement afoot to keep our children away from programming which is based on brand-name toys. We took that into account when we included these videos here. Although they are based on the Fisher Price toy characters, these fun videos have high production quality and also promote positive values, such as friendship. 30 minutes each. Age

Recommendation: T (Toddler; Ages Birth-3 years); S (Starting school, starting to read, starting pre-school, starting kindergarten; Ages 4-5).

Little People: Christmas Fun
VHS: S24806. $14.95.

Little People: Favorite Songs
VHS: S24807. $14.95.

Little People: Fun with Words
VHS: S24808. $14.95.

Little People: Three Favorite Stories
VHS: S24809. $14.95.

Little Sister Rabbit

A colorful, witty portrait of the activities and movements of Big Brother Rabbit and his fiercely individualistic younger sister. 25 minutes. Age Recommendation: S (Starting school, starting to read, starting pre-school, starting kindergarten; Ages 4-5); P (Primary grades, grades 1-3; Ages 6-9).
VHS: S18022. $12.98.

Living and Working in Space: The Countdown Has Begun
(© Anthony Friedkin/FASE Productions)

Living and Working in Space: The Countdown Has Begun

Famous calculus teacher Jaime Escalante and a former student look at outer space activities and conduct interviews with space professionals. 60 minutes. Age Recommendation: P (Primary grades, grades 1-3; Ages 6-9); I (Intermediate grades, grades 4-6; Ages 10-12).

VHS: S24982. $19.95.

Look Around Endangered Animals, A

Did you know that rhinos don't see very well? That elephants like to have a lot of company? That the panda isn't a bear at all? Discover all this and more in *A Look Around Endangered Animals*. Included are segments on the Siberian Tiger, the Gray Wolf, and others, along with information about helping endangered animals. 14 minutes. Age Recommendation: P (Primary grades, grades 1-3; Ages 6-9); I (Intermediate grades, grades 4-6; Ages 10-12).

VHS: S16345. $44.95.

Look What I Found

Teacher Amy Purcell teaches children how to develop analytical skills and problem solving through constructing codes, fingerprint games, tin can telephones, and treasure hunts. 45 minutes. Age Recommendation: P (Primary grades, grades 1-3; Ages 6-9); I (Intermediate grades, grades 4-6; Ages 10-12).

VHS: S17885. Currently out of print. May be available for rental in some video stores.

Look What I Grew

Instructor Amy Purcell leads an informative and revealing introductory lesson on gardening, with suggestions on sprouting vegetable tops, seed viewers and seed packs, apple finger puppets, terrariums, and the keeping of garden journals. This video is recommended by the National Gardening Association. 45 minutes. Age Recommendation: P (Primary grades, grades 1-3; Ages 6-9); I (Intermediate grades, grades 4-6; Ages 10-12).

VHS: S17886. Currently out of print. May be available for rental in some video stores.

Look What I Made

This award-winning interactive video, hosted by teacher Amy Purcell, is an instructive and highly valuable tool for educating children about arts and crafts, with instructions on constructing piñatas, flower bouquets, paper hats, origami and newspaper hammocks. 45 minutes. Age Recommendation: S (Starting school, starting to read, starting pre-school, starting kindergarten; Ages 4-5); P (Primary grades, grades 1-3; Ages 6-9); I (Intermediate grades, grades 4-6; Ages 10-12).

VHS: S17884. Currently out of print. May be available for rental in some video stores.

Lovely Butterfly — Pepar Nechmad

This series designed for children of primary age is entirely in Hebrew and uses puppets, games, songs and stories to tell children about Jewish holidays and traditions. In elementary Hebrew *without* subtitles. Each program is about 30 minutes. Age Recommendation: S (Starting school, starting to read, starting pre-school, starting kindergarten; Ages 4-5); P (Primary grades, grades 1-3; Ages 6-9).

Chanukah
VHS: S10456. $29.95.

Flowers for the Independence Day
VHS: S10460. $29.95.

Passover
VHS: S10455. $29.95.

Purim
VHS: S10458. $29.95.

Tishrei Month Holidays (Rosh Hashana and Sukkot)
VHS: S10457. $29.95.

Tu B'Shvat
VHS: S10459. $29.95.

Lyle, Lyle Crocodile: The House on East 88th Street

Based on the book by Bernard Waber. He cooks! He cleans! But he's a crocodile....and he's living in the bathtub of the Primm's new house. Narrated by Tony Randall. Fully animated musical. 25 minutes. Age Recommendation: S (Starting school, starting to read, starting pre-school, starting kindergarten; Ages 4-5); P (Primary grades, grades 1-3; Ages 6-9).

VHS: S11237. $14.95.

Madame C.J. Walker (1867-1919) — Entrepreneur

From *The Black Americans of Achievement Series*. This video is based upon the acclaimed book by A'Lelia Bundles, drawing from the expertise of a brilliant group of consultants and experts. This biography of the life of the famous cosmetics entrepreneur includes archival footage, photographs and period music to tell the story of the first female African American millionaire. This video was designed for classroom use. 30 minutes. Age Recommendation: P (Primary grades, grades 1-3; Ages 6-9); I (Intermediate grades, grades 4-6; Ages 10-12).

VHS: S17391. $39.95.

Madeline

Everyone's favorite French schoolgirl is the subject of this charming adaptation of Ludwig Bemelmans' classic story. Madeline becomes the envy of her schoolmates after her trip to the hospital to have her appendix removed. This version is told in rhyme, and is close to the original story. 8 minutes. Age Recommendation: S (Starting school, starting to read, starting pre-school, starting kindergarten; Ages 4-5); P (Primary grades, grades 1-3; Ages 6-9); I (Intermediate grades, grades 4-6; Ages 10-12).

VHS: S08396. $65.00.

Madeline (Narrated by Christopher Plummer)

Her heart was big, her size was small, and Madeline was loved by all! A best-loved children's classic by Ludwig Bemelmans. Fully animated. 30 minutes. Age Recommendation: S (Starting school, starting to read, starting pre-school, starting kindergarten; Ages 4-5); P (Primary grades, grades 1-3; Ages 6-9); I (Intermediate grades, grades 4-6; Ages 10-12).

VHS: S11235. $14.95.

Madeline and the Dog Show

Based on the book by Ludwig Bemelmans. Madeline arrives to register Genevieve the dog for a dog show, but Genevieve is rejected for lack of a pedigree. Find out how she wins anyway! Narrated by Christopher Plummer. 30 minutes. Age Recommendation: S (Starting school, starting to read, starting pre-school, starting kindergarten; Ages 4-5); P (Primary grades, grades 1-3; Ages 6-9); I (Intermediate grades, grades 4-6; Ages 10-12).

VHS: S24764. $12.95.

Madeline and the Easter Bonnet

Madeline and the girls become the hit of the fashion show when their horse's tattered hat is transformed into a wonderful Easter bonnet. Narrated by Christopher Plummer. 30 minutes. Age Recommendation: S (Starting school, starting to read, starting pre-school, starting kindergarten; Ages 4-5); P (Primary grades, grades 1-3; Ages 6-9); I (Intermediate grades, grades 4-6; Ages 10-12).

VHS: S24997. $12.95.

Madeline and the Toy Factory

The girls go on a tour of a toy factory. Madeline poses as a doll herself and becomes the prized possession of a sad and lonely little girl. Narrated by Christopher Plummer. 30 minutes. Age Recommendation: S (Starting school, starting to read, starting pre-school, starting kindergarten; Ages 4-5); P (Primary grades, grades 1-3; Ages 6-9); I (Intermediate grades, grades 4-6; Ages 10-12).

VHS: S24998. $12.95.

Madeline at Cooking School

Madeline enrolls in France's most famous cooking school, and makes a very important choice. On graduation day, she serves up the most important ingredient of all — kindness! Narrated by Christopher Plummer. 1994. 30 minutes. Age Recommendation: S (Starting school, starting to read, starting pre-school, starting kindergarten; Ages 4-5); P (Primary grades, grades 1-3; Ages 6-9); I (Intermediate grades, grades 4-6; Ages 10-12).

VHS: S24888. $12.95.

Madeline in London

Madeline and the rest of the boarding school visit her friend Pepito in London. Madeline gets caught-up in adventures and even receives a medal from the Queen. Narrated by Christopher Plummer. 30 minutes. Age Recommendation: S (Starting school, starting to read, starting pre-school, starting kindergarten; Ages 4-5); P (Primary grades, grades 1-3; Ages 6-9); I (Intermediate grades, grades 4-6; Ages 10-12).

VHS: S24548. $12.95.

Madeline's Christmas

Everyone at the boarding school is sick, so Madeline changes her holiday plans to help them. The show ends with a rhyme about love. Narrated by

Christopher Plummer. 24 minutes. Age Recommendation: S (Starting school, starting to read, starting pre-school, starting kindergarten; Ages 4-5); P (Primary grades, grades 1-3; Ages 6-9); I (Intermediate grades, grades 4-6; Ages 10-12).

VHS: S24549. $12.95.

Madeline's Rescue and Other Stories About Madeline

These three animated shorts are based on the outstanding children's books by Ludwig Bemelmans. *Madeline's Rescue* is the story of Genevieve the dog who saves Madeline and then joins the school, *Madeline and the Bad Hat* is about a bad boy (Pepito) turned good, and *Madeline and the Gypsies* is about a circus. 1988. 23 minutes. Age Recommendation: S (Starting school, starting to read, starting pre-school, starting kindergarten; Ages 4-5); P (Primary grades, grades 1-3; Ages 6-9); I (Intermediate grades, grades 4-6; Ages 10-12).

VHS: S13334. $14.95.

Madeline and the Easter Bonnet
(Western Publishing Co., Inc.)

Madre Tierra

From The Multi-Coloured Workshop in Uruguay, this nine-part series of animated films is the product of a unique collaborative experience between Danish and Uruguayan animators and students from Bolivia, Ecuador, Brazil and Peru. With an emphasis on Mother Earth and our environment, the tape includes nine four-minute animated films. Also included are film clips of the production studio and the artists at work. 57 minutes. Age Recommendation: P (Primary grades, grades 1-3; Ages 6-9); I (Intermediate grades, grades 4-6; Ages 10-12). Includes Public Performance Rights.

VHS: S24742. $39.95.

Magic of Discovery, The

A collection of seven films for pre-schoolers by the National Film Board of Canada. *Body Talking* is a musical journey in body language, showing how you can "not say a word and still be heard." *The Animal Movie* shows a boy discovering each animal's specialization, and his own talent as well! *Adventures* is about a little raccoon who strays too far from home. *The Sky Is Blue* follows a little boy who explores the sky and outer space riding on the tail of a kite. *A Sense of Touch* goes from bath water to bubble gum, from bananas to beards, with a nice musical score. *Matrioska* brings to life nesting Russian dolls, who perform a Russian folk dance. *Dimensions* looks at proportions, starting with a girl and boy who don't fit in furniture. 60 minutes. Age Recommendation: S (Starting school, starting to read, starting pre-school, starting kindergarten; Ages 4-5).

VHS: S24556. $99.00.

Magic School Bus

Based on the books by Joanna Cole. Ms. Frizzle's adventures on the magic bus bring a host of scientific problems and principles to life. Lily Tomlin is the voice of Ms. Frizzle, the go-getting heroine of this animated science series, based on Scholastic's award winning books. The series first aired on PBS, and also features the voices of Malcolm Jamal Warner, Little Richard, Ed Begley, Jr., Robby Benson, Carol Channing, Tyne Daly and Dom DeLuise. Each video is 30 minutes. Age Recommendation: S (Starting school, starting to read, starting pre-school, starting kindergarten; Ages 4-5); P (Primary grades, grades 1-3; Ages 6-9; I (Intermediate grades, grades 4-6; Ages 10-12).

The Magic School Bus: For Lunch
VHS: S23296. $12.95.

The Magic School Bus: Gets Eaten
VHS: S25109. $12.95.

The Magic School Bus: Gets Lost in Space
VHS: S23297. $12.95.

The Magic School Bus: Hops Home
VHS: S25108. $12.95.

The Magic School Bus: Inside Ralphie
VHS: S25110. $12.95.

Magic Thinking Cap, The

The puppets at The Judy Theatre help children develop skills for living. In this video about a family, Dad almost becomes abusive. The Wise Old Owl's magic thinking cap helps the family analyze the problem, cope with negative emotions and uncover a loving solution. 30 minutes. Age Recommendation: P (Primary grades, grades 1-3; Ages 6-9); I (Intermediate grades, grades 4-6; Ages 10-12) (and families).

VHS: S21275. $19.95.

Magical Coqui — Puerto Rico — Mi Tierra!

This video contains a delightful original story about a small boy and his pet Coqui (tree frog) in Puerto Rico. There is also a presentation of music and beautiful pictures about Puerto Rican life and culture. The program is presented first in English, and then repeated in Spanish. 40 minutes. Age Recommendation: S (Starting school, starting to read, starting pre-school, starting kindergarten; Ages 4-5); P (Primary grades, grades 1-3; Ages 6-9); I (Intermediate grades, grades 4-6; Ages 10-12).

VHS: S10789. $59.95.

Making Music with Children

Children's Video Report called this the "Video Series of the Year!" Music educator John Langstaff, author of 22 children's books and song collections, engages a racially diverse group of children in fun with music. Each video is 60 minutes.

Program 1. Making Music with Children: Ages 3-7
Includes singing games, rhythm and movement activities, music from different cultures and folk songs. Age Recommendation: S (Starting school, starting to read, starting pre-school, starting kindergarten; Ages 4-5); P (Primary grades, grades 1-3; Ages 6-9); I (Intermediate grades, grades 4-6; Ages 10-12).
VHS: S23681. $24.95.

Program 2. Making Music with Children: Ages 7-11
Includes folk song rounds, percussion accompaniment, music from different cultures, and more. 60 minutes. Age Recommendation: P (Primary grades, grades 1-3; Ages 6-9); I (Intermediate grades, grades 4-6; Ages 10-12).
VHS: S23682. $24.95.

Program 3. Making Music in the Classroom: Ages 3-7
Similar to *Program 1*, but features a classroom setting. Age Recommendation: S (Starting school, starting to read, starting pre-school, starting kindergarten; Ages 4-5); P (Primary grades, grades 1-3; Ages 6-9).
VHS: S23683. $24.95.

Program 4. Making Music in the Classroom: Ages 7-11
Similar to *Program 2*, but features a classroom setting. Age Recommendation: P (Primary grades, grades 1-3; Ages 6-9); I (Intermediate grades, grades 4-6; Ages 10-12).
VHS: S23684. $24.95.

Maricela

This film gets special mention from Latino evaluators for its relevance to Latino culture. The story concerns a 13 year-old girl from El Salvador who tries to adjust to life in the United States. Because this video touches on the violence of prejudice, adults might want to watch it *with* children, to help them make sense of things. It is difficult to make an age recommendation, though if adults are present, kids as young as 6 will be interested. 55 minutes. Age Recommendation: I (Intermediate grades, grades 4-6; Ages 10-12).
VHS: S15787. $29.95.

Mary McLeod Bethune (1875-1955) — Educator

From *The Black Americans of Achievement Series*. This video is based upon the acclaimed book by Malu Halasa, drawing from the expertise of a brilliant group of consultants and experts. With informative interviews, archival footage, photographs and period music. This biography was designed for classroom use. 30 minutes. Age Recommendation: P (Primary grades, grades 1-3; Ages 6-9); I (Intermediate grades, grades 4-6; Ages 10-12).
VHS: S24105. $39.95.

Mary Poppins

This beloved Disney film combines brilliant, animated sequences with a delightful story about an independent magical nanny (Julie Andrews) who transforms the lives of the children in her care. The film also features a stong mother in the suffragist movement, addressing women's rights issues. With Dick Van Dyke, Glynis Johns, Ed Wynn. Robert Stevenson, USA, 1964. 140 minutes. Age Recommendation: P (Primary grades, grades 1-3; Ages 6-9); I (Intermediate grades, grades 4-6; Ages 10-12).
VHS: S01589. $26.99.
Laser: LD71132. $44.99.

Math...Who Needs It?

Meet the famous calculus teacher Jaime Escalante (who inspired the film *Stand and Deliver*), along with several of his students. This made-for-TV special features Bill Cosby, Dizzy Gillespie and other guest celebrities. 60 minutes. Age Recommendation: P (Primary grades, grades 1-3; Ages 6-9); I (Intermediate grades, grades 4-6; Ages 10-12).

VHS: S24980. $19.95.

Mathnet: The Case of The Unnatural

In the *Mathnet* series by the Children's Television Workshop, a young detective team investigates answers while learning concepts related to math. Warning: many of the other plots in this series center on robberies, bombers and other violent incidents. This case concerns a baseball pitcher who sends coded messages to his friend. 62 minutes. Age Recommendation: P (Primary grades, grades 1-3; Ages 6-9); I (Intermediate grades, grades 4-6; Ages 10-12).

VHS: S24550. $9.95.

Where the Wild Things Are (from the Maurice Sendak Library)
(©Weston Woods/Children's Circle Home Video)

Maurice Sendak Library, The

The video opens with four little poems from Sendak's *The Nutshell Library* set to music, including *Alligators All Around* (Note: Native American evaluators were offended by Sendak's "Imitating Indians," featuring a red colored cartoon "Indian" holding a tomahawk and dancing around a campfire shouting "woo woo!"), *Pierre, One Was Johnny,* and *Chicken Soup with Rice.* Next, Sendak's classic *Where the Wild Things Are* is brought to life. (Even the youngest children weren't scared by these monsters.) Finally, in Sendak's *In the Night Kitchen,* a little boy dreams of a special place where bakers bake cakes, dough airplanes fly, and everyone dances to deliciously syncopated music. (Children may find the frontal nudity of the cartoon boy from *In The*

Night Kitchen to be embarrassing.) The tape includes *Getting to Know Maurice Sendak*, a personal talk with the author and illustrator. 35 minutes. Age Recommendation: S (Starting school, starting to read, starting pre-school, starting kindergarten; Ages 4-5); P (Primary grades, grades 1-3; Ages 6-9). VHS: S11229. $14.95.

Max's Chocolate Chicken and Other Stories for Young Children

Rosemary Wells wrote the title story in this video of good book-based stories, including Janet and Allan Ahlberg's *Each Peach Plum*, Emily Arnold McCully's *Picnic*, and Maud and Minska Petersham's *The Circus Baby*. 36 minutes. Age Recommendation: S (Starting school, starting to read, starting pre-school, starting kindergarten; Ages 4-5); P (Primary grades, grades 1-3; Ages 6-9). VHS: S22163. $14.95.

Meet Your Animal Friends

Lynn Redgrave hosts this wonderful visit with baby animals. Infants and toddlers will giggle with glee at the funny antics of sheep, deer, horses, dogs and other species. Winner of the Film Advisory Board's Award of Excellence, the California Children's Book Award and the Video Award. 60 minutes. Age Recommendation: T (Toddler; Ages Birth-3 years); S (Starting school, starting to read, starting pre-school, starting kindergarten; Ages 4-5). VHS: S17013. $12.95.

Mighty Pawns, The

A teacher tries to help city youth in an unusual fashion — with chess! A look at the excitement of the game and its positive influence. The cast includes Paul Winfield and Alfonso Ribiero. Winner of the Silver Plaque at the 1987 Chicago International Film Festival, the CEBA Award for distinction, and an NAACP Image Awards Finalist. From the WonderWorks series, originally aired on PBS. Eric Laneuville, USA, 1987. 60 minutes. Age Recommendation: P (Primary grades, grades 1-3; Ages 6-9); I (Intermediate grades, grades 4-6; Ages 10-12). VHS: S13238. $29.95.

Mike Mulligan and His Steam Shovel

Three treasured children's books are adapted into three animated video pieces. In *Burt Dow: Deep Water Man* (written by Robert McCloskey), a whale swallows Burt Dow. *Moon Man* (written by Tomi Ungerer) is the story of the man in the moon visiting the Earth (set to a jazzy musical score), and in the collection's title piece, the duo of Mike and Mary Anne the steam shovel are helped by a little boy (based on the book by Virginia L. Burton). Morton Schindel, USA, 1986. 30 minutes. Age Recommendation: S (Starting school, starting to read, starting pre-school, starting kindergarten; Ages 4-5); P (Primary grades, grades 1-3; Ages 6-9).

VHS: S00854. $14.95.

Mine and Yours

From the *Learn About Living Series*, designed to help children sort out the challenges of growing up. Live-action and animated stories and songs in this colorful well-produced video carry a message about sharing and cooperation. In *Mine and Yours*, Katie wants to keep Renee's birthday present. This story invites kids to sing along. Other titles in the series include *How Come?*, *Never Talk to Strangers* and *Who Will Be My Friend?*. 25 minutes. Age Recommendation: S (Starting school, starting to read, starting pre-school, starting kindergarten; Ages 4-5).

VHS: S24554. $9.95.

Moira's Birthday (plus Blackberry Subway Jam)

Moira's birthday is coming and she wants a big party! The video also includes *Blackberry Subway Jam*, about a subway that pulls into Jonathan's house where all the passengers pile out. Animated stories by Robert Munsch. 25 minutes. Age Recommendation: T (Toddler; Ages Birth-3 years); S (Starting school, starting to read, starting pre-school, starting kindergarten; Ages 4-5).

VHS: S24996. $12.95.

The Mole Series

Created by Czech animator Zdenek Miller in 1957, the award-winning Mole series is known and loved by children and adults around the world. Non-verbal. Each video is 32 minutes. Age Recommendation: S (Starting school, starting to read, starting pre-school, starting kindergarten; Ages 4-5); P (Primary grades, grades 1-3; Ages 6-9).

The Mole and The Green Star
This tape features three stories. In the title piece, the Mole unearths a bright, shiny object while cleaning his underground home. In *The Mole and the Chewing Gum*, the Mole burrows into a littered campsite and finds himself in a sticky situation. In the third story, *The Mole and the Car*, he discovers a creative way to recycle a broken toy automobile.

VHS: S23680. $14.95.

The Mole in Town
The Mole and his friends are out enjoying berries in the sun one day, when a rumble startles them. They discover that their forest home is quickly being turned into a city. The three friends learn together that life in town can be fun and full of adventure, but it's not long before they want to go back to nature!
VHS: S23679. $14.95.

Mommy's Office

Based on the book by Barbara Shook. A delightful story of a little girl who spends the day with her mother at work and sees the similarities between mommy's office and her own school experience. 7 minutes. Age Recommendation: S (Starting school, starting to read, starting pre-school, starting kindergarten; Ages 4-5).
VHS: S22348. $39.95.

Monkey Moves

This marvelous musical exercise and movement tape, based on the principles of Dr. Moshe Feldenkrais, helps children develop balance, coordination and motor sequencing skills while moving to original songs and music. (Also see *Move Like the Animals*). 25 minutes. Age Recommendation: S (Starting school, starting to read, starting pre-school, starting kindergarten; Ages 4-5); P (Primary grades, grades 1-3; Ages 6-9).
VHS: S24552. $19.95.

Mop Top
(Live Oak Media)

The Monkey People (Rabbit Ears)

The great Puerto Rican actor Raul Julia brilliantly narrates this fantastic fable from the Amazon rainforest about a village of people whose extreme laziness has hilarious and devastating consequences. Music by Lee Ritenour. 30 minutes. Age Recommendation: S (Starting school, starting to read, starting pre-school, starting kindergarten; Ages 4-5); P (Primary grades, grades 1-3; Ages 6-9); I (Intermediate grades, grades 4-6; Ages 10-12).

VHS: S15641. $9.95.

Mop Top

Based on the story by Don Freeman. Moppy finally sees himself as others do. (His head is literally mistaken for a mop!) He begins to appreciate a neat-looking appearance. 10 minutes. Age Recommendation: S (Starting school, starting to read, starting pre-school, starting kindergarten; Ages 4-5); P (Primary grades, grades 1-3; Ages 6-9).

VHS: S24555. $37.95.

More Pre-School Power

Pre-school age "teachers" show viewers how to tie shoes, brush teeth, make fruit salad and play with shadow puppets. Packed with songs, music, jokes and tongue-twisters. Recommended by *Parents Magazine*, and winner of the Parents' Choice Award and the California Children's Video Award. (Also see listings for *Pre-School Power: Jacket Flips & Other Tips* and *Pre-School Power #3*.). 30 minutes. Age Recommendation: T (Toddler; Ages Birth-3 years); S (Starting school, starting to read, starting pre-school, starting kindergarten; Ages 4-5).

VHS: S17008. $14.95.

Morris the Moose: Goes to School/Gets a Cold

Morris decides that school will be a fun place to learn to read and count. Boris the Bear helps Morris recover from his cold. Two wonderful stories based on the beginner's reading books by Bernard Wiseman. 30 minutes. Age Recommendation: S (Starting school, starting to read, starting pre-school, starting kindergarten; Ages 4-5).

VHS: S23278. $12.95.

Mose The Fireman (Rabbit Ears)

Michael Keaton narrates this animated story of a legendary fire fighter. With music by John Beasley and Walter Becker. 23 minutes. Age

---

Recommendation: S (Starting school, starting to read, starting pre-school, starting kindergarten; Ages 4-5); P (Primary grades, grades 1-3; Ages 6-9); I (Intermediate grades, grades 4-6; Ages 10-12).
VHS: S24039. $9.98.

Mouse and the Motorcycle, The

On vacation, a lonely boy meets a talkative little mouse named Ralph. When the boy shares his fancy toy motorcycle with Ralph, our very tiny hero embarks on a very big adventure. Based on the book by Beverly Cleary. Winner of numerous awards. Live-action and puppet animation. Ron Underwood, USA, 1987. (Also, see the listing for the sequel, *Runaway Ralph*). 41 minutes. Age Recommendation: S (Starting school, starting to read, starting pre-school, starting kindergarten; Ages 4-5); P (Primary grades, grades 1-3; Ages 6-9); I (Intermediate grades, grades 4-6; Ages 10-12).
VHS: S16579. $9.98.

Move Like the Animals

In this creative tape, kids learn movement from animals, while incorporating the learning methods of Dr. Moshe Feldenkrais. The video is put together by Dr. Stephen Rosenholtz, a well-qualified educator, known also for his Feldenkrais movement videos for adults (see also *Monkey Moves*). 25 minutes. Age Recommendation: S (Starting school, starting to read, starting pre-school, starting kindergarten; Ages 4-5); P (Primary grades, grades 1-3; Ages 6-9).
VHS: S24551. $19.95.

Moving Machines

One of the award-winning Bo Peep Productions, this video moves back and forth between heavy machinery (dump trucks, cranes, bulldozers) on real work sites, and pre-schoolers playing with toys in the sand box. This tape features percussion rhythms, nice sound effects and enjoyable comments from multi-ethnic boys and girls. 25 minutes. Age Recommendation: T (Toddler; Ages Birth-3 years); S (Starting school, starting to read, starting pre-school, starting kindergarten; Ages 4-5).
VHS: S22380. $19.95.

Mr. Rogers Videos

Mr. Rogers gets a very special mention in this book for both entertaining pre-schoolers and for imparting positive lessons in living. His award-winning public television program is probably the one most researchers rely on in studies of the positive social effects television can have upon children. Designed for pre-schoolers, Mr. Rogers' videos focus primarily on social and emotional development, and are noted for imparting positive outlooks and skills related to sharing, cooperation, helping, understanding others' feelings, social interaction, and valuing individual differences. The "Neighborhood" format provides a learning environment for the immediate world close to pre-schoolers. Age Recommendation: T (Toddler; Ages Birth-3 years); S (Starting school, starting to read, starting pre-school, starting kindergarten; Ages 4-5).

Mr. Rogers: Dinosaurs & Monsters
Mister Rogers helps young people understand what scary monsters are and are not about. Mister Rogers visits a museum to show dinosaurs, and with the help of Lady Aberlin and Handyman Negri, he clears up confusion about what is real and what is fantasy. USA, 1986. 64 minutes. Age Recommendation: T (Toddler; Ages Birth-3 years); S (Starting school, starting to read, starting pre-school, starting kindergarten; Ages 4-5).
VHS: S00893. $19.98.

Mr. Rogers: Music and Feelings
Mister Rogers, aided by musician Ella Jenkins, explores the many moods of music. Also features cellist Yo Yo Ma and the entire gang from the Neighborhood of Make-Believe. 65 minutes. Age Recommendation: T (Toddler; Ages Birth-3 years); S (Starting school, starting to read, starting pre-school, starting kindergarten; Ages 4-5).
VHS: S05012. $19.98.

Mr. Rogers: Musical Stories
Mister Rogers invites children into a land of musical make-believe with two musical stories for children. In *Potato and Cows*, a cow learns to feel good about herself. In *A Granddad for Daniel*, a family has a reunion. 59 minutes. Age Recommendation: T (Toddler; Ages Birth-3 years); S (Starting school, starting to read, starting pre-school, starting kindergarten; Ages 4-5).
VHS: S05897. $19.98.

Mr. Rogers: What About Love
A trolley will take you to the enchanting Neighborhood of Make Believe in this reassuring program about the value of love and the confusing feelings that can accompany it. 51 minutes. Age Recommendation: T (Toddler; Ages Birth-3 years); S (Starting school, starting to read, starting pre-school, starting kindergarten; Ages 4-5).
VHS: S05011. $19.98.

Mr. Rogers: When Parents Are Away
Mister Rogers advises parents and their children on how to handle the times of separation. It covers going to babysitters and to day-care. With songs, outings and a special visit to the "Neighborhood of Make-Believe" with King Friday and Queen Sara Saturday. Can you say "We'll be back soon?" USA, 1987. 66 minutes. Age Recommendation: T (Toddler; Ages Birth-3 years); S (Starting school, starting to read, starting pre-school, starting kindergarten; Ages 4-5).
VHS: S04380. $19.98.

Mr. Rogers' Neighborhood: Circus Fun
Mr. Rogers helps children see how circus performers rehearse to entertain others. The video also explores aspects of the circus which may frighten children. For example, the Neighbors help Daniel Tiger with his fear of clowns and costumes. The episode includes a visit with baby chicks, and the music of a circus band. USA, 1995. 28 minutes. Age Recommendation: T (Toddler; Ages Birth-3 years); S (Starting school, starting to read, starting pre-school, starting kindergarten; Ages 4-5).
VHS: S23024. $9.98.

Mr. Rogers' Neighborhood: Kindness
Broadway star Tommy Tune joins Mr. Rogers in an exploration of kindness as an outlook, a value, and a way of being. The episode includes an accordion player and music-making with rhythm-band instruments. USA, 1995. 28 minutes. Age Recommendation: T (Toddler; Ages Birth-3 years); S (Starting school, starting to read, starting pre-school, starting kindergarten; Ages 4-5).
VHS: S23023. $9.98.

Mr. Rogers' Neighborhood: Love
Who could explain the complexities of this central emotion better than Mr. Rogers? Perhaps his teddy bear, who helps in this exploration of feelings. The episode includes a visit to a music store and a Ukrainian lullaby played on mandolin. USA, 1995. 28 minutes. Age Recommendation: T (Toddler; Ages Birth-3 years); S (Starting school, starting to read, starting pre-school, starting kindergarten; Ages 4-5).
VHS: S23026. $9.98.

Mr. Rogers' Neighborhood: Making Music
Share in the healthy feelings music can offer in this tape featuring Mr. Rogers' visit with world-famous cellist Yo Yo Ma, who shows how he uses music to express a wide range of feelings. The episode includes a bass violin festival in the Neighborhood and a behind-the-scenes visit to a bass violin factory. USA, 1995. 28 minutes. Age Recommendation: T (Toddler; Ages Birth-3 years); S (Starting school, starting to read, starting pre-school, starting kindergarten; Ages 4-5).
VHS: S23025. $9.98.

Multicultural Peoples of North America Video Series

This series celebrates the cultural heritage of fifteen different cultural groups. The videos were based on the highly acclaimed *Peoples of North America* books and were created in consultation with an impressive list of experts, including people from each culture under discussion.

Each video traces the history of the group's origins in North America and looks at their unique traditions and contributions. In addition to interviews, archival footage and stills, viewers take a look inside the life of a real family, meeting three generations of family members. Designed for classroom use. This is a set you might want to watch *with* children, in order to help them get perspective on historical events, which can be disturbing. 30 minutes each video. Age Recommendation: I (Intermediate grades, grades 4-6; Ages 10-12).

African Americans
Based on the book by Howard Smead.
VHS: S20359. $39.95.

The Amish
Based on the book by Fred L. Israel.
VHS: S20360. $39.95.

Arab Americans
Based on the book by Alixa Naff.
VHS: S20361. $39.95.

Central Americans
Based on the book by Faren Bachelis.
VHS: S20362. $39.95.

Chinese Americans
Based on the book by William Daley.
VHS: S20363. $39.95.

German Americans
Based on the book by Anne Balicich.
VHS: S20364. $39.95.

Greek Americans
Based on the book by Dimitus Monas.
VHS: S20365. $39.95.

Irish Americans
Based on the book by J.F. Watts.
VHS: S20366. $39.95.

Italian Americans
Based on the book by J. Philip di Franco.
VHS: S20367. $39.95.

Japanese Americans
Based on the book by Harry Kitano.
VHS: S20368. $39.95.

Jewish Americans
Based on the book by Howard Muggamin.
VHS: S20369. $39.95.

Korean Americans
Based on the book by Brian Lehrer.
VHS: S20370. $39.95.

Mexican Americans
Based on the book by Julie Catalano.
VHS: S20371. $39.95.

Polish Americans
Based on the book by Stan Dolan.
VHS: S20372. $39.95.

Puerto Ricans
Based on the book by Jerome J. Aliotta.
VHS: S20373. $39.95.

Multicultural Peoples of North America Video Series 15 Volume Set
VHS: S24408. $599.25.

Murmel, Murmel, Murmel (plus The Boy in the Drawer)

The story of a little girl who discovers a baby in her sandbox. The tape includes the story *The Boy in the Drawer*, about a boy the size of a sock who lives in Shelly's dresser drawer. Animated stories by Robert Munsch. 30 minutes. Age Recommendation: T (Toddler; Ages Birth-3 years); S (Starting school, starting to read, starting pre-school, starting kindergarten; Ages 4-5).
VHS: S24986. $12.95.

Music and Magic

"Positive Music Videos for Today's Kids." These MTV-style videos promote positive values. 30 minutes. Age Recommendation: S (Starting school, starting to read, starting pre-school, starting kindergarten; Ages 4-5); P (Primary grades, grades 1-3; Ages 6-9); I (Intermediate grades, grades 4-6; Ages 10-12).
VHS: S24714. $9.98.

Music Mania/Professor Iris

Professor Iris gets his class tuning-up musical instruments from around the world, and leads activities with music, song and dance. This video is part of the *Ready, Set, Learn* series which first aired on The Learning Channel, and which has been recommended by the National Educational Association and the PTA. See listings for *Birthday! Party/Professor Iris, Creepy Critters/Professor Iris, Lets Do It!/Professor Iris* and for *Space Cadets/Professor Iris*. 40 minutes. Age Recommendation: T (Toddler; Ages Birth-3 years); S (Starting school, starting to read, starting pre-school, starting kindergarten; Ages 4-5).
VHS: S23016. $19.95.

My First Activity Series

A fun, intellectually stimulating series of videos adapted from the *My First Book* series, providing instructional, easy-to-follow guidelines to a series of activities. Children learn the construction of musical instruments, awareness of ecology and environmental issues, unlocking creativity, understanding nature, conducting science experiments andmaking fun things to eat. Backed by lively musical accompaniment. "The production is excellent, with carefully spoken narration and clear, simple cinematography," (*Video Review*). Age Recommendation: S (Starting school, starting to read, starting pre-school, starting kindergarten; Ages 4-5); P (Primary grades, grades 1-3; Ages 6-9).

My First Activity Video.
50 minutes.
VHS: S20295. $14.98.

My First Cooking Video.
50 minutes.
VHS: S20298. $14.98.

My First Green Video.
40 minutes.
VHS: S20294. $14.98.

My First Music Video.
50 minutes.
VHS: S20293. $14.98.

My First Nature Video.
40 minutes.
VHS: S20296. $14.98.

My First Science Video.
45 minutes.
VHS: S20297. $14.98.

My Friend Walter

This fantastic children's tale, based on the book by Michael Morpurgo, merges the supernatural and lyrical. While visiting the Tower of London, Bess encounters the ghost of her ancestor — Sir Walter Raleigh. Bess enlists Raleigh's help to save her family's farm. With Ronald Pickup, Prunella Scales and Polly Grant. 93 minutes. Age Recommendation: I (Intermediate grades, grades 4-6; Ages 10-12).
VHS: S19509. $29.95.

My Neighbor Totoro

This Japanese animated film features the fuzzy creatures called Totoros, who help sisters Satsuki and Lucy when they get into mischief. Hayao Miyazaki, Japan, 1993. Fantasy antics. 87 minutes. Age Recommendation: S (Starting school, starting to read, starting pre-school, starting kindergarten; Ages 4-5).
VHS: S21354. $19.98.

My New York

Premiere folk artists reveal vibrant New York City through vivid and detailed illustrations in this read-along video. Central Park Zoo, Chinatown, the ferry to Ellis Island and the Empire State Building are depicted. This video shows urban culture well. 15 minutes. Age Recommendation: P (Primary grades, grades 1-3; Ages 6-9).
VHS: S22350. $39.95.

My Principal Lives Next Door

Ben Johnson thought life was a breeze until Mrs. Strictly, the school's principal, moved in next door, setting off a panic in Ben. After experiencing trouble with his math papers, he discovers that the principal is a nice person to turn to. Written and illustrated by third-grade students of Sanibel, Florida Elementary School. 8 minutes. Age Recommendation: S (Starting school, starting to read, starting pre-school, starting kindergarten; Ages 4-5); P (Primary grades, grades 1-3; Ages 6-9).
VHS: S19599. $39.00.

My Sesame Street Home Videos

Featuring the cast of *Sesame Street Muppets* and *Sesame Street Live*, created by Jim Henson.

The Alphabet Game
Sunny Friendly is the host of a new game show, *Alphabet Treasure Hunt*.
There are prizes and surprises, and children can play along. 30 minutes. Age
Recommendation: T (Toddler; Ages Birth-3 years); S (Starting school, start-
ing to read, starting pre-school, starting kindergarten; Ages 4-5).
VHS: S08172. $9.98.

Bedtime Stories & Songs
Big Bird, Kermit the Frog and the Cookie Monster tell stories and sing lulla-
bies that children will ask for night after night. 30 minutes. Age
Recommendation: T (Toddler; Ages Birth-3 years); S (Starting school, start-
ing to read, starting pre-school, starting kindergarten; Ages 4-5).
VHS: S02836. $9.98.

The Best of Elmo
From the Children's Television Workshop comes the furry Elmo and some
charming songs for pre-schoolers. 30 minutes. Age Recommendation: T
(Toddler; Ages Birth-3 years); S (Starting school, starting to read, starting
pre-school, starting kindergarten; Ages 4-5).
VHS: S24511. $9.98.

The Best of Ernie and Bert
When *Sesame Street*'s Big Bird turns the pages of Ernie's scrapbook, each
picture comes to life and everyone relives the adventures of Bert and Ernie.
30 minutes. Age Recommendation: T (Toddler; Ages Birth-3 years); S
(Starting school, starting to read, starting pre-school, starting kindergarten;
Ages 4-5).
VHS: S07711. $9.98.

Big Bird's Favorite Party Games
30 minutes. Age Recommendation: T (Toddler; Ages Birth-3 years); S
(Starting school, starting to read, starting pre-school, starting kindergarten;
Ages 4-5).
VHS: S07710. $9.98.

Big Bird's Story Time
30 minutes. Age Recommendation: T (Toddler; Ages Birth-3 years); S
(Starting school, starting to read, starting pre-school, starting kindergarten;
Ages 4-5).
VHS: S24630. $9.98.

Count It Higher: Great Music Videos from Sesame Street
Enjoy the "Doo Wop Hop" and other music videos! 30 minutes. Age
Recommendation: T (Toddler; Ages Birth-3 years); S (Starting school, start-
ing to read, starting pre-school, starting kindergarten; Ages 4-5).
VHS: S07712. $9.98.

Getting Ready for School
The crowd shares basic skills for getting along in school. 30 minutes. Age Recommendation: T (Toddler; Ages Birth-3 years); S (Starting school, starting to read, starting pre-school, starting kindergarten; Ages 4-5).
VHS: S24631. $9.98.

Getting Ready to Read
Big Bird, Bert and Ernie present songs, stories and rhymes designed to show children how some words look and sound, and how letters can be blended to become words. 30 minutes. Age Recommendation: T (Toddler; Ages Birth-3 years); S (Starting school, starting to read, starting pre-school, starting kindergarten; Ages 4-5).
VHS: S02832. $9.98.

I'm Glad I'm Me
Big Bird, Bert and Ernie encourage children to identify parts of their own bodies, to develop a sense of pride and self-esteem, and to feel good about themselves. 30 minutes. Age Recommendation: T (Toddler; Ages Birth-3 years); S (Starting school, starting to read, starting pre-school, starting kindergarten; Ages 4-5).
VHS: S02835. $9.98.

Learning About Letters
Big Bird and his friend Alphabet Day introduce the entire alphabet, with help from the rest of the Muppets. Cookie Monster's favorite letter is "C," of course, because it stands for "cookie." 30 minutes. Age Recommendation: T (Toddler; Ages Birth-3 years); S (Starting school, starting to read, starting pre-school, starting kindergarten; Ages 4-5).
VHS: S02833. $9.98.

Learning About Numbers
Children will learn to count from 1 to 20 with the help of The Count and Big Bird. 30 minutes. Age Recommendation: T (Toddler; Ages Birth-3 years); S (Starting school, starting to read, starting pre-school, starting kindergarten; Ages 4-5).
VHS: S02834. $9.98.

Learning to Add and Subtract
30 minutes. Age Recommendation: T (Toddler; Ages Birth-3 years); S (Starting school, starting to read, starting pre-school, starting kindergarten; Ages 4-5).
VHS: S24632. $9.98.

New Baby in My House, A
Mrs. Snuffleupagus helps older brother Snuffy understand his feelings about his new baby sister. Includes a story within the story and six little musical numbers. From the Children's Television Workshop. 30 minutes.

Age Recommendation: T (Toddler; Ages Birth-3 years); S (Starting school, starting to read, starting pre-school, starting kindergarten; Ages 4-5).
VHS: S24557. $9.98.

Play-Along Games & Songs
Big Bird and his friends present some of their most popular games which familiarize children with counting, reading and reasoning skills. 30 minutes. Age Recommendation: T (Toddler; Ages Birth-3 years); S (Starting school, starting to read, starting pre-school, starting kindergarten; Ages 4-5).
VHS: S02837. $9.98.

National Geographic Kids Videos

This National Geographic series features documentaries aimed at school-aged children and takes kids to exotic locations to see how the animals they love really live. Narrated by an animated globe called Spin, featuring the voice of Dudley Moore. Age Recommendation: P (Primary grades, grades 1-3; Ages 6-9); I (Intermediate grades, grades 4-6; Ages 10-12).

Adventures in Asia
Spin leads children on a whirlwind tour of the largest continent. There are huge manta rays in the Red Sea, rare panda bears in China, reclusive orang-utangs in Borneo and elephants on the Indian subcontinent. 40 minutes.
VHS: S21212. $14.95.

Amazing North America
In the frozen North there are white wolves and polar bears, but in the swamps near the Gulf of Mexico, alligators lie in wait submerged beneath murky, warm waters. This great diversity also includes some of the most commonplace of animals, like the ground squirrel. 47 minutes.
VHS: S21214. $14.95.

Deep Sea Dive
The Earth's last great frontier is also home to some of the world's most fascinating creatures. Whales, dolphins and sharks share this wildlife refuge. Underwater photography lets you see these animals in action. 45 minutes.
VHS: S20613. $14.95.

Swinging Safari
This safari through the Serengeti Plain and the Kalahari Desert reveals the wildlife of Africa. Cheetahs, crocodiles, rhinos, lions, and chimpanzees are all seen in their natural environments. 44 minutes.
VHS: S20611. $14.95.

Totally Tropical Rainforest

The rainforest is home to a greater variety of living things than any other eco-system on Earth. From this abundance, a variety of curious creatures stand out. Spin reveals tarantulas, aggressive piranha fish and the strange, slow-moving sloths that are just some of the animals unique to these forests. 45 minutes.

VHS: S21213. $14.95.

Wonders Down Under

Weird creatures from the unique Australian eco-systems star, including kangaroos, platypuses and koala bears. The video shows how Australia's unusual animals are a result of this continent's comparative isolation from the rest of the world. 45 minutes.

VHS: S20612. $14.95.

National Geographic Kids Videos: GeoKids

This series of National Geographic videos is aimed at children under six years old. A combination of entertaining characters, music, graphics and marvelous wildlife camera-work. Each video is 33 minutes. Age Recommendation: S (Starting school, starting to read, starting pre-school, starting kindergarten; Ages 4-5).

GeoKids: Bear Cubs, Baby Ducks and Kooky Kookaburras

After Sunny Honeypossum and Bobby Bushbaby see a mother monkey caring for her baby, Balzac de Chameleon tells them about all different kinds of animal babies and how they grow up.

VHS: S21961. $12.95.

GeoKids: Cool Cats, Raindrops, and Things That Live in Holes

During a game of hide-and-go-seek, the animal hosts discover a tree hole, prompting Balzac de Chameleon to tell them about the variety of animals that live in holes.

VHS: S21962. $12.95.

GeoKids: Flying, Trying and Honking Around

Ever wish you could fly? Balzac de Chameleon knows just the fascinating feathery creatures you should know.

VHS: S21960. $12.95.

National Velvet

Evaluators hailed this as a classic women's and girls' empowerment tale. Elizabeth Taylor and Mickey Rooney play the kids determined to win the

Grand National Horse Race. Anne Revere won a Best Supporting Actress Oscar for her performance as the wise mother, who provides an excellent role model (She pays the entrance fee with money she won years earlier for swimming the English Channel). Angela Lansbury also gives a winning performance. In addition to a captivating story, we see a strong independent mother and a powerful mother-daughter relationship. 1944. 125 minutes. Special fiftieth anniversary edition. Age Recommendation: P (Primary grades, grades 1-3; Ages 6-9); I (Intermediate grades, grades 4-6; Ages 10-12).

VHS: S01789. $19.98.

Laser: LD70636. $69.98.

Native Indian Folklore

This tape showcases five stories from the National Film Board of Canada: (1) *Christmas at Moose Factory*, which shows Christmas in the Native American Cree settlement, presented through children's drawings; (2) *Salmon People*, a West Coast legend of the Salmon Princess, contrasted with today's native-owned fishing boats and canneries (a 25 minute piece); (3) *The Man, the Snake and The Fox*, which presents a puppet enactment of an Ojibwa tale; (4) *Medoonak the Stormmaker*, which presents an exciting stage performance of an ancient Micmac legend about taming the weather; and (5) *Summer Legend*, an animated version of the Micmac legend which explains the cycle of the seasons. 71 minutes. Age Recommendation: P (Primary grades, grades 1-3; Ages 6-9); I (Intermediate grades, grades 4-6; Ages 10-12).

VHS: S24775. $99.00.

Never Talk to Strangers

From the *Learn About Living* series, designed to help children sort out the challenges of growing up. This tape teaches children to use caution when approached by strangers, and uses animals as the "strangers," which helps to make the subject less frightening. Other segments are *I Had a Bad Dream*, about the scary subject of nightmares, and *The House That Had Enough*, about a messy girl. Topics are explored in an entertaining way, through songs, live-action and animation. It is best for adults to watch this video *with* kids, to help kids sort out the messages and their feelings. Other titles in the series include *How Come?*, *Mine and Yours* and *Who Will Be My Friend?*. 30 minutes. Age Recommendation: S (Starting school, starting to read, starting pre-school, starting kindergarten; Ages 4-5); P (Primary grades, grades 1-3; Ages 6-9).

VHS: S24994. $9.95.

New Friends and Other Stories

This tape presents *New Friends* and three other stories by author James Stevenson, well known for his gentle books about friendship. 30 minutes. Age Recommendation: S (Starting school, starting to read, starting pre-school, starting kindergarten; Ages 4-5); P (Primary grades, grades 1-3; Ages 6-9). VHS: S16308. $14.95.

The Night Before Christmas (Rabbit Ears)

Meryl Streep narrates this traditional retelling of the holiday classic. The program also includes some of the best loved yuletide carols sung by the Edwin Hawkins Singers, the Christ Church Cathedral Choir and the Oscar-winning Ms. Streep. USA, 1992. 30 minutes. Age Recommendation: P (Primary grades, grades 1-3; Ages 6-9); I (Intermediate grades, grades 4-6; Ages 10-12). VHS: S16813. $9.95.

Noah and the Ark (Rabbit Ears)

Kelly McGillis narrates the poetic and heroic tale of Noah. Illustrated by Lori Lohstoeter, with music by Paul Winter Consort. 25 minutes. Age Recommendation: S (Starting school, starting to read, starting pre-school, starting kindergarten; Ages 4-5); P (Primary grades, grades 1-3; Ages 6-9); I (Intermediate grades, grades 4-6; Ages 10-12). VHS: S18003. $12.98.

Noah's Ark (James Earl Jones)

Embark on one of the greatest adventures of all time as Academy Award-nominee James Earl Jones narrates this beautifully animated adaptation of Peter Spiers' acclaimed children's book, complemented by a dynamic, evocative score from Grammy-winner Stewart Copeland. Winner of the Action for Children's Television Award and CINE Golden Eagle. Recommended by American Library Association and *Video Librarian*. 27 minutes. Age Recommendation: P (Primary grades, grades 1-3; Ages 6-9); I (Intermediate grades, grades 4-6; Ages 10-12). VHS: S11415. $12.98.

Noel

Noel is the story of a magical Christmas tree ornament that comes to life as it is passed down from one generation to the next. 25 minutes. Age

Recommendation: S (Starting school, starting to read, starting pre-school, starting kindergarten; Ages 4-5); P (Primary grades, grades 1-3; Ages 6-9).
VHS: S24612. $12.95.

Nonsense and Lullabyes: Nursery Rhymes

A collection of eighteen nursery rhymes updated with new twists and beautifully animated by renowned filmmaker Michael Sporn. Original music and songs are by Caleb Sampson and the all-star roster of narrators includes Karen Allen, Eli Wallach, Linda Hunt, Courtney Vance, Heidi Stallings and Phillip Schopper. Watch out for the story of *The Little Boy Who Cried Wolf*, the only scary tale of the collection. 27 minutes. Age Recommendation: S (Starting school, starting to read, starting pre-school, starting kindergarten; Ages 4-5).
VHS: S16466. $9.98.

Nonsense and Lullabyes: Poems for Children

Classic poems like Edward Lear's "The Owl and the Pussycat" and Robert Louis Stevenson's "Autumn Fires" are featured with new children's poems like Russell Hoban's "Homework" in this incredible collection. Each poem becomes its own animated short. Featuring the voices of Karen Allen, Eli Wallach, and Linda Hunt. Directed by Michael Sporn. 27 minutes. Age Recommendation: S (Starting school, starting to read, starting pre-school, starting kindergarten; Ages 4-5).
VHS: S16467. $9.98.

Noah and the Ark
(Illustrated by Lori Lohstoeter/Rabbit Ears Productions)

Norman the Doorman and Other Stories

Although Norman's job is to guard the mouse entrance to the Museum of Art, his ambition is to become an artist in this animated adaptation of the story by Don Freeman. Other animated stories include William Steig's *Brave Irene*, who defies blinding snows to help out her sick mother, and Robert McCloskey's *Lentil*, about a boy who buys a harmonica. USA. 30 minutes. Age Recommendation: S (Starting school, starting to read, starting pre-school, starting kindergarten; Ages 4-5); P (Primary grades, grades 1-3; Ages 6-9).
VHS: S11228. $14.95.

"Not Now!" Said the Cow

Find out what's on the cow's mind in this story which is similar to the *Little Red Hen* tale. From the *Bank Street Read-Along Story Video Series*. The story is told twice — once to familiarize children with the characters and story, and the second time, with words printed onscreen so children can "read-along." 30 minutes. Age Recommendation: S (Starting school, starting to read, starting pre-school, starting kindergarten; Ages 4-5); P (Primary grades, grades 1-3; Ages 6-9).
VHS: S13531. $14.99.

Now I Know My Aleph Bet

Through Torah tales, popular Hebrew songs, simple crafts and a wealth of exciting information, three teachers take their play-group students (and the viewing audience of children) on a wonderful journey through the letters of the Hebrew alphabet. Two-volume video set: *Volume 1* is 45 minutes and

Volume 2 is 51 minutes. Age Recommendation: S (Starting school, starting to read, starting pre-school, starting kindergarten; Ages 4-5); P (Primary grades, grades 1-3; Ages 6-9).
VHS: S24803. $45.00.

On Our Way to School

Shari Lewis, Lamb Chop and friends lead kids in a romp through activities which help prepare pre-schoolers for school. 30 minutes. Age Recommendation: T (Toddler; Ages Birth-3 years); S (Starting school, starting to read, starting pre-school, starting kindergarten; Ages 4-5).
VHS: S24613. $9.95.

Opus n' Bill: A Wish for Wings That Work

Opus the penguin learns to appreciate his own qualities (even though he can't fly) when he and his friend Bill the cat are enlisted to help Father Christmas. Based on the comic series *Bloom County* by Berkeley Breathed. Directed by Skip Jones, USA, 1991, 30 minutes. Age Recommendation: P (Primary grades, grades 1-3; Ages 6-9).
VHS: S19592. $12.98.

Orca Whales and Mermaid Tales

Meet the huge orca whales and the mysterious manatees, once thought to be mermaids! Watch a baby manatee and find out about the orca's blowhole. 25 minutes. Age Recommendation: S (Starting school, starting to read, starting pre-school, starting kindergarten; Ages 4-5); P (Primary grades, grades 1-3; Ages 6-9); I (Intermediate grades, grades 4-6; Ages 10-12).
VHS: S24614. $14.95.

Original Tales and Tunes

Little K.J. is the guide for a song-filled journey combining live-action and puppetry. 30 minutes. Age Recommendation: T (Toddler; Ages Birth-3 years); S (Starting school, starting to read, starting pre-school, starting kinder-garten; Ages 4-5).
VHS: S24615. $14.95.

Other Way to Listen, The

From *Will Rogers Jr. Presents: Stories of American Indian Culture*. This second volume in the stories of Native American culture explores the wonders of the natural world. Have you ever heard corn sing? Or heard what a rock has to say to a lizard? A wise old man takes a young boy on an informative hike through the desert to learn its secrets. Narrated by Will Rogers Jr. USA, 1990. 20 minutes. Age Recommendation: S (Starting school, starting to read, starting pre-school, starting kindergarten; Ages 4-5); P (Primary grades, grades 1-3; Ages 6-9); I (Intermediate grades, grades 4-6; Ages 10-12).

VHS: S13295. $14.99.

Owl Moon and Other Stories

These five short animated films based upon popular children's literature tell stories of people and animals learning about themselves. The title piece, by Jane Yolen, shows a child who looks for the great Horned Owl with her father. Also included are Jack Kent's *The Caterpillar and the Polliwog*, Mwenye Iladithi's *Hot Hippo*, and Robert McCloskey's *Time of Wonder*. 35 minutes. Age Recommendation: S (Starting school, starting to read, starting pre-school, starting kindergarten; Ages 4-5); P (Primary grades, grades 1-3; Ages 6-9).

VHS: S13969. $14.95.

Opus n' Bill: A Wish for Wings That Work
Courtesy of

Paul Bunyan (Rabbit Ears)

P

Jonathan Winters reads this story which captures the spirit of the early U.S. The hilariously exaggerated exploits of Paul's logging adventures in the northern United States represent the proud tradition of American storytelling. 30 minutes. Age Recommendation: S (Starting school, starting to read, starting pre-school, starting kindergarten; Ages 4-5); P (Primary grades, grades 1-3; Ages 6-9); I (Intermediate grades, grades 4-6; Ages 10-12).

VHS: S12473. $14.95.

Laser: LD71820. $24.95.

Paws, Claws, Feathers and Fins

Dogs, cats, gerbils, hamsters....even a pony! An award-winning video to help families consider the ups and down of owning a pet. 30 minutes. Age Recommendation: S (Starting school, starting to read, starting pre-school, starting kindergarten; Ages 4-5); P (Primary grades, grades 1-3; Ages 6-9).

VHS: S24617. $14.95.

Pecos Bill (Rabbit Ears)

One of the most popular tall tales of the old Wild West — the legend of Pecos Bill, raised by coyotes from an early age until he discovered cowboys and became king of the range. This is the least-violent "cowboy film" we've seen. While nearly all characters are male, it shows positive friendships and does feature one good, stong female. Nice early American dialect. Narrated by Robin Williams, with illustrations by Tim Raglin. 30 minutes. Age Recommendation: S (Starting school, starting to read, starting pre-school, starting kindergarten; Ages 4-5); P (Primary grades, grades 1-3; Ages 6-9); I (Intermediate grades, grades 4-6; Ages 10-12).

VHS: S07166. $14.95.

Peep and the Big Wide World

Three simple award-winning, amusing and fresh episodes on the adventures of Peep, a newly hatched chick. Quack, a cantankerous duck and the excitable robin Chirp accompany Peep on her thrilling travels. Sure to enrich the imaginations of the very young. Smart animation, featuring the voice of Peter Ustinov. 30 minutes. Age Recommendation: S (Starting school, starting to read, starting pre-school, starting kindergarten; Ages 4-5); P (Primary grades, grades 1-3; Ages 6-9).

VHS: S15790. $14.95.

Pegasus

Mia Farrow tells the enchanting story of Pegasus, the winged horse from Greek mythology that was transformed into a dazzling star constellation. *Parents Magazine* selected this shimmering animated adventure for its Best of the Year List. Winner of the Parent's Choice Award. 25 minutes. Age Recommendation: P (Primary grades, grades 1-3; Ages 6-9); I (Intermediate grades, grades 4-6; Ages 10-12).

VHS: S16162. $12.98.

Pepito's Dream

Latino evaluators (adults and children) gave this film the highest marks! An adaptation of the *Pepito* trilogy (three books by John and Margaret Travers-Moore), this heartwarming tale chronicles a young boy's determination to quell the violence and discord in his neighborhood, and of his long-held dream to deliver a speech before the United Nations. 27 minutes. Age Recommendation: P (Primary grades, grades 1-3; Ages 6-9); I (Intermediate grades, grades 4-6; Ages 10-12).

VHS: S17280. $14.95.

Pete Seeger's Family Concert

Join the live outdoor concert in this mix of folk songs, favorite kids songs and originals from the folk master, Pete Seeger. 45 minutes. Age Recommendation: S (Starting school, starting to read, starting pre-school, starting kindergarten; Ages 4-5); P (Primary grades, grades 1-3; Ages 6-9); I (Intermediate grades, grades 4-6; Ages 10-12).

VHS: S24620. $14.95.

A Picture Book of Martin Luther King, Jr.
(Live Oak Media)

Picture Book of Martin Luther King, Jr., A

Based on the book by David A. Adler. A straightforward, fact-filled text joins with warm, realistic illustrations to capture the life and times of Dr. King, fostering an appreciation and understanding of his efforts to secure equal rights for all people. This video deals with historical events in a positive manner. 9 minutes. Age Recommendation: P (Primary grades, grades 1-3; Ages 6-9); I (Intermediate grades, grades 4-6; Ages 10-12).

VHS: S24618. $37.95.

Piggy Banks to Money Markets

A group of kids share the facts about saving, investing, spending, and earning money. Produced with consultation from the American Banking Association, the National Council on Economic Education and *Inc. Magazine*. This tape includes original songs, computer graphics and a fun group of kids. 30 minutes. Age Recommendation: P (Primary grades, grades 1-3; Ages 6-9); I (Intermediate grades, grades 4-6; Ages 10-12).

VHS: S24619. $14.95.

Pigs (plus David's Father)

Join the chase when Megan lets the pigs out, then join Julie when she meets her neighbor's unusual dad. 30 minutes. Age Recommendation: S (Starting school, starting to read, starting pre-school, starting kindergarten; Ages 4-5); P (Primary grades, grades 1-3; Ages 6-9).

VHS: S24766. $12.95.

Pinocchio (Rabbit Ears)

Danny Aiello narrates this enchanting animated version of the story by Italian author Carlo Collodi. This is the timeless story of the lonely, frustrated toymaker named Gepeto and his astonishing creation, the wooden marionette who comes to life. Music by the Les Miserables Brass Band. 30 minutes. Age Recommendation: S (Starting school, starting to read, starting pre-school, starting kindergarten; Ages 4-5); P (Primary grades, grades 1-3; Ages 6-9); I (Intermediate grades, grades 4-6; Ages 10-12).

VHS: S18132. $9.95.

P.J. Funnybunny

This witty, comical tale tells the story of a young rabbit who learns to outwit bullies and get respect from his overbearing siblings. 21 minutes. Age Recommendation: S (Starting school, starting to read, starting pre-school, starting kindergarten; Ages 4-5); P (Primary grades, grades 1-3; Ages 6-9).

VHS: S16582. Currently out of print. May be available for rental in some video stores.

Poky Little Puppy's First Christmas

Sweet little Poky is now on video. While the family searches for the perfect Christmas tree, Poky wanders off, falls into a deep hole and meets his rescuer, a little skunk named Herman. Narrated by Donald Sutherland. 30 minutes. Age Recommendation: T (Toddler; Ages Birth-3 years); S (Starting school, starting to read, starting pre-school, starting kindergarten; Ages 4-5).

VHS: S25001. $9.95.

Poky's Favorite Stories

These Golden Book favorites are now on video. This compilation features the animated stories *The Poky Little Puppy and The Patchwork Blanket* (written by Jean Chandler), *The Sailor Dog* (written by Margaret Wise Brown) and *Little Toad to the Rescue* (written by Leonard Shortall). 30 minutes. Age Recommendation: T (Toddler; Ages Birth-3 years); S (Starting school, starting to read, starting pre-school, starting kindergarten; Ages 4-5).

VHS: S24990. $5.95.

Pollyanna (BBC)

A poignant adaptation of Eleanor Porter's book about a resilient and charming young orphan who withstands her despair, faces disability, and wins the hearts of the cold and lonely eccentrics of an English community. Elizabeth Archand stars as Pollyanna. Great Britain, 1973. 155 minutes. Age Recommendation: I (Intermediate grades, grades 4-6; Ages 10-12).

VHS: S19093. $24.98.

Postman Pat's 123 Story

Postman Pat teaches young children the basics of counting in this humorous, simple tale. 30 minutes. Age Recommendation: T (Toddler; Ages Birth-3 years); S (Starting school, starting to read, starting pre-school, starting kindergarten; Ages 4-5).

VHS: S19422. $12.98.

Postman Pat's ABC Story

A delightful, educational program about the charming postman who teaches children about the power of language, thought and action. 30 minutes. Age Recommendation: T (Toddler; Ages Birth-3 years); S (Starting school, starting to read, starting pre-school, starting kindergarten; Ages 4-5).
VHS: S19421. $12.98.

Pre-School Power #3

Pre-schoolers learn to do things for themselves — things like putting on gloves, making a paper fan, sweeping-up spills, making French bread, making giant bubbles, and setting up dominoes. Imagination and cooperation are emphasized. Recommended by the American Library Association (Also see listings for *Pre-School Power: Jacket Flips and Other Tips* and *More Pre-School Power*). 30 minutes. Age Recommendation: T (Toddler; Ages Birth-3 years); S (Starting school, starting to read, starting pre-school, starting kindergarten; Ages 4-5).
VHS: S17010. $14.95.

Pre-School Power:
Jacket Flips & Other Tips

This tape shares the techniques of how to button, buckle, zip, wash hands, put on jackets, tidy rooms, make snacks and pour without spilling a drop. It features pre-schoolers sharing the methods of educator Maria Montessori; youngsters will learn the lasting gift of self-reliance. Winner of the New York Film Festival Award. Recommended by the American Library Association (Also see listings for *More Pre-School Power* and *Pre-School Power #3*). 30 minutes. Age Recommendation: T (Toddler; Ages Birth-3 years); S (Starting school, starting to read, starting pre-school, starting kindergarten; Ages 4-5).
VHS: S17009. $14.95.

Princess Scargo and the
Birthday Pumpkin (Rabbit Ears)

Geena Davis recounts this haunting work based on the Native American myth about the selfless act of a young girl who refuses her priceless birthday gift in order to help her village. With music by Michael Hedges. 30 minutes. Age Recommendation: P (Primary grades, grades 1-3; Ages 6-9); I (Intermediate grades, grades 4-6; Ages 10-12).
VHS: S18131. $9.95.

Princess Scargo and The Birthday Pumpkin
(Illustrated by Karen Barbour/Rabbit Ears Productions)

Puppy Pals

A heartwarming, evocative and tender program about the joy and spirit of puppies, especially their attraction to children, which encourages a friendship between youngsters and animals. With a sing-along soundtrack. 30 minutes. Age Recommendation: S (Starting school, starting to read, starting preschool, starting kindergarten; Ages 4-5).

VHS: S18264. $14.95.

Puss in Boots (Rabbit Ears)

Tracey Ullman's comedic genius and veteran jazz violinist Jean Luc Ponty's spirited score animate this hilarious version of the beloved French story. 30 minutes. Age Recommendation: P (Primary grades, grades 1-3; Ages 6-9); I (Intermediate grades, grades 4-6; Ages 10-12).

VHS: S15640. $9.95.

R Raffi in Concert with the Rise and Shine Band

A young children's concert with the incomparable Raffi and his Rise and Shine Band. Songs include "Baby Beluga," "Time to Sing," "Bathtime," "Apples and Bananas" and "Everything Grows." Great fun with this truly wonderful performer! 50 minutes. Age Recommendation: T (Toddler; Ages Birth-3 years); S (Starting school, starting to read, starting pre-school, starting kindergarten; Ages 4-5).

VHS: S14110. $19.95.

Laser: LD71290. $29.98.

Raffi: Young People's Concert with Raffi

A live performance in Toronto, with "Shake My Sillies Out," "Wheels on The Bus" and "Bumping Up and Down." The internationally acclaimed Raffi is a treasure for children. David Devine, USA, 1984. 45 minutes. Age Recommendation: T (Toddler; Ages Birth-3 years); S (Starting school, starting to read, starting pre-school, starting kindergarten; Ages 4-5).

VHS: S01524. $19.95.

Rainbow of My Own, A

Based on the book by Don Freeman. After a rainy afternoon of playing imaginary games with a rainbow, a boy goes home to find a real rainbow waiting in his room. 5 minutes. Age Recommendation: S (Starting school, starting to read, starting pre-school, starting kindergarten; Ages 4-5); P (Primary grades, grades 1-3; Ages 6-9).

VHS: S24621. $37.95.

Rainy Day Games

Includes *Soap Bubble Magic, A Secret Language, Kite Flying*, and *String Figures*. Each activity can be done at home with simple household materials. 30 minutes. Age Recommendation: P (Primary grades, grades 1-3; Ages 6-9).

VHS: S08105. $26.95.

Rainy Day Magic Show

Magician Mark Mazzarella instills a sense of wonder in children while demonstrating how to turn everyday things into a complete magic show. USA. 30 minutes. Age Recommendation: P (Primary grades, grades 1-3; Ages 6-9); I (Intermediate grades, grades 4-6; Ages 10-12).

VHS: S14952. $19.95.

Ramona

Here's Ramona, the title character of Beverly Cleary's best-selling children's classics, brought to life on video. Meet Sarah Polley as the spunky and

---

lovable Ramona. Watch Ramona, her older sister Beezus and the Quimbys come to life in these stories based upon Cleary favorites. The live-action series shows a multicultural world and conflict in the context of resolution. Age Recommendation: P (Primary grades, grades 1-3; Ages 6-9); I (Intermediate grades, grades 4-6; Ages 10-12).

Ramona: Goodbye, Hello
Based on *Ramona Forever*, this story deals with Ramona and her older sister. Together, they face the death of their cat. 28 minutes.
VHS: S10969. $14.95.

Ramona: Great Hair Argument
Ramona's older sister Beezus has a "bad hair day" with a professional hair cut. 28 minutes.
VHS: S10971. $14.95.

Ramona: New Pajamas
Ramona wears her new pajamas under her clothes to school. 28 minutes.
VHS: S10972. $14.95.

Ramona: The Patient
Ramona is embarrased by throwing-up in front of her class. Later, she returns to class excited by her presentation. 28 minutes.
VHS: S10974. $14.95.

Ramona: Perfect Day and Bad Day
The tape includes two complete episodes. *Perfect Day* is about Aunt Bea's new husband, whom Ramona dislikes. *A Bad Day* combines a bad day at school with parents fighting at home. 60 minutes.
VHS: S06863. $29.95.

Ramona: Rainy Sunday
A dull, rainy Sunday turns fascinating when the family meets a stranger. 28 minutes.
VHS: S10970. $14.95.

Ramona: Ramona's Bad Day
It's a bad day all around, both at school and at home. 28 minutes.
VHS: S10973. $14.95.

Ramona: Siblingitis
There is a third child expected in the Quimby family, and third grader Ramona is having difficulty sorting out her place. 28 minutes.
VHS: S10975. $14.95.

Ramona: Squeakerfoot and Goodbye, Hello
The tape includes two complete episodes. In *Squeakerfoot*, Ramona is embarrassed when she literally winds up with egg on her face. *Goodbye,*

Hello concerns Ramona and her older sister. Their conflicting feelings for each other become less important as they face the death of their cat. 60 minutes.
VHS: S06861. $29.95.

Reach for the Sky

A realistic look at a young girl's sacrifice in training to become a champion gymnast. 60 minutes. Age Recommendation: S (Starting school, starting to read, starting pre-school, starting kindergarten; Ages 4-5); P (Primary grades, grades 1-3; Ages 6-9); I (Intermediate grades, grades 4-6; Ages 10-12).
VHS: S24622. $19.95.

Real Story Videos Series, The

Celebrities are the voices for characters in this series based on well known children's stories, songs and rhymes. While the actual story may be short, the videos imagine an entire life surrounding the material. Contemporary, upbeat, imaginative and surprising. Each video is approximately 25 minutes. Age Recommendation: S (Starting school, starting to read, starting pre-school, starting kindergarten; Ages 4-5); P (Primary grades, grades 1-3; Ages 6-9).

The Real Story of Baa Baa Black Sheep
VHS: S25047. $12.95.

The Real Story of Happy Birthday to You
VHS: S25045. $12.95.

The Real Story of I'm A Little Teapot
VHS: S25042. $12.95.

The Real Story of Itsy Bitsy Spider
Recommended. With *Cosby* show star Malcolm Jamal-Warner and singer Patti LaBelle. Very engaging.
VHS: S25041. $12.95.

The Real Story of Rain, Rain Go Away
VHS: S25044. $12.95.

The Real Story of Three Little Kittens
VHS: S25043. $12.95.

The Real Story of Twinkle Twinkle Little Star
VHS: S25046. $12.95.

Red Shoes, The (Animation)

The Red Shoes, a story by Hans Christian Andersen, is a charming favorite that receives a hip and delightful updating by animator Michael Sporn with music by reggae star Jimmy Cliff. As today's story goes, Lisa and Jennie are best friends. They share everything until Lisa's parents win the lottery and the now jealous and selfish Lisa steals a pair of magical red shoes from Jennie. With the shoes on her feet, she is caught in an energetic dance which she can stop only when she realizes that friendship is the most precious gift of all. Michael Sporn, USA, 1990. 30 minutes. Age Recommendation: P (Primary grades, grades 1-3; Ages 6-9); I (Intermediate grades, grades 4-6; Ages 10-12).
VHS: S12353. $9.98.

Reluctant Dragon

One of Disney's best — the story of the gentle dragon who'd rather sip tea and sing slap-happy songs than do battle. A wonderful reversal of the dragons and knights stories. Hilarious, surprising. USA. 28 minutes. Age Recommendation: S (Starting school, starting to read, starting pre-school, starting kindergarten; Ages 4-5); P (Primary grades, grades 1-3; Ages 6-9).
VHS: S03040. $14.95.

Richard Scarry Series

These videos are as enjoyable as the popular books on which they are based. Join the fun in Busytown with Huckle Cat, Lowly Worm and friends. Age Recommendation: T (Toddler; Ages Birth-3 years); S (Starting school, starting to read, starting pre-school, starting kindergarten; Ages 4-5).

Richard Scarry's Best Busy People Video
A fun look at jobs and occupations in Busytown. 30 minutes.
VHS: S24623. $9.95.

Richard Scarry's Best Counting Video
The friends are back all over town — count down! 20 minutes.
VHS: S24625. $9.95.

Richard Scarry's Best Ever ABC Video
This time, the fun is centered at the Busytown School. 20 minutes.
VHS: S24624. $9.95.

Richard Scarry's Best Learning Songs Ever
Join the Busytown crowd singing about letters, numbers, shapes and other fun things. 30 minutes.
VHS: S24626. $9.95.

Rights from the Heart/Droits au Coeur

A collection of short, animated, non-verbal films produced by the National Film Board of Canada. Vignettes illustrate the ten "Rights of the Child," adopted by the United Nations in 1990. International in outlook, these films stress the values of peace, dignity, tolerance, freedom and equality. 40 minutes. Includes public performance rights. Age Recommendation: P (Primary grades, grades 1-3; Ages 6-9); I (Intermediate grades, grades 4-6; Ages 10-12).
VHS: S18966. $39.95.

Make Way for Ducklings (from the Robert McCloskey Library)
(© Weston Woods/Children's Circle Home Video)

Robert McCloskey Library

This tape includes six short adaptations of books by Robert McCloskey. *Lentil* is the story of a boy who buys a harmonica, *Make Way for Ducklings* is about a mother duck and her urban chicks, *Blueberries for Sal* is the story of Sal, who meets a bear cub, *Time of Wonder* is about experiences of life on an island, and *Burt Dow: Deep-Water Man* is about a man swallowed by a whale. Also included is a short documentary about Robert McCloskey. 55 minutes. Age Recommendation: S (Starting school, starting to read, starting pre-school, starting kindergarten; Ages 4-5); P (Primary grades, grades 1-3; Ages 6-9).
VHS: S13335. $19.95.

Roxaboxen

Based on the book by Alice McLerran. Roxaboxen is just a rocky hill, but Marian, her sisters and the other neighbors create a wonderful imaginative town. A nice story about using your imagination. 9 minutes. Age Recommendation: S (Starting school, starting to read, starting pre-school, starting kindergarten; Ages 4-5); P (Primary grades, grades 1-3; Ages 6-9).
VHS: S16353. $44.95.

Runaway Ralph

In this sequel to *The Mouse and the Motorcycle*, Fred Savage plays a kid at summer camp who has no friends until he meets the rambunctious mouse named Ralph. Based on the book by Beverly Cleary. 42 minutes. Age Recommendation: S (Starting school, starting to read, starting pre-school, starting kindergarten; Ages 4-5); P (Primary grades, grades 1-3; Ages 6-9); I (Intermediate grades, grades 4-6; Ages 10-12).

VHS: S16580. $9.98.

Rupert

The animated adventures of Rupert the Bear, the favorite British cartoon character, and his friends Bill Badger, Tiger-Lilly and Jack Frost. They live in a faraway land of dragons and sea-serpents, which can only be reached by the animal underground railway. Narrated by Ray Brooks. 57 minutes. Age Recommendation: S (Starting school, starting to read, starting pre-school, starting kindergarten; Ages 4-5); P (Primary grades, grades 1-3; Ages 6-9).

VHS: S13204. $14.98.

Rupert and the Frog Song

A McCartney family project: Paul wrote the songs for the British Rupert, a little bear who discovers a magical cave where the forest frogs put on a musical show; Linda contributed with "Seaside Woman" (set to a calypso beat) and "Oriental Nightfish." Great Britain, 1985. 30 minutes. Age Recommendation: S (Starting school, starting to read, starting pre-school, starting kindergarten; Ages 4-5); P (Primary grades, grades 1-3; Ages 6-9).

VHS: S02571. Currently out of print. May be available for rental in some video stores.

Rupert and the Runaway Dragon

More stories about Rupert the British bear, in a world where dragons run away, red robins turn yellow, and eggs hatch fire-birds. 37 minutes. Age Recommendation: S (Starting school, starting to read, starting pre-school, starting kindergarten; Ages 4-5); P (Primary grades, grades 1-3; Ages 6-9).

VHS: S13205. $14.98.

Ruth Heller's Nature Stories

Questions about plants and animals are asked and answered in meaningful and amusing stories that young children will love. Includes four programs: *Animals Born Alive and Well, Chickens Aren't the Only Ones, Plants That*

Never Ever Bloom and *The Reason for a Flower*. 18 minutes. Age Recommendation: P (Primary grades, grades 1-3; Ages 6-9); I (Intermediate grades, grades 4-6; Ages 10-12).

VHS: S14175. $139.95.

Sammy and Other Songs from Getting to Know Myself

Singer and songwriter Hap Palmer encourages the audience to join in this exploration of body movement and feelings. 30 minutes. Age Recommendation: S (Starting school, starting to read, starting pre-school, starting kindergarten; Ages 4-5); P (Primary grades, grades 1-3; Ages 6-9).

VHS: S24627. $19.95.

Sand Castle, The

This 1977 Academy Award-winner is a fable of great humor and appeal, directed by Co Hoedemann. The Sandman sculpts magical creatures who build a castle and then celebrate their new home, but an uninvited guest arrives to start the wind blowing. The tape includes the delightful animated shorts *The North Wind and the Sun, Alphabet* and *The Owl and the Lemming*. Canada, 1977. 30 minutes. Age Recommendation: S (Starting school, starting to read, starting pre-school, starting kindergarten; Ages 4-5); P (Primary grades, grades 1-3; Ages 6-9); I (Intermediate grades, grades 4-6; Ages 10-12).

VHS: S15795. $19.98.

Savior Is Born, The (Rabbit Ears)

Actor Morgan Freeman gives a resonant reading of the first Christmas from the actual gospels of Matthew and Luke (Note that this includes the terrible violence of King Herod). For parents looking for a story close to the biblical original, this is an excellent choice. Quite awe-inspiring. Beautifully illustrated by Robert Van Nuit. Music by the Christ Church Cathedral Choir of Oxford, England. From *The Greatest Stories Ever Told Collection*. 27 minutes. Age Recommendation: P (Primary grades, grades 1-3; Ages 6-9); I (Intermediate grades, grades 4-6; Ages 10-12).

VHS: S18002. $12.98.

Say No to Drugs!

Called "an essential weapon in parents' fight against adolescent drug and alcohol abuse" by the National Foundation of Parents for Drug-Free Youth. 50 minutes. Age Recommendation: I (Intermediate grades, grades 4-6; Ages 10-12).

VHS: S05024. Currently out of print. May be available for rental in some video stores.

Science Primer

These special science programs help children understand the five senses, the animal world and the four elements that compose matter. Age Recommendation: S (Starting school, starting to read, starting pre-school, starting kindergarten; Ages 4-5); P (Primary grades, grades 1-3; Ages 6-9).

Earth, Air, Water, Fire
From ancient civilization, the four basic elements make up matter. This video helps children understand the elements of the world they inhabit. 19 minutes.
VHS: S19955. $49.95.

The Five Senses
The five senses process signals to the brain and keep us attuned to our environment and are aptly referred to as the "windows of the world." This program helps children understand the feelings and information their senses convey. 27 minutes.
VHS: S19956. $49.95.

Habitats
Children are introduced to the habitats of plants and animals. The program studies plants and animals in their natural environments, above and below ground, in the sea and in the air. 35 minutes.
VHS: S19957. $49.95.

Science Primer Series
The collection of three programs. 110 minutes.
VHS: S19958. $129.00.

Scuffy the Tugboat and Friends

Remember the Golden Books you read as a kid? *Scuffy the Tugboat* is now in video format. Also included on this tape are the Golden Book titles *What Was That!* and *Theodore Mouse Goes to Sea*. 30 minutes. Age

Recommendation: T (Toddler; Ages Birth-3 years); S (Starting school, starting to read, starting pre-school, starting kindergarten; Ages 4-5). VHS: S24989. $5.95.

Seasons and Holidays Around the World

Colorful and dramatic stories tell how real people celebrate the holidays. 6 minutes each story; set of 4 is 24 minutes. Age Recommendation: P (Primary grades, grades 1-3; Ages 6-9); I (Intermediate grades, grades 4-6; Ages 10-12).

Chinese New Year
Chin and his dad discuss Chinese New Year both in New York's Chinatown and in ancient China.
VHS: S16364. $34.95.

Christmas in Mexico
Enter a Mexican home and celebrate Christmas with Carmen and her family.
VHS: S16363. $34.95.

Christmas in Sweden
A brother and sister tell us about their favorite Christmas story — Jultomten arriving in his sleigh pulled by Julbockar.
VHS: S16365. $34.95.

Halloween in Britain
A party for a holiday that has its origins in the Druidic religious traditions.
VHS: S16362. $34.95.

Secret Garden, The (Agnieszka Holland)

A haunting adaptation of Frances Hodgson Burnett's 1909 classic about the orphaned girl Kate Maberly sent to her uncle's remote English estate. With the help of her painfully withdrawn cousin (Heydon Prowse) and a local boy (Andrew Knott), she discovers an enchanting garden and watches it come to life. Maggie Smith plays the tyrannical housekeeper. Director Agnieszka Holland captures beautifully the painful social isolation of childhood. USA. 1993. 102 minutes. Age Recommendation: P (Primary grades, grades 1-3; Ages 6-9); I (Intermediate grades, grades 4-6; Ages 10-12).
VHS: S20217. $19.98.

Laser: LD72328. $34.98.

Secret Garden, The (BBC)

A faithful adaptation of Frances Hodgson Burnett's classic children's novel about a a girl's strength and a garden's power to transform the life of a sickly boy. A BBC production starring Sarah Hollis Andrews and David Patterson. England. 1984. 107 minutes. Age Recommendation: P (Primary grades, grades 1-3; Ages 6-9); I (Intermediate grades, grades 4-6; Ages 10-12).

VHS: S07181. $14.98.

Secret Garden, The (MGM)

An interesting and well-made early adaptation of Frances Hodgson Burnett's classic children's novel about the transcendent powers and astonishing capabilities of a young girl to change and influence the dark and foreboding residents of a depressed Victorian estate. This film classic is shot mostly in black and white. With Margaret O'Brien, Herbert Marshall, Dean Stockwell and Gladys Cooper. Fred M. Wilcox, USA, 1949. 92 minutes. Age Recommendation: P (Primary grades, grades 1-3; Ages 6-9); I (Intermediate grades, grades 4-6; Ages 10-12).

VHS: S18564. $19.98.

See How They Grow

Based on the best-selling books of Dorling Kindersley, this collection of four tapes takes children inside the mysteries of animal behavior — charting from infancy to adulthood the growth of pets, farm animals, wild animals and insects and spiders. Each video contains four different animals, and is offset by musical accompaniment. "This timeless video collection will bring kids and parents back again and again," (*The Playground*). 30 minutes each video. Age Recommendation: P (Primary grades, grades 1-3; Ages 6-9).

See How They Grow: Farm Animals
VHS: S20290. $14.98.

See How They Grow: Insects and Spiders
VHS: S20291. $14.98.

See How They Grow: Pets
VHS: S20289. $14.98.

See How They Grow: Wild Animals
VHS: S20292. $14.98.

Sesame Songs Series

Stories, games, songs and the wonderful Sesame Street crowd. Each video is 30 minutes. Age Recommendation: T (Toddler; Ages Birth-3 years); S (Starting school, starting to read, starting pre-school, starting kindergarten; Ages 4-5).

Sesame Songs: Dance Along!
The Muppets and other Sesame Street characters demonstrate such dances as The Count's "Batty Bat" and Bert's favorite, "Doin' the Pigeon." 30 minutes. Age Recommendation: T (Toddler; Ages Birth-3 years); S (Starting school, starting to read, starting pre-school, starting kindergarten; Ages 4-5).
VHS: S12769. $9.98.

Sesame Songs: Elmo's Sing-Along Guessing Game
Kids sing-along the clues as they try to guess the answers to Elmo's questions in this TV game show take-off. 1991.
VHS: S24628. $9.98.

Sesame Songs: Monster Hits!
Ten Sesame Street hit songs performed by the loveable and furry monsters. Sing along with "C is for Cookie," "That Furry Blue Mommy of Mine" and "Fuzzy and Blue."
VHS: S12264. $9.98.

Sesame Songs: Rock & Roll!
Sesame Street characters call-in their requests to D.J. Jackman Wolf. Songs include "Count up to Nine," "The Word Is No," and "It's Hip to Be Square."
VHS: S12768. $9.98.

Sesame Songs: Sing Yourself Silly!

James Taylor is the musical guest for this potpourri of Sesame Street's silliest songs, including the "Honker Duckie Dinger Jamboree," "The Everything Is in the Wrong Place Ball," "Jellyman Kelly," and the ever popular "Lady Bug Picnic." Also includes visits from Pete Seeger, Paul Simon and Rhea Perlman.

VHS: S12265. $9.98.

Sesame Songs: Sing, Hoot and Howl

Big Bird hosts such sing-along favorites as "Proud to Be a Cow," "The Insects in Your Neighborhood," and "Cluck Around the Clock."

VHS: S24629. $9.98.

Sesame Songs: Sing-Along Earth Songs

Join Sesame Street's Grover to find out about the importance of protecting the Earth. 30 minutes. Age Recommendation: T (Toddler; Ages Birth-3 years); S (Starting school, starting to read, starting pre-school, starting kindergarten; Ages 4-5).

VHS: S24649. $9.98.

Sesame Songs: We All Sing Together

The Sesame Street crowd is back! This time, Herry the "anchor-monster" discovers the variety of shapes, colors and sizes of different kids. Full of songs, fun and other favorite Sesame Street characters. 30 minutes. Age Recommendation: T (Toddler; Ages Birth-3 years); S (Starting school, starting to read, starting pre-school, starting kindergarten; Ages 4-5).

VHS: S24656. $9.98.

Sesame Street
Home Video Visits

Pre-schoolers love Sesame Street's "get-acquainted" approach to making places like the firehouse and the hospital less frightening. Age Recommendation: T (Toddler; Ages Birth-3 years); S (Starting school, starting to read, starting pre-school, starting kindergarten; Ages 4-5); P (Primary grades, grades 1- 3; Ages 6-9).

Sesame Street Home Video Visits: The Firehouse

After Oscar's trash can goes on fire, the crew visits the firehouse. 30 minutes. VHS: S24634. $9.98.

Sesame Street Home Video Visits: The Hospital

Big Bird is afraid when he has to go to the hospital, but after he learns more about the hospital he feels better. 30 minutes.

Sesame Street Specials

Travel with Big Bird and the Sesame Street gang to exciting and often far-away places such as China, Japan, and the Metropolitan Museum of Art in these award-winning Sesame Street specials.

Sesame Street Specials: Big Bird in China
Big Bird's desire to find the legendary Chinese phoenix bird leads him and Barkley the Dog to an exciting adventure in China. Along the way, they visit with Chinese school children and learn some Chinese words and songs. This is a good informative cultural program for all ages. 75 minutes. Age Recommendation: T (Toddler; Ages Birth-3 years); S (Starting school, starting to read, starting pre-school, starting kindergarten; Ages 4-5); P (Primary grades, grades 1- 3; Ages 6-9).

VHS: S05373. $12.98.

Sesame Street Specials: Big Bird in Japan
Join Big Bird and Barkley the Dog on their visit to Japan. Meet with Japanese people as well. This is a good informative cultural program for all ages. 75 minutes. Age Recommendation: T (Toddler; Ages Birth-3 years); S (Starting school, starting to read, starting pre-school, starting kindergarten; Ages 4-5); P (Primary grades, grades 1- 3; Ages 6-9).

VHS: S24633. $12.98.

Sesame Street Specials: Celebrates Around the World
Join the party as the Sesame Street crowd celebrates New Year's Eve around the world in Mexico, Japan, Portugal, Israel, Norway and Germany. 30 minutes. Age Recommendation: T (Toddler; Ages Birth-3 years); S (Starting school, starting to read, starting pre-school, starting kindergarten; Ages 4-5); P (Primary grades, grades 1-3; Ages 6-9).

VHS: S23129. $12.95.

Sesame Street Specials: Christmas Eve on Sesame Street
Holiday skits and songs, with Big Bird figuring out "How does Santa Claus, who is 'built like a dump truck', get down all those skinny little chimneys?" The whole gang is involved in this charming story which uncovers the true Christmas spirit. 60 minutes. Age Recommendation: T (Toddler; Ages Birth-3 years); S (Starting school, starting to read, starting pre-school, starting kindergarten; Ages 4-5); P (Primary grades, grades 1- 3; Ages 6-9).

VHS: S05379. $12.98.

Sesame Street Specials: Don't Eat the Pictures — Sesame Street Visits the Metropolitan Museum of Art
This one-hour musical follows the adventures of Big Bird, Snuffy, Cookie Monster, and the rest of the Sesame Street gang as they find themselves accidentally locked in the New York Metropolitan Museum overnight. 60

---

minutes. Age Recommendation: T (Toddler; Ages Birth-3 years); S (Starting school, starting to read, starting pre-school, starting kindergarten; Ages 4-5); P (Primary grades, grades 1- 3; Ages 6-9).
VHS: S05374. $12.98.

Sesame Street Specials: Put Down the Duckie
Sesame Street's Ernie learns to play the saxophone. 30 minutes. Age Recommendation: T (Toddler; Ages Birth-3 years); S (Starting school, starting to read, starting pre-school, starting kindergarten; Ages 4-5).
VHS: S23130. $12.98.

Sesame Street Specials: Sesame Street's 25th Birthday: A Musical Celebration
A musical birthday party featuring an hour of musical favorites. This tape features 20 musical numbers, including favorites like Ernie's "Rubber Duckie," and also includes new magic, like a finale with the South African a capella singing group Ladysmith Black Mambazo. 60 minutes. Age Recommendation: T (Toddler; Ages Birth-3 years); S (Starting school, starting to read, starting pre-school, starting kindergarten; Ages 4-5); P (Primary grades, grades 1-3; Ages 6-9).
VHS: S24636. $12.98.

Sesame Street Start to Read Videos

These videos are based on the popular *Start to Read Books* series. Large print permits children to read along with the ever popular Big Bird. Each tape features three stories. Each video is 30 minutes. Age Recommendation: S (Starting school, starting to read, starting pre-school, starting kindergarten; Ages 4-5).

Don't Cry, Big Bird and Other Stories
VHS: S21949. $14.95.

Ernie's Big Mess and Other Stories
VHS: S21950. $14.95.

Ernie's Little Lie and Other Stories
VHS: S21951. $14.95.

I Want to Go Home! and Other Stories
VHS: S21952. $14.95.

Sesame Street: Plaza Sesamo

Sesame Street is finally available in Spanish! For use in teaching Spanish, the videos can work for ages 2-12. Each video is 30 minutes. Age

Recommendation: T (Toddler; Ages Birth-3 years); S (Starting school, starting to read, starting pre-school, starting kindergarten; Ages 4-5); P (Primary grades, grades 1- 3; Ages 6-9).

De Compamento Con Montoya: Big Bird Goes Camping
VHS: S19757. $25.00.

El Alfabeto De Montoya: Learn the Alphabet with Bert and Ernie
VHS: S19760. $25.00.

Plaza Sesamo Canta: Favorite Songs from Past Shows
VHS: S19758. $25.00.

Vamos a Imaginar: Learn About Sounds and Shapes
VHS: S19759. $25.00.

Viaja Con Nosotros: Big Bird and Oscar Go to Venezuela and Mexico
VHS: S19756. $25.00.

The Plaza Sesamo Complete Set.
150 minutes.
VHS: S19761. $89.75.

Sesame Street Specials: Put Down the Duckie
(©1995 Children's Television Workshop. Courtesy of Western Publishing.)

Shalom Sesame

It's a long way from Sesame Street to Israel! Violinist Itzhak Perlman and Broadway and television star Bonnie Franklin team up with the Muppets and the Israeli casts of *Rechov Sumsum*, the Israeli version of *Sesame Street*, to introduce American children to the people, places, cultures and languages of Israel. The tapes are in English, though many of the tapes include some basic Hebrew instruction. Each program is 30 minutes. Age Recommendation: S (Starting school, starting to read, starting pre-school, starting kindergarten; Ages 4-5); P (Primary grades, grades 1-3; Ages 6-9); I (Intermediate grades, grades 4-6; Ages 10-12).

Aleph-Bet Telethon
Subtitled *Discovering the Hebrew Letters.* Kippi ben Kippod and Jerry Stiller are called to action when the Hebrew alphabet mysteriously vanishes. The two respond by holding a special telethon to track down the mysterious letters.
VHS: S17122. $22.95.

Chanukah
This tape looks at the ritual and power of the Festival of Lights. Viewers explore memory and time in the land of the Maccabees with Jeremy Miller.
VHS: S17119. $22.95.

Jerusalem
Experience the golden beauty of Israel's City of Peace as Itzhak Perlman, Bonnie Franklin and their young Israeli friends take you on a tour of Jerusalem, from the Old City's Jewish, Christian, Moslem and Armenian Quarters to the differing cultures of East and West Jerusalem.
VHS: S08386. $22.95.

Journey to Secret Places
Jeremy Miller and Kippi ben Kippod move through a strange, eerie tunnel that transports them into the vibrant culture of Israel's exotic, mysterious regions.
VHS: S17121. $22.95.

Kibbutz
Bonnie Franklin travels to Kibbutz Ein Gedi on the shore of the Dead Sea and shares with the kibbutz kids their unique way of life.
VHS: S08384. $22.95.

Kids Sing Israel
In this glorious finale, Kippi ben Kippod, Sarah Jessica Parker (*L.A. Story)* and the children of Israel host a rousing mixture of traditional Israeli and Hebrew songs with the best-loved Sesame Street tunes.
VHS: S17124. $22.95.

Land of Israel
Meet your new Israeli friends from *Rechov Sumsum*, including an oversized porcupine named Kippy ben Kipod, Moishe Oofnick, the neighborhood grouch, Bentz and Arik. Mary Tyler Moore joins Bonnie Franklin and Itzhak Perlman in this tour of Israel.
VHS: S08382. $22.95.

Passover
Also known as *Jerusalem Jones and the Lost Afikoman*. The talented young actress Sarah Jessica Parker stars as Jerusalem Jones in this program geared toward the Passover theme. Parker must find a lost afikoman and determine whether Miriam's bread will rise.
VHS: S17123. $22.95.

People of Israel
They came from Sweden, Russia, Ethiopia, Egypt, India and America; now they're *Israeli* kids. Join them and Itzhak Perlman as they explore the colorful mix that makes up Israel's people.
VHS: S08385. $22.95.

Sing Around The Seasons
In this educational program about the landscape, people and culture of Israel, the *Sesame Street* gang orchestrates a sing-along celebrating the country's changing seasons, exploring its flair for celebration, ritual, holidays and festivals.
VHS: S17120. $22.95.

Tel Aviv
Itzhak Perlman introduces his hometown, including the colorful, bustling Carmel Market, the Tel Aviv boardwalk and beach, and the ancient city of Jaffa.
VHS: S08383. $22.95.

Shamu & You Series

Shamu the whale is just one of the fascinating creatures kids meet in this series which explores the wonders of animals. Featuring live-action, animation, and wildlife footage and songs. 30 minutes each video. Age Recommendation: S (Starting school, starting to read, starting pre-school, starting kindergarten; Ages 4-5); P (Primary grades, grades 1-3; Ages 6-9); I (Intermediate grades, grades 4-6; Ages 10-12).

Shamu & You: Exploring the World of Birds
VHS: S24637. $14.98.

Shamu & You: Exploring the World of Fish
VHS: S24638. $14.98.

Shamu & You: Exploring the World of Mammals
VHS: S24639. $14.98.

Shamu & You: Exploring the World of Reptiles
VHS: S24640. $14.98.

Shari Lewis: 101 Things for Kids to Do

A fun activity tape which includes arts and crafts, games, magic tricks and more. 60 minutes. Age Recommendation: S (Starting school, starting to read, starting pre-school, starting kindergarten; Ages 4-5); P (Primary grades, grades 1-3; Ages 6-9).
VHS: S24642. $9.95.

Shari Lewis: Don't Wake Your Mom

This innovative program gives kids something to do for 45 minutes while a parent takes that needed break. With characteristic charm, Shari Lewis makes magic out of the classic question, "Is it time yet?". 45 minutes. Age Recommendation: S (Starting school, starting to read, starting pre-school, starting kindergarten; Ages 4-5); P (Primary grades, grades 1-3; Ages 6-9).
VHS: S16158. $14.95.

Shari Lewis: Kooky Classics

Join Shari and friends as they tour the world of classical music, from Brahms to Mozart. 55 minutes. Age Recommendation: S (Starting school, starting to read, starting pre-school, starting kindergarten; Ages 4-5); P (Primary grades, grades 1-3; Ages 6-9).
VHS: S24641. $19.95.

Shari Lewis: Lamb Chop in the Land of No Manners

Shari Lewis, with her sassy sidekick the puppet Lamb Chop, takes youngsters on a magical journey to a place where they don't have to follow any rules or take turns. 44 minutes. Age Recommendation: S (Starting school, starting to read, starting pre-school, starting kindergarten; Ages 4-5); P (Primary grades, grades 1-3; Ages 6-9).
VHS: S14519. $19.95.

Shari Lewis: Lamb Chop's Play-Along

Lamb Chop, the wonderful hand puppet, gets top billing over her friend and creator Shari Lewis in this children's video that combine songs and games for the audience at home to join in. You too can interact with Shari and her talented Lamb Chop. Includes the music videos "Betchas, Tricks and Silly Stunts," "Jokes, Riddles, Knock-Knocks and Funny Poems," "Action Songs" and "Action Stories." 45 minutes. Age Recommendation: S (Starting school, starting to read, starting pre-school, starting kindergarten; Ages 4-5); P (Primary grades, grades 1-3; Ages 6-9).

VHS: S07704. $9.95.

Shari Lewis: You Can Do It!

Puppets Hush Puppy, Charley and Lamb Chop join Shari in teaching kids how to make their own puppet shows and how to do magic tricks. 56 minutes. Age Recommendation: S (Starting school, starting to read, starting pre-school, starting kindergarten; Ages 4-5); P (Primary grades, grades 1-3; Ages 6-9).

VHS: S04441. $19.95.

Shari's Christmas Concert

Shari Lewis and her cuddly and often very shy friend Lamb Chop ring in the holiday season in this video for children of all ages. Shari conducts a symphony orchestra, sings, dances and provides the "Merry" in "Merry Christmas!" Colorful family entertainment. 50 minutes. Age Recommendation: S (Starting school, starting to read, starting pre-school, starting kindergarten; Ages 4-5); P (Primary grades, grades 1-3; Ages 6-9).

VHS: S07718. $9.95.

Sharon, Lois & Bram's Elephant Show

This remarkable singing group (and their life-sized puppet elephant) have brought years of outstanding entertainment to children around the world. This multiple award-winning series was designed to impart social skills, to strengthen pre-school developmental abilities and to provide pre-reading and language experiences in a fun manner. These tapes feature music, sing-alongs, games, live-action, and on-location visits to interesting places. "Contagious! The trio's affection for children comes across instantly... demonstrating that music is an integral part of life." (*Variety*) Each video is 30 minutes. Age Recommendation: S (Starting school, starting to read, starting pre-school, starting kindergarten; Ages 4-5).

Back by Popular Demand
More live concert performances compiled from the award-winning *Elephant Show*. Ten songs, including "Jelly, Jelly in My Belly," "Keep on the Sunny Side" and "Chugga-Chugga."

VHS: S16493. $14.95.

Live in Your Living Room
Featuring live concert performances compiled from the award-winning *Elephant Show*. Ten songs, including "Little Rabbit Foo Foo," "Pufferbellies" and "Canadian Jig Medley."
VHS: S16492. $14.95.

Pet Fair
The neighborhood kids are excited about entering their pets in the upcoming pet fair. Songs include "Rags (My Little Puppy)," "One Elephant, Deux Elephant" and "Hercules, King of Fleas."
VHS: S24645. $14.95.

Radio Show
When their television goes on the blink, the kids pull a magic, old-fashioned radio out of the closet and become transfixed by the broadcast. Songs include "Sambalele," "The Erie Canal" and "Skinnamarink."
VHS: S24646. $14.95.

Sleepover
A mime group, The Potato People, perform a bedtime story. The 12 songs include "Where's My Pajamas," "Ham 'n Eggs" and "Ten in the Bed."
VHS: S16491. $14.95.

Soap Box Derby
The children construct a soap box car and enter an exciting soap box derby. The 10 songs include, "Get Out and Get Under," "Going to Kentucky" and "I'm a Little Piece of Tin."
VHS: S16496. $14.95.

Treasure Island
The kids discover a treasure map and follow a musical hunt, featuring a visit by Naomi Tyrell. With 9 songs, including "Lots of Worms," "Going Over The Sea" and "The Shanty Medley."
VHS: S16494. $14.95.

Who Stole the Cookies
Lois bakes 60 cookies, and 59 disappear! Elephant plays detective in *The Case of The Missing Cookies*. The 10 songs include "Cookie Jar," "My Little Rooster" and "Apple Pickers Red."
VHS: S16495. $14.95.

Shelley Duvall Presents Mrs. Piggle-Wiggle

This series of videos features Jean Stapleton as a lovable lady with a knack for helping kids — and their parents — out of jams. She wears platform tennis shoes and finds uncommon solutions to the common everyday challenges of growing up. These tapes teach children about life in a wonderful, whimsical way and feature a multi-ethnic, multi-talented cast of children. Each tape includes two episodes. 57 minutes each. Age Recommendation: P (Primary grades, grades 1-3; Ages 6-9); I (Intermediate grades, grades 4-6; Ages 10-12).

The Answer Backer Cure and The Chores Cure
VHS: S22874. $12.98.

The Not-Truthful Cure and the Radish Cure
VHS: S22872. $12.98.

The Pet Forgetters Cure and The Never-Want-To-Go-To-Bedders Cure
VHS: S22873. $12.98.

Shelley Duvall's Bedtime Stories: Aunt Ippy's Museum of Junk

Jodi and Jimi love visiting Aunt Ippy's shop, a hotbed of recycling and rebuilding. One day they explore the entire fascinating kingdom in search of a special object. Narrated by Kathy Bates. *Uncle Wizmo's New Car*, the story of Jodi and Jimi in a used car lot, is also included on the tape. Ed Begley, Jr. narrates. 26 minutes. Age Recommendation: S (Starting school, starting to read, starting pre-school, starting kindergarten; Ages 4-5); P (Primary grades, grades 1-3; Ages 6-9); I (Intermediate grades, grades 4-6; Ages 10-12).
VHS: S21806. $12.98.

Shelley Duvall's Bedtime Stories: Elizabeth and Larry/Bill and Pete

Narrated by Jean Stapleton and based on the book by Marilyn Sadler, *Elizabeth and Larry* is the charming story of an older woman and her beloved pet alligator. *Bill and Pete* is another story of friendship and cooperation, this time between a crocodile and a bird, based on the book by Tomie De Paola. 25 minutes. Age Recommendation: S (Starting school, starting to read, starting pre-school, starting kindergarten; Ages 4-5); P (Primary grades, grades 1-3; Ages 6-9); I (Intermediate grades, grades 4-6; Ages 10-12).
VHS: S16993. $12.98.

Shelley Duvall's Bedtime Stories: The Little Rabbit Who Wanted Red Wings

Shelley Duvall narrates the title story of an imaginative rabbit who gets his wish for wings, only to discover that being yourself is really the best thing. In *Katy No-Pocket* (written by Emmy Payne), a mother kangaroo has a problem. With no pouch to carry her baby, things are difficult — until Katy finds the perfect all-purpose pocket. Narrated by Mary Steenburgen. 26 minutes. Age Recommendation: S (Starting school, starting to read, starting pre-school, starting kindergarten; Ages 4-5); P (Primary grades, grades 1-3; Ages 6-9).
VHS: S21804. $12.98.

Shelley Duvall's Bedtime Stories: Moe the Dog in Tropical Paradise

Moe, the family dog, works at an ice cream factory in the frozen north. He and a friend dream of an expensive tropical holiday. Narrated by Richard Dreyfuss. The tape also includes Morgan Freeman narrating *Amos, The Story of an Old Dog and His Couch* (written by Susan Seligson). 26 minutes. Age Recommendation: S (Starting school, starting to read, starting pre-school, starting kindergarten; Ages 4-5); P (Primary grades, grades 1-3; Ages 6-9); I (Intermediate grades, grades 4-6; Ages 10-12).
VHS: S21771. $12.98.

Sign Songs: Fun Songs to Sign and Sing

Sign language can enhance learning for all children. This is a great tape for all kids, who can learn new songs, new signs and how to sign-along. Featuring 11 delightful songs by Ken Longquist, who sings and plays guitar, with sign interpretation by John Kinstler. 29 minutes. Age Recommendation: S (Starting school, starting to read, starting pre-school, starting kinder-garten; Ages 4-5); P (Primary grades, grades 1-3; Ages 6-9).
VHS: S24983. $49.95.

Sign-Me-a-Story

Any child, hearing-impaired or hearing, would enjoy these two tales told in American Sign Language. Sesame Street's Linda Bove, deaf herself, is a won-derful narrator and role model. Along the way, we learn a few signs ourselves! 60 minutes. Age Recommendation: S (Starting school, starting to read, start-ing pre-school, starting kindergarten; Ages 4-5); P (Primary grades, grades 1-3; Ages 6-9); I (Intermediate grades, grades 4-6; Ages 10-12).
VHS: S24643. $14.95.

Silly Tales and Tunes

Disc jockey K.J. is back, hosting comical stories and sing-along songs. 30 minutes. Age Recommendation: T (Toddler; Ages Birth-3 years); S (Starting school, starting to read, starting pre-school, starting kindergarten; Ages 4-5); P (Primary grades, grades 1-3; Ages 6-9).

VHS: S24644. $12.95.

Simon the Lamb

Simon the lamb turns bright blue. The rest of the flock reject him because he's different. Find out how they come to accept him. 30 minutes. Age Recommendation: S (Starting school, starting to read, starting pre-school, starting kindergarten; Ages 4-5); P (Primary grades, grades 1-3; Ages 6-9).

VHS: S24936. $12.95.

Smile for Auntie and Other Stories
(Weston Woods/Children's Circle Home Video)

Simply Magic: Episode 2

Joanie Bartell is a substitute teacher who leads students on journeys to different places, times and planets. 45 minutes. Age Recommendation: S (Starting school, starting to read, starting pre-school, starting kindergarten; Ages 4-5); P (Primary grades, grades 1-3; Ages 6-9).

VHS: S24648. $14.98.

Simply Magic: The Rainy Day Adventure

Joanie Bartell leads a sing-along program about a poolside party and a magical car. 1993. 45 minutes. Age Recommendation: S (Starting school, starting to read, starting pre-school, starting kindergarten; Ages 4-5); P (Primary grades, grades 1-3; Ages 6-9).

VHS: S24647. $14.98.

Skating Safe for Kids

With the phenomenal rise in numbers of kids using the speedy in-line and Roller Blade skates, this fun instructional tape encourages children to learn basic techniques and methods. This tape shows how to use safety equipment, how to stop(!), and teaches ten Rules of The Road in a program created by professional skaters. 20 minutes. Age Recommendation: P (Primary grades, grades 1-3; Ages 6-9); I (Intermediate grades, grades 4-6; Ages 10-12). VHS: S23858. $24.95.

Smile for Auntie and Other Stories

Smile for Auntie (written by Diane Paterson) is the hilarious tale of a silly Auntie who sings, dances and does anything to make a baby smile. Other films on the tape are *Make Way for Ducklings* (written by Robert McCloskey), in which a mother duck shows her chicks how to survive the urban jungle as they head for the pond, *The Snowy Day* (written by Ezra Jack Keats), in which a young African American boy comes to understand snow, and *Wynken, Blynken and Nod* (written by Eugene Field), the story of three men who sail the sky in a wooden shoe. 27 minutes. Age Recommendation: S (Starting school, starting to read, starting pre-school, starting kindergarten; Ages 4-5); P (Primary grades, grades 1-3; Ages 6-9). VHS: S01218. $19.95.

Snowman, The

Based on the story by Raymond Briggs. An Academy-Award Nominee, this delightful animated story weaves a spell of magic enchantment as a young boy's snowman comes to life and escorts the boy on a fantasy dream visit to the North Pole. No narration. John Coates, USA, 1989. 30 minutes. Age Recommendation: S (Starting school, starting to read, starting pre-school, starting kindergarten; Ages 4-5); P (Primary grades, grades 1-3; Ages 6-9). VHS: S01222. $14.95.

Sojourner Truth (1797-1883) — Abolitionist Leader

From *The Black Americans of Achievement Series*. This video is based upon the acclaimed book by Peter Krass, drawing from the knowledge of a brilliant group of consultants and experts. Born a slave named Isabella, Sojourner Truth became a traveling preacher and famous leader in the abolitionist movement. The strength and presence of her electrifying speeches against oppression and for women's rights inspired Frederick Douglas, William Lloyd Garrison and Abraham Lincoln. This video deals with powerful positive

responses to violent reality, and frames historical events well. 30 minutes. Age Recommendation: P (Primary grades, grades 1-3; Ages 6-9); I (Intermediate grades, grades 4-6; Ages 10-12).
VHS: S17393. $39.95.

Something Good (plus Mortimer)

This is the tale of Tyya, a little girl whose dad refuses to buy her any "good stuff" like cookies and candy. Also included is *Mortimer*, the story of a boy who's unwilling to be quiet and go to bed. Animated stories by Robert Munsch. 30 minutes. Age Recommendation: T (Toddler; Ages Birth-3 years); S (Starting school, starting to read, starting pre-school, starting kindergarten; Ages 4-5).
VHS: S24987. $12.95.

Song of Sacajawea, The (Rabbit Ears)

Based on the true story of the seventeen year-old Native American woman who used her courage and backwoods know-how to guide the Lewis and Clark expedition over the Rocky Mountains to the Pacific Ocean. This is a film to watch *with* children, who are often confused about "the founding of the Americas." 25 minutes. Age Recommendation: P (Primary grades, grades 1-3; Ages 6-9); I (Intermediate grades, grades 4-6; Ages 10-12).
VHS: S24043. $9.98.

Sounds Around

One of the award-winning Bo Peep Productions, this video explores the various sounds made by toys, household appliances, animals and the sounds people make, including musical sounds. A wide variety of children are shown involved with and creating these sounds. The multicultural cast includes a child with Downs Syndrome. Live-action. 28 minutes. Age Recommendation: T (Toddler; Ages Birth-3 years); S (Starting school, starting to read, starting pre-school, starting kindergarten; Ages 4-5).
VHS: S22382. $19.95.

Space Cadets/Professor Iris

Professor Iris turns his classroom into a rocket ship as he helps young kids understand science. This video is part of the *Ready, Set, Learn* series which first aired on The Learning Channel, and which has been recommended by the National Educational Association and the PTA. Also see listings for *Birthday! Party/Professor Iris, Creepy Critters/Professor Iris, Lets Do It!/Professor Iris* and for *Music Mania/Professor Iris*. 40 minutes.

Age Recommendation: T (Toddler; Ages Birth-3 years); S (Starting school, starting to read, starting pre-school, starting kindergarten; Ages 4-5). VHS: S24650. $12.95.

Spanish Club: Fiesta!

A live-action video featuring Señora Reyes and her Spanish language club as they explore the meaning of fiesta. The program uses traditional songs and stories to teach culture as well as language. 30 minutes. Age Recommendation: T (Toddler; Ages Birth-3 years); S (Starting school, starting to read, starting pre-school, starting kindergarten; Ages 4-5); P (Primary grades, grades 1-3; Ages 6-9).
VHS: S21923. $19.95.

Spanish Club: Los Animales!

Señora Reyes and the Spanish Club Kids explore the world of animals in the second installment of this series, which uses traditional songs and stories to teach culture and language. 40 minutes. Age Recommendation: T (Toddler; Ages Birth-3 years); S (Starting school, starting to read, starting pre-school, starting kindergarten; Ages 4-5); P (Primary grades, grades 1-3; Ages 6-9).
VHS: S21924. $19.95.

Sparky's Magic Piano

When a magic piano grants a little boy the ability to play like a master, the boy learns a lesson in modesty. With voices by William Schallert, Mel Blanc and Vincent Price. 1988. 51 minutes. Age Recommendation: S (Starting school, starting to read, starting pre-school, starting kindergarten; Ages 4-5); P (Primary grades, grades 1-3; Ages 6-9).
VHS: S24651. $9.95.

Speeches of Martin Luther King, Jr., The

A collection of six actual speeches by the revered leader of the Civil Rights Movement. This video includes statements concerning non-violence and the famed "I Have a Dream" speech. See it *with* kids to help them understand the historical conflict which was the backdrop for Dr. King's speeches. 60 minutes. Age Recommendation: P (Primary grades, grades 1-3; Ages 6-9); I (Intermediate grades, grades 4-6; Ages 10-12).
VHS: S07027. $19.95.

Spirits of the Rainforest

Children boat down an actual river, sharing myths, magic and legends of the Michiguenga Indians, who still live in the rainforest. 90 minutes. Age Recommendation: P (Primary grades, grades 1-3; Ages 6-9); I (Intermediate grades, grades 4-6; Ages 10-12).

VHS: S24767. $19.95.

Spoonbill Swamp

Based on the book by Brenda Z. Guiberson. Kids will find out about two fascinating swamp creatures, an alligator and a spoonbill bird, in this story of two mothers teaching their young how to survive. 10 minutes. Age Recommendation: S (Starting school, starting to read, starting pre-school, starting kindergarten; Ages 4-5); P (Primary grades, grades 1-3; Ages 6-9).

VHS: S22354. $39.95.

The Song of Sacajawea
(Illustrated by Jack Molloy/Rabbit Ears Productions)

Spot

These animated tales are valuable educational tools. Spot relates the familiar objects and activities he views, mirroring the experience of his young viewers. "Students relate to Spot and his adventures because his experiences are very similar to those of the audience," (*Media and Methods*). 30 minutes each video. Age Recommendation: S (Starting school, starting to read, starting pre-school, starting kindergarten; Ages 4-5); P (Primary grades, grades 1-3; Ages 6-9).

Spot's Adventure - French

VHS: S19795. Currently out of print. May be available for rental in some video stores.

Spot's Adventure - German
VHS: S19854. $29.95.

Spot's Adventure - Spanish
VHS: S19825. $29.95.

Spot's First Video - French
VHS: S19794. $29.95.

Spot's First Video - German
VHS: S19853. $29.95.

Spot's First Video - Spanish
VHS: S19824. $29.95.

Spot Goes to School

Based on the ever-popular books by Eric Hill, featuring every toddler's favorite puppy. Five animated stories follow Spot on gentle adventures at school, on the playground and at home. 30 minutes. Age Recommendation: T (Toddler; Ages Birth-3 years); S (Starting school, starting to read, starting pre-school, starting kindergarten; Ages 4-5).
VHS: S22974. $14.99.

Squiggles, Dots and Lines

Ed Emberly presents his drawing alphabet, a tool for kids to unlock their creativity. Fourteen kids share in the fun, telling stories and creating a giant mural. Winner of the Parents' Choice Award, and a *TV Guide* Top Ten Pick. 30 minutes. Age Recommendation: P (Primary grades, grades 1-3; Ages 6-9); I (Intermediate grades, grades 4-6; Ages 10-12).
VHS: S10147. $14.95.
Public Performance Rights. VHS: S17153. $34.90.

Story of the Dancing Frog

Aunt Gertrude's life is amazing! Animator Michael Sporn directed this charming story about George, who is no ordinary frog. He is a multi-talented entertainer whose leaps and bounds bring him to fame and fortune. George and his devoted friend Gertrude set out to dance their way around the world in this adventure based on the story by Quentin Blake, narrated by Amanda Plummer. Michael Sporn, USA, 1986. 30 minutes. Age Recommendation: S

(Starting school, starting to read, starting pre-school, starting kindergarten; Ages 4-5); P (Primary grades, grades 1-3; Ages 6-9); I (Intermediate grades, grades 4-6; Ages 10-12).

VHS: S12003. $14.95.

Strega Nonna and Other Stories

Based on the book by Tomie De Paola. Big Anthony finds himself ankle-deep in trouble (and pasta) when he tries to use Strega Nonna's magic pasta pot without her permission. A Blue Ribbon winner at the American Film Festival. The video also includes Arlene Mosel's *Tikki Tikki Tembo* (an effort to explain why Chinese children have short names), the award-winning *Foolish Frog* (written by Pete & Charles Seeger) sung by Pete Seeger, and Gail Haley's African folktale *A Story—A Story*, set to African music, featuring the spider man, who is rewarded by the African gods with stories for the world. 35 minutes. Age Recommendation: S (Starting school, starting to read, starting pre-school, starting kindergarten; Ages 4-5); P (Primary grades, grades 1-3; Ages 6-9).

VHS: S14491. $14.95.

Sun, the Wind and the Rain, The

This is the story of two mountains. One created by the Earth and the other made by Elizabeth while wearing her yellow sun hat. Lisa Westberg Peters describes the creation and evolution of mountains by comparing the centuries-long geological process to Elizabeth's sand sculptures. Ted Rand's spectacular paintings illuminate the basic concepts of the story. The result is an unusually evocative first lesson in geology. 7 minutes. Age Recommendation: P (Primary grades, grades 1-3; Ages 6-9).

VHS: S16355. $44.95.

Sweet 15

This film gets special mention as a rare, realistic look at Latino culture. The story concerns a Mexican American girl preparing for her traditional quinceanera party celebrating her 15th birthday, when she discovers that her father is not a legal resident. Our Mexican reviewers (ages 4-adult) all loved it! This is a good film to watch *with* children, to help them understand the issues involved. From the acclaimed WonderWorks Series. 108 minutes. Age Recommendation: I (Intermediate grades, grades 4-6; Ages 10-12).

VHS: S12400. $29.95.

T Tadpole and the Whale

An extraordinary live-action story about a 12 year-old girl and her relationship with some of the world's most spectacular undersea creatures, including Elvar the dolphin, her best friend in the world. Winner of the Academy of Canadian Television and Cinema Award, the London Film Festival Award, and the International Ecological Film Festival Award. 90 minutes. Age Recommendation: P (Primary grades, grades 1-3; Ages 6-9); I (Intermediate grades, grades 4-6; Ages 10-12).
VHS: S17134. $29.95.

Talking Eggs, The

Written by Robert San Souci and illustrated by Jerry Pinkney, this video presentation of the 1990 Caldecott Honor book tells the magical folktale of sweet Blanche, her spoiled sister and her greedy mother. Blanche's kindness is rewarded by an old witch who transports her to a miraculous world where talking eggs dramatize that the plainest of objects may conceal wondrous treasures. 1990. 21 minutes. Public Performance Rights included. Age Recommendation: P (Primary grades, grades 1-3; Ages 6-9); I (Intermediate grades, grades 4-6; Ages 10-12).
VHS: S13894. $65.00.

Tall Tales: Darlin' Clementine

Shelley Duvall stars as a lone female in the camps of the Gold Rush days in this lively version of the story behind a legendary American folk song. With Edward Asner, David Dukes, John Matuszak and Gordon Jump, narrated (and title song performed by) Randy Newman, this whimsically clever tale makes the West come alive with a positive message. 49 minutes. Age Recommendation: P (Primary grades, grades 1-3; Ages 6-9); I (Intermediate grades, grades 4-6; Ages 10-12).
VHS: S10749. $9.98.

Tawny Scrawny Lion's Jungle Tales

These Golden Book favorites are back, now on video. This tape includes the classics *The Saggy Baggy Elephant* (written by Sergey Prokofiev), *The Tawny Scrawny Lion*, and *Rupert the Rhinoceros*. 30 minutes. Age Recommendation: T (Toddler; Ages Birth-3 years); S (Starting school, starting to read, starting pre-school, starting kindergarten; Ages 4-5).
VHS: S25002. $5.95.

Teddy Bear's Picnic, The

The teddy bears come alive at a party in the forest for one day each year. This time, a real girl, Amanda, gets to attend. 30 minutes. Age Recommendation: S (Starting school, starting to read, starting pre-school, starting kindergarten; Ages 4-5); P (Primary grades, grades 1-3; Ages 6-9). VHS: S24652. $9.95.

Teddy Bears' Jamboree

Gary Rosen and Bill Shontz present 15 of their greatest hits live in concert. Great humor and smart songs entertain the live concert audience of kids, parents and bears. 60 minutes. Age Recommendation: T (Toddler; Ages Birth-3 years); S (Starting school, starting to read, starting pre-school, starting kindergarten; Ages 4-5); P (Primary Grades, Grades 1- 3; Ages 6-9). VHS: S24653. $12.98.

There Goes a Bulldozer

A children's video which features a live-action introduction to heavy construction. Foreman Dave guides youngsters around the heavy machinery that shapes our environment. 30 minutes. Age Recommendation: S (Starting school, starting to read, starting pre-school, starting kindergarten; Ages 4-5); P (Primary grades, grades 1-3; Ages 6-9). VHS: S20605. $10.95.

There Goes a Fire Truck

Fireman Dave indulges children's fascination with all the trappings of fire fighting, including fire department trucks, boats, and even helicopters. Yes, a female firefighter does make an appearance. 30 minutes. Age Recommendation: S (Starting school, starting to read, starting pre-school, starting kindergarten; Ages 4-5); P (Primary grades, grades 1-3; Ages 6-9). VHS: S20606. $10.95.

There Goes a Police Car

Officers Becky and Dave lead children through the paces that these hard-working cars endure everyday. Kids will be thrilled to see the inside of these vehicles that serve the nation's lawmakers as they do their duty. 35 minutes. Age Recommendation: S (Starting school, starting to read, starting pre-school, starting kindergarten; Ages 4-5); P (Primary grades, grades 1-3; Ages 6-9). VHS: S21253. $10.95.

There Goes a Train

Engineer Dave stars in this videotape aimed at children. Kids will learn about the ways trains work, how they travel and how they are powered, as well as about the job a train engineer does. 35 minutes. Age Recommendation: S (Starting school, starting to read, starting pre-school, starting kindergarten; Ages 4-5); P (Primary grades, grades 1-3; Ages 6-9).

VHS: S21251. $10.95.

There Goes a Truck

Dave is joined by Becky in this jaunt aboard a large truck capable of travel-ing many miles with a heavy load. These machines carry nearly everything we use. Kids will be fascinated by their power and the ingenuity of their design. 35 minutes. Age Recommendation: S (Starting school, starting to read, starting pre-school, starting kindergarten; Ages 4-5); P (Primary grades, grades 1-3; Ages 6-9).

VHS: S21254. $10.95.

There's a Cricket in the Library

Written by fifth-grade students of McKee School in Oakdale, Pennsylvania, this charming tale follows the rude adventures of a cricket caught in the library, who displays no manners or good library behavior and has to be reminded by the children about the need to obey rules. Illustrated by Morgan Windsheimer. 4 minutes. Age Recommendation: P (Primary grades, grades 1-3; Ages 6-9); I (Intermediate grades, grades 4-6; Ages 10-12).

VHS: S19601. $39.00.

Thirteen Moons on Turtle's Back

Subtitled *A Native American Year of Moons*, Abenaki Indian Joseph Bruchac and poet Jonathan London discuss the history of Native American legend and mythology, focused on the belief of the thirteen moons of the year. The writers contrast legends within different Native American tribes to show how the cultures identified the cycles of the moon with the seasons. 17 minutes. Age Recommendation: S (Starting school, starting to read, starting pre-school, starting kindergarten; Ages 4-5); P (Primary grades, grades 1-3; Ages 6-9); I (Intermediate grades, grades 4-6; Ages 10-12).

VHS: S20002. $44.95.

This Pretty Planet

Tom Chapin's award-winning live performance of 13 songs combined with nature shots. "These songs are wittier and catchier than most in kid-dom, and Chapin may be the most charming performer on earth," (*Forbes Newspapers*). 50 minutes. Age Recommendation: S (Starting school, starting to read, starting pre-school, starting kindergarten; Ages 4-5); P (Primary grades, grades 1-3; Ages 6-9); I (Intermediate grades, grades 4-6; Ages 10-12).
VHS: S20299. $14.98.

Thomas the Tank Engine & Friends

From *Shining Time Station*, the award-winning PBS children's show that is heralded for presenting a fascinating learning environment, filled with positive values. Very young kids everywhere have fallen in love with Thomas the Tank Engine, whose character was popularized in *The Railway Series*, written by Reverend W. Awdry. 40 minutes each tape. Age Recommendation: T (Toddler; Ages Birth-3 years); S (Starting school, starting to read, starting pre-school, starting kindergarten; Ages 4-5).

Better Late Than Never and Other Stories
Stories include fun little lessons on pride, bad manners, and jumping to conclusions.
VHS: S16490. $12.98.

Christmas Party
VHS: S21987. $12.98.

James Learns a Lesson & Other Stories
James switches from hauling freight to hauling coaches. The tape also includes *Thomas Goes Fishing*.
VHS: S16487. $12.98.

Percy's Ghostly & Other Stories
VHS: S21986. $12.98.

Tenders & Turntables & Other Stories
The engines go on strike! The tape also includes *Thomas Comes to Breakfast* and *The Flying Kipper*, which features Henry.
VHS: S16488. $12.98.

Thomas Breaks the Rules & Other Stories
Thomas gets a ticket! Other stories show how everyone has good and bad points.
VHS: S16489. Currently out of print. May be available for rental in some video stores.

Thomas Gets Bumped

This tape focuses on stories of rivalry and friendship.

VHS: S24654. Currently out of print. May be available for rental in some video stores.

Thomas Gets Tricked & Other Stories

This tape focuses on appreciating others, cooperation and patience.

VHS: S16486. $12.98.

Trust Thomas & Other Stories

These stories center on forgiveness, keeping promises, cooperation and trust.

VHS: S16485. $12.98.

Three Sesame Street Stories

Included in this collection are three tales starring Big Bird, Oscar the Grouch and the Cookie Monster. 30 minutes. Age Recommendation: T (Toddler; Ages Birth-3 years); S (Starting school, starting to read, starting pre-school, starting kindergarten; Ages 4-5).

VHS: S24991. $5.95.

Thunder Cake

A loud clap of thunder booms and rattles the windows of Grandma's old farmhouse. "This is Thunder Cake baking weather," calls Grandma, as she and her granddaughter scurry around the farm gathering the necessary ingredients. A real Thunder Cake must reach the oven before the storm arrives — but the list of ingredients is long, not easy to follow and the storm is coming closer every minute. From the award-winning story by Patricia Polacco. 14 minutes. Age Recommendation: S (Starting school, starting to read, starting pre-school, starting kindergarten; Ages 4-5); P (Primary grades, grades 1-3; Ages 6-9); I (Intermediate grades, grades 4-6; Ages 10-12).

VHS: S16358. $44.95.

Tickle Tune Typhoon: Let's Be Friends

This live concert by the Tickle Tune Typhoon entourage features a "typhoon" of award-winning songs with messages ranging from racial tolerance to an understanding of differently-abled persons. The song "Skin" reveals a harmony in our multiracial society, "Everyone Is Differently Abled" focuses on what people can do, not what they can't, and "Pearly White Waltz" stresses the importance of brushing one's teeth. 60 minutes. Age Recommendation: S (Starting school, starting to read, starting pre-school, starting kindergarten; Ages 4-5); P (Primary grades, grades 1-3; Ages 6-9).

VHS: S16758. $14.98.

Timmy's Special Delivery

Timmy the Angel is touched when a brother and sister make their Christmas wishes and each wishes that the other will receive a gift. 30 minutes. Age Recommendation: T (Toddler; Ages Birth-3 years); S (Starting school, starting to read, starting pre-school, starting kindergarten; Ages 4-5).
VHS: S25003. $12.95.

Tinka's Planet

This film is an entertaining introduction for elementary school children to the need for recycling. When Tinka discovers that not all trash needs to be thrown away, she begins to collect her family's cans, bottles and newspapers. On her first visit to the local recycling center, she learns how recycling can help preserve the environment. Inspired to do something more for the environment, she convinces other kids in the neighborhood to join her in a recycling campaign. Ben Swets/Donna Worden, USA, 1990. 12 minutes. Age Recommendation: P (Primary grades, grades 1-3; Ages 6-9); I (Intermediate grades, grades 4-6; Ages 10-12).
VHS: S12321. $24.95.

Today Was a Terrible Day
(Live Oak Media)

To Bathe a Boa

Based on the book by C. Imbior Kudrna. Kids build vocabulary in this read-along video, while following the story of a reluctant boa who wants to avoid a bath. 8 minutes. Age Recommendation: S (Starting school, starting to read, starting pre-school, starting kindergarten; Ages 4-5); P (Primary grades, grades 1-3; Ages 6-9).

VHS: S22355. $39.95.

Today Was a Terrible Day

Based on the book by Patricia Reilly Giff. On a day with one mishap after another, young Ronald finally finds a reason to smile when he discovers he can read by himself. 8 minutes. Age Recommendation: S (Starting school, starting to read, starting pre-school, starting kindergarten; Ages 4-5); P (Primary grades, grades 1-3; Ages 6-9).

VHS: S24655. $37.95.

Tommy Tricker and the Stamp Traveller

From the producer of *Bach and Broccoli* and *The Dog Who Stopped the War*, a fast-paced family delight in which stamp collecting becomes anything but a passive hobby for the smooth-talking Tommy Tricker when he snatches a valuable stamp. The theft unveils the secret of travelling on the head of a postage stamp and sends Tommy and his pal on a whirlwind adventure around the globe. Michael Rubbo, Canada, 1987. 101 minutes. Age Recommendation: P (Primary grades, grades 1-3; Ages 6-9); I (Intermediate grades, grades 4-6; Ages 10-12).

VHS: S07816. $14.95.

Treasury of Children's Stories: Stories to Help Us Grow

Beginning with an alligator who learns not to be scared of the dark, this collection of three delightfully illustrated stories shows how other friendly animals deal with common problems of insecurity. 25 minutes. Age Recommendation: S (Starting school, starting to read, starting pre-school, starting kindergarten; Ages 4-5); P (Primary grades, grades 1-3; Ages 6-9).

VHS: S10315. $29.95.

'Twas the Night Before Christmas

It's that favorite Christmas poem in a wonderful presentation. 27 minutes. Age Recommendation: T (Toddler; Ages Birth-3 years); S (Starting school, starting to read, starting pre-school, starting kindergarten; Ages 4-5); P (Primary grades, grades 1-3; Ages 6-9); I (Intermediate grades, grades 4-6; Ages 10-12).

VHS: S24944. $14.98.

Velveteen Rabbit, The (Christopher Plummer)

Christopher Plummer narrates this charming, animated adaptation of Margery Williams' timeless story. 25 minutes. Age Recommendation: T (Toddler; Ages Birth-3 years); S (Starting school, starting to read, starting pre-school, starting kindergarten; Ages 4-5); P (Primary grades, grades 1-3; Ages 6-9).

VHS: S09891. $14.95.

Velveteen Rabbit, The (Rabbit Ears)

Meryl Streep narrates this Margery Williams children's classic, first published in 1922, about the rabbit who becomes real when loved by a child for a long time. George Winston provides the music, David Jorgensen the illustrations. Mark Sottnick, USA, 1985. 30 minutes. Age Recommendation: T (Toddler; Ages Birth-3 years); S (Starting school, starting to read, starting pre-school, starting kindergarten; Ages 4-5); P (Primary grades, grades 1-3; Ages 6-9).

VHS: S05108. $14.95.

Vincent and Me

A live-action mystery ensues when a girl's paintings are good enough to pass for those of the acclaimed 19th century painter, Vincent Van Gogh. This Emmy Award-winning film is highly imaginative, colorful and comical. 100 minutes. Age Recommendation: P (Primary grades, grades 1-3; Ages 6-9); I (Intermediate grades, grades 4-6; Ages 10-12).

VHS: S25851. $19.95.

Vincent and Me
(Hemdale Home Video)

W A Walk in the Wild

Based on the book by Lorraine Ward, this video is based on an actual visit by third graders to a national wildlife refuge. Kids join in the exploration of the natural wonders, finding out about ecology and the environment. 10 minutes. Age Recommendation: S (Starting school, starting to read, starting pre-school, starting kindergarten; Ages 4-5); P (Primary grades, grades 1-3; Ages 6-9); I (Intermediate grades, grades 4-6; Ages 10-12).
VHS: S22357. $39.95.

Walking on Air

A brilliant film starring kids with disabilities. Confined to a wheelchair, young Danny's greatest dream is to be able to fly. During a swimming class he discovers the wonderful feeling of weightlessness that swimming can bring. Taking his dream one more step, Danny fights friends, family and NASA so that he and his disabled friends can become part of the space program. Starring Lynn Redgrave as a fascinating science teacher, this realistic drama is based on a story idea by Ray Bradbury and won the Red Ribbon at the American Film Festival. 60 minutes. Age Recommendation: P (Primary grades, grades 1-3; Ages 6-9); I (Intermediate grades, grades 4-6; Ages 10-12).
VHS: S12397. $14.95.

Water Is Wet

This very special children's film was made to engage the imagination and learning spirit of the youngest children. Produced by the Erikson Institute for Early Childhood Education, the video is a visual and auditory exploration of simple elements, always striving to engage the child's imagination and sense of discovery about learning. The film's unique accomplishment is showing a multicultural world, populated by real people, not actors. See mothers and their kids having fun together. Watch real kids engaged in creative movement, drama and song activities. Gordon Weisenborn, USA, 1968. 65 minutes. Age Recommendation: T (Toddler; Ages Birth-3 years); S (Starting school, starting to read, starting pre-school, starting kindergarten; Ages 4-5).
VHS: S03490. $39.95.

Way to Start a Day, The

From *Will Rogers Jr. Presents: Stories of American Indian Culture*. Based on the book by Byrd Baylor, this animated children's video looks at how people in various countries all over the world get up in the morning. It is the dawn of a new day! Winner of the CINE 1989 Golden Eagle Award. USA, 1990. 12 minutes. Age Recommendation: S (Starting school, starting to read, starting pre-school, starting kindergarten; Ages 4-5); P (Primary grades, grades 1-3; Ages 6-9); I (Intermediate grades, grades 4-6; Ages 10-12).

VHS: S13293. $14.99.

We Learn About the World

Available in both an English and a Spanish version, this tape introduces young viewers into the world of shapes, colors, feelings, and concepts of big and little numbers. 26 minutes. Age Recommendation: S (Starting school, starting to read, starting pre-school, starting kindergarten; Ages 4-5); P (Primary grades, grades 1-3; Ages 6-9).

English Version. VHS: S06727. $29.95.

Spanish Version. VHS: S06728. $29.95.

Wee Sing Series

Written and created by Pamela Conn Beall and Susan Hagen Nipp. This series of videos continues the positive tradition of the popular book and audiocassette series which has brought music to so many. Each tape is 60 minutes. Age Recommendation: T (Toddler; Ages Birth-3 years); S (Starting school, starting to read, starting pre-school, starting kindergarten; Ages 4-5).

Wee Sing in Sillyville
This video features a girl and a boy who bring harmony to the land of Yellow Spurtlegurgles and Green Jingleheimers. Twenty nonsense songs (Adults will remember some of these classic songs).

VHS: S24842. $12.95.

Wee Sing Together
Sally's stuffed toys surprise her by coming to life and throwing a birthday party for her. The tape encourages kids to sing along with this mixture of live-action and special effects.

VHS: S24841. $12.95.

Wee Sing Train
Kids ride along, singing, dancing, learning, and making exciting stops along the way.

VHS: S24844. $12.95.

Wee Sing: Grandpa's Magical Toys
Grandpa leads diverse children into a special live-action world where toys come alive and songs are fun to sing.

VHS: S24843. $12.95.

Where in The World/Kids Explore

With a pen pal and a secret clubhouse, viewers join the live-action journey to some interesting spots around the world. Using a combination of colorful graphics, animation and dance, we see real kids finding out about the culture, geography, geology, ecology and history of each destination. Each video is 30 minutes. Age Recommendation: S (Starting school, starting to read, starting pre-school, starting kindergarten; Ages 4-5); P (Primary grades, grades 1-3; Ages 6-9); I (Intermediate grades, grades 4-6; Ages 10-12).

Volume 1. Kids Explore Mexico
Investigate the mysteries of the Aztec and Mayan ruins, have dinner with a fun-loving Mexican family, join guitar players and flamenco dancers, see festivals, visit Mexico City, and have fun!
VHS: S24945. $9.95.

Volume 2. Kids Explore Alaska
Pan for gold, join "Gold Rush Days," race with a dog sled team, share a little Eskimo life, meet the Coastal Indians and visit a wilderness bush family.
VHS: S24946. $9.95.

Volume 3. Kids Explore Kenya
Meet nomadic herders, unearth ancient skulls in the Great Rift Valley, find out about tribal family life, enjoy music, dance, and visit the city of Nairobi.
VHS: S24947. $9.95.

Volume 4. Kids Explore America's National Parks
Explore the rain forests and seashore of Olympic, see the granite walls and giant Sequoia trees of Yosemite and look at pioneer life at Fort Vancouver. Visit Yellowstone, the Grand Canyon, the Everglades and more — experience walks, wildlife, waterfalls...whew!
VHS: S24948. $9.95.

Where's Spot

This is a well-regarded set of stories featuring a puppy who has entertaining adventures. Based on the books by Eric Hill, the six stories on this tape include *Spot Goes Splash*, *Spot Finds a Key*, and more. 30 minutes. Age Recommendation: T (Toddler; Ages Birth-3 years); S (Starting school, starting to read, starting pre-school, starting kindergarten; Ages 4-5).
VHS: S24657. $14.99.

Which Way, Weather?

One of the award-winning Bo Peep Productions. This video is made with the developmental needs of the youngest viewers in mind. The tape features several types of weather, and demonstrates ways for young children to enjoy weather conditions. See multicultural children swimming, sailing, flying kites, ice skating, sledding, pumpkin picking, puddle stomping and more. 30 minutes. Age Recommendation: T (Toddler; Ages Birth-3 years); S (Starting school, starting to read, starting pre-school, starting kindergarten; Ages 4-5). VHS: S24658. $19.95.

Where in the World: Kids Explore Mexico
(IVN Communications, Inc.)

White Cat, The (Rabbit Ears)

Famed British actress Emma Thompson tells the tale of a charming creature. Music by Joe Jackson. 26 minutes. Age Recommendation: S (Starting school, starting to read, starting pre-school, starting kindergarten; Ages 4-5); P (Primary grades, grades 1-3; Ages 6-9); I (Intermediate grades, grades 4-6; Ages 10-12).
VHS: S24050. $9.98.

Who Will Be My Friend?

From the *Learn About Living* series, designed to help children sort out the challenges of growing up, this film helps kids deal with starting school. Molly brings her toy dinosaur to school, and discovers new friends. This tape is full of songs, live-action and animation. Other titles in the series include *How Come?*, *Mine and Yours* and *Never Talk to Strangers*. 25 minutes. Age Recommendation: S (Starting school, starting to read, starting pre-school, starting kindergarten; Ages 4-5).
VHS: S24659. $9.95.

Why the Sun and the Moon Live in the Sky

Adapted from the book by Elphinstone Dayrell, this video tells the Nigerian legend of the time when the Sun and Moon existed on land. When Water emerges, accompanied by people and animals, the Sun and Moon seek refuge in the sky. 11 minutes. Age Recommendation: P (Primary grades, grades 1-3; Ages 6-9); I (Intermediate grades, grades 4-6; Ages 10-12). VHS: S20003. $49.95.

Wild Christmas Reindeer, The

Based on the story by Jan Brett. A very interesting, unique Christmas story, giving a look at tundra life. Santa asks young Teeka to get his reindeer ready to fly on Christmas Eve. Teeka is excited and worried because she has never worked with the reindeer before and they've been running wild and free on the tundra. She has to catch, groom and train them. 10 minutes. Age Recommendation: S (Starting school, starting to read, starting pre-school, starting kindergarten; Ages 4-5); P (Primary grades, grades 1-3; Ages 6-9). VHS: S16359. $44.95.

Wildlife Symphony

This tape combines symphony music with animals at play in their natural habitats. 60 minutes. Age Recommendation: T (Toddler; Ages Birth-3 years); S (Starting school, starting to read, starting pre-school, starting kindergarten; Ages 4-5); P (Primary grades, grades 1-3; Ages 6-9); I (Intermediate grades, grades 4-6; Ages 10-12). VHS: S24814. $29.95.

Winnie the Pooh

This is the story of young Christopher Robin and his adventures with his wonderful toy animals: the bear, the donkey, the pig, the tiger. Using the original illustrations of E.H. Shepard, this video includes four stories from the classic A.A. Milne books: *Kanga and Roo Come to the Forest, Pooh Invents a New Game, Rabbit Has a Busy Day* and *An Enchanted Place*. USA. 60 minutes. Age Recommendation: S (Starting school, starting to read, starting pre-school, starting kindergarten; Ages 4-5); P (Primary grades, grades 1-3; Ages 6-9). VHS: S13206. $14.98.

Winnie the Pooh and a Day for Eeyore

This video adapts the Winnie the Pooh chapter "In Which Eeyore Has a Birthday and Gets Two Presents." Animated, Disney, USA. 25 minutes. Age Recommendation: S (Starting school, starting to read, starting pre-school, starting kindergarten; Ages 4-5); P (Primary grades, grades 1-3; Ages 6-9). VHS: S03039. $14.95.

Winnie the Pooh and the Blustery Day

This story of heroism in the face of a horrible flood is based on the chapter "In Which Tigger Comes to the Forest and Has Breakfast" from *The House at Pooh Corner*. Academy Award-winner. Animated, Disney, USA. 24 minutes. Age Recommendation: S (Starting school, starting to read, starting pre-school, starting kindergarten; Ages 4-5); P (Primary grades, grades 1-3; Ages 6-9). VHS: S03042. $14.95.

Winnie the Pooh and the Honey Tree

This video adapts the chapter "In Which We are Introduced to Winnie-the-Pooh" from *The House At Pooh Corner*. The story concerns the dilemmas of a boy, the charming Pooh bear, and other animals. Animated. Disney, USA. 24 minutes. Age Recommendation: S (Starting school, starting to read, starting pre-school, starting kindergarten; Ages 4-5); P (Primary grades, grades 1-3; Ages 6-9). VHS: S03041. $14.95.

Winnie the Pooh and Tigger Too

This story about self-acceptance and about the value of uniqueness is based on the chapter "In Which Tigger is Unbounced" from *The House at Pooh Corner*. Animated, Disney, USA. 25 minutes. Age Recommendation: S (Starting school, starting to read, starting pre-school, starting kindergarten; Ages 4-5); P (Primary grades, grades 1-3; Ages 6-9). VHS: S03043. $14.95.

Winnie the Pooh: Making Friends, Learning

Featuring Pooh, Piglet and Tigger, these three stories explore "sharing, caring and growing up." Animated, Disney. USA. 27 minutes. Age Recommendation: T (Toddler; Ages Birth-3 years); S (Starting school, starting to read, starting pre-school, starting kindergarten; Ages 4-5). VHS: S24660. $12.99.

Winnie the Pooh/The New Adventures (Series/Walt Disney)

Disney created new animated stories based on the old friends. Animated, Disney, USA. 44 minutes each video. Age Recommendation: S (Starting school, starting to read, starting pre-school, starting kindergarten; Ages 4-5); P (Primary grades, grades 1-3; Ages 6-9).

Volume 1. The Great Honey Pot Robbery
VHS: S24661. $12.99.

Volume 2. The Wishing Bear
VHS: S24662. $12.99.

Volume 3. Newfound Friends
VHS: S24937. $12.95.

Wish That Changed Christmas, The

An enchanting animated adaptation of Rumer Godden's *The Story of Holly and Ivy*. Ivy, a disillusioned orphan, boards a train on Christmas Eve and entertains no thoughts of happiness until she receives a mysterious message that catapults her on a magical odyssey to find the grandmother she's always longed for. With the voices of Paul Winfield and Jonathan Winters. 23 minutes. Age Recommendation: P (Primary grades, grades 1-3; Ages 6-9).
VHS: S19178. $12.98.

Woman's Place, A

This documentary features biographies of many great women, with a special focus on "firsts" in arts, science, business and athletics. Featuring women such as Helen Keller, Barbara Jordan, Susan B. Anthony, Margaret Mead, Joan Ganz Cooney and Harriet Tubman. Narrated by Julie Harris, the video includes rare historical footage and photographs to highlight this uplifting celebration of women who dared to be the best. 1989. 25 minutes. Age Recommendation: I (Intermediate grades, grades 4-6; Ages 10-12).
VHS: S05745. $39.95.

Workout with Daddy & Me

This workout video combines physical activities with games and songs to enhance learning, coordination and socialization. *Workout with Daddy and Me* provides a fun and easy way to exercise with your child. The video comes with an activity book. 30 minutes. Age Recommendation: T (Toddler; Ages Birth-3 years); S (Starting school, starting to read, starting pre-school, starting kindergarten; Ages 4-5).
VHS: S16483. $12.98.

Workout with Mommy & Me

Millions of parents have attended *Mommy and Me* classes for more than 15 years. Now you and your child can take the class at home. Complete with an activity book, this fun-filled exercise program is led by award-winning gymnastics and dance instructor Barbara Peterson Davis. 30 minutes. Age Recommendation: T (Toddler; Ages Birth-3 years); S (Starting school, starting to read, starting pre-school, starting kindergarten; Ages 4-5).

VHS: S16482. $12.98.

World Alive, A

Spectacular wildlife footage encourages children to appreciate the diverse lives and beauties of this planet's creatures. Narrated by James Earl Jones, this video received the National Educational Film Festival Award and includes a dramatic musical score by Kit Walker. 25 minutes. Age Recommendation: S (Starting school, starting to read, starting pre-school, starting kindergarten; Ages 4-5); P (Primary grades, grades 1-3; Ages 6-9); I (Intermediate grades, grades 4-6; Ages 10-12).

VHS: S13839. $14.95.

Public Performance Rights. VHS: S17146. $34.95.

Worlds Below, The

Sweeping sea lions, snowstorms of plankton, starfish in motion and forests as majestic as any on land. Swim with a newborn seal and slide into a wondrous journey of wave-swept rocks, vast submerged plains, and the mysterious depths of the ocean. Recommended by *The Video Rating Guide*. 50 minutes. Age Recommendation: P (Primary grades, grades 1-3; Ages 6-9); I (Intermediate grades, grades 4-6; Ages 10-12).

VHS: S17135. $19.95.

Public Performance Rights. VHS: S17147. $34.95.

You Can Choose! Series

This series reminds us that positive social values can be imparted through media. This is all done in a fun, engaging, and dramatic manner. This series combines comedy, drama, music, peer-education and a diverse group of child role models. One of the animated characters faces a dilemma and must make a tough choice. A group of real elementary school children meet in an unrehearsed problem-solving session to figure out what the character should do, facilitated by comedian and youth counselor Michael Pritchard. We then return to the animated story, in which the character follows the kids' advice. Each video is 30 minutes. Age Recommendation: P (Primary grades, grades 1-3; Ages 6-9); I (Intermediate grades, grades 4-6; Ages 10-12).

Volume 1. Cooperation

Moose learns how to cooperate so he can keep his singing quartet going. Age Recommendation: P (Primary grades, grades 1-3; Ages 6-9); I (Intermediate grades, grades 4-6; Ages 10-12).
VHS: S24701. $59.95.

Volume 2. Being Responsible

Rhonda Bird must choose between having a good time and being responsible to her friends. Age Recommendation: S (Starting school, starting to read, starting pre-school, starting kindergarten; Ages 4-5); P (Primary grades, grades 1-3; Ages 6-9).
VHS: S24702. $59.95.

Volume 3. Dealing with Feelings

When Tuggy Turtle tries to hide his fears about going on a weekend camp-out, his friendship with Moose is almost ruined. Together, they discover the importance of accepting feelings and expressing them honestly and positively. Age Recommendation: P (Primary grades, grades 1-3; Ages 6-9); I (Intermediate grades, grades 4-6; Ages 10-12).
VHS: S24703. $59.95.

Volume 4. Saying No

Missie Mouse has to choose whether to say "no" to a friend or do something she knows is wrong. When Missie's best friend Rhonda tries to pressure her into smoking cigarettes, Missie agonizes over her options before discovering that there are many ways to say no. Age Recommendation: P (Primary grades, grades 1-3; Ages 6-9); I (Intermediate grades, grades 4-6; Ages 10-12).
VHS: S24704. $59.95.

Volume 5. Doing the Right Thing

Two girls struggle over a money-filled wallet, which they found on the playground. Age Recommendation: P (Primary grades, grades 1-3; Ages 6-9); I (Intermediate grades, grades 4-6; Ages 10-12).
VHS: S24705. $59.95.

Volume 6. Dealing with Disappointment

When her baseball team falls into last place, Missie Mouse must learn to handle disappointments in a positive way. Age Recommendation: P (Primary grades, grades 1-3; Ages 6-9); I (Intermediate grades, grades 4-6; Ages 10-12).
VHS: S24706. $59.95.

Volume 7. Appreciating Yourself

Tuggy learns that being himself is better than pretending to be something he's not. When Tuggy becomes troubled by feelings of inadequacy, his friends help him to recognize and appreciate his positive inner qualities. Age Recommendation: P (Primary grades, grades 1-3; Ages 6-9); I (Intermediate grades, grades 4-6; Ages 10-12).

VHS: S24707. $59.95.

Volume 8. Asking for Help

Moose learns not to let pride or embarassment get in the way of asking for help. After ruining a group science project, Moose finds that the only good way to cope with his secret reading problem is to get the help he needs to overcome it. Age Recommendation: P (Primary grades, grades 1-3; Ages 6-9); I (Intermediate grades, grades 4-6; Ages 10-12).

VHS: S24708. $59.95.

Volume 9. Being Friends

Rhonda, Missie and Fiona learn about the complex nature of friendship. When Missie is not invited to the "in" party, the three girls are forced to deal with differences in their relationships with each other. Age Recommendation: P (Primary grades, grades 1-3; Ages 6-9); I (Intermediate grades, grades 4-6; Ages 10-12).

VHS: S24709. $59.95.

Volume 10. Resolving Conflicts

Tuggy and Rhonda learn that there are ways to resolve disagreements without fighting. When a dispute between them puts their class art project in jeopardy, Tuggy and Rhonda learn to work out interpersonal conflicts in a peaceful and positive way. Age Recommendation: P (Primary grades, grades 1-3; Ages 6-9); I (Intermediate grades, grades 4-6; Ages 10-12).

VHS: S24710. $59.95.

"You Can" Video Series

This series of unique, reality-based family and educational programs aim at empowerment through positive, nurturing messages. They are expressedly non-violent, and make an effort to show girls and boys equally. Each video is 30 minutes. Age Recommendation: S (Starting school, starting to read, starting pre-school, starting kindergarten; Ages 4-5); P (Primary grades, grades 1-3; Ages 6-9).

You Can Fly a Kite

Join the You Can kids as they introduce children to the magical world of kites. Through teamwork and friendship, children learn about kites — their history, building kites, acrobatic kite flying, safety tips and more.

VHS: S24939. $12.95.

Zeezel the Zowie Zoon in the Color Chase
(©Zeezel Pix)

You Can Ride a Horse
Come along with the You Can kids as they visit a stable, watch a blacksmith at work, learn about horseback riding and more. Full of fascinating facts about horses, with catchy sing-alongs and a nice musical backdrop.
VHS: S24770. $12.95.

You Must Remember This

Robert Guillaume is Uncle Buddy, a former independent filmmaker who doubts the worth of his past work. His niece refuses to let him forget his past so easily. She researches African American cinema and discovers that Uncle Buddy was a big part of history. Also starring Tim Reid (*WKRP in Cincinnati*), Vonetta McGee, Tyra Ferrell and Vonte Sweet. Deals with historical injustices in a very positive manner. From the WonderWorks series, originally aired on PBS. Helaine Head, USA, 1992. 110 minutes. Age Recommendation: I (Intermediate grades, grades 4-6; Ages 10-12).
VHS: S16011. $29.95.

You on Kazoo!

The video comes with a kazoo. Seven kids have a blast inviting the viewers to join the kazoo fun as they mimic animals and machines. 30 minutes. Age Recommendation: S (Starting school, starting to read, starting pre-school, starting kindergarten; Ages 4-5); P (Primary grades, grades 1-3; Ages 6-9).
VHS: S25037. $14.95.

Zeezel the Zowie Zoon in the Color Chase

Eartha the Colorfly magically changes everything to black and white. She takes Zeezel on a chase to find the missing colors. As Zeezel follows along, the 8 original songs and colorful sets help him (and the child watching) to learn the colors. 30 minutes. Age Recommendation: T (Toddler; Ages Birth-3 years).
VHS: S24859. $12.98.

Zillions TV: A Kid's Guide to Toys and Games

A bit of a media literacy guide of its own, *Zillions TV* aims to debunk the linkage of money and quality. This program teaches kids how to use science, math and problem-solving capabilities in order to assess the quality of video games, walkie-talkies, food, movie tickets, boom boxes and mountain bikes, among other products. The work features two songs: "Check It Out," a rap music video, and "Shop Around," a take-off of the classic song that promotes comparison shopping. 30 minutes. Age Recommendation: P (Primary grades, grades 1-3; Ages 6-9); I (Intermediate grades, grades 4-6; Ages 10-12).
VHS: S20024. $19.95.

Zoobilee Zoo Series

This Emmy Award-winning series hosted by Ben Vereen uses stories to encourage and educate children about their own self-worth. Endorsed by the American Federation of Teachers and recommended by the National Education Association. Each tape contains three full episodes and is 70 minutes long. Age Recommendation: S (Starting school, starting to read, starting pre-school, starting kindergarten; Ages 4-5); P (Primary grades, grades 1-3; Ages 6-9).

Blue Ribbon Zooble and Other Stories
Learning that honesty is its own reward or discovering that even when it's difficult, doing the right thing is worth the effort, are just some of the lessons brought up by the Blue Ribbon Zooble. Children will see that accepting friends means accepting their similarities and differences. 70 minutes.
VHS: S20676. $9.95.

Lady Whazzat and Other Stories
The Zooble family has a great time as they perform songs, dances and rhymes. Simultaneously they experience important lessons, such as learning that it's best to live up to your own possibilities, and that taking care of yourself is the best medicine.
VHS: S20679. $9.95.

Laughland and Other Stories
The entertaining Zoobles encourage children to sing along with titles which include "The Alphabet Song," "I'm a Little Teapot," and "Twinkle Twinkle Little Star." The songs also show kids that sometimes it is more fun to give than to receive and that it never pays to jump to conclusions. 70 minutes.
VHS: S20673. $9.95.

Zoobadoobas and Other Stories
Friendship is more valuable than fame, as the Zoobles find out. Working together and being creative are important abilities highlighted by this episode, while friendship emerges as the best gift of all.
VHS: S20678. $9.95.

Zooble Hop and Other Stories
Children will be keen to get up and dance the Zooble dance steps, but they will also understand that even those who can't dance should be treated nicely. Another lesson in this interactive tape concerns "doing something for yourself, compared with having someone do it for you."
VHS: S20674. $9.95.

Title Index

Abuela's Weave 1

Action Songs (Shari Lewis: Lamb Chop's Play-Along) 132, 133

Action Stories (Shari Lewis: Lamb Chop's Play-Along) 132, 133

Adventures (Magic of Discovery, The) 84

African Story Magic 1

Afro-Classic Folk Tales 2

Afro-Classic Folk Tales, Volume 1   2

Afro-Classic Folk Tales, Volume 2   2

Alejandro's Gift 2

Alexander and the Terrible, Horrible, No Good, Very Bad Day 2

Alice Walker (1944-Present) — Author 2, 3

All About ABC's 3

Alligators All Around (Maurice Sendak Library, The) 87

Alphabet (Sand Castle, The) 121

Alphabet Library 3

Alphabet Library: Alphabet City 3

Alphabet Library: Alphabet House 3

Alphabet Library: Alphabet Zoo 3

Amazing Bone and Other Stories, The 3

Amazing Things 4

Amazing Things, Volume 1   4

Amazing Things, Volume 2   4

American Women of Achievement Video Collection 4

American Women of Achievement Video Collection: Abigail Adams (1744 - 1818) — Women's Rights Advocate 4

American Women of Achievement Video Collection: Jane Addams (1860 - 1935) — Social Worker 4

American Women of Achievement Video Collection: Marian Anderson (1902 - 1993) — Singer 4, 5

American Women of Achievement Video Collection: Susan B. Anthony (1820 - 1906) — Woman Suffragist 5

American Women of Achievement Video Collection: Clara Barton (1821 - 1912) — Founder, American Red Cross 5

American Women of Achievement Video Collection: Emily Dickinson (1830 - 1890) — Poet 5

American Women of Achievement Video Collection: Amelia Earhart (1897 - Disappeared in 1937) — Aviator 5

American Women of Achievement Video Collection: Helen Keller (1880 - 1968) — Humanitarian 5

American Women of Achievement Video Collection: Sandra Day O'Connor (1930 - Present) — Supreme Court Justice 5

American Women of Achievement Video Collection: Wilma Rudolph (1940 - Present) — Champion Athlete 5, 6

American Women of Achievement 10 Volume Set   6

Amos, The Story of an Old Dog and His Couch (Shelley Duvall's Bedtime Stories: Moe the Dog in Tropical Paradise) 136

Anansi (Rabbit Ears) 6, 6

Anansi Goes Fishing 6

And the Children Shall Lead 7

Andy and the Lion (Animal Stories) 7

Angela's Airplane (plus The Fire Station) 7

Animal Alphabet 7

Animal Babies in the Wild 7

Animal Movie, The (Magic of Discovery, The) 84

Animal Stories 7

Animals Are Beautiful People 8

Animals Born Alive and Well (Ruth Heller's Nature Stories) 120, 121

Animating Harold (Harold and the Purple Crayon) 52

Anna Maria's Blanket 8

Anne of Green Gables 8

Annie Oakley (Rabbit Ears) 8, 9

Are You My Mother? 9

Are You My Mother?: English Version 9

Are You My Mother?: Spanish Version, Eres Tu Mi Mama? 9

Art Lessons for Children 9

Art Lessons for Children: Volume 1: Easy Watercolor Techniques 9

Art Lessons for Children: Volume 2: Easy Art Projects 9

Art Lessons for Children: Volume 3: More Fun with Watercolors 10

Art Lessons for Children: Volume 4: Felt Pen Fun 10

Art Lessons for Children: Volume 5: Animals of the Rain Forest 10

Art Lessons for Children: Volume 6: Plants of the Rain Forest 10

Astronomy 101: A Family Adventure 10

At Home in the Coral Reef 10

At Home in the Coral Reef: English Version 10

At Home in the Coral Reef: Spanish Version 10

At the Zoo 11

Attic-in-the-Blue 11

Aunt Ippy's Museum of Junk (Shelley Duvall's Bedtime Stories: Aunt Ippy's Museum of Junk) 135

Baby Animal Fun 11

Baby Animals Just Want to Have Fun 11

Baby Goes...Songs to Take Along 12

Baby Song Series 12

Baby Songs 1   12

Baby Songs 2: More Baby Songs 12

Baby Songs Christmas 12

Baby Songs Presents: Follow Along Songs with Hap Palmer 12

Baby Songs Presents: John Lithgow's Kid-Size Concert 13

Baby Songs: Even More Baby Songs 12

Baby Songs: Sing Together 13

Baby Songs: Super Baby Songs 13

Baby Vision 13

Baby Vision Volume 1 13

Baby Vision Volume 2 13

Baby's Bedtime 13

Baby's Lap Book, The (Baby's Nursery Rhymes) 14

Baby's Morningtime 14

Baby's Nursery Rhymes 14

Baby-Sitters Club Videos 14

Baby-Sitters Club, The: Christmas Special (1991) 14

Baby-Sitters Club, The: Claudia and the Missing Jewels 15

Baby-Sitters Club, The: Claudia and the Mystery of the Secret Passage 15

Baby-Sitters Club, The: Dawn and the Dream Boy 15

Baby-Sitters Club, The: Dawn and the Haunted House 15

Baby-Sitters Club, The: Dawn Saves the Trees 15

Baby-Sitters Club, The: Jessi and the Mystery of the Stolen Secrets 15

Baby-Sitters Club, The: Kristy and the Great Campaign 15

Baby-Sitters Club, The: Mary Ann and the Brunettes (1990) 15

Baby-Sitters Club, The: Stacey Takes a Stand 15

Baby-Sitters Club, The: Stacey's Big Break 16

Baby-Sitters Club, The: The Baby-Sitters and the Boy Sitters 14

Baby-Sitters Club, The: The Baby-Sitters Remember 14

Bach and Broccoli 16

Bad Day, A (Ramona: Perfect Day and Bad Day) 116

Ballet Shoes 16

Bank Street Read-Along Story Video Series (Dozen Dizzy Dogs, A) 36

Bank Street Read-Along Story Video Series ("Not Now!" Said the Cow) 106

Barney and the Backyard Gang 16

Barney and the Backyard Gang: Barney Goes to School 16

Barney and the Backyard Gang: Barney in Concert 17

Barney and the Backyard Gang: Barney's Best Manners 17

Barney and the Backyard Gang: Barney's Birthday 17

Barney and the Backyard Gang: Barney's Campfire Sing-Along 17

Barney and the Backyard Gang: Barney's Home Sweet Homes 17

Barney and the Backyard Gang: Barney's Imagination Island 17

Barney and the Backyard Gang: Barney's Magical Musical Adventure 17

Barney and the Backyard Gang: Barney's Safety Video 17

Barney and the Backyard Gang: Rock with Barney 17

Barney and the Backyard Gang: Waiting for Santa 18

Barry's Scrapbook: A Window into Art 18

Basil Hears a Noise 18

Beady Bear 18

Bear Who Slept Through Christmas, The 18

Bearly There At All (Land of Pleasant Dreams, The: Bearly There At All) 71

Beethoven Lives Upstairs 19

Beginner's Guide to The Night Sky, A (Astronomy 101: A Family Adventure) 10

Ben's Dream (Fun in a Box, Volume 1: Ben's Dream) 48

Berenstain Bears and the Missing Dinosaur Bone (Berenstain Bears: No Girls Allowed and the Missing Dinosaur Bone) 20

Berenstain Bears Videos 19

Berenstain Bears Videos: Berenstain Bears and the Messy Room 19

Berenstain Bears Videos: Berenstain Bears and the Trouble with Friends 19

Berenstain Bears Videos: Berenstain Bears and the Truth 19

Berenstain Bears Videos: Berenstain Bears and Too Much Birthday and To the Rescue 19

Berenstain Bears Videos: Berenstain Bears Christmas Tree 19

Berenstain Bears Videos: Berenstain Bears Easter Surprise 20

Berenstain Bears Videos: Berenstain Bears Get in a Fight 20

Berenstain Bears Videos: Berenstain Bears in the Dark 20

Berenstain Bears Videos: Berenstain Bears Learn About Strangers 20

Berenstain Bears Videos: Berenstain Bears: No Girls Allowed and the Missing Dinosaur Bone 20

Best Friends 20, *21*

Best Friends Part I 20

Best Friends Part II 21

Best Nest, The (Are You My Mother?) 9

Best of Beakman's World, The 21

Betchas, Trick and Silly Stunts (Shari Lewis: Lamb Chop's Play-Along) 132, 133

Bethie's Really Silly Clubhouse 21

Big Bird Brings Spring to Sesame Street (Five Sesame Street Stories) 45

Big Bird's Favorite Party Games 22

Biggest Bears!, The 22, *22*

Biggest Little Girl, The (Land of Pleasant Dreams, The: Is It Soup Yet?) 71

Bill and Pete (Shelley Duvall's Bedtime Stories: Elizabeth and Larry/Bill and Pete) 135

Bill Cosby's Picturepages 22

Bill Cosby's Picturepages: What Goes Where? 23

Bill Cosby's Picturepages: What's Different? 23

Bill Cosby's Picturepages: What's Missing? 23

Bill Cosby's Picturepages: What's That Shape? 23

Bill Cosby's Picturepages: Who's Counting? 23

Bill Nye the Science Guy 23

Bill Nye: Dinosaurs/Those Big Boneheads 23

Bill Nye: Outer Space/Way Out There 23

Bill Nye: The Human Body/The Inside Scoop 23

Birds of a Feather (I'm Not Oscar's Friend Anymore and Other Stories) 58

Birthday Dragon 23

Birthday! Party (Birthday! Party/Professor Iris) 23, 24

Birthday! Party/Professor Iris 23, 24

Black Americans of Achievement Series (Mary McLeod Bethune (1875 - 1955) — Educator 86

Black Americans of Achievement Series, Set II, The (Alice Walker (1944 - Present) — Author) 2, 3

Black Americans of Achievement Series, The (Harriet Tubman (1820 - 1913) — Anti-Slavery Activist) 52

Black Americans of Achievement Series, The (Madame C.J. Walker (1867 - 1919) — Entrepreneur) 81

Black Americans of Achievement Series, The (Sojourner Truth (1797 - 1883) — Abolitionist Leader) 138, 139

Blackberry Subway Jam (Moira's Birthday (plus Blackberry Subway Jam)) 89

Blueberries for Sal (Corduroy Bear) 31

Blueberries for Sal (Robert McCloskey Library) 119

Body Talk (Indoor Fun) 59, 60

Body Talking (Magic of Discovery, The) 84

Book About Adjectives, A (Language Stories: Many Luscious Lollipops) 73

Boy in The Drawer, The (Murmel, Murmel, Murmel (plus The Boy in the Drawer)) 96

Boy Who Loved Trolls, The 24

Brave Irene (Norman the Doorman and Other Stories) 106

Brave Little Toaster, The 24

Brer Rabbit and the Wonderful Tar Baby (Rabbit Ears) 24

Bubbe's Boarding House Series 25

Bubbe's Boarding House Series: Chanuka at Bubbe's 25

Bubbe's Boarding House Series: Passover at Bubbe's 25

Bugs Don't Bug Us 25

Bump — My First Video 25

Burt Dow: Deep Water Man (Mike Mulligan and His Steam Shovel) 88, 89

Burt Dow: Deep-Water Man (Robert McCloskey Library) 119

Camel Who Took a Walk (Danny and the Dinosaur and Other Stories) 33

Can I Be Good? 26

Candles, Snow and Mistletoe 26

Caps for Sale (Five Stories for the Very Young) 46, 46

Caribbean Kids 26

Caribbean Kids: English Version 26

Caribbean Kids: Spanish Version 26

Carlitos, Dani y Luis Alfredo 26

Casey's Revenge (Human Race Club: A Story About Fights between Brothers and Sisters) 57

Cat in the Hat Comes Back, The (Dr. Seuss Videos: Dr. Seuss: Cat in the Hat Comes Back, The) 37

Caterpillar and The Polliwog, The (Owl Moon and Other Stories) 108

Caterpillar's Wish, A 27

Changes (Five Stories for the Very Young) 46

Chanter Pour S'Amuser 27

Chanter Pour S'Amuser: Chanter Pour S'Amuser Set 27

Chanter Pour S'Amuser: L'Album de Marie-Soleil 27

Chanter Pour S'Amuser: Une Journée Avec Marie-Soleil 27

Charles the Clown 27

Cherries and Cherry Pits 28

Chicken Soup with Rice (Maurice Sendak Library, The) 87

Chicken Sunday 28

Chickens Aren't the Only Ones (Ruth Heller's Nature Stories) 120, 121

Child of Mine: The Lullaby Video 28

Child's Christmas in Wales, A 28

Christmas at Moose Factory (Native Indian Folklore) 103

Circus Baby, The (Max's Chocolate Chicken and Other Stories for Young Children) 88

Classroom Holidays 29

Classroom Holidays: Bee My Valentine: A Valentine's Day Story 29

Classroom Holidays: Classroom Holidays Set 29

Classroom Holidays: Don't Eat Too Much Turkey: A Thanksgiving Story 29

Classroom Holidays: Liar, Liar, Pants on Fire: A Christmas/Chanukah Story 29

Classroom Holidays: Starring First Grade: An Anytime Celebration 29

Clean Your Room, Harvey Moon! 29

Clifford's Fun With....Series 30

Clifford's Fun with Letters 30

Clifford's Fun with Numbers 30

Clifford's Fun with Opposites 30

Clifford's Fun with Rhymes 30

Clifford's Fun with Shapes and Colors 30

Clifford's Fun with Sounds 30

Clifford's Sing-a-Long Adventure 30

Close Look at Volcanoes, A (Indoor Fun) 59, 60

Cloudy with a Chance of Meatballs 30

Corduroy Bear 31, 32

Coughing Catfish, The (Berenstain Bears Videos: Berenstain Bears and the Trouble with Friends) 19

Creative Dance for Preschoolers 31

Creative Movement: A Step Towards Intelligence 31

Creepy Critters (Creepy Critters/Professor Iris) 31

Creepy Critters/Professor Iris 31

Creole (I'm Not Oscar's Friend Anymore and Other Stories) 58

Cri-Cri: El Grillito Cantor 32

Curious George Rides a Bike (Doctor De Soto and Other Stories) 34, 35

Curious George Videos 32

Curious George Videos: Curious George 32

Curious George Videos: Curious George Goes to Town 32

Curious George Videos: Curious George: Fun in the Sun 32

Daisy-Head Mayzie 33

Dan Crow's Oops! 33

Dancing with the Indians 33, 34

Danny and the Dinosaur and Other Stories 33

David's Father (Pigs (plus David's Father)) 111

Desert Scene (Art Lessons for Children: Volume 1: Easy Watercolor Techniques) 9

Dimensions (Magic of Discovery, The) 84

Discovery Stories 34

Divorce Can Happen to the Nicest People 34

Doctor De Soto (Doctor De Soto and Other Stories) 34, 35

Doctor De Soto and Other Stories 34, 35

Dog Who Had Kittens, The 35

Dog Who Stopped the War, The 35

Doing Things: Eating, Washing, in Motion 35

Don Cooper: Mother Nature's Songs 36

Dozen Dizzy Dogs, A 36

Dr. Seuss Videos 36

Dr. Seuss Videos: Dr. Seuss Video Festival 36

Dr. Seuss Videos: Dr. Seuss: Butter Battle Book, The 36

Dr. Seuss Videos: Dr. Seuss: Cat in the Hat Comes Back, The 37

Dr. Seuss Videos: Dr. Seuss: Green Eggs and Ham 37

Dr. Seuss Videos: Dr. Seuss: Hoober-Bloob Highway 37

Dr. Seuss Videos: Dr. Seuss: Hop on Pop 37

Dr. Seuss Videos: Dr. Seuss: Horton Hatches the Egg 37, 38

Dr. Seuss Videos: Dr. Seuss: Horton Hears a Who 37, 38

Dr. Seuss Videos: Dr. Seuss: How the Grinch Stole Christmas 38, 38

Dr. Seuss Videos: Dr. Seuss: I am NOT Going to Get Up Today! 38

Dr. Seuss Videos: Dr. Seuss: Lorax, The 39

Dr. Seuss Videos: Dr. Seuss: One Fish Two Fish Red Fish Blue Fish: English Version 39

Dr. Seuss Videos: Dr. Seuss: One Fish Two Fish Red Fish Blue Fish: Spanish Version: Un Pez Dos Peces Pez Rojo Pez Azul 39

Dr. Seuss Videos: Dr. Seuss: Pontoffel Pock 39

Dr. Seuss Videos: Dr. Seuss' ABC 39

Dr. Seuss Videos: Dr. Seuss' Cat in the Hat 39

Dr. Seuss Videos: Dr. Seuss' Sleep Book 40

Dragons and Giants (Frog and Toad Together) 48

Dreadlocks and the Three Bears 40

Drug Free Kids 40

Drummer Hoff (Five Stories for the Very Young) 46

Each Peach Plum (Max's Chocolate Chicken and Other Stories for Young Children) 88

Eco, You, and Simon, Too! 40

Eight Super Stories from Sesame Street 41

Elizabeth and Larry (Shelley Duvall's Bedtime Stories: Elizabeth and Larry/Bill and Pete) 135

Ella Jenkins Live! At the Smithsonian 41

Ella Jenkins: For the Family 41

Emperor and Nightingale (Rabbit Ears) 41, 42

Emperor's New Clothes (Rabbit Ears) 42

Empty Pot, The 42

Enchanted Place, An (Winnie the Pooh) 156

Ezra Jack Keats Library 42

Fair Weather Friend, The (Human Race Club: A Story About Making Friends, A Story About Prejudice and Discrimination) 57

Family Farm 43

Farmer's Huge Carrot, The 43

Fence Too High, A (Land of Pleasant Dreams, The: Fence Too High, A) 71

50 Below Zero (plus Thomas' Snowsuit) 43

Fingermouse, Yoffy and Friends 43

Finn McCoul (Rabbit Ears) 44

Fire and Rescue 44

Fire Station, The (Angela's Airplane (plus The Fire Station)) 7

Fireman Sam: The Hero Next Door 44

First and Second Grade Feelings 44

First and Second Grade Feelings: Jim's Dog, Muffins 44

First and Second Grade Feelings: The Real-Skin Rubber Monster Mask 45

First and Second Grade Feelings: See You in Second Grade! 45

First and Second Grade Feelings: So What? 45

First and Second Grade Feelings Set 45

Fish (Fun in a Box, Volume 1: Ben's Dream) 48

Five Lionni Classics 45

Five Sesame Street Stories 45

Five Stories for the Very Young 46, 46

Flying Kipper, The (Thomas the Tank Engine & Friends: Tenders & Turntables & Other Stories) 147

Foil Art and Printmaking (Art Lessons for Children: Volume 2: Easy Art Projects 9

Folk Games 46

Follow That Bunny! 47

Follow the Drinking Gourd (Rabbit Ears) 47

Foolish Frog (Strega Nonna and Other Stories) 143

Foot Book, The (Dr. Seuss Videos: Dr. Seuss: One Fish Two Fish Red Fish Blue Fish) 39

Fox in Socks (Dr. Seuss Videos: Dr. Seuss: Cat in the Hat Comes Back, The) 37

Free to Be...You and Me 47

Frog and Toad Are Friends 47

Frog and Toad Together 48

Fun in a Box 48

Fun in a Box Volume 1: Ben's Dream 48

Fun in a Box Volume 2: New Friends and Other Stories 48

Fun in a Box Volume 3: Birthday Movie, The 48

Gateway to the Mind 49

Get Ready for School 49

Getting to Know Ezra Jack Keats (Ezra Jack Keats Library) 42

Getting to Know Maurice Sendak (Maurice Sendak Library, The) 87

Gift of Amazing Grace, The 49

Gift of the Whales 49

Gingerbread Christmas, A (Rabbit Ears) 49, 50

Gingham Dog and the Calico Cat, The (Rabbit Ears) 50

Girl With The Pop-Up Garden, A (Land of Pleasant Dreams, The: Bearly There At All) 71

Go, Dog, Go! (Are You My Mother?) 9

Good Morning Miss Toliver 50, 51

Good Morning Sunshine 51

Good Morning, Good Night: A Day on The Farm 50

Goodbye, Hello (Ramona: Squeakerfoot and Goodbye, Hello) 116, 117

Granddad for Daniel, A (Mr. Rogers: Musical Stories) 93

Granpa 51

Great Day for Up (Dr. Seuss Videos: Dr. Seuss: I am NOT Going to Get Up Today!) 38

Gryphon 51

Happy Birdy 52

Happy Lion (Danny and the Dinosaur and Other Stories) 33

Harold and The Purple Crayon 52

Harold's Fairy Tale (Five Stories for the Very Young) 46

Harold's Fairy Tale (Harold and the Purple Crayon) 52

Harriet Tubman (1820-1913) — Anti-Slavery Activist 52

Hat, The (Doctor De Soto and Other Stories) 34, 35

Hawk, I'm Your Brother 52, 53

Here We Go 53

Here We Go — Volume 1 53

Here We Go — Volume 2 53

Here We Go Again 53

Hey, What About Me? 53

Hideaways, The 54

High Price to Pay, A (Human Race Club: A Story About Self-Esteem) 57

Hip Hop Animal Rock Workout 54

Hispanics of Achievement Video Collection, The (Joan Baez (1941 - Present) — Mexican American Folksinger) 64

Hoboken Chicken Emergency 54

Holidays for Children Video Series 54, 55

Holidays for Children: Arbor Day 55

Holidays for Children: Chinese New Year 55

Holidays for Children: Christmas 55

Holidays for Children: Cinco De Mayo 55

Holidays for Children: Easter 55

Holidays for Children: Halloween 55

Holidays for Children: Hanukkah/Passover 55

Holidays for Children: Independence Day 55

Holidays for Children: Kwanzaa 55

Holidays for Children: Rosh Hashanah/Yom Kippur 55

Holidays for Children: Thanksgiving 55

Holidays for Children: Valentine's Day 55

Holidays for Children/Set of 12 Videos 55

Hop on Pop (Dr. Seuss Videos: Dr. Seuss: Hop on Pop) 37

Horton Hears a Who (Dr. Seuss Videos: Dr. Seuss Video Festival) 36

Horton Hears a Who (Dr. Seuss Videos: Dr. Seuss: Horton Hears a Who) 37, 38

Hot Hippo (Owl Moon and Other Stories) 108

House That Had Enough, The (Never Talk to Strangers) 103

How Come? 55, 56

How the Grinch Stole Christmas (Dr. Seuss Videos: Dr. Seuss Video Festival 36, 38

How the Leopard Got His Spots (Rabbit Ears) 56

How to Hide a Butterfly and Other Insects 56

How to Hide a Crocodile and Other Reptiles 56

How to Hide a Gray Treefrog and Other Amphibians 56

How to Hide a Polar Bear and Other Mammals 56

How to Hide a Whip-Poor-Will and Other Birds 56

How to Hide an Octopus and Other Sea Creatures 56

How to Hide Stories 56

How to Hide Stories Set 56

Howard (Fun in a Box Volume 2: New Friends and Other Stories) 48

Hug Me (I'm Not Oscar's Friend Anymore and Other Stories) 58

Human Race Club: A Story About Fights between Brothers and Sisters 57

Human Race Club: A Story About Making Friends, A Story About Prejudice and Discrimination 57

Human Race Club: A Story About Self-Esteem 57

Human Race Club Series 57

I Am NOT Going to Get Up Today! (Dr. Seuss Videos: Dr. Seuss: I Am NOT Going to Get Up Today!) 38

I Can Build 57

I Can Read With My Eyes Shut (Dr. Seuss Videos: Dr. Seuss' ABC) 39

I Dig Fossils 57, 58

I Had A Bad Dream (Never Talk to Strangers) 103

I Have a Friend 58

I Need a Hug! 58

I Want to Be an Artist When I Grow Up 58

I'm Not Oscar's Friend Anymore and Other Stories 58

Imaginaria: A Computer Animation Music Video for Children 59

Imagine That! 59

In a People House (Dr. Seuss Videos: Dr. Seuss: I am NOT Going to Get Up Today!) 38

In the Company of Whales 59

In the Night Kitchen (Maurice Sendak Library, The) 87

In the Tall, Tall Grass 59

Indoor Fun 59, 60

Introducing: the Flying Fruit Fly Circus 60

Ira Says Goodbye 60, 60

Ira Sleeps Over 60

Is It Soup Yet? (Land of Pleasant Dreams, The: Is It Soup Yet?) 71

Island of Skog, The (Danny and the Dinosaur and Other Stories) 33

It Zwibble: Earthday Birthday 61

It's Not Always Easy Being a Kid 61

It's Not Easy Being Green 61

It's the Muppets! Series 61

It's the Muppets!: Meet the Muppets! 61

It's the Muppets!: More Muppets! 61

Jack and The Beanstalk (Faerie Tale Theatre) 62

Jack and the Beanstalk (Rabbit Ears) 62

Jacob Have I Loved (Amanda Plummer) 62

Jacob Have I Loved (Bridget Fonda) 62

James Learns a Lesson (Thomas the Tank Engine & Friends: James Learns a Lesson & Other Stories) 147

Janey Junkfood's Fresh Adventure 62, 63

Jay Jay the Jet Plane and His Flying Friends Series 63

Jay Jay the Jet Plane and His Flying Friends: Volume 1. Jay Jay's First Flight and Three Other Stories 63

Jay Jay the Jet Plane and His Flying Friends: Volume 1. Tito Turbinitis Y Sus Amigos Voladores 63

Jay Jay the Jet Plane and His Flying Friends: Volume 2. Old Oscar Leads the Parade and Three Other Stories 63

Jay O'Callahan: Herman & Marguerite 63

Jay O'Callahan: Master Class in Storytelling, A 63

Jay O'Callahan: Six Stories About Little Heroes 64

Jazz Time Tale 64

Jessi Sings Songs from Around the World 64

Joan Baez (1941-Present) — Mexican American Folksinger 64

Joan Baez (1941-Present) — Mexican American Folksinger: English Version 64

Joan Baez (1941-Present) — Mexican American Folksinger: Spanish Version 64

Joe Scruggs First Video 65

Joe Scruggs in Concert 65

John Henry (Rabbit Ears) 65, 66

Johnny Appleseed (Rabbit Ears) 65

Jokes, Riddles, Knock-Knocks and Funny Poems (Shari Lewis: Lamb Chop's Play-Along) 132, 133

Josephine's Imagination 65, 66

Joshua's Masai Mask 66

Juggle Time 67

Jumanji 67

Junglies: First Day at School 67

Just Grandma and Me 67

Just Me and My Dad 67

Kanga and Roo Come to the Forest (Winnie the Pooh) 156

Katy No-Pocket (Shelley Duvall's Bedtime Stories: Little Rabbit Who Wanted Red Wings, The) 136

Kids Get Cooking: The Egg 68

Kids Kitchen: Making Good Eating Great Fun for Kids! 68

Kidsongs Music Video Stories 69

Kidsongs Music Video Stories: Boppin' with Biggles 69

Kidsongs Music Video Stories: Cars, Boats, Trains and Planes 69

Kidsongs Music Video Stories: Country Sing-Along 69

Kidsongs Music Video Stories: Day at Camp, A 69

Kidsongs Music Video Stories: Day at Old MacDonald's Farm, A 69

Kidsongs Music Video Stories: Day at the Circus, A 69

Kidsongs Music Video Stories: Day with the Animals, A 69

Kidsongs Music Video Stories: Good Night, Sleep Tight 69

Kidsongs Music Video Stories: I'd Like to Teach the World to Sing 69

Kidsongs Music Video Stories: If We Could Talk to the Animals 69

Kidsongs Music Video Stories: Let's Play Ball! 69

Kidsongs Music Video Stories: Ride the Roller Coaster 69

Kidsongs Music Video Stories: Sing Out, America! 70

Kidsongs Music Video Stories: Very Silly Songs 70

Kidsongs Music Video Stories: We Wish You a Merry Christmas 70

Kidsongs Music Video Stories: What I Want to Be! 70

Kidsongs Music Video Stories: Wonderful World of Sports, The 70

King Midas and the Golden Touch (Rabbit Ears) 70

Kite Flying (Rainy Day Games) 115

Kitten Companions 70

Knots on a Counting Rope 70

Koi and the Kola Nuts (Rabbit Ears) 68, 71

Land of Pleasant Dreams, The 71

Land of Pleasant Dreams, The: Bearly There At All 71

Land of Pleasant Dreams, The: Fence Too High, A 71

Land of Pleasant Dreams, The: Is It Soup Yet? 71

Land of Sweet Taps, The 71

Language Primer 72

Language Primer Set 72

Language Primer: Adventuresome Max: Discovering the World 72

Language Primer: Max in Motion: Developing Language Skills 72

Language Primer: Max's Library: Beginning to Write 72

Language Stories 72

Language Stories Set 73

Language Stories: Cache of Jewels and Other Collective Nouns, A 72

Language Stories: Kites Sail High 73

Language Stories: Many Luscious Lollipops 73

Language Stories: Merry-Go-Round 73

Lean Mean Machine, The (Human Race Club: A Story About Fights Between Brothers and Sisters) 57

Learn About Living Series (How Come?) 55, 56

Learn About Living Series (Mine and Yours) 89

Learn About Living Series (Never Talk to Strangers) 103

Learn About Living Series (Who Will Be My Friend?) 155, 156

Learning About Me 73

Learning About Me Set 74

Learning About Me: A Is for Autonomy 73

Learning About Me: B Is for Belonging 73

Learning About Me: Ipsilwhich Adventures 73

Lentil (Norman the Doorman and Other Stories) 106

Lentil (Robert McCloskey Library) 119

Let's Create Art Activities 74, 74

Let's Create for Pre-Schoolers 74

Let's Do It! (Let's Do It!/Professor Iris 74, 75

Let's Do It!/Professor Iris 74, 75

Let's Get a Move On! 75

Let's Sing Along 75

Letter on Light Blue Stationery, The (Human Race Club: A Story About Self-Esteem) 57

Letter to Amy, A (Ezra Jack Keats Library) 42

Letter, The (Frog and Toad Are Friends) 47

Lights: The Miracle of Chanukah 75

Linnea in Monet's Garden 75

Lion and the Lamb, The (Rabbit Ears) 76

Lion, the Witch, and the Wardrobe, The (Animated) 76

Lion, the Witch, and the Wardrobe, The (WonderWorks) 76

Little Crooked Christmas Tree, The 76, 77

Little Duck Tale, A 77

Little Engine That Could, The 77

Little Engine That Could, The: English Narration 77

Little Engine That Could, The: French Narration 77

Little Engine That Could, The: Spanish Narration 77

Little Lou and His Strange Little Zoo 77

Little People Videos 77, 78

Little People: Christmas Fun 78

Little People: Favorite Songs 78

Little People: Fun with Words 78

Little People: Three Favorite Stories 78

Little Rabbit Who Wanted Red Wings, The (Shelley Duvall's Bedtime Stories: The Little Rabbit Who Wanted Red Wings) 136

Little Sister Rabbit 78

Little Toad to the Rescue (Poky's Favorite Stories) 112

Living and Working in Space: The Countdown Has Begun 78, 79

Look Around Endangered Animals, A 79

Look What I Found 79

Look What I Grew 79

Look What I Made 79, 80

Lost Button, A (Frog and Toad Are Friends) 47

Lovely Butterfly — Pepar Nechmad 80

Lovely Butterfly — Pepar Nechmad: Chanukah 80

Lovely Butterfly — Pepar Nechmad: Flowers for the Independence 80

Lovely Butterfly — Pepar Nechmad: Passover 80

Lovely Butterfly — Pepar Nechmad: Purim 80

Lovely Butterfly — Pepar Nechmad: Tishrei Month Holidays (Rosh Hashana and Sukkot) 80

Lovely Butterfly — Pepar Nechmad: Tu B'Shvat 80

Lyle, Lyle Crocodile: The House on East 88th Street 80

Madame C.J. Walker (1867-1919) — Entrepreneur 81

Madeline 81

Madeline (Narrated by Christopher Plummer) 81

Madeline and the Bad Hat (Madeline's Rescue and Other Stories About Madeline) 83

Madeline and the Dog Show 81

Madeline and the Easter Bonnet 82, 83

Madeline and the Gypsies (Madeline's Rescue and Other Stories About Madeline) 83

Madeline and the Toy Factory 82

Madeline at Cooking School 82

Madeline in London 82

Madeline's Christmas 82, 83

Madeline's Rescue (Madeline's Rescue and Other Stories About Madeline) 83

Madeline's Rescue and Other Stories About Madeline 83

Madre Tierra 83

Magic of Discovery, The 84

Magic School Bus 84

Magic School Bus, The: For Lunch 84

Magic School Bus, The: Gets Eaten 84

Magic School Bus, The: Gets Lost in Space 84

Magic School Bus, The: Hops Home 84

Magic School Bus, The: Inside Ralphie 84

Magic Thinking Cap, The 85

Magical Coqui — Puerto Rico — Mi Tierra! 85

Make Way for Ducklings (Robert McCloskey Library) 119, 119

Make Way for Ducklings (Smile for Auntie and Other Stories) 119, 138

Making Faces (Indoor Fun) 59, 60

Making Music with Children 85

Making Music with Children: Program 1. Making Music with Children: Ages 3 - 7 85

Making Music with Children: Program 2. Making Music with Children: Ages 7 - 11 85

Facets Non-Violent, Non-Sexist Children's Video Guide

Making Music with Children: Program 3. Making Music in the Classroom: Ages 3 - 7 85

Making Music with Children: Program 4. Making Music in the Classroom: Ages 7 - 11 86

Making of Daisy-Head Mayzie, The (Daisy-Head Mayzie) 33

Man, The Snake and The Fox, The (Native Indian Folklore) 103

Many Luscious Lollipops (Language Stories: Many Luscious Lollipops) 73

Maricela 86

Marvin K. Mooney, Will You Please Go Now! (Dr. Seuss Videos: Dr. Seuss: Hop on Pop) 37

Mary McLeod Bethune (1875-1955) — Educator 86

Mary Poppins 86

Math...Who Needs It? 86, 87

Mathnet: The Case of The Unnatural 87

Matrioska (Magic of Discovery, The) 84

Maurice Sendak Library, The 87, 87, 88

Max's Chocolate Chicken (Max's Chocolate Chicken and Other Stories for Young Children) 88

Max's Chocolate Chicken and Other Stories for Young Children 88

Medoonak The Stormmaker (Native Indian Folklore) 103

Meet Your Animal Friends 88

Metal Dogs of India (Fun in a Box Volume 2: New Friends and Other Stories) 48

Mighty Pawns, The 88

Mike Mulligan and His Steam Shovel 88, 89

Mine and Yours 89

Moe the Dog in Tropical Paradise (Shelley Duvall's Bedtime Stories: Moe the Dog in Tropical Paradise) 136

Moira's Birthday (Moira's Birthday (plus Blackberry Subway Jam)) 89

Moira's Birthday (plus Blackberry Subway Jam) 89

Mole and The Car, The (Mole and The Green Star, The) 89

Mole and the Chewing Gum, The (Mole and The Green Star, The) 89

Mole and The Green Star, The 89

Mole in Town, The 90

Mole Series, The 89

Mommy's Office 90

Monkey Moves 90

Monkey People, The (Rabbit Ears) 91

Moon Man (Mike Mulligan and His Steam Shovel) 89

Mop Top 90, 91

More Pre-School Power 91

Morris the Moose: Goes to School/Gets a Cold 91

Mortimer (Something Good (plus Mortimer)) 139

Mose The Fireman (Rabbit Ears) 91, 92

Mouse and the Motorcycle, The 92

Move Like the Animals 92

Moving Machines 92

Mr. Brown Can Moo — Can You? (Dr. Seuss Videos: Dr. Seuss' ABC) 39

Mr. Rogers Videos 92, 93, 94

Mr. Rogers: Dinosaurs & Monsters 93

Mr. Rogers: Music and Feelings 93

Mr. Rogers: Musical Stories 93

Mr. Rogers: What About Love 93

Mr. Rogers: When Parents Are Away 93

Mr. Rogers' Neighborhood: Circus Fun 94

Mr. Rogers' Neighborhood: Kindness 94

Mr. Rogers' Neighborhood: Love 94

Mr. Rogers' Neighborhood: Making Music 94

Multicultural Peoples of North America Video Series 94, 95

Multicultural Peoples of North America Video Series: 15 Volume Set 96

Multicultural Peoples of North America Video Series: African Americans 95

Multicultural Peoples of North America Video Series: Amish, The 95

Multicultural Peoples of North America Video Series: Arab Americans 95

Multicultural Peoples of North America Video Series: Central Americans 95

Multicultural Peoples of North America Video Series: Chinese Americans 95

Multicultural Peoples of North America Video Series: German Americans 95

Multicultural Peoples of North America Video Series: Greek Americans 95

Multicultural Peoples of North America Video Series: Irish Americans 95

Multicultural Peoples of North America Video Series: Italian Americans 95

Multicultural Peoples of North America Video Series: Japanese Americans 95

Multicultural Peoples of North America Video Series: Jewish Americans 96

Multicultural Peoples of North America Video Series: Korean Americans 96

Multicultural Peoples of North America Video Series: Mexican Americans 96

Multicultural Peoples of North America Video Series: Polish Americans 96

Multicultural Peoples of North America Video Series: Puerto Ricans 96

Murmel, Murmel, Murmel (Murmel, Murmel, Murmel (plus The Boy in the Drawer)) 96

Murmel, Murmel, Murmel (plus The Boy in the Drawer) 96

Music and Magic 96

Music Mania (Music Mania/Professor Iris) 97

Music Mania/Professor Iris 97

My First Activity Series 97

My First Activity Video 97

My First Cooking Video 97

My First Green Video 97

My First Music Video 97

My First Nature Video 97

My First Science Video 97

My Friend Walter 98

My Neighbor Totoro 98

My New York 98

My Principal Lives Next Door 98

My Sesame Street Home Videos 98, 99, 100, 101

My Sesame Street Home Videos: Alphabet Game, The 99

My Sesame Street Home Videos: Bedtime Stories & Songs 99

My Sesame Street Home Videos: Best of Elmo, The 99

My Sesame Street Home Videos: Best of Ernie and Bert, The 99

My Sesame Street Home Videos: Big Bird's Favorite Party Games 99

My Sesame Street Home Videos: Big Bird's Story Time 99

My Sesame Street Home Videos: Count It Higher: Great Music Videos from Sesame Street 99

My Sesame Street Home Videos: Getting Ready for School 100

My Sesame Street Home Videos: Getting Ready to Read 100

My Sesame Street Home Videos: I'm Glad I'm Me 100

My Sesame Street Home Videos: Learning About Letters 100

My Sesame Street Home Videos: Learning About Numbers 100

My Sesame Street Home Videos: Learning to Add and Subtract 100

My Sesame Street Home Videos: New Baby in My House, A 100, 101

My Sesame Street Home Videos: Play-Along Games & Songs 101

National Geographic Kids Videos 101, 102

National Geographic Kids Videos: Adventures in Asia 101

National Geographic Kids Videos: Amazing North America 101

National Geographic Kids Videos: Deep Sea Dive 101

National Geographic Kids Videos: GeoKids 102

National Geographic Kids Videos: GeoKids: Bear Cubs, Baby Ducks and Kooky Kookaburras 102

National Geographic Kids Videos: GeoKids: Cool Cats, Raindrops, and Things that Live in Holes 102

National Geographic Kids Videos: GeoKids: Flying, Trying and Honking Around 102

National Geographic Kids Videos: Swinging Safari 101

National Geographic Kids Videos: Totally Tropical Rainforest 102

National Geographic Kids Videos: Wonders Down Under 102

National Velvet 102, 103

Native American Year of Moons, A (Thirteen Moons on Turtle's Back) 146

Native Indian Folklore 103

Never Talk to Strangers 103

New Friends (Fun in a Box Volume 2: New Friends and Other Stories) 48

New Friends and Other Stories 104

Night Before Christmas, The (Rabbit Ears) 104

No Girls Allowed (Berenstain Bears Videos: Berenstain Bears: No Girls Allowed and The Missing Dinosaur Bone) 20

Noah and the Ark (Rabbit Ears) 104, *105*

Noah's Ark (James Earl Jones) 104

Noel 104, 105

Nonsense and Lullabyes: Nursery Rhymes 105

Nonsense and Lullabyes: Poems for Children 105

Norman the Doorman (Norman the Doorman and Other Stories) 106, *106*

Norman the Doorman and Other Stories 106, *106*

North Wind and the Sun, The (Sand Castle, The) 121

"Not Now!" Said the Cow 106

Now I Know My Aleph Bet 106, 107

Oh Say Can You Say? (Dr. Seuss Videos: Dr. Seuss: Hop on Pop) 37

Oh, The Thinks You Can Think (Dr. Seuss Videos: Dr. Seuss: One Fish Two Fish Red Fish Blue Fish) 39

On Our Way to School 107

One Fish Two Fish Red Fish Blue Fish (Dr. Seuss Videos: Dr. Seuss: One Fish Two Fish Red Fish Blue Fish) 39

One Was Johnny (Maurice Sendak Library, The) 87

Opaque Watercolors (Art Lessons for Children: Volume 1: Easy Watercolor Techniques) 9

Opus n' Bill: A Wish for Wings That Work 107, *108*

Orca Whales and Mermaid Tales 107

Original Tales and Tunes 107

Other Way to Listen, The 108

Owl and The Lemming, The (Sand Castle, The) 121

Owl Moon (Owl Moon and Other Stories) 108

Owl Moon and Other Stories 108

Panama (Corduroy Bear) 31

Pastel (Art Lessons for Children: Volume 2: Easy Art Projects) 9

Patrick (Doctor De Soto and Other Stories) 34, 35

Paul Bunyan (Rabbit Ears) 109

Paws, Claws, Feathers and Fins 109

Pecos Bill (Rabbit Ears) 109

Peep and the Big Wide World 109

Pegasus 110

Pepito's Dream 110

Perfect Day (Ramona: Perfect Day and Bad Day) 116

Pet Show! (Ezra Jack Keats Library) 42

Pete Seeger's Family Concert 110

Peter's Chair (Ezra Jack Keats Library) 42

Petunia, the Silly Goose (Animal Stories) 7

Picnic (Max's Chocolate Chicken and Other Stories for Young Children) 88

Picture Book of Martin Luther King, Jr., A *110*, 111

Picture for Harold's Room, A (Harold and the Purple Crayon) 52

Pierre (Maurice Sendak Library, The) 87

Piggy Banks to Money Markets 111

Pigs (Pigs (plus David's Father)) 111

Pigs (plus David's Father) 111

Pinocchio (Rabbit Ears) 111

P.J. Funnybunny 112

Plants That Never Ever Bloom (Ruth Heller's Nature Stories) 120, 121

Poky Little Puppy and The Patchwork Blanket, The (Poky's Favorite Stories) 112

Poky Little Puppy's First Christmas 112

Poky's Favorite Stories 112

Pollyanna (BBC) 112

Pooh Invents a New Game (Winnie the Pooh) 156

Postman Pat's 123 Story 112

Postman Pat's ABC Story 113

Potato and Cows (Mr. Rogers: Musical Stories) 93

Pre-School Power #3 113

Pre-School Power: Jacket Flips & Other Tips 113

Princess Scargo and the Birthday Pumpkin (Rabbit Ears) 113, *114*

Professor Iris (Birthday! Party/Professor Iris) 23, 24

Professor Iris (Creepy Critters/Professor Iris) 31

Professor Iris (Let's Do It!/Professor Iris) 74, 75

Professor Iris (Music Mania/Professor Iris) 97

Professor Iris (Space Cadets/Professor Iris) 139, 140

Puppy Pals 114

Puss in Boots (Rabbit Ears) 114

Rabbit Has a Busy Day (Winnie the Pooh) 156

Raffi in Concert with the Rise and Shine Band 114, 115

Raffi: Young People's Concert with Raffi 115

Rainbow of My Own, A 115

Rainy Day Games 115

Rainy Day Magic Show 115

Ramona 115, 116, 117

Ramona: Goodbye, Hello 116

Ramona: Great Hair Argument 116

Ramona: New Pajamas 116

Ramona: Patient, The 116

Ramona: Perfect Day and Bad Day 116

Ramona: Rainy Sunday 116

Ramona: Ramona's Bad Day 116

Ramona: Siblingitis 116

Ramona: Squeakerfoot and Goodbye, Hello 116, 117

Reach for the Sky 117

Ready, Set, Learn (Birthday! Party/Professor Iris) 23, 24

Ready, Set, Learn (Creepy Critters/Professor Iris) 31

Ready, Set, Learn (Let's Do It!/Professor Iris) 74, 75

Ready, Set, Learn (Music Mania/Professor Iris) 97

Ready, Set, Learn (Space Cadets/Professor Iris) 139, 140

Real Story of Baa Baa Black Sheep, The 117

Real Story of Happy Birthday to You, The 117

Real Story of I'm A Little Teapot, The 117

Real Story of Itsy Bitsy Spider, The 117

Real Story of Rain, Rain Go Away, The 117

Real Story of Three Little Kittens, The 117

Real Story of Twinkle Twinkle Little Star, The 117

Real Story Videos Series, The 117

Reason for a Flower, The (Ruth Heller's Nature Stories) 120, 121

Red Shoes, The (Animation) 118

Reluctant Dragon 118

Richard Scarry Series 118

Richard Scarry's Best Busy People Video 118

Richard Scarry's Best Counting Video 118

Richard Scarry's Best Ever ABC Video 118

Richard Scarry's Best Learning Songs Ever 118

Rights from the Heart/Droits au Coeur 119

Robert McCloskey Library 119, 119

Roxaboxen 119

Runaway Ralph 120

Rupert 120

Rupert and the Frog Song 120

Rupert and the Runaway Dragon 120

Rupert the Rhinoceros (Tawny Scrawny Lion's Jungle Tales) 144

Ruth Heller's Nature Stories 120, 121

Saggy Baggy Elephant, The (Tawny Scrawny Lion's Jungle Tales) 144

Sailor Dog, The (Poky's Favorite Stories) 112

Salmon People (Native Indian Folklore) 103

Sammy and Other Songs from Getting to Know Myself 121

Sand Castle, The 121

Savior Is Born, The (Rabbit Ears) 121

Say No to Drugs! 122

Science Primer 122

Science Primer Series 122

Science Primer: Earth, Air, Water, Fire 122

Science Primer: Five Senses, The 122

Science Primer: Habitats 122

Scuffy the Tugboat (Scuffy the Tugboat and Friends) 122, 123

Scuffy the Tugboat and Friends 122, 123

Seasons and Holidays Around the World 123

Seasons and Holidays Around the World: Chinese New Year 123

Seasons and Holidays Around the World: Christmas in Mexico 123

Seasons and Holidays Around the World: Christmas in Sweden 123

Seasons and Holidays Around the World: Halloween in Britain 123

Secret Garden, The (Agnieszka Holland) 123

Secret Garden, The (BBC) 124

Secret Garden, The (MGM) 124, 125

Secret Language, A (Rainy Day Games) 115

See How They Grow 124

See How They Grow: Farm Animals 124

See How They Grow: Insects and Spiders 124

See How They Grow: Pets 124

See How They Grow: Wild Animals 124

Sense of Touch, A (Magic of Discovery, The) 84

Sesame Songs Series 125, 126

Sesame Songs: Dance Along! 125

Sesame Songs: Elmo's Sing-Along Guessing Game 125

Sesame Songs: Monster Hits! 125

Sesame Songs: Rock & Roll! 125

Sesame Songs: Sing Yourself Silly! 126

Sesame Songs: Sing, Hoot and Howl 126

Sesame Songs: Sing-Along Earth Songs 126

Sesame Songs: We All Sing Together 126

Sesame Street Home Video Visits 126

Sesame Street Home Video Visits: The Firehouse 126

Sesame Street Home Video Visits: The Hospital 126

Sesame Street Specials 127, 128

Sesame Street Specials: Big Bird in China 127

Sesame Street Specials: Big Bird in Japan 127

Sesame Street Specials: Celebrates Around the World 127

Sesame Street Specials: Christmas Eve on Sesame Street 127

Sesame Street Specials: Don't Eat the Pictures Sesame Street 127, 128

Sesame Street Specials: Put Down the Duckie 128, 129

Sesame Street Specials: Sesame Street's 25th Birthday: A Musical Celebration 128

Sesame Street Start to Read Videos 128

Sesame Street Start to Read Videos: Don't Cry, Big Bird and Other Stories 128

Sesame Street Start to Read Videos: Ernie's Big Mess and Other Stories 128

Sesame Street Start to Read Videos: Ernie's Little Lie and Other Stories 128

Sesame Street Start to Read Videos: I Want to Go Home! and Other Stories 128

Sesame Street: Plaza Sesamo 128, 129

Sesame Street: Plaza Sesamo: De Compamento Con Montoya: Big Bird Goes Camping 129

Sesame Street: Plaza Sesamo: El Alfabeto De Montoya: Learn the Alphabet with Bert and Ernie 129

Sesame Street: Plaza Sesamo: Plaza Sesamo Canta: Favorite Songs from Past Shows 129

Sesame Street: Plaza Sesamo: Vamos a Imaginar: Learn About Sounds and Shapes 129

Sesame Street: Plaza Sesamo: Viaja Con Nosotros: Big Bird and Oscar Go to Venezuela and Mexico 129

Sesame Street: Plaza Sesamo: The Plaza Sesamo Complete Set 129

Shalom Sesame 129, 130, 131

Shalom Sesame: Aleph-Bet Telethon 130

Shalom Sesame: Chanukah 130

Shalom Sesame: Jerusalem 130

Shalom Sesame: Journey to Secret Places 130

Shalom Sesame: Kibbutz 130

Shalom Sesame: Kids Sing Israel 130

Shalom Sesame: Land of Israel 130

Shalom Sesame: Passover 131

Shalom Sesame: People of Israel 131

Shalom Sesame: Sing Around The Seasons 131

Shalom Sesame: Tel Aviv 131

Shamu & You Series 131

Shamu & You: Exploring the World of Birds 131

Shamu & You: Exploring the World of Fish 131

Shamu & You: Exploring the World of Mammals 131

Shamu & You: Exploring the World of Reptiles 131

Shape of Me and Other Stuff, The (Dr. Seuss Videos: Dr. Seuss: I Am NOT Going to Get Up Today!) 38

Shari Lewis: 101 Things for Kids to Do 132

Shari Lewis: Don't Wake Your Mom 132

Shari Lewis: Kooky Classics 132

Shari Lewis: Lamb Chop in the Land of No Manners 132

Shari Lewis: Lamb Chop's Play-Along 132, 133

Shari Lewis: You Can Do It! 133

Shari's Christmas Concert 133

Sharon, Lois & Bram's Elephant Show 133, 134

Sharon, Lois & Bram's Elephant Show: Back by Popular Demand 133

Sharon, Lois & Bram's Elephant Show: Live in Your Living Room 134

Sharon, Lois & Bram's Elephant Show: Pet Fair 134

Sharon, Lois & Bram's Elephant Show: Radio Show 134

Sharon, Lois & Bram's Elephant Show: Sleepover 134

Sharon, Lois & Bram's Elephant Show: Soap Box Derby 134

Sharon, Lois & Bram's Elephant Show: Treasure Island 134

Sharon, Lois & Bram's Elephant Show: Who Stole the Cookies 134

Shelley Duvall Presents Mrs. Piggle-Wiggle 134, 135

Shelley Duvall Presents Mrs. Piggle-Wiggle: The Answer Backer Cure and the Chores Cure 135

Shelley Duvall Presents Mrs. Piggle-Wiggle: The Not-Truthful Cure and the Radish Cure 135

Shelley Duvall Presents Mrs. Piggle-Wiggle: The Pet Forgetters Cure and The Never-Want-To-Go-To-Bedders Cure 135

Shelley Duvall's Bedtime Stories: Aunt Ippy's Museum of Junk 135

Shelley Duvall's Bedtime Stories: Elizabeth and Larry/Bill and Pete 135

Shelley Duvall's Bedtime Stories: The Little Rabbit Who Wanted Red Wings 136

Shelley Duvall's Bedtime Stories: Moe the Dog in Tropical Paradise 136

Short Journey Into Space, A (Indoor Fun) 59, 60

Sign Songs: Fun Songs to Sign and Sing 136

Sign-Me-a-Story 136

Silly Tales and Tunes 137

Simon the Lamb 137

Simply Magic: Episode 2 137

Simply Magic: The Rainy Day Adventure 137

Skating Safe for Kids 138

Sky is Blue, The (Magic of Discovery, The) 84

Smile for Auntie (Smile for Auntie and Other Stories) 137, 138

Smile for Auntie and Other Stories 137, 138

Snowman, The 138

Snowy Day (Ezra Jack Keats Library) 42

Snowy Day, The (Smile for Auntie and Other Stories) 138

Soap Bubble Magic (Rainy Day Games) 115

Sojourner Truth (1797-1883) — Abolitionist Leader 138, 139

Something Good (plus Mortimer) 139

Something Good (Something Good (plus Mortimer)) 139

Song of Sacajawea, The (Rabbit Ears) 139, 141

Sounds Around 139

Space Cadets (Space Cadets/Professor Iris) 139

Space Cadets/Professor Iris 139, 140

Spanish Club: Fiesta! 140

Spanish Club: Los Animales! 140

Sparky's Magic Piano 140

Speeches of Martin Luther King, Jr., The 140

Spirits of the Rainforest 141

Spoonbill Swamp 141

Spot 141, 142

Spot Finds a Key (Where's Spot) 154

Spot Goes Splash (Where's Spot) 154

Spot Goes to School 142

Spot's Adventure - French 141

Spot's Adventure - German 142

Spot's Adventure - Spanish 142

Spot's First Video - French 142

Spot's First Video - German 142

Spot's First Video - Spanish 142

Spring (Frog and Toad Are Friends) 47

Squeakerfoot (Ramona: Squeakerfoot and Goodbye, Hello) 116, 117

Squiggles, Dots and Lines 142

Story of the Dancing Frog 142, 143

Story of the Underground Railroad, A (Follow the Drinking Gourd) 47

Story, The (Frog and Toad Are Friends) 47

Story—A Story, A (Strega Nonna and Other Stories) 143

Strega Nonna (Strega Nonna and Other Stories) 143

Strega Nonna and Other Stories 143

String Figures (Rainy Day Games) 115

Summer Legend (Native Indian Folklore) 103

Sun, the Wind and the Rain, The 143

Super-Grover (Five Sesame Street Stories) 45

Sweet 15   143

Swim, A (Frog and Toad Are Friends) 47

Tadpole and the Whale 144

Tailor-Made Friendship, A (Land of Pleasant Dreams, The: Fence Too High, A) 71

Talking Eggs, The 144

Tall Tales: Darlin' Clementine 144

Tawny Scrawny Lion, The (Tawny Scrawny Lion's Jungle Tales) 144

Tawny Scrawny Lion's Jungle Tales 144

Teddy Bear's Picnic, The 145

Teddy Bears' Jamboree 145

Tenders & Turntables (Thomas the Tank Engine & Friends: Tenders & Turntables) 147

Theodore Mouse Goes to Sea (Scuffy the Tugboat and Friends) 122, 123

There Goes a Bulldozer 145

There Goes a Fire Truck 145

There Goes a Police Car 145

There Goes a Train 146

There Goes a Truck 146

There's a Cricket in the Library 146

There's A Wocket in My Pocket (Dr. Seuss Videos: Dr. Seuss: Cat in the Hat Comes Back, The) 37

Thidwick the Big-Hearted Moose (Dr. Seuss Videos: Dr. Seuss: Horton Hears a Who) 37, 38

Thirteen Moons on Turtle's Back 146

This Pretty Planet 147

Thomas Comes to Breakfast (Thomas the Tank Engine & Friends: Tenders & Turntables & Other Stories) 147

Thomas Goes Fishing (Thomas the Tank Engine & Friends: James Learns a Lesson & Other Stories) 147

Thomas the Tank Engine & Friends 147, 148

Thomas the Tank Engine & Friends: Better Late Than Never and Other Stories 147

Thomas the Tank Engine & Friends: Christmas Party 147

Thomas the Tank Engine & Friends: James Learns a Lesson & Other Stories 147

Thomas the Tank Engine & Friends: Percy's Ghostly & Other Stories 147

Thomas the Tank Engine & Friends: Tenders & Turntables & Other Stories 147

Thomas the Tank Engine & Friends: Thomas Breaks the Rules & Other Stories 147

Thomas the Tank Engine & Friends: Thomas Gets Bumped 148

Thomas the Tank Engine & Friends: Thomas Gets Tricked & Other Stories 148

Thomas the Tank Engine & Friends: Trust Thomas & Other Stories 148

Thomas' Snow Suit (50 Below Zero (plus Thomas' Snowsuit)) 43

Three Sesame Street Stories 148

Thunder Cake 148

Tickle Tune Typhoon: Let's Be Friends 148

Tikki Tikki Tembo (Strega Nonna and Other Stories) 143

Time of Wonder (Owl Moon and Other Stories) 108

Time of Wonder (Robert McCloskey Library) 119

Timmy's Special Delivery 149

Tinka's Planet 149

To Bathe a Boa 149, 150

To The Rescue (Berenstain Bears Videos: Berenstain Bears and Too Much Birthday and To the Rescue) 19

Today Was a Terrible Day 149, 150

Tommy Tricker and the Stamp Traveller 150

Too Much Birthday (Berenstain Bears Videos: Berenstain Bears and Too Much Birthday and To the Rescue) 19

Treasury of Children's Stories: Stories to Help Us Grow 150

Trip, The (Ezra Jack Keats Library) 42

Trouble With Friends, The (Berenstain Bears Videos: Berenstain Bear 19

'Twas the Night Before Christmas 150

Uncle Wizmo's New Car (Shelley Duvall's Bedtime Stories: Aunt Ippy's Museum of Junk) 135

Unforgettable Pen Pal (Human Race Club: A Story About Making Friends, A Story About Prejudice and Discrimination) 57

Velveteen Rabbit, The (Christopher Plummer) 151

Velveteen Rabbit, The (Rabbit Ears) 151

Vincent and Me 151, 151

Walk in the Wild, A 152

Walking on Air 152

Water Is Wet 152

Watercolor Discovery (Art Lessons for Children: Volume 1: Easy Watercolor Techniques) 9

Watercolor Flowers (Art Lessons for Children: Volume 1: Easy Watercolor Techniques) 9

Way to Start a Day, The 152, 153

We Learn About the World 153

We Learn About the World: English Version 153

We Learn About the World: Spanish Version 153

Wee Sing Series 153

Wee Sing Series: Wee Sing in Sillyville 153

Wee Sing Series: Wee Sing Together 153

Wee Sing Series: Wee Sing Train 153

Wee Sing Series: Wee Sing: Grandpa's Magical Toys 153

What Was That! (Scuffy the Tugboat and Friends) 122, 123

Where in The World/Kids Explore 154

Where in The World/Kids Explore: Volume 1. Kids Explore Mexico 154, 155

Where in The World/Kids Explore: Volume 2. Kids Explore Alaska 154

Where in The World/Kids Explore: Volume 3. Kids Explore Kenya 154

Where in The World/Kids Explore: Volume 4. Kids Explore America 154

Where the Wild Things Are (Maurice Sendak Library, The) 87, 87

Where's Spot 154

Which Way, Weather? 154, 155

Whistle for Willie (Ezra Jack Keats Library) 42

Whistle for Willie (Five Stories for the Very Young) 46

White Cat, The (Rabbit Ears) 155

Who Will Be My Friend? 155

Why Cats Eat First (Fun in a Box Volume 2: New Friends and Other Stories) 48

Why Mosquitoes Buzz in People's Ears (Animal Stories) 7

Why the Sun and the Moon Live in the Sky 155, 156

Wild Christmas Reindeer, The 156

Wildlife Symphony 156

Will Rogers Jr. Presents: Stories of American Indian Culture 52, 108, 152

Will Rogers Jr. Presents: Stories of American Indian Culture (Hawk, I'm Your Brother) 52

Will Rogers Jr. Presents: Stories of American Indian Culture (Other Way to Listen, The) 108

Will Rogers Jr. Presents: Stories of American Indian Culture (Way to Start the Day, The) 152, 153

Winnie the Pooh 156

Winnie the Pooh and a Day for Eeyore 156

Winnie the Pooh and the Blustery Day 157

Winnie the Pooh and the Honey Tree 157

Winnie the Pooh and Tigger Too 157

Winnie the Pooh: Making Friends, Learning 157

Winnie the Pooh/The New Adventures (Series/Walt Disney) 157, 158

Winnie the Pooh/The New Adventures (Series/Walt Disney): Volume 1. The Great Honey Pot Robbery 158

Winnie the Pooh/The New Adventures (Series/Walt Disney): Volume 2. The Wishing Bear 158

Winnie the Pooh/The New Adventures (Series/Walt Disney): Volume 3. Newfound Friends 158

Wish That Changed Christmas, The 158

Woman's Place, A 158

Working with Oil (Art Lessons for Children: Volume 2: Easy Art Projects) 9

Workout with Daddy & Me 158

Workout with Mommy & Me 158, 159

World Alive, A 159

Worlds Below, The 159

Wynken, Blynken and Nod (Smile for Auntie and Other Stories) 138

You Can Choose! Series 159, 160, 161

You Can Choose! Series: Volume 1. Cooperation 160

You Can Choose! Series: Volume 2. Being Responsible 160

You Can Choose! Series: Volume 3. Dealing with Feelings 160

You Can Choose! Series: Volume 4. Saying No 160

You Can Choose! Series: Volume 5. Doing the Right Thing 160

You Can Choose! Series: Volume 6. Dealing with Disappointment 160

You Can Choose! Series: Volume 7. Appreciating Yourself 161

You Can Choose! Series: Volume 8. Asking for Help 161

You Can Choose! Series: Volume 9. Being Friends 161

You Can Choose! Series: Volume 10. Resolving Conflicts 161

"You Can" Video Series 161, 162

"You Can" Video Series: You Can Fly a Kite 161

"You Can" Video Series: You Can Ride a Horse 162

You Must Remember This 162

You on Kazoo! 163

Young People's Concert with Raffi (Raffi: Young People's Concert with Raffi) 115

Your Feets Too Big (Fun in a Box, Volume 1: Ben's Dream) 48

Zeezel the Zowie Zoon in the Color Chase 162, 163

Zillions TV: A Kid's Guide to Toys and Games 163

Zoobilee Zoo Series 163, 164

Zoobilee Zoo Series: Blue Ribbon Zooble and Other Stories 164

Zoobilee Zoo Series: Lady Whazzat and Other Stories 164

Zoobilee Zoo Series: Laughland and Other Stories 164

Zoobilee Zoo Series: Zoobadoobas and Other Stories 164

Zoobilee Zoo Series: Zooble Hop and Other Stories 164

Age Index

Toddlers: Ages birth - 3

AfroClassic Folk Tales, Volume 1

AfroClassic Folk Tales, Volume 2

All About ABC's

Alphabet City

Alphabet House

Alphabet Zoo

Angela's Airplane (plus The Fire Station)

Animal Alphabet

Animal Babies in the Wild

Anna Maria's Blanket

Are You My Mother?

At the Zoo

Baby Animal Fun

Baby Animals Just Want to Have Fun

Baby Goes...Songs to Take Along

Baby Song Series

Baby Songs 1

Baby Songs 2: More Baby Songs

Baby Songs Christmas

Baby Songs Presents: Follow Along Songs with Hap Palmer

Baby Songs Presents: John Lithgow's Kid-Size Concert

Baby Songs: Even More Baby Songs

Baby Songs: Sing Together

Baby Songs: Super Baby Songs

Baby Vision

Baby Vision Volume 1

Baby Vision Volume 2

Baby's Bedtime

Baby's Morningtime

Baby's Nursery Rhymes

Barney and the Backyard Gang

Barney and the Backyard Gang: Barney Goes to School

Barney and the Backyard Gang: Barney in Concert

Barney and the Backyard Gang: Barney's Best Manners

Barney and the Backyard Gang: Barney's Birthday Adventure

Barney and the Backyard Gang: Barney's Campfire Sing-Along

Barney and the Backyard Gang: Barney's Home Sweet Homes

Barney and the Backyard Gang: Barney's Imagination Island

Barney and the Backyard Gang: Barney's Magical Musical

Barney and the Backyard Gang: Barney's Safety Video

Barney and the Backyard Gang: Rock with Barney

Barney and the Backyard Gang: Waiting for Santa

Basil Hears a Noise

Bear Who Slept Through Christmas, The

Bethie's Really Silly Clubhouse

Big Bird's Favorite Party Games

Birthday! Party/ Professor Iris

Bugs Don't Bug Us

Caterpillar's Wish, A

Child of Mine: The Lullaby Video

Creepy Critters/ Professor Iris

Curious George

Curious George: Fun in the Sun

Curious George Goes to Town

Curious George Videos

Doing Things: Eating, Washing, in Motion

Dr. Seuss: I Am NOT Going to Get Up Today!

Dr. Seuss: One Fish, Two Fish, Red Fish, Blue Fish

Dr. Seuss' ABC

Dr. Seuss' Sleep Book

Eight Super Stories from Sesame Street

Eres Tu Mi Mama?

50 Below Zero (plus Thomas' Snowsuit)

Five Lionni Classics

Five Sesame Street Stories

Five Stories for the Very Young

Get Ready for School

Good Morning Sunshine

Good Morning, Good Night: A Day on the Farm

Here We Go

Here We Go — Volume 1

Here We Go Volume 2

Here We Go Again

Hey, What About Me?

I Can Build

I Have a Friend

It's Not Easy Being Green

Jay Jay the Jet Plane and His Flying Friends Series

Jay Jay the Jet Plane and His Flying Friends Volume 1. Jay Jay's First Flight and Three Other Stories

Jay Jay the Jet Plane and His Flying Friends Volume 1. Tito Turbinitas Y Sus Amigos Voladores

Jay Jay the Jet Plane and His Flying Friends Volume 2. Old Oscar Leads the Parade and Three Other Stories

Kidsongs Music Video Stories

Kidsongs Music Video Stories: Boppin' with Biggles

Kidsongs Music Video Stories: Cars, Boats, Trains and Planes

Kidsongs Music Video Stories: Country Sing-Along

Kidsongs Music Video Stories: A Day at Camp

Kidsongs Music Video Stories: A Day at Old MacDonald's Farm

Kidsongs Music Video Stories: A Day at the Circus

Kidsongs Music Video Stories: A Day with the Animals

Kidsongs Music Video Stories: Good Night, Sleep Tight

Kidsongs Music Video Stories: I'd Like to Teach the World to Sing

Kidsongs Music Video Stories: If We Could Talk to the Animals

Kidsongs Music Video Stories: Let's Play Ball!

Kidsongs Music Video Stories: Ride the Roller Coaster

Kidsongs Music Video Stories: Sing Out, America!

Kidsongs Music Video Stories: Very Silly Songs

Kidsongs Music Video Stories: We Wish You a Merry Christmas

Kidsongs Music Video Stories: What I Want to Be!

Kidsongs Music Video Stories: The Wonderful World of Sports

Land of Pleasant Dreams, The

Land of Pleasant Dreams, The: Bearly There At All

Land of Pleasant Dreams, The: Fence Too High, A

Land of Pleasant Dreams, The: Is It Soup Yet?

Let's Create for Pre-Schoolers

Let's Do It!/ Professor Iris

Let's Sing Along

Little People Videos

Little People: Christmas Fun

Little People: Favorite Songs

Little People: Fun with Words

Little People: Three Favorite Stories

Meet Your Animal Friends

Moira's Birthday (plus Blackberry Subway Jam)

More Pre-School Power

Moving Machines

Mr. Rogers Videos

Mr. Rogers: Dinosaurs & Monsters

Mr. Rogers: Music and Feelings

Mr. Rogers: Musical Stories

Mr. Rogers: What About Love

Mr. Rogers: When Parents Are Away

Mr. Rogers' Neighborhood: Circus Fun

Mr. Rogers' Neighborhood: Kindness

Mr. Rogers' Neighborhood: Love

Mr. Rogers' Neighborhood: Making Music

Murmel, Murmel, Murmel (plus The Boy in the Drawer)

Music Mania/ Professor Iris

My Sesame Street Home Videos

My Sesame Street Home Video: Alphabet Game, The

My Sesame Street Home Video: Big Bird's Favorite Party Games

My Sesame Street Home Video: Big Bird's Story Time

My Sesame Street Home Video: Best of Elmo, The

My Sesame Street Home Video: Best of Ernie and Bert, The

My Sesame Street Home Video: Bedtime Stories & Songs

My Sesame Street Home Video: Count It Higher: Great Music Videos

My Sesame Street Home Video: Getting Ready for School

My Sesame Street Home Video: Getting Ready to Read

My Sesame Street Home Video: I'm Glad I'm Me

My Sesame Street Home Video: Learning About Letters

My Sesame Street Home Video: Learning About Numbers

My Sesame Street Home Video: Learning to Add and Subtract

My Sesame Street Home Video: Play-Along Games & Songs

My Sesame Street Home Video: New Baby in My House, A

On Our Way to School

Original Tales and Tunes

Poky Little Puppy's First Christmas

Poky's Favorite Stories

Postman Pat's 123 Story

Postman Pat's ABC Story

Pre-School Power #3

Pre-School Power: Jacket Flips & Other Tips

Raffi in Concert with the Rise and Shine Band

Raffi: Young People's Concert with Raffi

Richard Scarry's Best Counting Video

Richard Scarry's Best Ever ABC Video

Richard Scarry Series

Richard Scarry's Best Learning Songs Ever

Richard Scarry's Best Busy People Video

Scuffy the Tugboat and Friends

Sesame Songs Series

Sesame Songs: Dance Along!

Sesame Songs: Elmo's Sing-Along Guessing Game

Sesame Songs: Monster Hits!

Sesame Songs: Rock & Roll!

Sesame Songs: Sing Yourself Silly!

Sesame Songs: Sing, Hoot and Howl

Sesame Songs: Sing-Along Earth Songs

Sesame Songs: We All Sing Together

Sesame Street: Plaza Sesamo

Sesame Street: Plaza Sesamo: De Compamento Con Montoya: Big Bird Goes Camping

Sesame Street: Plaza Sesamo: El Alfabeto De Montoya: Learn the Alphabet with Bert and Ernie

Sesame Street: Plaza Sesamo: Plaza Sesamo Canta: Favorite Songs From Past Shows

Sesame Street: Plaza Sesamo: Vamos a Imaginar: Learn About Sounds and Shapes

Sesame Street: Plaza Sesamo: Viaja Con Nosotros: Big Bird and Oscar Go to Venezuela and Mexico

Sesame Street: Plaza Sesamo: The Plaza Sesamo Complete Set

Sesame Street Specials: Big Bird in China

Sesame Street Specials: Big Bird in Japan

Sesame Street Specials: Celebrates Around the World

Sesame Street Specials: Christmas Eve on Sesame Street

Sesame Street Specials: Don't Eat the Pictures — Sesame Street Visits the Metropolitan Museum of Art

Sesame Street Specials: Put Down the Duckie

Sesame Street Specials: Sesame Street's 25th Birthday: A Musical Celebration

Sesame Street Visits: The Firehouse

Sesame Street Visits: The Hospital

Silly Tales and Tunes

Something Good (plus Mortimer)

Sounds Around

Space Cadets/Professor Iris

Spanish Club: Fiesta!

Spanish Club: Los Animales!

Spot Goes to School

Tawny Scrawny Lion's Jungle Tales

Teddy Bears' Jamboree

Thomas the Tank Engine & Friends

Thomas the Tank Engine & Friends: Better Late Than Never and Other Stories

Thomas the Tank Engine & Friends: Christmas Party

Thomas the Tank Engine & Friends: James Learns a Lesson & Other Stories

Thomas the Tank Engine & Friends: Percy's Ghostly & Other Stories

Thomas the Tank Engine & Friends: Tenders & Turntables & Other Stories

Thomas the Tank Engine & Friends: Thomas Breaks the Rules & Other Stories

Thomas the Tank Engine & Friends: Thomas Gets Bumped

Thomas the Tank Engine & Friends: Thomas Gets Tricked & Other Stories

Thomas the Tank Engine & Friends: Trust Thomas & Other Stories

Three Sesame Street Stories

Timmy's Special Delivery

'Twas the Night Before Christmas

Un Pez, Dos Peces

Velveteen Rabbit, The (Plummer)

Velveteen Rabbit, The (Rabbit Ears)

Water Is Wet

Wee Sing in Sillyville

Wee Sing Series

Wee Sing Together

Wee Sing Train

Wee Sing: Grandpa's Magical Toys

Where's Spot

Which Way, Weather?

Wildlife Symphony

Winnie the Pooh: Making Friends, Learning

Workout with Daddy & Me

Workout with Mommy & Me

Young People's Concert with Raffi

Zeezel the Zowie Zoon in the Color Chase

Starting school: ages 4 - 5 (starting to read, starting pre-school, starting kindergarten)

Abuela's Weave

African Story Magic

AfroClassic Folk Tales, Volume 1

AfroClassic Folk Tales, Volume 2

Alejandro's Gift

Alexander and the Terrible, Horrible, No Good, Very Bad Day

All About ABC's

Alphabet City

Alphabet House

Alphabet Zoo

Anansi Goes Fishing

Angela's Airplane (plus The Fire Station)

Animal Alphabet

Animal Babies in the Wild

Animal Stories

Anna Maria's Blanket

Annie Oakley (Rabbit Ears)

Are You My Mother?

At the Zoo

Attic in the Blue

Baby Animal Fun

Baby Animals Just Want to Have Fun

Baby Goes...Songs to Take Along

Baby Song Series

Baby Songs 1

Baby Songs 2: More Baby Songs

Baby Songs Christmas

Baby Songs Presents: Follow Along Songs with Hap Palmer

Baby Songs Presents: John Lithgow's Kid-Size Concert

Baby Songs: Even More Baby Songs

Baby Songs: Sing Together

Baby Songs: Super Baby Songs

Baby's Bedtime

Baby's Morningtime

Baby's Nursery Rhymes

Barney and the Backyard Gang

Barney and the Backyard Gang: Barney Goes to School

Barney and the Backyard Gang: Barney in Concert

Barney and the Backyard Gang: Barney's Best Manners

Barney and the Backyard Gang: Barney's Birthday Adventure

Barney and the Backyard Gang: Barney's Campfire Sing-Along

Barney and the Backyard Gang: Barney's Home Sweet Homes

Barney and the Backyard Gang: Barney's Imagination Island

Barney and the Backyard Gang: Barney's Magical Musical

Barney and the Backyard Gang: Barney's Safety Video

Barney and the Backyard Gang: Waiting for Santa

Barney and the Backyard Gang: Rock with Barney

Barry's Scrapbook: A Window into Art

Basil Hears a Noise

Beady Bear

Bear Who Slept Through Christmas, The

Ben's Dream and Other Stories

Berenstain Bears and the Messy Room

Berenstain Bears and the Trouble with Friends

Berenstain Bears and the Truth

Berenstain Bears and Too Much Birthday and to the Rescue

Berenstain Bears Christmas Tree

Berenstain Bears Easter Surprise

Berenstain Bears Get in a Fight

Berenstain Bears in the Dark

Berenstain Bears Learn About Strangers

Berenstain Bears Videos

Berenstain Bears: No Girls Allowed and The Missing Dinosaur Bone

Best Friends

Best Friends Part I

Best Friends Part II

Bethie's Really Silly Clubhouse

Big Bird's Favorite Party Games

Biggest Bears!, The

Bill Cosby's Picturepages

Bill Cosby's Picturepages: What Goes Where?

Bill Cosby's Picturepages: What's Different?

Bill Cosby's Picturepages: What's Missing?

Bill Cosby's Picturepages: What's That Shape?

Bill Cosby's Picturepages: Who's Counting?

Birthday Dragon

Birthday! Party/ Professor Iris

Brave Little Toaster, The

Brer Rabbit and the Wonderful Tar Baby (Rabbit Ears)

Bubbe's Boarding House Series

Bugs Don't Bug Us

Bump My First Video

Can I Be Good?

Candles, Snow and Mistletoe

Caribbean Kids: English Version

Caribbean Kids: Spanish Version

Carlitos, Dani y Luis Alfredo

Chanter Pour S'Amuser

Chanter Pour S'Amuser Set

Chanter Pour S'Amuser: L'Album de Marie-Soleil

Chanter Pour S'Amuser: Une Journee Avec Marie-Soleil

Chanuka at Bubbe's

Charles the Clown

Cherries and Cherry Pits

Child of Mine: The Lullaby Video

Classroom Holidays

Classroom Holidays: Bee My Valentine: A Valentine's Day Story

Classroom Holidays: Classroom Holidays Set

Classroom Holidays: Don't Eat Too Much Turkey: A Thanksgiving Story

Classroom Holidays: Liar, Liar, Pants on Fire: A Christmas/Chanukah Story

Classroom Holidays: Starring First Grade: An Anytime Celebration

Clean Your Room, Harvey Moon!

Clifford's Fun with Rhymes

Clifford's Fun with Letters

Clifford's Fun with Opposites

Clifford's Fun with Shapes and Colors

Clifford's Fun with Sounds

Clifford's Fun With....Series

Clifford's Sing Along Adventure

Cloudy with a Chance of Meatballs

Corduroy Bear

Creative Dance for Preschoolers

Creative Movement: A Step Towards Intelligence

Creepy Critters/ Professor Iris

CriCri: El Grillito Cantor

Curious George

Curious George Goes to Town

Curious George Videos

Curious George: Fun in the Sun

Daisy-Head Mayzie

Dan Crow's Oops!

Danny and the Dinosaur and Other Stories

Discovery Stories

Doctor De Soto and Other Stories

Dog Who Had Kittens, The

Doing Things: Eating, Washing, in Motion

Don Cooper: Mother Nature's Songs

Dozen Dizzy Dogs, A

Dr. Seuss Video Festival

Dr. Seuss Videos

Dr. Seuss: Green Eggs and Ham

Dr. Seuss: HooberBloob Highway

Dr. Seuss: Hop on Pop

Dr. Seuss: Horton Hatches the Egg

Dr. Seuss: Horton Hears a Who

Dr. Seuss: How the Grinch Stole Christmas

Dr. Seuss: I Am NOT Going to Get Up Today!

Dr. Seuss: One Fish, Two Fish, Red Fish, Blue Fish

Dr. Seuss: Pontoffel Pock

Dr. Seuss: The Butter Battle Book

Dr. Seuss: The Cat in the Hat Comes Back

Dr. Seuss: The Lorax

Dr. Seuss' ABC

Dr. Seuss' Cat in the Hat

Dr. Seuss' Sleep Book

Dreadlocks and the Three Bears

Eco, You, and Simon, Too!

Eight Super Stories from Sesame Street

Ella Jenkins Live! At the Smithsonian

Ella Jenkins: For the Family

Eres Tu Mi Mama?

Ezra Jack Keats Library

Farmer's Huge Carrot, The

50 Below Zero (plus Thomas' Snowsuit)

Fingermouse, Yoffy and Friends

Fire and Rescue

Fireman Sam: The Hero Next Door

First and Second Grade Feelings

First and Second Grade Feelings: First and Second Grade Feelings Set

First and Second Grade Feelings: Jim's Dog, Muffins

First and Second Grade Feelings: See You in Second Grade!

First and Second Grade Feelings: So What?

First and Second Grade Feelings: The RealSkin Rubber Monster Mask

Five Lionni Classics

Five Sesame Street Stories

Five Stories for the Very Young

Follow That Bunny!

Foolish Frog and Other Stories

Free to Be...You and Me

Frog and Toad Are Friends

Frog and Toad Together

Fun in a Box

Fun in a Box Volume 1: Ben's Dream

Fun in a Box Volume 2: New Friends and Other Stories

Gingerbread Christmas, A (Rabbit Ears)

Gingham Dog and the Calico Cat (Rabbit Ears), The

Good Morning Sunshine

Good Morning, Good Night: A Day on the Farm

Granpa

Happy Birdy

Harold and the Purple Crayon

Here We Go

Here We Go — Volume 1

Here We Go — Volume 2

Here We Go Again

Hey, What About Me?

Holidays for Children Video Series

Holidays for Children Video Series: 12-Tape Set

Holidays for Children Video Series: Arbor Day

Holidays for Children Video Series: Chinese New Year

Holidays for Children Video Series: Cinco De Mayo

Holidays for Children Video Series: Easter

Holidays for Children Video Series: Halloween

Holidays for Children Video Series: Hanukkah/Passover

Holidays for Children Video Series: Independence Day

Holidays for Children Video Series: Kwanzaa

Holidays for Children Video Series: Rosh Hashanah/Yom Kippur

Holidays for Children Video Series: Thanksgiving

Holidays for Children Video Series: Valentine's Day

How Come?

How the Leopard Got His Spots (Rabbit Ears)

How to Hide a Butterfly and Other Insects

How to Hide a Crocodile and Other Reptiles

How to Hide a Gray Treefrog and Other Amphibians

How to Hide a Polar Bear and Other Mammals

How to HIde a WhipPoorWill and Other Birds

How to Hide an Octopus and Other Sea Creatures

How to Hide Stories

How to Hide Stories 6-Tape Set

I Can Build

I Dig Fossils

I Have a Friend

I Need a Hug!

I Want to Be an Artist When I Grow Up

I'm Not Oscar's Friend Anymore and Other Stories

Imaginaria: A Computer Animation Music Video for Children

Imagine That!

In the Tall, Tall Grass

Ira Says Goodbye

Ira Sleeps Over

It Zwibble: Earthday Birthday

It's Not Easy Being Green

It's the Muppets: More Muppets!

It's the Muppets! Series

It's the Muppets!: Meet the Muppets!

Jack and the Beanstalk (Rabbit Ears)

Janey Junkfood's Fresh Adventure

Jay Jay the Jet Plane and His Flying Friends Series

Jay Jay the Jet Plane and His Flying Friends Volume 1. Jay Jay's First Flight and Three Other Stories

Jay Jay the Jet Plane and His Flying Friends Volume 1. Tito Turbinitas Y Sus Amigos Voladores

Jay Jay the Jet Plane and His Flying Friends Volume 2. Old Oscar Leads the Parade and Three Other Stories

Jay O'Callahan: Herman & Marguerite

Jessi Sings Songs from Around the World

Joe Scruggs First Video

Joe Scruggs in Concert

John Henry (Rabbit Ears)

Johnny Appleseed (Rabbit Ears)

Josephine's Imagination

Joshua's Masai Mask

Junglies: First Day at School

Just Grandma and Me

Just Me and My Dad

Kids Get Cooking: The Egg

Kids Kitchen: Making Good Eating Great Fun for Kids!

Kidsongs Music Video Stories

Kidsongs Music Video Stories: A Day at the Circus

Kidsongs Music Video Stories: Boppin' with Biggles

Kidsongs Music Video Stories: Cars, Boats, Trains and Planes

Kidsongs Music Video Stories: Country Sing-Along

Kidsongs Music Video Stories: A Day at Camp

Kidsongs Music Video Stories: A Day at Old MacDonald's Farm

Kidsongs Music Video Stories: A Day with the Animals

Kidsongs Music Video Stories: Good Night, Sleep Tight

Kidsongs Music Video Stories: I'd Like to Teach the World to Sing

Kidsongs Music Video Stories: If We Could Talk to the Animals

Kidsongs Music Video Stories: Let's Play Ball!

Kidsongs Music Video Stories: Ride the Roller Coaster

Kidsongs Music Video Stories: Sing Out, America!

Kidsongs Music Video Stories: Very Silly Songs

Kidsongs Music Video Stories: We Wish You a Merry Christmas

Kidsongs Music Video Stories: What I Want to Be!

Kidsongs Music Video Stories: The Wonderful World of Sports

Kitten Companions

Knots on a Counting Rope

Land of Pleasant Dreams, The

Land of Pleasant Dreams, The: Bearly There At All

Land of Pleasant Dreams, The: Fence Too High, A

Land of Pleasant Dreams, The: Is It Soup Yet?

Land of Sweet Taps, The

Language Primer

Language Primer: Adventuresome Max: Discovering the World

Language Primer: Language Primer Set

Language Primer: Max in Motion: Developing Language Skills

Language Primer: Max's Library: Beginning to Write

Learning About Me

Learning About Me Set

Learning About Me: A Is for Autonomy

Learning About Me: B Is for Belonging

Learning About Me: Ipsilwhich Adventures

Let's Create Art Activities

Let's Create for Pre-Schoolers

Let's Do It!/ Professor Iris

Let's Get a Move On!

Let's Sing Along

Lights: The Miracle of Chanukah

Lion and the Lamb, The (Rabbit Ears)

Little Crooked Christmas Tree, The

Little Engine That Could, The: English Narration

Little Engine That Could, The: French Narration

Little Engine That Could, The: Spanish Narration

Little People Videos

Little People: Christmas Fun

Little People: Favorite Songs

Little People: Fun with Words

Little People: Three Favorite Stories

Little Sister Rabbit

Look What I Made

Lovely Butterfly — Papar Nechmad

Lovely Butterfly — Papar Nechmad: Chanukah

Lovely Butterfly — Papar Nechmad: Flowers for the Independence Day

Lovely Butterfly — Papar Nechmad: Passover

Lovely Butterfly — Papar Nechmad: Purim

Lovely Butterfly — Papar Nechmad: Tishrei Month Holidays (Rosh Hashana and Sukkot)

Lovely Butterfly — Papar Nechmad: Tu B'Shvat

Lyle, Lyle Crocodile: The House on East 88th Street

Madeline

Madeline (Christopher Plummer)

Madeline and the Dog Show

Madeline and the Easter Bonnet

Madeline and the Toy Factory

Madeline at Cooking School

Madeline in London

Madeline's Christmas

Madeline's Rescue and Other Stories About Madeline

Magic of Discovery, The

Magic School Bus, The

Magic School Bus, The: For Lunch

Magic School Bus, The: Gets Eaten

Magic School Bus, The: Gets Lost in Space

Magic School Bus, The: Hops Home

Magic School Bus, The: Inside Ralphie

Magical Coqui Puerto Rico Mi Tierra!

Making Music with Children

Making Music with Children, Program 1.

Making Music with Children: Ages 3-7

Making Music with Children, Program 3.

Making Music in the Classroom: Ages 3-7

Maurice Sendak Library, The

Max's Chocolate Chicken and Other Stories for Young Children

Meet Your Animal Friends

Mike Mulligan and His Steam Shovel

Mine and Yours

Moira's Birthday (plus Blackberry Subway Jam)

Mole and the Green Star, The

Mole in Town, The

Mole Series, The

Mommy's Office

Monkey Moves

Monkey People (Rabbit Ears), The

Mop Top

More Pre-School Power

Morris the Moose: Goes to School/Gets a Cold

Mose the Fireman (Rabbit Ears)

Mouse and the Motorcycle, The

Move Like the Animals

Moving Machines

Mr. Rogers Videos

Mr. Rogers: Dinosaurs & Monsters

Mr. Rogers: Music and Feelings

Mr. Rogers: Musical Stories

Mr. Rogers: What About Love

Mr. Rogers: When Parents Are Away

Mr. Rogers' Neighborhood: Circus Fun

Mr. Rogers' Neighborhood: Kindness

Mr. Rogers' Neighborhood: Love

Mr. Rogers' Neighborhood: Making Music

Murmel, Murmel, Murmel (plus The Boy in the Drawer)

Music and Magic

Music Mania/ Professor Iris

My First Activity Series

My First Activity Series: My First Activity Video

My First Activity Series: My First Cooking Video

My First Activity Series: My First Green Video

My First Activity Series: My First Music Video

My First Activity Series: My First Nature Video

My First Activity Series: My First Science Video

My Principal Lives Next Door

My Neighbor Totoro

My Sesame Street Home Videos

My Sesame Street Home Video: Alphabet Game, The

My Sesame Street Home Video: Bedtime Stories & Songs

My Sesame Street Home Video: Best of Elmo, The

My Sesame Street Home Video: Best of Ernie and Bert, The

My Sesame Street Home Video: Big Bird's Favorite Party Games

My Sesame Street Home Video: Big Bird's Story Time

My Sesame Street Home Video: Count It Higher: Great Music Videos

My Sesame Street Home Video: Getting Ready for School

My Sesame Street Home Video: Getting Ready to Read

My Sesame Street Home Video: I'm Glad I'm Me

My Sesame Street Home Video: Learning About Letters

My Sesame Street Home Video: Learning About Numbers

My Sesame Street Home Video: Learning to Add and Subtract

My Sesame Street Home Video: New Baby in My House, A

My Sesame Street Home Video: Play-Along Games & Songs

National Geographic Kids Videos: GeoKids

National Geographic Kids Videos: GeoKids: Bear Cubs, Baby Ducks and Kooky

National Geographic Kids Videos: GeoKids: Cool Cats, Raindrops, and Things That Live in Holes

National Geographic Kids Videos: GeoKids: Flying, Trying and Honking Around

Never Talk to Strangers

New Friends and Other Stories

Noah and the Ark (Rabbit Ears)

Noel

Nonsense and Lullabies: Nursery Rhymes

Nonsense and Lullabies: Poems for Children

Norman the Doorman and Other Stories

"Not Now!" Said the Cow

Now I Know My Aleph Bet

On Our Way to School

Orca Whales and Mermaid Tales

Original Tales and Tunes

Other Way to Listen, The

Owl Moon and Other Stories

P.J. Funnybunny

Passover at Bubbe's

Paul Bunyan (Rabbit Ears)

Paws, Claws, Feathers and Fins

Pecos Bill (Rabbit Ears)

Peep and the Big Wide World

Pete Seeger's Family Concert

Pigs (plus David's Father)

Pinocchio (Rabbit Ears)

Poky Little Puppy's First Christmas

Poky's Favorite Stories

Postman Pat's 123 Story

Postman Pat's ABC Story

Pre-School Power: Jacket Flips & Other Tips

Pre-School Power #3

Puppy Pals

Raffi in Concert with the Rise and Shine Band

Raffi: Young People's Concert with Raffi

Rainbow of My Own, A

Reach for the Sky

Real Story of Baa Baa Black Sheep, The

Real Story of Happy Birthday to You, The

Real Story of I'm a Little Teapot, The

Real Story of Itsy Bitsy Spider, The

Real Story of Rain, Rain Go Away, The

Real Story of Three Little Kittens, The

Real Story of Twinkle Twinkle Little Star, The

Real Story Videos Series, The

Reluctant Dragon, The

Richard Scarry Series

Richard Scarry's Best Busy People Video

Richard Scarry's Best Counting Video

Richard Scarry's Best Ever ABC Video

Richard Scarry's Best Learning Songs Ever

Robert McCloskey Library

Roxaboxen

Runaway Ralph

Rupert

Rupert and the Frog Song

Rupert and the Runaway Dragon

Sammy and Other Songs from Getting to Know Myself

Sand Castle, The

Science Primer

Science Primer Series

Science Primer: Earth, Air, Water, Fire

Science Primer: The Five Senses

Science Primer: Habitats

Scuffy the Tugboat and Friends

Sesame Songs Series

Sesame Songs: Dance Along!

Sesame Songs: Elmo's Sing-Along Guessing Game

Sesame Songs: Monster Hits!

Sesame Songs: Rock & Roll!

Sesame Songs: Sing, Hoot and Howl

Sesame Songs: Sing-Along Earth Songs

Sesame Songs: We All Sing Together

Sesame Street Specials: Big Bird in China

Sesame Street Specials: Big Bird in Japan

Sesame Street Specials: Celebrates Around the World

Sesame Street Specials: Christmas Eve on Sesame Street

Sesame Street Specials: Don't Eat the Pictures — Sesame Street Visits the Metropolitan Museum of Art

Sesame Street Specials: Put Down the Duckie

Sesame Street Specials: Sesame Street's 25th Birthday: A Musical Celebration

Sesame Street Visits: The Firehouse

Sesame Street Visits: The Hospital

Sesame Street Start to Read Videos

Sesame Street Start to Read Videos: Don't Cry, Big Bird and Other Stories

Sesame Street Start to Read Videos: Ernie's Big Mess and Other Stories

Sesame Street Start to Read Videos: Ernie's Little Lie and Other Stories

Sesame Street Start to Read Videos: I Want to Go Home! and Other Stories

Sesame Street: Plaza Sesamo

Sesame Street: Plaza Sesamo: De Compamento Con Montoya: Big Bird Goes Camping

Sesame Street: Plaza Sesamo: El Alfabeto De Montoya: Learn the Alphabet with Bert and Ernie

Sesame Street: Plaza Sesamo: Plaza Sesamo Canta: Favorite Songs From Past Shows

Sesame Street: Plaza Sesamo: The Plaza Sesamo Complete Set

Sesame Street: Plaza Sesamo: Vamos a Imaginar: Learn About Sounds and Shapes

Sesame Street: Plaza Sesamo: Viaja Con Nosotros: Big Bird and Oscar Go to Venezuela and Mexico

Shalom Sesame

Shalom Sesame: Aleph-Bet Telethon

Shalom Sesame: Chanukah

Shalom Sesame: Jerusalem

Shalom Sesame: Journey to Secret Places

Shalom Sesame: Kibbutz

Shalom Sesame: Kids Sing Israel

Shalom Sesame: Land of Israel

Shalom Sesame: Passover

Shalom Sesame: People of Israel

Shalom Sesame: Tel Aviv

Shalom Sesame: Sing Around the Seasons

Shamu & You Series

Shamu & You: Exploring the World of Birds

Shamu & You: Exploring the World of Fish

Shamu & You: Exploring the World of Mammals

Shamu & You: Exploring the World of Reptiles

Shari Lewis: 101 Things for Kids to Do

Shari Lewis: Don't Wake Your Mom

Shari Lewis: Kooky Classics

Shari Lewis: Lamb Chop in the Land of No Manners

Shari Lewis: Lamb Chop's Play Along

Shari Lewis: You Can Do It!

Shari's Christmas Concert

Sharon, Lois & Bram's: Elephant Show

Sharon, Lois & Bram's: Elephant Show: Back by Popular Demand

Sharon, Lois & Bram's: Elephant Show: Live in your Living Room

Sharon, Lois & Bram's: Elephant Show: Pet Fair

Sharon, Lois & Bram's: Elephant Show: Radio Show

Sharon, Lois & Bram's: Elephant Show: Sleepover

Sharon, Lois & Bram's: Elephant Show: Soap Box Derby

Sharon, Lois & Bram's: Elephant Show: Treasure Island

Sharon, Lois & Bram's: Elephant Show: Who Stole the Cookies

Shelley Duvall's Bedtime Stories: Elizabeth and Larry/ Bill and Pete

Shelley Duvall's Bedtime Stories: The Little Rabbit Who Wanted Red Wings

Shelley Duvall's Bedtime Stories: Moe the Dog in Tropical Paradise

Shelley Duvall's Bedtime Stories: Aunt Ippy's Museum of Junk

Sign Songs: Fun Songs to Sign and Sing

Sign-Me-A-Story

Silly Tales and Tunes

Simon the Lamb

Simply Magic: Episode 2

Simply Magic: The Rainy Day Adventure

Sing-Along, Dance-Along, Do-along

Smile for Auntie and Other Stories

Snowman, The

Something Good (plus Mortimer)

Sounds Around

Space Cadets/ Professor Iris

Spanish Club: Fiesta!

Spanish Club: Los Animales!

Sparky's Magic Piano

Spoonbill Swamp

Spot

Spot Goes to School

Spot's Adventure - French

Spot's Adventure - German

Spot's Adventure - Spanish

Spot's First Video - French

Spot's First Video - German

Spot's First Video - Spanish

Story of the Dancing Frog

Strega Nonna and Other Stories

Tawny Scrawny Lion's Jungle Tales

Teddy Bear's Picnic, The

Teddy Bears' Jamboree

There Goes a Bulldozer

There Goes a Fire Truck

There Goes a Police Car

There Goes a Train

There Goes a Truck

Thirteen Moons on Turtle's Back

This Pretty Planet

Thomas the Tank Engine & Friends

Thomas the Tank Engine & Friends: Better Late Than Never and Other Stories

Thomas the Tank Engine & Friends: Christmas Party

Thomas the Tank Engine & Friends: James Learns a Lesson & Other Stories

Thomas the Tank Engine & Friends: Percy's Ghostly & Other Stories

Thomas the Tank Engine & Friends: Tenders & Turntables & Other Stories

Thomas the Tank Engine & Friends: Thomas Breaks the Rules & Other Stories

Thomas the Tank Engine & Friends: Thomas Gets Bumped

Thomas the Tank Engine & Friends: Thomas Gets Tricked & Other Stories

Thomas the Tank Engine & Friends: Trust Thomas & Other Stories

Three Sesame Street Stories

Thunder Cake

Tickle Tune Typhoon: Let's Be Friends

Timmy's Special Delivery

To Bathe a Boa

Today Was a Terrible Day

Treasury of Children's Stories: Stories to Help Us Grow

`Twas the Night Before Christmas

Un Pez, Dos Peces

Velveteen Rabbit, The (Plummer)

Velveteen Rabbit, The (Rabbit Ears)

Walk in the Wild, A

Water Is Wet

Way to Start a Day, The

We Learn About the World: English Version

We Learn About the World: Spanish Version

Wee Sing in Sillyville

Wee Sing Series

Wee Sing Together

Wee Sing Train

Wee Sing: Grandpa's Magical Toys

Where in the World/ Kids Explore

Where in the World/ Kids Explore: Volume 1. Kids Explore Mexico

Where in the World/ Kids Explore: Volume 2. Kids Explore Alaska

Where in the World/ Kids Explore: Volume 3. Kids Explore Kenya

Where in the World/ Kids Explore: Volume 4. Kids Explore America's National Parks

Where's Spot

Which Way, Weather?

White Cat, The (Rabbit Ears)

Who Will Be My Friend?

Wild Christmas Reindeer, The

Wildlife Symphony

Winnie the Pooh

Winnie the Pooh and the Blustery Day

Winnie the Pooh and a Day for Eeyore

Winnie the Pooh and the Honey Tree

Winnie the Pooh and Tigger Too

Winnie the Pooh/ The New Adventures (Series/Walt Disney)

Winnie the Pooh/ The New Adventures Volume 1. The Great Honey Pot Robbery

Winnie the Pooh/ The New Adventures Volume 2. The Wishing Bear

Winnie the Pooh/ The New Adventures Volume 3. Newfound Friends

Winnie the Pooh: Making Friends, Learning

Workout with Daddy & Me

Workout with Mommy & Me

World Alive, A

You Can Choose!: Volume 2. Being Responsible

"You Can" Video Series

You Can Fly a Kite

You Can Ride a Horse

You On Kazoo!

Young People's Concert with Raffi

Zoobilee Zoo

Zoobilee Zoo: Blue Ribbon Zooble and Other Stories

Zoobilee Zoo: Lady Whazzat and Other Stories

Zoobilee Zoo: Laughland and Other Stories

Zoobilee Zoo: Zoobadoobas and Other Stories

Zoobilee Zoo: Zooble Hop and Other Stories

Primary grades: ages 6 - 9 (grades 1 - 3)

Abuela's Weave

African Story Magic

AfroClassic Folk Tales, Volume 1

AfroClassic Folk Tales, Volume 2

Alejandro's Gift

Alexander and the Terrible, Horrible, No Good, Very Bad Day

Amazing Bone and Other Stories, The

Amazing Things, Volume 1

Amazing Things, Volume 2

Anansi (Rabbit Ears)

Anansi Goes Fishing

And the Children Shall Lead

Animal Stories

Animals Are Beautiful People

Annie Oakley (Rabbit Ears)

Art Lessons for Children

Art Lessons for Children Volume 1: Easy Watercolor Techniques

Art Lessons for Children Volume 2: Easy Art Projects

Art Lessons for Children Volume 3: More Fun with Watercolors

Art Lessons for Children Volume 4: Felt Pen Fun

Art Lessons for Children Volume 5: Animals of the Rain Forest

Art Lessons for Children Volume 6: Plants of the Rain Forest

Astronomy 101: A Family Adventure

At Home in the Coral Reef

Attic in the Blue

Baby Animal Fun

Baby-Sitters Club Videos

Baby-Sitters Club, The: The Baby-Sitters Remember

Baby-Sitters Club, The: The Baby-Sitters and the Boy Sitters

Baby-Sitters Club, The: Christmas Special (1991)

Baby-Sitters Club, The: Claudia and the Missing Jewels

Baby-Sitters Club, The: Claudia and the Mystery of the Secret Passage

Baby-Sitters Club, The: Dawn and the Dream Boy

Baby-Sitters Club, The: Dawn and the Haunted House

Baby-Sitters Club, The: Dawn Saves the Trees

Baby-Sitters Club, The: Jessi and the Mystery of the Stolen Secrets

Baby-Sitters Club, The: Kristy and the Great Campaign

Baby-Sitters Club, The: Mary Ann and the Brunettes (1990)

Baby-Sitters Club, The: Stacey Takes a Stand

Baby-Sitters Club, The: Stacey's Big Break

Bach and Broccoli

Ballet Shoes

Barry's Scrapbook: A Window into Art

Beady Bear

Beethoven Lives Upstairs

Ben's Dream and Other Stories

Berenstain Bears and the Messy Room

Berenstain Bears and the Trouble with Friends

Berenstain Bears and the Truth

Berenstain Bears and Too Much Birthday and to the Rescue

Berenstain Bears Christmas Tree

Berenstain Bears Easter Surprise

Berenstain Bears Get in a Fight

Berenstain Bears in the Dark

Berenstain Bears Learn About Strangers

Berenstain Bears Videos

Berenstain Bears: No Girls Allowed and The Missing Dinosaur Bone

Best Friends

Best Friends Part I

Best Friends Part II

Best of Beakman's World, The

Biggest Bears!, The

Boy Who Loved Trolls, The

Brave Little Toaster, The

Brer Rabbit and the Wonderful Tar Baby (Rabbit Ears)

Bubbe's Boarding House Series

Caribbean Kids: English Version

Caribbean Kids: Spanish Version

Carlitos, Dani y Luis Alfredo

Chanter Pour S'Amuser

Chanter Pour S'Amuser Set

Chanter Pour S'Amuser: L'Album de Marie-Soleil

Chanter Pour S'Amuser: Une Journee Avec Marie-Soleil

Chanuka at Bubbe's

Charles the Clown

Cherries and Cherry Pits

Chicken Sunday

Child's Christmas in Wales, A

Classroom Holidays

Classroom Holidays: Bee My Valentine: A Valentine's Day Story

Classroom Holidays: Classroom Holidays Set

Classroom Holidays: Don't Eat Too Much Turkey: A Thanksgiving Story

Classroom Holidays: Liar, Liar, Pants on Fire: A Christmas/Chanukah Story

Classroom Holidays: Starring First Grade: An Anytime Celebration

Clean Your Room, Harvey Moon!

Cloudy with a Chance of Meatballs

Corduroy Bear

Creative Movement: A Step Towards Intelligence

Cri Cri: El Grillito Cantor

Daisy-Head Mayzie

Dan Crow's Oops!

Dancing with the Indians

Danny and the Dinosaur and Other Stories

Discovery Stories

Divorce Can Happen to the Nicest People

Doctor De Soto and Other Stories

Dog Who Had Kittens, The

Dog Who Stopped the War, The

Dozen Dizzy Dogs, A

Dr. Seuss Video Festival

Dr. Seuss Videos

Dr. Seuss: The Butter Battle Book

Dr. Seuss: The Cat in the Hat Comes Back

Dr. Seuss: Green Eggs and Ham

Dr. Seuss: HooberBloob Highway

Dr. Seuss: Horton Hatches the Egg

Dr. Seuss: Horton Hears a Who

Dr. Seuss: How the Grinch Stole Christmas

Dr. Seuss: The Lorax

Dr. Seuss: Pontoffel Pock

Dr. Seuss' Cat in the Hat

Dreadlocks and the Three Bears

Eco, You, and Simon, Too!

Ella Jenkins Live! At the Smithsonian

Ella Jenkins: For the Family

Emperor and Nightingale (Rabbit Ears)

Emperor's New Clothes (Rabbit Ears)

Empty Pot, The

Ezra Jack Keats Library

Family Farm

Farmer's Huge Carrot, The

Fingermouse, Yoffy and Friends

Finn McCoul (Rabbit Ears)

Fire and Rescue

First and Second Grade Feelings

First and Second Grade Feelings: First and Second Grade Feelings Set

First and Second Grade Feelings: Jim's Dog, Muffins

First and Second Grade Feelings: The RealSkin Rubber Monster Mask

First and Second Grade Feelings: See You in Second Grade!

First and Second Grade Feelings: So What?

Folk Games

Follow That Bunny!

Follow the Drinking Gourd (Rabbit Ears)

Foolish Frog and Other Stories

Free to Be...You and Me

Frog and Toad Are Friends

Frog and Toad Together

Fun in a Box

Fun in a Box Volume 1: Ben's Dream

Fun in a Box Volume 2: New Friends and Other Stories

Fun in a Box Volume 3: The Birthday Movie

Gateway to the Mind

Gift of Amazing Grace, The

Gift of the Whales

Gingerbread Christmas (Rabbit Ears), A

Gingham Dog and the Calico Cat, The (Rabbit Ears)

Good Morning Miss Toliver

Granpa

Gryphon

Happy Birdy

Harold and the Purple Crayon

Harriet Tubman (1820-1913) — Anti-Slavery Activist

Hawk, I'm Your Brother

Hideaways, The

Hip Hop Animal Rock Workout

Hoboken Chicken Emergency

Holidays for Children Video Series

Holidays for Children Video Series: 12-Tape Set

Holidays for Children Video Series: Arbor Day

Holidays for Children Video Series: Chinese New Year

Holidays for Children Video Series: Cinco De Mayo

Holidays for Children Video Series: Easter

Holidays for Children Video Series: Halloween

Holidays for Children Video Series: Hanukkah/Passover

Holidays for Children Video Series: Independence Day

Holidays for Children Video Series: Kwanzaa

Holidays for Children Video Series: Rosh Hashanah/Yom Kippur

Holidays for Children Video Series: Thanksgiving

Holidays for Children Video Series: Valentine's Day

How to Hide a Butterfly and Other Insects

How to Hide a Crocodile and Other Reptiles

How to Hide a Gray Treefrog and Other Amphibians

How to Hide a Polar Bear and Other Mammals

How to HIde a WhipPoorWill and Other Birds

How to Hide an Octopus and Other Sea Creatures

How to Hide Stories

How to Hide Stories 6-Tape Set

How the Leopard Got His Spots (Rabbit Ears)

Human Race Club/Series

Human Race Club: A Story About Fights between Brothers and Sisters

Human Race Club: A Story About Making Friends, A Story About Prejudice and Discrimination

Human Race Club: A Story About Self-Esteem

I Dig Fossils

I Need a Hug!

I Want to Be an Artist When I Grow Up

I'm Not Oscar's Friend Anymore and Other Stories

Imaginaria: A Computer Animation Music Video for Children

In the Company of Whales

In the Tall, Tall Grass

Indoor Fun

Introducing: The Flying Fruit Fly Circus

Ira Says Goodbye

Ira Sleeps Over

It Zwibble: Earthday Birthday

It's Not Always Easy Being a Kid

It's the Muppets: More Muppets!

It's the Muppets! Series

It's the Muppets!: Meet the Muppets!

Jack and the Beanstalk (Faerie Tale Theatre)

Jack and the Beanstalk (Rabbit Ears)

Janey Junkfood's Fresh Adventure

Jay O'Callahan: Herman & Marguerite

Jay O'Callahan: A Master Class in Storytelling

Jay O'Callahan: Six Stories About Little Heroes

Jazz Time Tale

Jessi Sings Songs from Around the World

Joe Scruggs First Video

Joe Scruggs in Concert

John Henry (Rabbit Ears)

Johnny Appleseed (Rabbit Ears)

Josephine's Imagination

Joshua's Masai Mask

Juggle Time

Jumanji

Just Grandma and Me

Just Me and My Dad

Kids Get Cooking: The Egg

Kids Kitchen: Making Good Eating Great Fun for Kids!

Kidsongs Music Video Stories

Kidsongs Music Video Stories: Boppin' with Biggles

Kidsongs Music Video Stories: Cars, Boats, Trains and Planes

Kidsongs Music Video Stories: Country Sing-Along

Kidsongs Music Video Stories: A Day at Camp

Kidsongs Music Video Stories: A Day at Old MacDonald's Farm

Kidsongs Music Video Stories: A Day at the Circus

Kidsongs Music Video Stories: A Day with the Animals

Kidsongs Music Video Stories: Good Night, Sleep Tight

Kidsongs Music Video Stories: I'd Like to Teach the World to Sing

Kidsongs Music Video Stories: If We Could Talk to the Animals

Kidsongs Music Video Stories: Let's Play Ball!

Kidsongs Music Video Stories: Ride the Roller Coaster

Kidsongs Music Video Stories: Sing Out, America!

Kidsongs Music Video Stories: Very Silly Songs

Kidsongs Music Video Stories: We Wish You a Merry Christmas

Kidsongs Music Video Stories: What I Want to Be!

Kidsongs Music Video Stories: The Wonderful World of Sports

King Midas and the Golden Touch

Kitten Companions

Knots on a Counting Rope

Koi and the Kola Nuts (Rabbit Ears)

Land of Sweet Taps, The

Language Primer

Language Primer: Adventuresome Max: Discovering the World

Language Primer: Language Primer Set

Language Primer: Max in Motion: Developing Language Skills

Language Primer: Max's Library: Beginning to Write

Language Stories

Language Stories: A Cache of Jewels and Other Collective Nouns

Language Stories: Kites Sail High

Language Stories: Language Stories Set

Language Stories: Many Luscious Lollipops

Language Stories: Merry GoRound

Learning About Me

Learning About Me Set

Learning About Me: A Is for Autonomy

Learning About Me: B Is for Belonging

Learning About Me: Ipsilwhich Adventures

Let's Create Art Activities

Let's Get a Move On!

Lights: The Miracle of Chanukah

Linnea in Monet's Garden

Lion and the Lamb, The (Rabbit Ears)

Lion, the Witch, and the Wardrobe, The (Animated)

Lion, the Witch, and the Wardrobe, The (Live action)

Little Crooked Christmas Tree, The

Little Duck Tale, A

Little Engine That Could, The: English Narration

Little Engine That Could, The: French Narration

Little Engine That Could, The: Spanish Narration

Little Lou and His Strange Little Zoo

Little Sister Rabbit

Living and Working in Space: The Countdown Has Begun

Look Around Endangered Animals, A

Look What I Found

Look What I Grew

Look What I Made

Lovely Butterfly — Papar Nechmad

Lovely Butterfly — Papar Nechmad: Chanukah

Lovely Butterfly — Papar Nechmad: Flowers for the Independence Day

Lovely Butterfly — Papar Nechmad: Passover

Lovely Butterfly — Papar Nechmad: Purim

Lovely Butterfly — Papar Nechmad: Tishrei Month Holidays (Rosh Hashana and Sukkot)

Lovely Butterfly — Papar Nechmad: Tu B'Shvat

Lyle, Lyle Crocodile: The House on East 88th Street

Madame C.J. Walker (1867-1919) — Entrepreneur

Madeline

Madeline (Christopher Plummer)

Madeline and the Dog Show

Madeline and the Easter Bonnet

Madeline and the Toy Factory

Madeline at Cooking School

Madeline in London

Madeline's Rescue and Other Stories About Madeline

Madeline's Christmas

Madre Tierra

Magic School Bus

Magic School Bus, The: For Lunch

Magic School Bus, The: Gets Eaten

Magic School Bus, The: Gets Lost in Space

Magic School Bus, The: Hops Home

Magic School Bus, The: Inside Ralphie

Magic Thinking Cap, The

Magical Coqui Puerto Rico Mi Tierra!

Making Music with Children

Making Music with Children

Making Music with Children, Program 1.

Making Music with Children: Ages 3-7

Making Music with Children, Program 3.

Making Music in the Classroom: Ages 3-7

Making Music with Children: Program 2.

Making Music with Children: Ages 7-11

Making Music with Children: Program 4.

Making Music in the Classroom: Ages 7-11

Mary McLeod Bethune (1875-1955) — Educator

Mary Poppins

Math...Who Needs It?

Mathnet/ The Case of the Unnatural

Maurice Sendak Library, The

Max's Chocolate Chicken and Other Stories for Young Children

Mighty Pawns, The

Mike Mulligan and His Steam Shovel

Mole and the Green Star, The

Mole in Town, The

Mole Series, The

Monkey Moves

Monkey People, The (Rabbit Ears)

Mop Top

Mose the Fireman (Rabbit Ears)

Mouse and the Motorcycle, The

Move Like the Animals

Music and Magic

My First Activity Series

My First Activity Series: My First Activity Video

My First Activity Series: My First Cooking Video

My First Activity Series: My First Green Video

My First Activity Series: My First Music Video

My First Activity Series: My First Nature Video

My First Activity Series: My First Science Video

My New York

My Principal Lives Next Door

National Geographic Kids Videos

National Geographic Kids Videos: Adventures in Asia

National Geographic Kids Videos: Amazing North America

National Geographic Kids Videos: Deep Sea Dive

National Geographic Kids Videos: Swinging Safari

National Geographic Kids Videos: Totally Tropical Rainforest

National Geographic Kids Videos: Wonders Down Under

Native Indian Folklore

Never Talk to Strangers

New Friends and Other Stories

Night Before Christmas, The (Rabbit Ears)

Noah and the Ark (Rabbit Ears)

Noah's Ark

Noel

Norman the Doorman and Other Stories

"Not Now!" Said the Cow

Now I Know My Aleph Bet

Opus n' Bill: A Wish for Wings That Work

Orca Whales and Mermaid Tales

Other Way to Listen, The

Owl Moon and Other Stories

P.J. Funnybunny

Passover at Bubbe's

Paul Bunyan (Rabbit Ears)

Paws, Claws, Feathers and Fins

Pecos Bill (Rabbit Ears)

Peep and the Big Wide World

Pegasus

Pepito's Dream

Pete Seeger's Family Concert

Picture Book of Martin Luther King, Jr., A

Piggy Banks to Money Markets

Pigs (plus David's Father)

Pinocchio (Rabbit Ears)

Princess Scargo and the Birthday Pumpkin

Puss in Boots (Rabbit Ears)

Rainbow of My Own, A

Rainy Day Games

Rainy Day Magic Show

Ramona

Ramona: Goodbye, Hello

Ramona: Great Hair Argument

Ramona: New Pajamas

Ramona: The Patient

Ramona: Perfect Day and Bad Day

Ramona: Rainy Sunday

Ramona: Ramona's Bad Day

Ramona: Siblingitis

Ramona: Squeakerfoot and Goodbye, Hello

Reach for the Sky

Real Story of Baa Baa Black Sheep, The

Real Story of Happy Birthday to You, The

Real Story of I'm a Little Teapot, The

Real Story of Itsy Bitsy Spider, The

Real Story of Rain, Rain Go Away, The

Real Story of Three Little Kittens, The

Real Story of Twinkle Twinkle Little Star, The

Real Story Videos Series, The

Red Shoes, The (Animation)

Reluctant Dragon, The

Rights from the Heart/Droits au Coeur

Robert McCloskey Library

Roxaboxen

Runaway Ralph

Rupert

Rupert and the Frog Song

Rupert and the Runaway Dragon

Ruth Heller's Nature Stories

Sammy and Other Songs from Getting to Know Myself

Sand Castle, The

Savior Is Born, The (Rabbit Ears)

Science Primer

Science Primer Series

Science Primer: Earth, Air, Water, Fire

Science Primer: The Five Senses

Science Primer: Habitats

Seasons and Holidays Around the World

Seasons and Holidays Around the World: Chinese New Year

Seasons and Holidays Around the World: Christmas in Mexico

Seasons and Holidays Around the World: Christmas in Sweden

Seasons and Holidays Around the World: Halloween in Britain

Secret Garden, The (A. Holland)

Secret Garden, The (BBC)

Secret Garden, The (MGM)

See How They Grow

See How They Grow: Farm Animals

See How They Grow: Insects and Spiders

See How They Grow: Pets

See How They Grow: Wild Animals

Sesame Street: Plaza Sesamo

Sesame Street: Plaza Sesamo: De Compamento Con Montoya: Big Bird Goes Camping

Sesame Street: Plaza Sesamo: El Alfabeto De Montoya: Learn the Alphabet with Bert and Ernie

Sesame Street: Plaza Sesamo: Plaza Sesamo Canta: Favorite Songs From Past Shows

Sesame Street: Plaza Sesamo: The Plaza Sesamo Complete Set

Sesame Street: Plaza Sesamo: Vamos a Imaginar: Learn About Sounds and Shapes

Sesame Street: Plaza Sesamo: Viaja Con Nosotros: Big Bird and Oscar Go to Venezuela and Mexico

Sesame Street Home Video Visits: The Firehouse

Sesame Street Home Video Visits: The Hospital

Sesame Street Specials: Big Bird in China

Sesame Street Specials: Big Bird in Japan

Sesame Street Specials: Celebrates Around the World

Sesame Street Specials: Christmas Eve on Sesame Street

Sesame Street Specials: Don't Eat the Pictures — Sesame Street Visits the Museum of Art

Sesame Street Specials: Sesame Street's 25th Birthday: A Musical Celebration

Shalom Sesame

Shalom Sesame: Aleph-Bet Telethon

Shalom Sesame: Chanukah

Shalom Sesame: Jerusalem

Shalom Sesame: Journey to Secret Places

Shalom Sesame: Kibbutz

Shalom Sesame: Kids Sing Israel

Shalom Sesame: Land of Israel

Shalom Sesame: Passover

Shalom Sesame: People of Israel

Shalom Sesame: Sing Around the Seasons

Shalom Sesame: Tel Aviv

Shamu & You Series

Shamu & You: Exploring the World of Birds

Shamu & You: Exploring the World of Fish

Shamu & You: Exploring the World of Mammals

Shamu & You: Exploring the World of Reptiles

Shari Lewis: 101 Things for Kids to Do

Shari Lewis: Kooky Classics

Shari Lewis: Don't Wake Your Mom

Shari Lewis: Lamb Chop in the Land of No Manners

Shari Lewis: Lamb Chop's Play Along

Shari Lewis: You Can Do It!

Shari's Christmas Concert

Shelley Duvall's Bedtime Stories: Elizabeth and Larry/ Bill and Pete

Shelley Duvall's Bedtime Stories: The Little Rabbit Who Wanted Red Wings

Shelley Duvall's Bedtime Stories: Moe the Dog in Tropical Paradise

Shelley Duvall Presents Mrs. Piggle-Wiggle

Shelley Duvall Presents Mrs. Piggle-Wiggle: The Answer Backer Cure and The Chores Cure

Shelley Duvall Presents Mrs. Piggle-Wiggle: The Not-Truthful Cure and The Radish Cure

Shelley Duvall Presents Mrs. Piggle-Wiggle: The Pet Forgetters Cure and The Never-Want-To-Go-To-Bedders Cure

Shelley Duvall's Bedtime Stories: Aunt Ippy's Museum of Junk

Sign Songs: Fun Songs to Sign and Sing

Sign-Me-A-Story

Silly Tales and Tunes

Simon the Lamb

Simply Magic: Episode 2

Simply Magic: The Rainy Day Adventure

Skating Safe for Kids

Smile for Auntie and Other Stories

Snowman, The

Sojourner Truth (1797-1883) — Abolitionist Leader

Song of Sacajawea (Rabbit Ears)

Spanish Club: Fiesta!

Spanish Club: Los Animales!

Sparky's Magic Piano

Speeches of Martin Luther King, Jr., The

Spirits of the Rainforest

Spoonbill Swamp

Spot

Spot's Adventure — French

Spot's Adventure — German

Spot's Adventure — Spanish

Spot's First Video — French

Spot's First Video — German

Spot's First Video — Spanish

Squiggles, Dots and Lines

Story of the Dancing Frog

Strega Nonna and Other Stories

Sun, the Wind and the Rain, The

Tadpole and the Whale

Talking Eggs, The

Tall Tales: Darlin' Clementine

Teddy Bear's Picnic, The

Teddy Bears' Jamboree

There Goes a Bulldozer

There Goes a Fire Truck

There Goes a Police Car

There Goes a Train

There Goes a Truck

There's a Cricket in the Library

Thirteen Moons on Turtle's Back

This Pretty Planet

Thunder Cake

Tickle Tune Typhoon: Let's Be Friends

Tinka's Planet

To Bathe a Boa

Today Was a Terrible Day

Tommy Tricker and the Stamp Traveller

Treasury of Children's Stories: Stories to Help Us Grow

'Twas the Night Before Christmas

Velveteen Rabbit, The (Christopher Plummer)

Velveteen Rabbit, The (Rabbit Ears)

Vincent and Me

Walk in the Wild, A

Walking on Air

Way to Start a Day, The

We Learn About the World: English Version

We Learn About the World: Spanish Version

Where in the World/ Kids Explore

Where in the World/ Kids Explore: Volume 1. Kids Explore Mexico

Where in the World/ Kids Explore: Volume 2. Kids Explore Alaska

Where in the World/ Kids Explore: Volume 3. Kids Explore Kenya

Where in the World/ Kids Explore: Volume 4. Kids Explore America's National Parks

White Cat, The (Rabbit Ears)

Why the Sun and the Moon Live in the Sky

Wild Christmas Reindeer, The

Wildlife Symphony

Winnie the Pooh

Winnie the Pooh and the Blustery Day

Winnie the Pooh and a Day for Eeyore

Winnie the Pooh and the Honey Tree

Winnie the Pooh and Tigger Too

Winnie the Pooh/ The New Adventures (Series/Walt Disney)

Winnie the Pooh/ The New Adventures Volume 1. The Great Honey Pot Robbery

Winnie the Pooh/ The New Adventures Volume 2. The Wishing Bear

Winnie the Pooh/ The New Adventures Volume 3. Newfound Friends

Wish That Changed Christmas, The

World Alive, A

Worlds Below, The

You Can Choose!/Series

You Can Choose!: Volume 1. Cooperation

You Can Choose!: Volume 2. Being Responsible

You Can Choose!: Volume 3. Dealing with Feelings

You Can Choose!: Volume 4. Saying No

You Can Choose!: Volume 5. Doing the Right Thing

You Can Choose!: Volume 6. Dealing with Disappointment

You Can Choose!: Volume 7. Appreciating Yourself

You Can Choose!: Volume 8. Asking for Help

You Can Choose!: Volume 9. Being Friends

You Can Choose!: Volume 10. Resolving Conflicts

"You Can" Video Series

You Can Fly a Kite

You Can Ride a Horse

You On Kazoo!

Zillions TV: A Kid's Guide to Toys and Games

Zoobilee Zoo

Zoobilee Zoo: Blue Ribbon Zooble and Other Stories

Zoobilee Zoo: Lady Whazzat and Other Stories

Zoobilee Zoo: Laughland and Other Stories

Zoobilee Zoo: Zoobadoobas and Other Stories

Zoobilee Zoo: Zooble Hop and Other Stories

Intermediate grades: ages 10 - 12 (grades 4-6)

Abigail Adams (1744-1818) — Women's Rights Advocate

Abuela's Weave

Alice Walker (1944-Present) — Author

Amazing Things, Volume 1

Amazing Things, Volume 2

Amelia Earhart (1897-Disappeared in 1937) — Aviator

American Women of Achievement

American Women of Achievement Video Collection

Anansi (Rabbit Ears)

And the Children Shall Lead

Animals Are Beautiful People

Anne of Green Gables

Annie Oakley (Rabbit Ears)

Art Lessons for Children

Art Lessons for Children Volume 1: Easy Watercolor Techniques

Art Lessons for Children Volume 2: Easy Art Projects

Art Lessons for Children Volume 3: More Fun with Watercolors

Art Lessons for Children Volume 4: Felt Pen Fun

Art Lessons for Children Volume 5: Animals of the Rain Forest

Art Lessons for Children Volume 6: Plants of the Rain Forest

Astronomy 101: A Family Adventure

At Home in the Coral Reef

Baby-Sitters Club Videos

Baby-Sitters Club, The: The Baby-Sitters and the Boy Sitters

Baby-Sitters Club, The: The Baby-Sitters Remember

Baby-Sitters Club, The: Christmas Special (1991)

Baby-Sitters Club, The: Claudia and the Missing Jewels

Baby-Sitters Club, The: Claudia and the Mystery of the Secret Passage

Baby-Sitters Club, The: Dawn and the Dream Boy

Baby-Sitters Club, The: Dawn and the Haunted House

Baby-Sitters Club, The: Dawn Saves the Trees

Baby-Sitters Club, The: Jessi and the Mystery of the Stolen Secrets

Baby-Sitters Club, The: Kristy and the Great Campaign

Baby-Sitters Club, The: Mary Ann and the Brunettes (1990)

Baby-Sitters Club, The: Stacey Takes a Stand

Baby-Sitters Club, The: Stacey's Big Break

Bach and Broccoli

Ballet Shoes

Barry's Scrapbook: A Window into Art

Beethoven Lives Upstairs

Best of Beakman's World, The

Bill Nye the Science Guy

Bill Nye: Dinosaurs/Those Big Boneheads

Bill Nye: The Human body/ The Inside Scoop

Bill Nye: Outer Space/Way Out There

Boy Who Loved Trolls, The

Brave Little Toaster, The

Brer Rabbit and the Wonderful Tar Baby (Rabbit Ears)

Bubbe's Boarding House Series

Caribbean Kids: English Version

Caribbean Kids: Spanish Version

Chanter Pour S'Amuser

Chanter Pour S'Amuser Set

Chanter Pour S'Amuser: L'Album de Marie-Soleil

Chanter Pour S'Amuser: Une Journee Avec Marie-Soleil

Chanuka at Bubbe's

Cherries and Cherry Pits

Chicken Sunday

Child's Christmas in Wales, A

Clara Barton (1821-1912) — Founder, American Red Cross

Creative Movement: A Step Towards Intelligence

Cri Cri: El Grillito Cantor

Daisy-Head Mayzie

Dan Crow's Oops!

Dancing with the Indians

Divorce Can Happen to the Nicest People

Dog Who Stopped the War, The

Dr. Seuss Video Festival

Dr. Seuss Videos

Dr. Seuss: The Butter Battle Book

Dr. Seuss: The Cat in the Hat Comes Back

Dr. Seuss: Green Eggs and Ham

Dr. Seuss: HooberBloob Highway

Dr. Seuss: Horton Hatches the Egg

Dr. Seuss: Horton Hears a Who

Dr. Seuss: How the Grinch Stole Christmas

Dr. Seuss: The Lorax

Dr. Seuss: Pontoffel Pock

Dr. Seuss' Cat in the Hat

Drug Free Kids

Emily Dickinson (1830-1890) — Poet

Emperor and Nightingale (Rabbit Ears)

Emperor's New Clothes (Rabbit Ears)

Family Farm

Fingermouse, Yoffy and Friends

Finn McCoul (Rabbit Ears)

Fire and Rescue

First and Second Grade Feelings

First and Second Grade Feelings: First and Second Grade Feelings Set

First and Second Grade Feelings: Jim's Dog, Muffins

First and Second Grade Feelings: The Real Skin Rubber Monster Mask

First and Second Grade Feelings: See You in Second Grade!

First and Second Grade Feelings: So What?

Folk Games

Follow the Drinking Gourd (Rabbit Ears)

Fun in a Box Volume 3: The Birthday Movie

Gateway to the Mind

Gift of Amazing Grace, The

Gift of the Whales

Gingerbread Christmas, A (Rabbit Ears)

Gingham Dog and the Calico Cat, The (Rabbit Ears)

Good Morning Miss Toliver

Gryphon

Harriet Tubman (1820-1913) — Anti-Slavery Activist

Hawk, I'm Your Brother

Helen Keller (1880-1968) — Humanitarian

Hideaways, The

Hoboken Chicken Emergency

Holidays for Children Video Series

Holidays for Children Video Series: 12-Tape Set

Holidays for Children Video Series: Arbor Day

Holidays for Children Video Series: Chinese New Year

Holidays for Children Video Series: Cinco De Mayo

Holidays for Children Video Series: Easter

Holidays for Children Video Series: Halloween

Holidays for Children Video Series: Hanukkah/Passover

Holidays for Children Video Series: Independence Day

Holidays for Children Video Series: Kwanzaa

Holidays for Children Video Series: Rosh Hashanah/Yom Kippur

Holidays for Children Video Series: Thanksgiving

Holidays for Children Video Series: Valentine's Day

How the Leopard Got His Spots (Rabbit Ears)

How to Hide a Butterfly and Other Insects

How to Hide a Crocodile and Other Reptiles

How to Hide a Gray Treefrog and Other Amphibians

How to Hide a Polar Bear and Other Mammals

How to Hide a WhipPoorWill and Other Birds

How to Hide an Octopus and Other Sea Creatures

How to Hide Stories

How to Hide Stories 6-Tape Set

Human Race Club/Series

Human Race Club: A Story About Fights between Brothers and Sisters

Human Race Club: A Story About Making Friends, A Story About Prejudice and Discrimination

Human Race Club: A Story About Self-Esteem

I Dig Fossils

I Want to Be an Artist When I Grow Up

Imaginaria: A Computer Animation Music Video for Children

In the Company of Whales

Indoor Fun

Introducing: The Flying Fruit Fly Circus

Ira Says Goodbye

Ira Sleeps Over

It's Not Always Easy Being a Kid

Jack and the Beanstalk (Faerie Tale Theatre)

Jack and the Beanstalk (Rabbit Ears)

Jacob Have I Loved (Amanda Plummer)

Jacob Have I Loved (Bridget Fonda)

Jane Addams (1860-1935) — Social Worker

Janey Junkfood's Fresh Adventure

Jay O'Callahan: Herman & Marguerite

Jay O'Callahan: A Master Class in Storytelling

Jay O'Callahan: Six Stories About Little Heroes

Jazz Time Tale

Jessi Sings Songs from Around the World

Joan Baez (1941-Present) — Mexican American Folksinger

John Henry (Rabbit Ears)

Johnny Appleseed (Rabbit Ears)

Joshua's Masai Mask

Juggle Time

Jumanji

Kids Get Cooking: The Egg

Kids Kitchen: Making Good Eating Great Fun for Kids!

King Midas and the Golden Touch

Knots on a Counting Rope

Koi and the Kola Nuts (Rabbit Ears)

Language Stories

Language Stories: A Cache of Jewels and Other Collective Nouns

Language Stories: Kites Sail High

Language Stories: Language Stories Set

Language Stories: Many Luscious Lollipops

Language Stories: Merry GoRound

Let's Create Art Activities

Let's Get a Move On!

Lights: The Miracle of Chanukah

Linnea in Monet's Garden

Lion and the Lamb, The (Rabbit Ears)

Lion, the Witch, and the Wardrobe, The (Animated)

Lion, the Witch, and the Wardrobe, The (Live action)

Living and Working in Space: The Countdown Has Begun

Look Around Endangered Animals, A

Look What I Found

Look What I Grew

Look What I Made

Madame C.J. Walker (1867-1919) — Entrepreneur

Madeline

Madeline (Christopher Plummer)

Madeline and the Dog Show

Madeline and the Easter Bonnet

Madeline and the Toy Factory

Madeline at Cooking School

Madeline in London

Madeline's Christmas

Madeline's Rescue and Other Stories About Madeline

Madre Tierra

Magic Thinking Cap, The

Magic School Bus

Magic School Bus, The: For Lunch

Magic School Bus, The: Gets Eaten

Magic School Bus, The: Gets Lost in Space

Magic School Bus, The: Hops Home

Magic School Bus, The: Inside Ralphie

Magical Coqui Puerto Rico Mi Tierra

Making Music with Children

Making Music with Children: Program 2. Making Music with Children: Ages 7-11

Making Music with Children: Program 4. Making Music in the Classroom: Ages 7-11 Marian Anderson (1902-1993) — Singer

Maricela

Mary McLeod Bethune (1875-1955) — Educator

Mary Poppins

Math...Who Needs It?

Mathnet/ The Case of the Unnatural

Mighty Pawns, The

Monkey People, The (Rabbit Ears)

Mose the Fireman (Rabbit Ears)

Mouse and the Motorcycle, The

Multicultural Peoples of North America Video Series

Multicultural Peoples of North America Video Series 15 Volume Set

Multicultural Peoples of North America: African Americans

Multicultural Peoples of North America: The Amish

Multicultural Peoples of North America: Arab Americans

Multicultural Peoples of North America: Central Americans

Multicultural Peoples of North America: Chinese Americans

Multicultural Peoples of North America: German Americans

Multicultural Peoples of North America: Greek Americans

Multicultural Peoples of North America: Irish Americans

Multicultural Peoples of North America: Italian Americans

Multicultural Peoples of North America: Japanese Americans

Multicultural Peoples of North America: Jewish Americans

Multicultural Peoples of North America: Korean Americans

Multicultural Peoples of North America: Mexican Americans

Multicultural Peoples of North America: Polish Americans

Multicultural Peoples of North America: Puerto Ricans

Music and Magic

My Friend Walter

National Geographic Kids Videos

National Geographic Kids Videos: Adventures in Asia

National Geographic Kids Videos: Amazing North America

National Geographic Kids Videos: Deep Sea Dive

National Geographic Kids Videos: Swinging Safari

National Geographic Kids Videos: Totally Tropical Rainforest

National Geographic Kids Videos: Wonders Down Under

Native Indian Folklore

Night Before Christmas, The (Rabbit Ears)

Noah and the Ark (Rabbit Ears)

Noah's Ark

Orca Whales and Mermaid Tales

Other Way to Listen, The

Passover at Bubbe's

Paul Bunyan (Rabbit Ears)

Pecos Bill (Rabbit Ears)

Pegasus

Pepito's Dream

Pete Seeger's Family Concert

Picture Book of Martin Luther King, Jr., A

Piggy Banks to Money Markets

Pinocchio (Rabbit Ears)

Pollyanna (BBC)

Princess Scargo and the Birthday Pumpkin

Puss in Boots (Rabbit Ears)

Rainy Day Magic Show

Ramona

Ramona: Goodbye, Hello

Ramona: Great Hair Argument

Ramona: New Pajamas

Ramona: The Patient

Ramona: Perfect Day and Bad Day

Ramona: Rainy Sunday

Ramona: Ramona's Bad Day

Ramona: Siblingitis

Ramona: Squeakerfoot and Goodbye, Hello

Reach for the Sky

Red Shoes, The (Animation)

Rights from the Heart/Droits au Coeur

Runaway Ralph

Ruth Heller's Nature Stories

Sand Castle, The

Sandra Day O'Connor (1930-Present) — Supreme Court Justice

Savior Is Born, The (Rabbit Ears)

Say No to Drugs!

Seasons and Holidays Around the World

Seasons and Holidays Around the World: Chinese New Year

Seasons and Holidays Around the World: Christmas in Mexico

Seasons and Holidays Around the World: Christmas in Sweden

Seasons and Holidays Around the World: Halloween in Britain

Secret Garden, The (Agnieszka Holland)

Secret Garden, The (BBC)

Secret Garden, The (MGM)

Shalom Sesame

Shalom Sesame: Aleph-Bet Telethon

Shalom Sesame: Chanukah

Shalom Sesame: Jerusalem

Shalom Sesame: Journey to Secret Places

Shalom Sesame: Kibbutz

Shalom Sesame: Kids Sing Israel

Shalom Sesame: Land of Israel

Shalom Sesame: Passover

Shalom Sesame: People of Israel

Shalom Sesame: Sing Around the Seasons

Shalom Sesame: Tel Aviv

Shamu & You Series

Shamu & You: Exploring the World of Birds

Shamu & You: Exploring the World of Fish

Shamu & You: Exploring the World of Mammals

Shamu & You: Exploring the World of Reptiles

Shelley Duvall's Bedtime Stories: Elizabeth and Larry/ Bill and Pete

Shelley Duvall's Bedtime Stories: Moe the Dog in Tropical Paradise

Shelley Duvall Presents Mrs. Piggle-Wiggle

Shelley Duvall Presents Mrs. Piggle-Wiggle: The Answer Backer Cure and The Chores Cure

Shelley Duvall Presents Mrs. Piggle-Wiggle: The Not-Truthful Cure and The Radish Cure

Shelley Duvall Presents Mrs. Piggle-Wiggle: The Pet Forgetters Cure and The Never-Want-To-Go-To-Bedders Cure

Shelley Duvall's Bedtime Stories: Aunt Ippy's Museum of Junk

Sign-Me-A-Story

Skating Safe for Kids

Sojourner Truth (1797-1883) — Abolitionist Leader

Song of Sacajawea (Rabbit Ears)

Speeches of Martin Luther King, Jr., The

Spirits of the Rainforest

Squiggles, Dots and Lines

Story of the Dancing Frog

Susan B. Anthony (1820-1906) — Woman Suffragist

Sweet 15

Tadpole and the Whale

Talking Eggs, The

Tall Tales: Darlin' Clementine

There's a Cricket in the Library

Thirteen Moons on Turtle's Back

This Pretty Planet

Thunder Cake

Tinka's Planet

Tommy Tricker and the Stamp Traveller

'Twas the Night Before Christmas

Vincent and Me

Walk in the Wild, A

Walking on Air

Way to Start a Day, The

Where in the World/ Kids Explore

Where in the World/ Kids Explore: Volume 1. Kids Explore Mexico

Where in the World/ Kids Explore: Volume 2. Kids Explore Alaska

Where in the World/ Kids Explore: Volume 3. Kids Explore Kenya

Where in the World/ Kids Explore: Volume 4. Kids Explore America's National Parks

White Cat, The (Rabbit Ears)

Why the Sun and the Moon Live in the Sky

Wildlife Symphony

Wilma Rudolph (1940-Present) — Champion Athlete

Woman's Place, A

World Alive, A

Worlds Below, The

You Can Choose!/Series

You Can Choose!: Volume 1. Cooperation

You Can Choose!: Volume 3. Dealing with Feelings

You Can Choose!: Volume 4. Saying No

You Can Choose!: Volume 5. Doing the Right Thing

You Can Choose!: Volume 6. Dealing with Disappointment

You Can Choose!: Volume 7. Appreciating Yourself

You Can Choose!: Volume 8. Asking for Help

You Can Choose!: Volume 9. Being Friends

You Can Choose!: Volume 10. Resolving Conflicts

You Must Remember This

Zillions TV: A Kid's Guide to Toys and Games

Age Index

Listing of Subject Areas

Activities, Indoor Fun and Rainy Day Fun

Adventure

Africa and African Culture

African American Culture

Alphabet Videos

Amish Culture

Animals: Pets, Wild Animals, Farm Animals, Dinosaurs, Animal Stories

Anorexia

Arab American Culture

Arbor Day

Archeology

Art and Art Activities

Astronomy

Australia and Australian Culture

Authors and Illustrators — Documentaries on Makers of Children's Books and Videos

Bedtime Videos

Bible Stories

Biography

Birthday Videos

Book-Based

Canadian and French Canadian Culture

Careers

Chanukah

Children's Television Workshop and Muppet Videos

Chinese Culture, Chinese New Year and China

Christmas

Cinco de Mayo

Circus

City Life

Conflict Resolution and Cooperation

Construction

Consumer Education

Czech Videos

Dance and Creative Movement

Dating

Death

Disabilities

Divorce

Dr. Martin Luther King, Jr./Dr. Martin Luther King, Jr. Day

Dr. Seuss Videos

Drug Education

Earth Science, Ecology, Environment

Easter

English Videos and English Culture

Family Relationships

　　Videos Featuring Aunts and Uncles

　　Videos Featuring Cousins

　　Videos Featuring Grandparents

　　Videos Featuring Parents

　　Videos Featuring Siblings

Farm Life/Country Life

Feelings

Fire Safety

Folk Games and Folk Songs

Food and Cooking

Fourth of July/Independence Day

French Language and Folktales

Friendship

Gardening

German Language and German American Culture

Girls — Great Videos Featuring Girls

Greek American Culture and Greek Mythology

Growing Up

Halloween

Health & Safety

Hebrew Language

Hospital Stays

Independence Day/ Fourth of July

India and Indian Culture

Irish and Irish American Culture

Italian Videos, Italian and Italian American Culture, Folktales

Japanese Videos, Japanese and Japanese American Culture, Tales

Jewish Videos, Jewish and Jewish American Culture, Holidays

Juggling

Korean American Culture

Kwanzaa

Latin American, Caribbean and Hispanic Culture

Magic

Manners

Math and Numbers

Money Management

Moving To a New Home

Mr. Rogers Videos

Music: Sing-Alongs, Instruction, Making Music, Videos About Music

Mystery

Native American Culture

New Year's Eve

Non-Verbal (Videos Without Words)

Party Videos

Passover (Pesach)

Poetry and RhymesPolish American Culture

Polish American Culture

Prejudice and Discrimination

Purim

Quinceanera

Rabbit Ears Video Series

Reading/Pre-Reading, Writing and Concepts

Rosh Hashanah

Russian American Culture

Science

Seasons of the Year, Senses)

Seasons of the Year

Self-Image and Self-Esteem

Senses: Sight, Hearing, Taste, Smell, Touch

Sign Language

Skills For Living

Space

Sports

Starting School

Stories, Tales and Folk Tales

Stranger Danger

Sukkot

Swedish Culture

Thanksgiving

Transportation: Trains, Planes, Buses

Tu B'Shvat

Valentine's Day

Values

Westerns

Women's History

WonderWorks Video Series

Workout Videos

Yom Ha'atz Ma'ot

Yom Kippur

Subject Index

Activities, Indoor Fun and Rainy Day Fun (SEE ALSO Dance, Party Videos, Art)

Amazing Things

Amazing Things, Volume 1

Amazing Things, Volume 2

Art Lessons for Children

Art Lessons for Children Volume 1: Easy Watercolor Techniques

Art Lessons for Children Volume 2: Easy Art Projects

Art Lessons for Children Volume 3: More Fun with Watercolors

Art Lessons for Children Volume 4: Felt Pen Fun

Art Lessons for Children Volume 5: Animals of the Rain Forest

Art Lessons for Children Volume 6: Plants of the Rain Forest

Astronomy 101: A Family Adventure

Baby Goes...Songs to Take Along

Baby Songs 1

Baby Songs 2: More Baby Songs

Baby Songs: Even More Baby Songs

Baby Songs Christmas

Baby Songs Presents: Follow Along Songs with Hap Palmer

Baby Songs Presents: John Lithgow's Kid-Size Concert

Baby Songs: Sing Together

Baby Songs: Super Baby Songs

Bill Cosby's Picturepages

Bill Cosby's Picturepages: What Goes Where?

Bill Cosby's Picturepages: What's Different?

Bill Cosby's Picturepages: What's That Shape?

Bill Cosby's Picturepages: What's Missing?

Bill Cosby's Picturepages: Who's Counting?

Clifford's Fun with Letters

Clifford's Fun with Numbers

Clifford's Fun with Opposites

Clifford's Fun with Rhymes

Clifford's Fun with Shapes and Colors

Clifford's Fun with Sounds

Clifford's Sing-A-Long Adventure

Dr. Seuss' ABC

Good Morning, Good Night: A Day on the Farm

Indoor Fun

Jay O'Callahan: A Master Class in Storytelling

Juggle Time

Let's Create Art Activities

Let'sCreate for Pre-Schoolers

Let's Do It! Professor Iris

Look What I Found

Look What I Grew

Making Music with Children

Making Music with Children, Program 1: Making Music with Children: Ages 3-7

Making Music with Children, Program 2: Making Music with Children: Ages 7-11

Making Music with Children, Program 3: Making Music in the Classroom: Ages 3-7

Making Music with Children, Program 4: Making Music in the Classroom: Ages 7-11

More Pre-School Power

Music Mania Professor Iris

My First Activity Series: My First Activity Video

My First Activity Series: My First Cooking Video

My First Activity Series: My First Green Video

My First Activity Series: My First Music Video

My First Activity Series: My First Nature Video

My First Activity Series: My First Science Video

My Sesame Street Home Video: Play-Along Games & Songs

Pre-School Power: Jacket Flips & Other Tips

Pre-School Power #3

Rainy Day Games

Rainy Day Magic Show

Shari Lewis: Don't Wake Your Mom

Shari Lewis: Lamb Chop's Play-Along

Shari Lewis: 101 Things for Kids to Do

Shari Lewis: You Can Do It!

Simply Magic: The Rainy Day Adventure

Simply Magic: Episode 2

Sounds Around

Water Is Wet

Which Way, Weather?

Workout with Daddy & Me

Workout with Mommy & Me

"You Can" Video Series: You Can Ride a Horse

"You Can" Video Series: You Can Fly a Kite

You On Kazoo!

Adventure

Amazing Bone and Other Stories, The

Attic-in-the-Blue

Berenstain Bears and Too Much Birthday and to the Rescue

Boy Who Loved Trolls, The

Brave Little Toaster, The

Doctor De Soto and Other Stories

Dr. Seuss: Pontoffel Pock

Finn McCoul (Rabbit Ears)

Five Stories for the Very Young

Fun in a Box Volume 1: Ben's Dream

Hideaways, The

Hoboken Chicken Emergency

Jumanji

Madeline's Rescue and Other Stories About Madeline

Maurice Sendak Library, The

Mole in Town, The

Mouse and the Motorcycle, The

My Friend Walter

National Velvet

Runaway Ralph

Simply Magic: Episode 2

Story of the Dancing Frog

Tommy Tricker and the Stamp Traveller

Vincent and Me

Where in the World Kids Explore

Where in the World Kids Explore: Volume 1. Kids Explore Mexico

Where in the World Kids Explore: Volume 2. Kids Explore Alaska

Where in the World Kids Explore: Volume 3. Kids Explore Kenya

Where in the World Kids
Explore: Volume 4. Kids
Explore America's
National Parks

Africa and African Culture

Anansi (Rabbit Ears)

Anansi Goes Fishing

Animal Stories (Why
Mosquitoes Buzz in
People's Ears)

Animals Are Beautiful
People

Foolish Frog and Other
Stories (A Story—A Story)

How the Leopard Got His
Spots (Rabbit Ears)

Joshua's Masai Mask

Koi and the Kola Nuts
(Rabbit Ears)

National Geographic Kids
Videos: Swinging Safari

Owl Moon and Other
Stories (Hot Hippo)

Sesame Street Specials:
Sesame Street's 25th
Birthday: A Musical
Celebration

Strega Nonna and Other
Stories (A Story A Story)

Where in the World Kids
Explore: Volume 3. Kids
Explore Kenya

Why the Sun and the
Moon Live in the Sky

African American Culture

African Story Magic

Afro-Classic Folk Tales

Afro-Classic Folk Tales,
Volume 1

Afro-Classic Folk Tales,
Volume 2

Alice Walker (1944-
Present) — Author

American Women of
Achievement: Marian
Anderson (1902-1993) —
Singer

American Women of
Achievement: Susan B.
Anthony (1820-1906) —
Woman Suffragist

American Women of
Achievement: Wilma
Rudolph (1940-Present) —
Champion Athlete

And the Children Shall
Lead

Anansi (Rabbit Ears)

Anansi Goes Fishing

Brer Rabbit and the
Wonderful Tar Baby
(Rabbit Ears)

Clean Your Room, Harvey
Moon!

Corduroy Bear

Dancing with the Indians

Dreadlocks and the Three
Bears

Ella Jenkins: For the
Family

Ella Jenkins Live! At the
Smithsonian

Ezra Jack Keats Library

Follow the Drinking
Gourd (Rabbit Ears)

Fun in a Box Volume 1:
Ben's Dream (Your Feets
Too Big)

Gift of Amazing Grace,
The

Harriet Tubman (1820-
1913) — Anti-Slavery
Activist

Holidays for Children:
Kwanzaa

How the Leopard Got His
Spots (Rabbit Ears)

Jazz Time Tale

John Henry (Rabbit Ears)

Joshua's Masai Mask

Koi and the Kola Nuts
(Rabbit Ears)

Little Lou and His
Strange Little Zoo

Madame C.J. Walker
(1867-1919) —
Entrepreneur

Mary McLeod Bethune
(1875-1955) — Educator

Multicultural Peoples of
North America: African
Americans

Picture Book of Martin
Luther King, Jr., A

Sojourner Truth (1797-
1883) — Abolitionist
Leader

Speeches of Martin
Luther King, Jr., The

Woman's Place, A

You Must Remember This

Alphabet Videos (SEE Reading/Pre-Reading)

Amish Culture

Multicultural Peoples of
North America: The
Amish

Animals: Pets, Wild Animals, Farm Animals, Dinosaurs, Animal Stories

Afro-Classic Folk Tales

Afro-Classic Folk Tales,
Volume 1

Afro-Classic Folk Tales,
Volume 2

Alejandro's Gift

Alphabet Library:
Alphabet Zoo

Amazing Bone and Other
Stories, The

Anansi

Anansi Goes Fishing

Animal Alphabet

Animal Babies in the Wild

Animal Stories

Animals Are Beautiful
People

Are You My Mother?:
English Version

Are You My Mother?:
Spanish Version (Eres Tu
Mi Mama?)

Art Lessons for Children
Volume 5: Animals of the
Rain Forest

At Home in the Coral
Reef: English Version

At Home in the Coral
Reef: Spanish Version

At the Zoo

Baby Animals Just Want
to Have Fun

Baby Animal Fun

Barney and the Backyard
Gang

Barney and the Backyard
Gang: Barney Goes to
School

Barney and the Backyard
Gang: Barney in Concert

Barney and the Backyard
Gang: Barney's Best
Manners

Barney and the Backyard
Gang: Barney's Birthday

Barney and the Backyard
Gang: Barney's Campfire
Sing-Along

Barney and the Backyard
Gang: Barney's
Imagination Island

Barney and the Backyard
Gang: Barney's Home
Sweet Homes

Barney and the Backyard
Gang: Barney's Magical
Musical Adventure

Barney and the Backyard
Gang: Barney's Safety
Video

Barney and the Backyard
Gang: Rock with Barney

Barney and the Backyard
Gang: Waiting for Santa

Beady Bear

Bear Who Slept Through
Christmas, The

Berenstain Bears Videos

Berenstain Bears
Christmas Tree

Berenstain Bears in the
Dark

Berenstain Bears Easter
Surprise

Berenstain Bears Learn
About Strangers

Berenstain Bears and the
Messy Room

Berenstain Bears: No
Girls Allowed and The
Missing Dinosaur Bone

Berenstain Bears and Too
Much Birthday and to the
Rescue

Berenstain Bears and the
Trouble with Friends

Berenstain Bears and the
Truth

Berenstain Bears Get in a
Fight

Best Friends

Best Friends Part I

Best Friends Part II

Bethie's Really Silly
Clubhouse

Biggest Bears

Bill Nye the Science Guy:
Dinosaurs/Those Big
Boneheads

Birthday Dragon

Brer Rabbit and the
Wonderful Tar Baby
(Rabbit Ears)

Bugs Don't Bug Us

Bump — My First Video

Can I Be Good?

Caterpillar's Wish, A

Clifford's Fun with
Letters

Facets Non-Violent, Non-Sexist Children's Video Guide

Clifford's Fun with Numbers

Clifford's Fun with Opposites

Clifford's Fun with Rhymes

Clifford's Fun with Shapes and Colors

Clifford's Fun with Sounds

Clifford's Sing-A-Long Adventure

Corduroy Bear

Creepy Critters Professor Iris

Curious George Videos

Curious George

Curious George: Fun in the Sun

Curious George Goes to Town

Danny and the Dinosaur and Other Stories

Dog Who Had Kittens, The

Dog Who Stopped the War, The

Doing Things: Eating, Washing, in Motion

Dozen Dizzy Dogs, A

Dr. Seuss: The Cat in the Hat Comes Back

Dr. Seuss: Horton Hatches the Egg

Dr. Seuss: Horton Hears a Who

Dr. Seuss' ABC

Dr. Seuss' Cat in the Hat

Dreadlocks and the Three Bears

Emperor and Nightingale (Rabbit Ears)

Ezra Jack Keats Library

First and Second Grade Feelings: Jim's Dog, Muffins

Five Lionni Classics

Follow That Bunny!

Frog and Toad Are Friends

Frog and Toad Together

Fun in a Box Volume 2: New Friends and Other Stories

Gateway to the Mind

Gift of the Whales

The Gingham Dog and the Calico Cat (Rabbit Ears)

Good Morning, Good Night: A Day on the Farm

Hawk, I'm Your Brother

Hip Hop Animal Rock Workout

How to Hide Stories

How to Hide a Butterfly and Other Insects

How to Hide a Crocodile and Other Reptiles

How to Hide a Gray Treefrog and Other Amphibians

How to Hide a Polar Bear and Other Mammals

How to Hide a Whip-Poor-Will and Other Birds

How to Hide an Octopus and Other Sea Creatures

I'm Not Oscar's Friend Anymore and Other Stories

Imaginaria: A Computer Animation Music Video for Children

in the Company of Whales

in the Tall, Tall Grass

Jay O'Callahan: Herman & Marguerite

Kidsongs Music Video Stories: A Day with the Animals

Kidsongs Music Video Stories: If We Could Talk to the Animals

Kitten Companions

Land of Pleasant Dreams, The: Fence Too High, A

Land of Pleasant Dreams, The: Is It Soup Yet?

Lion and the Lamb, The (Rabbit Ears)

Little Duck Tale, A

Little Sister Rabbit

Look Around Endangered Animals, A

Lyle, Lyle Crocodile: The House on East 88th Street

Madeline and the Dog Show

Magic of Discovery, The (The Animal Movie)

Magical Coqui — Puerto Rico — Mi Tierra!

Maurice Sendak Library, The

Meet Your Animal Friends

The Mole and the Green Star

The Mole in Town

Monkey Moves

Move Like the Animals

Mr. Rogers: Dinosaurs & Monsters

National Geographic Kids Videos

National Geographic Kids Videos: Adventures in Asia

National Geographic Kids Videos: Amazing North America

National Geographic Kids Videos: Deep Sea Dive

National Geographic Kids Videos: GeoKids

National Geographic Kids Videos: GeoKids: Bear Cubs, Baby Ducks and Kooky Kookaburras

National Geographic Kids Videos: GeoKids: Cool Cats, Raindrops, and Things That Live in Holes

National Geographic Kids Videos: GeoKids: Flying, Trying and Honking Around

National Geographic Kids Videos: Swinging Safari

National Geographic Kids Videos: Totally Tropical Rainforest

National Geographic Kids Videos: Wonders Down Under

National Velvet

Native Indian Folklore

Opus & Bill: A Wish for Wings That Work

Orca Whales and Mermaid Tales

Owl Moon and Other Stories

Paws, Claws, Feathers and Fins

Peep and the Big Wide World

P.J. Funnybunny

Poky Little Puppy's First Christmas

Puppy Pals

Puss in Boots (Rabbit Ears)

Ramona: Goodbye, Hello

Ramona: Squeakerfoot and Goodbye, Hello

Real Story Videos: The Real Story of Itsy Bitsy Spider

Real Story Videos: The Real Story of Three Little Kittens

Reluctant Dragon

Richard Scarry's Best Busy People Video

Richard Scarry's Best Ever ABC Video

Richard Scarry's Best Counting Video

Richard Scarry's Best Learning Songs Ever

Robert McCloskey Library

Rupert

Rupert and the Frog Song

Rupert and the Runaway Dragon

Ruth Heller's Nature Stories

Sand Castle, The (The Owl & the Lemming)

Science Primer: Habitats

See How They Grow

See How They Grow: Farm Animals

See How They Grow: Insects and Spiders

See How They Grow: Pets

See How They Grow: Wild Animals

Shamu & You: Exploring the World of Birds

Shamu & You: Exploring the World of Fish

Shamu & You: Exploring the World of Mammals

Shamu & You: Exploring the World of Reptiles

Sharon, Lois & Bram's: Elephant Show: Pet Fair

Shelley Duvall's Bedtime Stories: Elizabeth and Larry Bill and Pete

Shelley Duvall's Bedtime Stories: The Little Rabbit Who Wanted Red Wings

Shelley Duvall's Bedtime Stories: Moe the Dog in Tropical Paradise

Simon the Lamb

Spoonbill Swamp

Spot Goes to School

Story of the Dancing Frog

Tadpole and the Whale

Tawny Scrawny Lion's Jungle Tales

Teddy Bear's Picnic, The

To Bathe a Boa

Treasury of Children's Stories: Stories to Help Us Grow

Velveteen Rabbit (Rabbit Ears)

Velveteen Rabbit (Plummer)

A Walk in the Wild

Where's Spot

White Cat, The (Rabbit Ears)

Wild Christmas Reindeer, The

Wildlife Symphony

World Alive, A

Worlds Below, The

"You Can" Video Series: You Can Ride a Horse

Anorexia

The Baby-Sitters Club: Stacey's Big Break

Arab American Culture

Multicultural Peoples of North America: Arab Americans

Arbor Day

Holidays for Children: Arbor Day

Johnny Appleseed (Rabbit Ears)

Archeology

I Dig Fossils

Art and Art Activities

Art Lessons for Children

Art Lessons for Children Volume 1: Easy Watercolor Techniques

Art Lessons for Children Volume 2: Easy Art Projects

Art Lessons for Children Volume 3: More Fun with Watercolors

Art Lessons for Children Volume 4: Felt Pen Fun

Art Lessons for Children Volume 5: Animals of the Rain Forest

Art Lessons for Children Volume 6: Plants of the Rain Forest

Barney and the Backyard Gang: Barney Goes to School

Barry's Scrapbook: A Window into Art

Good Morning Miss Toliver

Hideaways, The

I Want to Be an Artist When I Grow Up

Let'sCreate for Pre-Schoolers

Let's Create Art Activities

Linnea in Monet's Garden

Look What I Made

Sesame Street Specials: Don't Eat the Pictures — Sesame Street Visits the Metropolitan Museum of Art

Squiggles, Dots and Lines

Vincent and Me

You Must Remember This

Astronomy

Astronomy 101: A Family Adventure

Australia and Australian Culture

Introducing: The Flying Fruit Fly Circus

National Geographic Kids Videos: Wonders Down Under

Authors and Illustrators — Documentaries on Makers of Children's Books and Videos

Alice Walker (1944-Present) — Author

American Women of Achievement: Emily Dickinson (1830-1890) — Poet

Daisy-Head Mayzie (The Making of Daisy-Head Mayzie)

Ezra Jack Keats Library (Getting to Know Jack Keats)

Madre Tierra

Maurice Sendak Library, The (Getting to Know Maurice Sendak)

Robert McCloskey Library

Bedtime Videos

Baby's Bedtime

Child of Mine: The Lullaby Video

Dr. Seuss' Sleep Book

Kidsongs Music Video Stories: Good Night, Sleep Tight

Land of Pleasant Dreams, The

Land of Pleasant Dreams, The: Bearly There At All

Land of Pleasant Dreams, The: Fence Too High, A

Land of Pleasant Dreams, The: Is It Soup Yet?

My Sesame Street Home Video: Bedtime Stories & Songs

Sharon, Lois & Bram's: Elephant Show: Sleepover

Shelley Duvall Presents Mrs. Piggle-Wiggle: The Pet Forgetters Cure and The Never-Want-To-Go-To-Bedders Cure

Shelley Duvall's Bedtime Stories: Aunt Ippy's Museum of Junk

Shelley Duvall's Bedtime Stories: Elizabeth and Larry Bill and Pete

Shelley Duvall's Bedtime Stories: Moe the Dog in Tropical Paradise

Smile for Auntie and Other Stories (Wynken, Blynken & Nod)

Something Good (plus Mortimer)

Bible Stories

Gift of Amazing Grace, The

Noah and the Ark (Rabbit Ears)

Noah's Ark (James Earl Jones)

Savior Is Born, The (Rabbit Ears)

Biography

Alice Walker (1944-Present) — Author

American Women of Achievement Video Collection

American Women of Achievement: Abigail Adams (1744-1818) — Women's Rights Advocate

American Women of Achievement: Jane Addams (1860-1935) — Social Worker

American Women of Achievement: Marian Anderson (1902-1993) — Singer

American Women of Achievement: Susan B. Anthony (1820-1906) — Woman Suffragist

American Women of Achievement: Clara Barton (1821-1912) — Founder, American Red Cross

American Women of Achievement: Emily Dickinson (1830-1890) — Poet

American Women of Achievement: Amelia Earhart (1897-Disappeared in 1937) — Aviator

American Women of Achievement: Helen Keller (1880-1968) — Humanitarian

American Women of Achievement: Sandra Day O'Connor (1930-Present) — Supreme Court Justice

American Women of Achievement: Wilma Rudolph (1940-Present) — Champion Athlete

Beethoven Lives Upstairs

Child's Christmas in Wales, A

Ezra Jack Keats Library

Harriet Tubman (1820-1913) — Anti-Slavery Activist

Joan Baez (1941-Present) — Mexican American Folksinger: English

Joan Baez (1941-Present) — Mexican American Folksinger: Spanish

Madame C.J. Walker (1867-1919) — Entrepreneur

Mary McLeod Bethune (1875-1955) — Educator

Picture Book of Martin Luther King, Jr., A

Sojourner Truth (1797-1883) — Abolitionist Leader

Speeches of Martin Luther King, Jr., The

Woman's Place, A

Birthday Videos (SEE Party Videos)

Book-Based (SEE ALSO Poetry and Stories)

Abuela's Weave

Alexander and the Terrible, Horrible, No Good, Very Bad Day

Alejandro's Gift

Amazing Bone and Other Stories, The

Angela's Airplane (plus The Fire Station)

Anna Maria's Blanket

Anansi Goes Fishing

Anne of Green Gables

Are You My Mother?: English Version

Are You My Mother?: Spanish Version (Eres Tu Mi Mama?)

At Home in the Coral Reef: English Version

At Home in the Coral Reef: Spanish Version

Baby's Nursery Rhymes

Ballet Shoes

Beady Bear

Berenstain Bears Videos

Berenstain Bears Christmas Tree

Berenstain Bears in the Dark

Berenstain Bears Easter Surprise

Berenstain Bears Learn About Strangers

Berenstain Bears and the Messy Room

Berenstain Bears: No Girls Allowed and The Missing Dinosaur Bone

Berenstain Bears and Too Much Birthday and to the Rescue

Berenstain Bears and the Trouble with Friends

Berenstain Bears and the Truth

Berenstain Bears Get in a Fight

Boy Who Loved Trolls, The

Cherries and Cherry Pits

Chicken Sunday

Child's Christmas in Wales, A

Clean Your Room, Harvey Moon!

Clifford's Fun with Letters

Clifford's Fun with Numbers

Clifford's Fun with Opposites

Clifford's Fun with Rhymes

Clifford's Fun with Shapes and Colors

Clifford's Fun with Sounds

Clifford's Sing-A-Long Adventure

Cloudy with a Chance of Meatballs

Curious George Videos

Curious George

Curious George: Fun in the Sun

Curious George Goes to Town

Daisy-Head Mayzie

Dancing with the Indians

Danny and the Dinosaur and Other Stories

Doctor De Soto and Other Stories

Dog Who Had Kittens, The

Dr. Seuss Video Festival

Dr. Seuss Videos

Dr. Seuss: The Cat in the Hat Comes Back

Dr. Seuss: Green Eggs and Ham

Dr. Seuss: Hoober-Bloob Highway

Dr. Seuss: Hop on Pop

Dr. Seuss: Horton Hatches the Egg

Dr. Seuss: Horton Hears a Who

Dr. Seuss: How the Grinch Stole Christmas

Dr. Seuss: I Am NOT Going to Get Up Today!

Dr. Seuss: The Lorax

Dr. Seuss: One Fish Two Fish Red Fish Blue Fish: English Version

Dr. Seuss: One Fish Two Fish Red Fish Blue Fish: Spanish Version, Un Pez Dos Peces Pez Rojo Pez Azul

Dr. Seuss: Pontoffel Pock

Dr. Seuss' ABC

Dr. Seuss: The Butter Battle Book

Dr. Seuss' Cat in the Hat

Dr. Seuss' Sleep Book

Emperor and Nightingale (Rabbit Ears)

Empty Pot, The

Ezra Jack Keats Library

Family Farm

50 Below Zero (plus Thomas' Snowsuit)

First and Second Grade Feelings

First and Second Grade Feelings: Jim's Dog, Muffins.

First and Second Grade Feelings: The Real-Skin Rubber Monster Mask

First and Second Grade Feelings: See You in Second Grade!

First and Second Grade Feelings: So What?

Five Lionni Classics

Five Stories for the Very Young

Foolish Frog and Other Stories

Frog and Toad Are Friends

Frog and Toad Together

Fun in a Box Volume 1: Ben's Dream

Fun in a Box Volume 2: New Friends and Other Stories

Get Ready for School

Granpa

Gryphon

Harold and the Purple Crayon

Hideaways, The

Hoboken Chicken Emergency

Human Race Club: A Story About Fights between Brothers and Sisters

Human Race Club: A Story About Making Friends, A Story About Prejudice and Discrimination

Human Race Club: A Story About Self-Esteem

I'm Not Oscar's Friend Anymore and Other Stories

Ira Sleeps Over

Ira Says Goodbye

Jack and the Beanstalk (Rabbit Ears)

Jack and the Beanstalk (Faerie Tale Theatre)

Jacob Have I Loved (Bridget Fonda)

Jacob Have I Loved (Amanda Plummer)

Josephine's Imagination

Joshua's Masai Mask

Jumanji

Just Me and My Dad

Just Grandma and Me

Knots on a Counting Rope

Linnea in Monet's Garden

Lion, the Witch, and the Wardrobe, The (Animated)

Lion, the Witch, and the Wardrobe, The (live action)

Little Crooked Christmas Tree, The

Little Engine That Could, The: English Narration

Little Engine That Could, The: French Narration

Little Engine That Could, The: Spanish Narration

Little Lou and His Strange Little Zoo

Lyle, Lyle Crocodile: The House on East 88th Street

Madame C.J. Walker (1867-1919) — Entrepreneur

Madeline

Madeline (Christopher Plummer)

Madeline and the Dog Show

Madeline and the Easter Bonnet

Madeline and the Toy Factory

Madeline at Cooking School

Madeline in London

Madeline's Christmas

Madeline's Rescue and Other Stories About Madeline

Magic School Bus

The Magic School Bus: For Lunch

The Magic School Bus: Gets Eaten

The Magic School Bus: Gets Lost in Space

The Magic School Bus: Hops Home

The Magic School Bus: Inside Ralphie

Mary McLeod Bethune (1875-1955) — Educator

Maurice Sendak Library, The

Max's Chocolate Chicken and Other Stories for Young Children

Mike Mulligan and His Steam Shovel

Moira's Birthday (plus Blackberry Subway Jam)

Mommy's Office

Mop Top

Morris the Moose: Goes to School/Gets a Cold

Mouse and the Motorcycle, The

Multicultural Peoples of North America Video Series 15 Volume Set

Multicultural Peoples of North America: African Americans

Multicultural Peoples of North America: The Amish

Multicultural Peoples of North America: Arab Americans

Multicultural Peoples of North America: Central Americans

Multicultural Peoples of North America: Chinese Americans

Multicultural Peoples of North America: German Americans

Multicultural Peoples of North America: Greek Americans

Multicultural Peoples of North America: Irish Americans

Multicultural Peoples of North America: Italian Americans

Multicultural Peoples of North America: Japanese Americans

Multicultural Peoples of North America: Jewish Americans

Multicultural Peoples of North America: Korean Americans

Multicultural Peoples of North America: Mexican Americans

Multicultural Peoples of North America: Polish Americans

Multicultural Peoples of North America: Puerto Ricans

Murmel, Murmel, Murmel (plus The Boy in the Drawer)

My First Activity Series: My First Activity Video

My First Activity Series: My First Cooking Video

My First Activity Series: My First Green Video

My First Activity Series: My First Music Video

My First Activity Series: My First Nature Video

My First Activity Series: My First Science Video

My Friend Walter

New Friends and Other Stories

Noah's Ark (James Earl Jones)

Norman the Doorman and Other Stories

Opus n' Bill: A Wish for Wings That Work

Owl Moon and Other Stories

Pepito's Dream

Picture Book of Martin Luther King, Jr., A

Pinocchio (Rabbit Ears)

Poky Little Puppy's First Christmas

Poky's Favorite Stories

Pollyanna (BBC)

Rainbow of My Own, A

Ramona

Ramona: Goodbye, Hello

Ramona: Great Hair Argument

Ramona: New Pajamas

Ramona: The Patient

Ramona: Perfect Day and Bad Day

Ramona: Rainy Sunday

Ramona: Ramona's Bad Day

Ramona: Siblingitis

Ramona: Squeakerfoot and Goodbye, Hello

Red Shoes, The (Animation)

Richard Scarry's Best Busy People Video

Richard Scarry's Best Ever ABC Video

Richard Scarry's Best Counting Video

Richard Scarry's Best Learning Songs Ever

Robert McCloskey Library

Roxaboxen

Runaway Ralph

Scuffy the Tugboat and Friends

Secret Garden, The (Agnieszka Holland)

Secret Garden, The (BBC)

Secret Garden, The (MGM)

See How They Grow

See How They Grow: Farm Animals

See How They Grow: Insects and Spiders

See How They Grow: Pets

See How They Grow: Wild Animals

Shelley Duvall's Bedtime Stories: Aunt Ippy's Museum of Junk

Shelley Duvall's Bedtime Stories: Elizabeth and Larry Bill and Pete

Shelley Duvall's Bedtime Stories: Moe the Dog in Tropical Paradise

Shelley Duvall's Bedtime Stories: The Little Rabbit Who Wanted Red Wings

Snowman, The

Sojourner Truth (1797-1883) — Abolitionist Leader

Something Good (plus Mortimer)

Spoonbill Swamp

Spot Goes to School

Story of the Dancing Frog

Strega Nonna and Other Stories

Talking Eggs, The

Tawny Scrawny Lion's Jungle Tales

Thomas the Tank Engine & Friends

Thomas the Tank Engine & Friends: Better Late Than Never and Other Stories

Thomas the Tank Engine & Friends: Christmas Party

Thomas the Tank Engine & Friends: James Learns a Lesson & Other Stories

Thomas the Tank Engine & Friends: Percy's Ghostly & Other Stories

Thomas the Tank Engine & Friends: Tenders & Turntables & Other Stories

Thomas the Tank Engine & Friends: Thomas Breaks the Rules & Other Stories

Thomas the Tank Engine & Friends: Thomas Gets Bumped

Thomas the Tank Engine & Friends: Thomas Gets Tricked & Other Stories

Thomas the Tank Engine & Friends: Trust Thomas & Other Stories

Thunder Cake

To Bathe a Boa

Today Was a Terrible Day

Velveteen Rabbit (Rabbit Ears)

Velveteen Rabbit (Plummer)

Vincent and Me

A Walk in the Wild

Walking on Air

Way to Start a Day, The

Wee Sing in Sillyville

Wee Sing Together

Wee Sing Train

Wee Sing: Grandpa's Magical Toys

Where's Spot

Why the Sun and the Moon Live in the Sky

Wild Christmas Reindeer, The

Winnie the Pooh

Winnie the Pooh and the Blustery Day

Winnie the Pooh and a Day for Eeyore

Winnie the Pooh and the Honey Tree

Winnie the Pooh and Tigger Too

Winnie the Pooh: Making Friends, Learning

Winnie the Pooh The New Adventures: Volume 1. The Great Honey Pot Robbery

Winnie the Pooh The New Adventures: Volume 2. The Wishing Bear

Winnie the Pooh The New Adventures: Volume 3. Newfound Friends

Wish That Changed Christmas, The

Canadian and French Canadian Culture

Anne of Green Gables

Bach and Broccoli

Chanter Pour S'Amuser

Chanter Pour S'Amuser: L'Album de Marie-Soleil

Chanter Pour S'Amuser: Une Journee Avec Marie-Soleil

Chanter Pour S'Amuser Set

Child's Christmas in Wales, A

Dog Who Stopped the War, The

Magic of Discovery, The

Native Indian Folklore

Rights from the Heart/Droits au Coeur

Sand Castle, The

Tommy Tricker and the Stamp Traveller

Careers

Alice Walker (1944-Present) — Author

American Women of Achievement Video Collection

American Women of Achievement: Abigail Adams (1744-1818) — Women's Rights Advocate

American Women of Achievement: Jane Addams (1860-1935) — Social Worker

American Women of Achievement: Marian Anderson (1902-1993) — Singer

American Women of Achievement: Susan B. Anthony (1820-1906) — Woman Suffragist

American Women of Achievement: Clara Barton (1821-1912) — Founder, American Red Cross

American Women of Achievement: Emily Dickinson (1830-1890) — Poet

American Women of Achievement: Amelia Earhart (1897-Disappeared in 1937) — Aviator

American Women of Achievement: Helen Keller (1880-1968) — Humanitarian

American Women of Achievement: Sandra Day O'Connor (1930-Present) — Supreme Court Justice

American Women of Achievement: Wilma Rudolph (1940-Present) — Champion Athlete

Baby-Sitters Club Videos

The Baby-Sitters Club: The Baby-Sitters Remember

The Baby-Sitters Club: The Baby-Sitters and the Boy Sitters

The Baby-Sitters Club: Christmas Special (1991)

The Baby-Sitters Club: Claudia and the Missing Jewels

The Baby-Sitters Club: Claudia and the Mystery of the Secret Passage

The Baby-Sitters Club: Dawn and the Dream Boy

The Baby-Sitters Club: Dawn and the Haunted House

The Baby-Sitters Club: Dawn Saves the Trees

The Baby-Sitters Club: Jessi and the Mystery of the Stolen Secrets

The Baby-Sitters Club: Kristy and the Great Campaign

The Baby-Sitters Club: Mary Ann and the Brunettes (1990)

The Baby-Sitters Club: Stacey's Big Break

The Baby-Sitters Club: Stacey Takes a Stand

Ballet Shoes

Barry's Scrapbook: A Window into Art

Charles the Clown

Fire and Rescue

Fireman Sam: The Hero Next Door

Good Morning Miss Toliver

I Want to Be an Artist When I Grow Up

Introducing: The Flying Fruit Fly Circus

Josephine's Imagination

Kidsongs Music Video Stories

Kidsongs Music Video Stories: Cars, Boats, Trains and Planes

Kidsongs Music Video Stories: A Day at Camp

Kidsongs Music Video Stories: A Day at the Circus

Kidsongs Music Video Stories: A Day at Old MacDonald's Farm

Kidsongs Music Video Stories: A Day with the Animals

Kidsongs Music Video Stories: Boppin' with Biggles

Kidsongs Music Video Stories: Country Sing-Along

Kidsongs Music Video Stories: Good Night, Sleep Tight

Kidsongs Music Video Stories: I'd Like to Teach the World to Sing

Kidsongs Music Video Stories: If We Could Talk to the Animals

Kidsongs Music Video Stories: Let's Play Ball!

Kidsongs Music Video Stories: Ride the Roller Coaster

Kidsongs Music Video Stories: Sing Out, America!

Kidsongs Music Video Stories: Very Silly Songs

Kidsongs Music Video Stories: We Wish You a Merry Christmas

Kidsongs Music Video Stories: What I Want to Be!

Kidsongs Music Video Stories: The Wonderful World of Sports

Living and Working in Space: The Countdown Has Begun

Madame C.J. Walker (1867-1919) — Entrepreneur

Magic School Bus

The Magic School Bus: For Lunch

The Magic School Bus: Gets Eaten

The Magic School Bus: Gets Lost in Space

The Magic School Bus: Hops Home

The Magic School Bus: Inside Ralphie

Mary McLeod Bethune (1875-1955) — Educator

Mommy's Office

Mose the Fireman (Rabbit Ears)

Moving Machines

Mr. Rogers' Neighborhood: Circus Fun

Norman the Doorman and Other Stories

Postman Pat's 123 Story

Postman Pat's ABC Story

Reach for the Sky

Richard Scarry's Best Busy People Video

Shalom Sesame: Kibbutz

There Goes a Police Car

There Goes a Train

There Goes a Truck

Walking on Air

Woman's Place, A

"You Can" Video Series: You Can Ride a Horse

Caribbean Culture (SEE Latin American/Caribbean Culture)

Central American Culture (SEE Latin American/Caribbean Culture)

Chanukah

Bubbe's Boarding House Series: Chanuka at Bubbe's

Holidays for Children: Hanukkah/Passover

Lights: The Miracle of Chanukah

Lovely Butterfly — Pepar Nechmad: Chanukah

Shalom Sesame: Chanukah

Children's Television Workshop and Muppet Videos

Basil Hears a Noise

Big Bird's Favorite Party Games

Eight Super Stories from Sesame Street

Five Sesame Street Stories

It's the Muppets!: Meet the Muppets!

It's the Muppets!: More Muppets!

It's Not Easy Being Green

Mathnet The Case of the Unnatural

My Sesame Street Home Videos

My Sesame Street Home Video: Alphabet Game, The

My Sesame Street Home Video: Bedtime Stories & Songs

My Sesame Street Home Video: Best of Elmo, The

My Sesame Street Home Video: Best of Ernie and Bert, The

My Sesame Street Home Video: Big Bird's Favorite Party Games

My Sesame Street Home Video: Big Bird's Story Time

My Sesame Street Home Video: Count it Higher: Great Music Videos from Sesame Street

My Sesame Street Home Video: Getting Ready for School

My Sesame Street Home Video: Getting Ready to Read

My Sesame Street Home Video: I'm Glad I'm Me

My Sesame Street Home Video: Learning About Letters

My Sesame Street Home Video: Learning About Numbers

My Sesame Street Home Video: Learning to Add and Subtract

My Sesame Street Home Video: New Baby in My House, A

My Sesame Street Home Video: Play-Along Games & Songs

Put Down the Duckie

Sesame Songs: Dance Along!

Sesame Songs: Elmo's Sing-Along Guessing Game

Sesame Songs: Monster Hits!

Sesame Songs: Rock & Roll!

Sesame Songs: Sing, Hoot and Howl

Sesame Songs: Sing-Along Earth Songs

Sesame Songs: Sing Yourself Silly!

Sesame Songs: We All Sing Together

Sesame Street Specials: Big Bird in China

Sesame Street Specials: Big Bird in Japan

Sesame Street Specials: Celebrates Around the World

Sesame Street Specials: Christmas Eve on Sesame Street

Sesame Street Specials: Don't Eat the Pictures — Sesame Street Visits the Metropolitan Museum of Art

Sesame Street Specials: Sesame Street's 25th Birthday: A Musical Celebration

Sesame Street Start to Read Videos

Sesame Street Start to Read Videos: Don't Cry, Big Bird and Other Stories

Sesame Street Start to Read Videos: Ernie's Big Mess and Other Stories

Sesame Street Start to Read Videos: Ernie's Little Lie and Other Stories

Sesame Street Start to Read Videos: I Want to Go Home! and Other Stories

Sesame Street Visits: The Firehouse

Sesame Street Visits: The Hospital

Sesame Street: Plaza Sesamo

Sesame Street: Plaza Sesamo: De Compamento Con Montoya: Big Bird Goes Camping

Sesame Street: Plaza Sesamo: El Alfabeto De Montoya: Learn the Alphabet with Bert and Ernie

Sesame Street: Plaza Sesamo: Plaza Sesamo Canta: Favorite Songs From Past Shows

Sesame Street: Plaza Sesamo: Vamos a Imaginar: Learn About Sounds and Shapes

Sesame Street: Plaza Sesamo: Viaja Con Nosotros: Big Bird and Oscar Go to Venezuela and Mexico

Sesame Street: Plaza Sesamo: The Plaza Sesamo Complete Set

Shalom Sesame

Shalom Sesame: Aleph-Bet Telethon

Shalom Sesame: Chanukah

Shalom Sesame: Jerusalem

Shalom Sesame: Journey to Secret Places

Shalom Sesame: Kibbutz

Shalom Sesame: Kids Sing Israel

Shalom Sesame: Land of Israel

Shalom Sesame: Passover

Shalom Sesame: People of Israel

Shalom Sesame: Sing Around the Seasons

Shalom Sesame: Tel Aviv

Three Sesame Street Stories

Chinese Culture, Chinese New Year and China

Empty Pot, The

Folk Games

Holidays for Children: Chinese New Year

Multicultural Peoples of North America: Chinese Americans

National Geographic Kids Videos: Adventures in Asia

Seasons and Holidays Around the World: Chinese New Year

Sesame Street Specials: Big Bird in China

Christmas

The Baby-Sitters Club: Christmas Special (1991)

Barney and the Backyard Gang: Waiting for Santa

Bear Who Slept Through Christmas, The

Berenstain Bears Christmas Tree

Candles, Snow and Mistletoe

Child's Christmas in Wales, A

Classroom Holidays: Liar, Liar, Pants on Fire: A Christmas/Chanukah Story

Dr. Seuss: How the Grinch Stole Christmas

Dr. Seuss Video Festival (How the Grinch Stole Christmas)

A Gingerbread Christmas (Rabbit Ears)

The Gingham Dog and the Calico Cat (Rabbit Ears)

Kidsongs Music Video Stories: We Wish You a Merry Christmas

Little Crooked Christmas Tree, The

Little People: Christmas Fun

Madeline's Christmas

Native Indian Folklore (Christmas at Moose Factory)

The Night Before Christmas (Rabbit Ears)

Noel

Opus n' Bill: A Wish for Wings That Work

Poky Little Puppy's First Christmas

Savior Is Born, The (Rabbit Ears)

Seasons and Holidays Around the World: Christmas in Mexico

Seasons and Holidays Around the World: Christmas in Sweden

Sesame Street Specials: Christmas Eve on Sesame Street

Shari's Christmas Concert

Timmy's Special Delivery

`Twas the Night Before Christmas

Wild Christmas Reindeer, The

Wish That Changed Christmas, The

Cinco de Mayo

Holidays for Children: Cinco De Mayo

Circus

Charles the Clown

Introducing: The Flying Fruit Fly Circus

Kidsongs Music Video Stories: A Day at the Circus

Madeline's Rescue and Other Stories About Madeline

Max's Chocolate Chicken and Other Stories for Young Children (The Circus Baby)

Mr. Rogers' Neighborhood: Circus Fun

City Life

African Story Magic

Alphabet Library: Alphabet City

Curious George Goes to Town

Fun in a Box Volume 2: New Friends and Other Stories (Howard)

Good Morning Miss Toliver

Little Duck Tale, A

Little Lou and His Strange Little Zoo

Mighty Pawns, The

The Mole in Town

My New York

Pepito's Dream

Richard Scarry's Best Busy People Video

Seasons and Holidays Around the World: Chinese New Year

Shalom Sesame: Jerusalem

Shalom Sesame: Tel Aviv

Smile for Auntie and Other Stories (Make Way for Ducklings)

Conflict Resolution and Cooperation

The Baby-Sitters Club: Mary Ann and the Brunettes (1990)

Berenstain Bears and the Messy Room

Berenstain Bears Get in a Fight

Clean Your Room, Harvey Moon!

Danny and the Dinosaur and Other Stories (The Island of Skog)

Dog Who Stopped the War, The

Dr. Seuss: The Butter Battle Book

Family Farm

Harriet Tubman (1820-1913) — Anti-Slavery Activist

It's Not Always Easy Being a Kid

Kidsongs Music Video Stories

Kidsongs Music Video Stories: Cars, Boats, Trains and Planes

Kidsongs Music Video Stories: A Day at Camp

Kidsongs Music Video Stories: A Day at the Circus

Kidsongs Music Video Stories: A Day at Old MacDonald's Farm

Kidsongs Music Video Stories: A Day with the Animals

Kidsongs Music Video Stories: Boppin' with Biggles

Kidsongs Music Video Stories: Country Sing-Along

Kidsongs Music Video Stories: Good Night, Sleep Tight

Kidsongs Music Video Stories: I'd Like to Teach the World to Sing

Kidsongs Music Video Stories: If We Could Talk to the Animals

Kidsongs Music Video Stories: Let's Play Ball!

Kidsongs Music Video Stories: Ride the Roller Coaster

Kidsongs Music Video Stories: Sing Out, America!

Kidsongs Music Video Stories: Very Silly Songs

Kidsongs Music Video Stories: We Wish You a Merry Christmas

Kidsongs Music Video Stories: What I Want to Be!

Kidsongs Music Video Stories: The Wonderful World of Sports

Learning About Me: Ipsilwhich Adventures

Magic Thinking Cap, The

Mine and Yours

My Sesame Street Home Videos

My Sesame Street Home Video: Alphabet Game, The

My Sesame Street Home Video: Bedtime Stories & Songs

My Sesame Street Home Video: Best of Ernie and Bert, The

My Sesame Street Home Video: Big Bird's Favorite Party Games

My Sesame Street Home Video: Big Bird's Story Time

My Sesame Street Home Video: Count It Higher: Great Music Videos from Sesame Street

My Sesame Street Home Video: Getting Ready for School

My Sesame Street Home Video: Getting Ready to Read

My Sesame Street Home Video: I'm Glad I'm Me

My Sesame Street Home Video: Learning About Letters

My Sesame Street Home Video: Learning About Numbers

My Sesame Street Home Video: Learning to Add and Subtract

My Sesame Street Home Video: Play-Along Games & Songs

National Velvet

Pepito's Dream

Picture Book of Martin Luther King, Jr., A

Ramona: Great Hair Argument

Sesame Songs: Dance Along!

Sesame Songs: Elmo's Sing-Along Guessing Game

Sesame Songs: Monster Hits!

Sesame Songs: Rock & Roll!

Sesame Songs: Sing, Hoot and Howl

Sesame Songs: Sing Yourself Silly!

Sesame Street Specials: Big Bird in China

Sesame Street Specials: Big Bird in Japan

Sesame Street Specials: Celebrates Around the World

Sesame Street Specials: Christmas Eve on Sesame Street

Sesame Street Specials: Don't Eat the Pictures — Sesame Street Visits the Metropolitan Museum of Art

Sesame Street Specials: Sesame Street's 25th Birthday: A Musical Celebration

Sesame Street Start to Read Videos

Sesame Street Start to Read Videos: Don't Cry, Big Bird and Other Stories

Sesame Street Start to Read Videos: Ernie's Big Mess and Other Stories

Sesame Street Start to Read Videos: Ernie's Little Lie and Other Stories

Sesame Street Start to Read Videos: I Want to Go Home! and Other Stories

Sesame Street Start to Read Books

Sesame Street Visits: The Firehouse

Sesame Street Visits: The Hospital

Shalom Sesame

Shalom Sesame: Aleph-Bet Telethon

Shalom Sesame: Chanukah

Shalom Sesame: Jerusalem

Shalom Sesame: Journey to Secret Places

Shalom Sesame: Kibbutz

Shalom Sesame: Kids Sing Israel

Shalom Sesame: Land of Israel

Shalom Sesame: Passover

Shalom Sesame: People of Israel

Shalom Sesame: Sing Around the Seasons

Shalom Sesame: Tel Aviv

Shelley Duvall Presents Mrs. Piggle-Wiggle

Shelley Duvall Presents Mrs. Piggle-Wiggle: The Not-Truthful Cure and The Radish Cure

Shelley Duvall Presents Mrs. Piggle-Wiggle: The Pet Forgetters Cure and The Never-Want-To-Go-To-Bedders Cure

Shelley Duvall Presents Mrs. Piggle-Wiggle: The Answer Backer Cure and The Chores Cure

Simon the Lamb

Speeches of Martin Luther King, Jr., The

Thomas the Tank Engine & Friends

Thomas the Tank Engine & Friends: Better Late Than Never and Other Stories

Thomas the Tank Engine & Friends: Christmas Party

Thomas the Tank Engine & Friends: James Learns a Lesson & Other Stories

Thomas the Tank Engine & Friends: Percy's Ghostly & Other Stories

Thomas the Tank Engine & Friends: Tenders & Turntables & Other Stories

Thomas the Tank Engine & Friends: Thomas Breaks the Rules & Other Stories

Thomas the Tank Engine & Friends: Thomas Gets Bumped

Thomas the Tank Engine & Friends: Thomas Gets Tricked & Other Stories

Thomas the Tank Engine & Friends: Trust Thomas & Other Stories

Wee Sing in Sillyville

Winnie the Pooh: Making Friends, Learning

You Can Choose!: Volume 1. Cooperation

You Can Choose!: Volume 2. Being Responsible

You Can Choose!: Volume 3. Dealing with Feelings

You Can Choose!: Volume 4. Saying No

You Can Choose!: Volume 5. Doing the Right Thing

You Can Choose!: Volume 6. Dealing with Disappointment

You Can Choose!: Volume 7. Appreciating Yourself

You Can Choose!: Volume 8. Asking for Help

You Can Choose!: Volume 9. Being Friends

You Can Choose!: Volume 10. Resolving Conflicts

Construction

I Can Build

Mike Mulligan and His Steam Shovel

Moving Machines

There Goes a Bulldozer

Consumer Education

Zillions TV

Cooperation (SEE Conflict Resolution and Cooperation)

Cultures of the World SEE:

African American Culture

Africa and African Culture

Amish Culture

Arab American Culture

Australian Culture

Book-Based

Canadian Videos and French Canadian Culture

Caribbean Culture (SEE Latin American/ Caribbean Culture)

Central American Culture (SEE Latin American/ Caribbean Culture)

Chinese Culture

Czech Videos

English Videos and English Culture

Folk Games and Folk Songs

French Language and French Folk Tales

German Language and German American Culture

Greek American Culture and Greek Mythology

Haitian Culture (SEE Latin American/ Caribbean Culture)

Hebrew Language

Hispanic Culture (SEE Latin American/ Caribbean Culture)

Holidays (by name of holiday)

India and Indian Culture

Irish and Irish American Culture

Italian Videos, Italian and Italian American Culture, Folktales

Japanese Videos, Japanese and Japanese American Culture, Tales

Jewish Videos, Jewish and Jewish American Culture

Korean American Culture

Languages SEE:

  French Language

  German Language

  Hebrew Language

  Non-Verbal (Videos without words)

  Sign Language

  Spanish Language

Latin American, Caribbean and Hispanic Culture

Mexico and Mexican Culture (SEE Latin American/Caribbean Culture)

Native American Culture

Polish American Culture

Puerto Rican Culture (SEE Latin American/ Caribbean Culture)

Russian American Culture

South American Culture (SEE Latin American/Caribbean Culture)

Swedish Culture

Czech Videos

Mole and the Green Star, The

Mole in Town, The

Dance and Creative Movement

Ballet Shoes

Clifford's Sing-A-Long Adventure

Creative Dance for Preschoolers

Creative Movement: A Step Towards Intelligence

Fun in a Box Volume 1: Ben's Dream (Your Feets Too Big)

Land of Sweet Taps, The

Let's Do It! Professor Iris

Monkey Moves

Move Like the Animals

Music Mania Professor Iris

Red Shoes, The (Animation)

Sesame Songs: Dance Along!

Sing-Along, Dance-Along, Do-along

Water Is Wet

Zoobilee Zoo: Zooble Hop and Other Stories

Dating

The Baby-Sitters Club: Dawn and the Dream Boy

The Baby-Sitters Club: Mary Ann and the Brunettes

Death

Chicken Sunday

First and Second Grade Feelings: Jim's Dog, Muffins

Ramona: Goodbye, Hello

Ramona: Squeakerfoot and Goodbye, Hello

Disabilities

Abuela's Weave

American Women of Achievement: Helen Keller (1880-1968) — Humanitarian

American Women of Achievement: Wilma Rudolph (1940-Present) — Champion Athlete

The Baby-Sitters Club: Christmas Special (1991)

Beethoven Lives Upstairs

Knots on a Counting Rope

Pollyanna (BBC)

Secret Garden, The (Agnieszka Holland)

Secret Garden, The (BBC)

Secret Garden, The (MGM)

Sounds Around

Tickle Tune Typhoon: Let's Be Friends

Walking on Air

Woman's Place, A

Discrimination (SEE Prejudice)

Divorce

The Baby-Sitters Club: Stacey Takes a Stand

Divorce Can Happen to the Nicest People

Dr. Martin Luther King, Jr./Dr. Martin Luther King, Jr. Day

Picture Book of Martin Luther King, Jr., A

Speeches of Martin Luther King, Jr., The

Dr. Seuss Videos

Daisy-Head Mayzie

Dr. Seuss Video Festival

Dr. Seuss Videos

Dr. Seuss: The Cat in the Hat Comes Back

Dr. Seuss: Green Eggs and Ham

Dr. Seuss: Hoober-Bloob Highway

Dr. Seuss: Hop on Pop

Dr. Seuss: Horton Hatches the Egg

Dr. Seuss: Horton Hears a Who

Dr. Seuss: How the Grinch Stole Christmas

Dr. Seuss: I Am NOT Going to Get Up Today!

Dr. Seuss: The Lorax

Dr. Seuss: One Fish Two Fish Red Fish Blue Fish: English Version

Dr. Seuss: One Fish Two Fish Red Fish Blue Fish: Spanish Version, Un Pez Dos Peces Pez Rojo Pez Azul

Dr. Seuss: Pontoffel Pock

Dr. Seuss' ABC

Dr. Seuss: The Butter Battle Book

Dr. Seuss' Cat in the Hat

Dr. Seuss' Sleep Book

Drug Education

Drug Free Kids

It's Not Always Easy Being a Kid

Say No to Drugs!

You Can Choose!: Volume 4. Saying No

Earth Science, Ecology, Environment

Art Lessons for Children Volume 6: Plants of the Rain Forest

At Home in the Coral Reef: English Version

At Home in the Coral Reef: Spanish Version

The Baby-Sitters Club: Dawn Saves the Trees

Barry's Scrapbook: A Window into Art

Berenstain Bears and the Trouble with Friends

Best of Beakman's World, The

Biggest Bears

Bugs Don't Bug Us

Creepy Critters Professor Iris

Discovery Stories

Don Cooper: Mother Nature's Songs

Dr. Seuss: The Lorax

Eco, You, and Simon, Too!

Gift of the Whales

How to Hide Stories

How to Hide a Butterfly and Other Insects

How to Hide a Crocodile and Other Reptiles

How to Hide a Gray Treefrog and Other Amphibians

How to Hide a Polar Bear and Other Mammals

How to Hide a Whip-Poor-Will and Other Birds

How to Hide an Octopus and Other Sea Creatures

In the Company of Whales

Indoor Fun (A Close Look at Volcanoes)

It Zwibble: Earthday Birthday

Johnny Appleseed (Rabbit Ears)

Madre Tierra

The Mole and the Green Star

The Mole in Town

My First Activity Series: My First Green Video

My First Activity Series: My First Nature Video

National Geographic Kids Videos: Adventures in Asia

National Geographic Kids Videos: Amazing North America

National Geographic Kids Videos: Deep Sea Dive

National Geographic Kids Videos: GeoKids

National Geographic Kids Videos: GeoKids: Bear Cubs, Baby Ducks and Kooky Kookaburras

National Geographic Kids Videos: GeoKids: Cool Cats, Raindrops, and Things That Live in Holes

National Geographic Kids Videos: GeoKids: Flying, Trying and Honking Around

National Geographic Kids Videos: Swinging Safari

National Geographic Kids Videos: Totally Tropical Rainforest

National Geographic Kids Videos: Wonders Down Under

Orca Whales and Mermaid Tales

Other Way to Listen, The

Ruth Heller's Nature Stories

Science Primer: Earth, Air, Water, Fire

See How They Grow

See How They Grow: Farm Animals

See How They Grow: Insects and Spiders

See How They Grow: Pets

See How They Grow: Wild Animals

Sesame Songs: Sing-Along Earth Songs

Shamu & You: Exploring the World of Birds

Shamu & You: Exploring the World of Fish

Shamu & You: Exploring the World of Mammals

Shamu & You: Exploring the World of Reptiles

Shelley Duvall's Bedtime Stories: Aunt Ippy's Museum of Junk

Spirits of the Rainforest

Sun, the Wind and the Rain, The

Tadpole and the Whale

This Pretty Planet

Tinka's Planet

A Walk in the Wild

Way to Start a Day, The

Where in the World Kids Explore

Where in the World Kids Explore: Volume 1. Kids Explore Mexico

Where in the World Kids Explore: Volume 2. Kids Explore Alaska

Where in the World Kids Explore: Volume 3. Kids Explore Kenya

Where in the World Kids Explore: Volume 4. Kids Explore America's National Parks

Which Way, Weather?

World Alive, A

Worlds Below, The

Easter

Berenstain Bears Easter Surprise

Holidays for Children: Easter

Madeline and the Easter Bonnet

English Videos and English Culture

Child's Christmas in Wales, A

Fingermouse, Yoffy and Friends

Fireman Sam: The Hero Next Door

Folk Games

Jack and the Beanstalk (Rabbit Ears)

Lion, the Witch, and the Wardrobe, The (live action)

Madeline in London

My Friend Walter

Pollyanna (BBC)

Rupert

Rupert and the Frog Song

Rupert and the Runaway Dragon

Seasons and Holidays Around the World: Halloween in Britain

Secret Garden, The (Agnieszka Holland)

Secret Garden, The (BBC)

Secret Garden, The (MGM)

Fairy Tales (SEE Book-Based Videos and Stories)

Family Relationships (SEE ALSO Divorce, Death)

50 Below Zero (plus Thomas' Snowsuit)

Anne of Green Gables

Are You My Mother?

Astronomy 101: A Family Adventure

The Baby-Sitters Club: Stacey Takes a Stand

Bach and Broccoli

Berenstain Bears Videos

Berenstain Bears Christmas Tree

Berenstain Bears in the Dark

Berenstain Bears Easter Surprise

Berenstain Bears Learn About Strangers

Berenstain Bears and the Messy Room

Berenstain Bears: No Girls Allowed and the Missing Dinosaur Bone

Berenstain Bears and Too Much Birthday and to the Rescue

Berenstain Bears and the Trouble with Friends

Berenstain Bears and the Truth

Berenstain Bears Get in a Fight

Bubbe's Boarding House Series: Chanuka at Bubbe's

Bubbe's Boarding House Series: Passover at Bubbe's

Chicken Sunday

Child of Mine: The Lullaby Video

Dancing with the Indians

Eres Tu Mi Mama?

Family Farm

Free to Be...You and Me

Gift of the Whales

Hey, What About Me?

Human Race Club: A Story About Fights between Brothers and Sisters

I Can Build

I Dig Fossils

Jacob Have I Loved (Bridget Fonda)

Jacob Have I Loved (Amanda Plummer)

Joshua's Masai Mask

Just Me and My Dad

Just Grandma and Me

Knots on a Counting Rope

Little Sister Rabbit

Magic Thinking Cap, The

Mary Poppins

Mr. Rogers: Musical Stories

My Friend Walter

My Sesame Street Home Video: New Baby in My House, A

National Velvet

P.J. Funnybunny

Ramona

Ramona: Goodbye, Hello

Ramona: Great Hair Argument

Ramona: New Pajamas

Ramona: The Patient

Ramona: Perfect Day and Bad Day

Ramona: Rainy Sunday

Ramona: Ramona's Bad Day

Ramona: Siblingitis

Ramona: Squeakerfoot and Goodbye, Hello

Seasons and Holidays Around the World: Chinese New Year

Seasons and Holidays Around the World: Christmas in Mexico

Seasons and Holidays Around the World: Christmas in Sweden

Secret Garden, The (Agnieszka Holland)

Secret Garden, The (BBC)

Secret Garden, The (MGM)

Shelley Duvall's Bedtime Stories: Aunt Ippy's Museum of Junk

Smile for Auntie and Other Stories

Something Good (plus Mortimer)

Spoonbill Swamp

Sweet 15

Story of the Dancing Frog

Thunder Cake

Timmy's Special Delivery

Water Is Wet

Wee Sing: Grandpa's Magical Toys

Wish That Changed Christmas, The

Workout with Daddy & Me

Workout with Mommy & Me

Videos Featuring Aunts and Uncles

Bach and Broccoli

Joshua's Masai Mask

Secret Garden, The (Agnieszka Holland)

Secret Garden, The (BBC)

Secret Garden, The (MGM)

Shelley Duvall's Bedtime Stories: Aunt Ippy's Museum of Junk

Smile for Auntie and Other Stories

Story of the Dancing Frog

Videos Featuring Cousins

Secret Garden, The (Agnieszka Holland)

Secret Garden, The (BBC)

Secret Garden, The (MGM)

Videos Featuring Grandparents

Abuela's Weave

Bubbe's Boarding House Series: Chanuka at Bubbe's

Bubbe's Boarding House Series: Passover at Bubbe's

Chicken Sunday

Gift of the Whales

Just Grandma and Me

Knots on a Counting Rope

Mr. Rogers: Musical Stories

Thunder Cake

Wee Sing: Grandpa's Magical Toys

Videos Featuring Parents

Are You My Mother?

The Baby-Sitters Club: Stacey Takes a Stand

Child of Mine: The Lullaby Video

Eres Tu Mi Mama?

Just Me and My Dad

Magic Thinking Cap, The

National Velvet

Something Good (plus Mortimer)

Spoonbill Swamp

Sweet 15

Workout with Daddy & Me

Workout with Mommy & Me

Videos Featuring Siblings

Hey, What About Me?

Human Race Club: A Story About Fights between Brothers and Sisters

Jacob Have I Loved
(Bridget Fonda)

Jacob Have I Loved
(Amanda Plummer)

Little Sister Rabbit

My Sesame Street Home
Video: New Baby in My
House, A

P.J. Funnybunny

Timmy's Special Delivery

**Farm Life/Country
Life**

Doing Things: Eating,
Washing, in Motion

Family Farm

Farmer's Huge Carrot,
The

Good Morning, Good
Night: A Day on the Farm

Kidsongs Music Video
Stories: A Day at Old
MacDonald's Farm

Kidsongs Music Video
Stories: Country Sing-
Along

My Friend Walter

See How They Grow:
Farm Animals

Thunder Cake

Feelings

Basil Hears a Noise

Beady Bear

Berenstain Bears in the
Dark

Chicken Sunday

Classroom Holidays

Classroom Holidays: Bee
My Valentine: A
Valentine's Day Story

Classroom Holidays: Don't
Eat Too Much Turkey: A
Thanksgiving Story

Classroom Holidays: Liar,
Liar, Pants on Fire: A
Christmas/Chanukah
Story

Classroom Holidays:
Starring First Grade: An
Anytime Celebration

Divorce Can Happen to
the Nicest People

First and Second Grade
Feelings

First and Second Grade
Feelings: Jim's Dog,
Muffins.

First and Second Grade
Feelings: The Real-Skin
Rubber Monster Mask

First and Second Grade
Feelings: See You in
Second Grade!

First and Second Grade
Feelings: So What?

Get Ready for School

Hey, What About Me?

Human Race Club: A
Story About Fights
between Brothers and
Sisters

Human Race Club: A
Story About Making
Friends, A Story About
Prejudice and
Discrimination

Human Race Club: A
Story About Self-Esteem

I Need a Hug!

I Have a Friend

Ira Sleeps Over

Ira Says Goodbye

Mr. Rogers Videos

Mr. Rogers: Dinosaurs &
Monsters

Mr. Rogers: Music and
Feelings

Mr. Rogers: Musical
Stories

Mr. Rogers: What About
Love

Mr. Rogers: When Parents
Are Away

Mr. Rogers'
Neighborhood: Circus Fun

Mr. Rogers'
Neighborhood: Kindness

Mr. Rogers'
Neighborhood: Love

Mr. Rogers'
Neighborhood: Making
Music

My Sesame Street Home
Video: New Baby in My
House, A

Never Talk to Strangers

Ramona: New Pajamas

Ramona: The Patient

Ramona: Perfect Day and
Bad Day

Ramona: Ramona's Bad
Day

Ramona: Siblingitis

Ramona: Squeakerfoot
and Goodbye, Hello

Sesame Street Start to
Read Videos

Sesame Street Start to
Read Videos: Don't Cry,
Big Bird and Other
Stories

Sesame Street Start to
Read Videos: Ernie's Big
Mess and Other Stories

Sesame Street Start to
Read Videos: Ernie's
Little Lie and Other
Stories

Sesame Street Start to
Read Videos: I Want to Go
Home! and Other Stories

Today Was a Terrible Day

Treasury of Children's
Stories: Stories to Help Us
Grow

We Learn About the
World: English Version

We Learn About the
World: Spanish Version

You Can Choose!: Volume
1. Cooperation

You Can Choose!: Volume
2. Being Responsible

You Can Choose!: Volume
3. Dealing with Feelings

You Can Choose!: Volume
4. Saying No

You Can Choose!: Volume
5. Doing the Right Thing

You Can Choose!: Volume
6. Dealing with
Disappointment

You Can Choose!: Volume
7. Appreciating Yourself

You Can Choose!: Volume
8. Asking for Help

You Can Choose!: Volume
9. Being Friends

You Can Choose!: Volume
10. Resolving Conflicts

**Fire Safety (SEE
Health and Safety)**

**Folk Games and
Folk Songs**

Folk Games

Fun in a Box Volume 3:
The Birthday Movie

Jessi Sings Songs from
Around the World

Johnny Appleseed (Rabbit
Ears)

Shalom Sesame: Kids
Sing Israel

**Folk Tales (SEE
Book-Based Videos
and Stories)**

Food and Cooking

Eco, You, and Simon, Too!

Janey Junkfood's Fresh
Adventure

Kids Kitchen: Making
Good Eating Great Fun
for Kids!

Kids Get Cooking: The
Egg

Madeline at Cooking
School

The Magic School Bus:
For Lunch

The Magic School Bus:
Gets Eaten

More Pre-School Power

My First Activity Series:
My First Cooking Video

Pre-School Power: Jacket
Flips & Other Tips

Pre-School Power #3

Something Good (plus
Mortimer)

**Fourth of
July/Independence
Day**

Holidays for Children:
Independence Day

**French Language
and Folktales**

Chanter Pour S'Amuser

Chanter Pour S'Amuser:
L'Album de Marie-Soleil

Chanter Pour S'Amuser:
Une Journee Avec Marie-
Soleil

Chanter Pour S'Amuser
Set

Folk Games

Little Engine That Could,
The: French Narration

Madeline

Madeline (Narrated by
Christopher Plummer)

Puss in Boots (Rabbit
Ears)

Rights from the Heart
Droits au Coeur

Spot: Spot's First Video -
French

Spot: Spot's Adventure -
French

Friendship

Alejandro's Gift

Baby-Sitters Club Videos

The Baby-Sitters Club:
The Baby-Sitters
Remember

The Baby-Sitters Club: The Baby-Sitters and the Boy Sitters

The Baby-Sitters Club: Christmas Special (1991)

The Baby-Sitters Club: Claudia and the Missing Jewels

The Baby-Sitters Club: Claudia and the Mystery of the Secret Passage

The Baby-Sitters Club: Dawn and the Dream Boy

The Baby-Sitters Club: Dawn and the Haunted House

The Baby-Sitters Club: Dawn Saves the Trees

The Baby-Sitters Club: Jessi and the Mystery of the Stolen Secrets

The Baby-Sitters Club: Kristy and the Great Campaign

The Baby-Sitters Club: Mary Ann and the Brunettes (1990)

The Baby-Sitters Club: Stacey's Big Break

The Baby-Sitters Club: Stacey Takes a Stand

Bach and Broccoli

Berenstain Bears and the Trouble with Friends

Best Friends

Best Friends Part I

Best Friends Part II

Bump — My First Video

Caterpillar's Wish, A

Chicken Sunday

Classroom Holidays

Classroom Holidays: Bee My Valentine: A Valentine's Day Story

Classroom Holidays: Don't Eat Too Much Turkey: A Thanksgiving Story

Classroom Holidays: Liar, Liar, Pants on Fire: A Christmas/Chanukah Story

Classroom Holidays: Starring First Grade: An Anytime Celebration

Eco, You, and Simon, Too!

Fireman Sam: The Hero Next Door

First and Second Grade Feelings

First and Second Grade Feelings: Jim's Dog, Muffins.

First and Second Grade Feelings: The Real-Skin Rubber Monster Mask

First and Second Grade Feelings: See You in Second Grade!

First and Second Grade Feelings: So What?

First and Second Grade Feelings Set

Frog and Toad Are Friends

Get Ready for School

The Gingham Dog and the Calico Cat (Rabbit Ears)

Human Race Club: A Story About Making Friends, A Story About Prejudice and Discrimination

I'm Not Oscar's Friend Anymore and Other Stories

Ira Sleeps Over

Ira Says Goodbye

Jay Jay the Jet Plane and His Flying Friends, Volume 1: Jay Jay's First Flight and Three Other Stories

Jay Jay the Jet Plane and His Flying Friends, Volume 1: Tito Turbinitas Y Sus Amigos Voladores

Jay Jay the Jet Plane and His Flying Friends, Volume 2: Old Oscar Leads the Parade and Three Other Stories

Jay O'Callahan: Six Stories About Little Heroes

Jay O'Callahan: Herman & Marguerite

Kitten Companions

Learning About Me: B Is for Belonging

Little People: Three Favorite Stories

Madeline and the Toy Factory

Mine and Yours

Mouse and the Motorcycle, The

My Sesame Street Home Videos

My Sesame Street Home Video: Alphabet Game, The

My Sesame Street Home Video: Bedtime Stories & Songs

My Sesame Street Home Video: Best of Ernie and Bert, The

My Sesame Street Home Video: Big Bird's Favorite Party Games

My Sesame Street Home Video: Big Bird's Story Time

My Sesame Street Home Video: Count It Higher: Great Music Videos from Sesame Street

My Sesame Street Home Video: Getting Ready for School

My Sesame Street Home Video: Getting Ready to Read

My Sesame Street Home Video: I'm Glad I'm Me

My Sesame Street Home Video: Learning About Letters

My Sesame Street Home Video: Learning About Numbers

My Sesame Street Home Video: Learning to Add and Subtract

My Sesame Street Home Video: Play-Along Games & Songs

National Velvet

New Friends and Other Stories

Pecos Bill (Rabbit Ears)

Red Shoes, The (Animation)

Sesame Songs: Dance Along!

Sesame Songs: Elmo's Sing-Along Guessing Game

Sesame Songs: Monster Hits!

Sesame Songs: Rock & Roll!

Sesame Songs: Sing Yourself Silly!

Sesame Songs: Sing, Hoot and Howl

Sesame Street Specials: Big Bird in China

Sesame Street Specials: Big Bird in Japan

Sesame Street Specials: Celebrates Around the World

Sesame Street Specials: Christmas Eve on Sesame Street

Sesame Street Specials: Don't Eat the Pictures — Sesame Street Visits the Metropolitan Museum of Art

Sesame Street Visits: The Firehouse

Sesame Street Visits: The Hospital

Shelley Duvall's Bedtime Stories: Elizabeth and Larry Bill and Pete

Thomas the Tank Engine & Friends

Thomas the Tank Engine & Friends: Better Late Than Never and Other Stories

Thomas the Tank Engine & Friends: Christmas Party

Thomas the Tank Engine & Friends: James Learns a Lesson & Other Stories

Thomas the Tank Engine & Friends: Percy's Ghostly & Other Stories

Thomas the Tank Engine & Friends: Tenders & Turntables & Other Stories

Thomas the Tank Engine & Friends: Thomas Breaks the Rules & Other Stories

Thomas the Tank Engine & Friends: Thomas Gets Bumped

Thomas the Tank Engine & Friends: Thomas Gets Tricked & Other Stories

Thomas the Tank Engine & Friends: Trust Thomas & Other Stories

Velveteen Rabbit (Rabbit Ears)

Velveteen Rabbit (Plummer)

Who Will Be My Friend?

Winnie the Pooh

Winnie the Pooh and the Blustery Day

Winnie the Pooh and a Day for Eeyore

Winnie the Pooh and the Honey Tree

Winnie the Pooh and Tigger Too

Winnie the Pooh: Making Friends, Learning

Winnie the Pooh The New Adventures: Volume 1. The Great Honey Pot Robbery

Winnie the Pooh The New Adventures: Volume 2. The Wishing Bear

Winnie the Pooh The New Adventures: Volume 3. Newfound Friends

"You Can" Video Series: You Can Fly a Kite

You Can Choose!: Volume 1. Cooperation

You Can Choose!: Volume 2. Being Responsible

You Can Choose!: Volume 3. Dealing with Feelings

You Can Choose!: Volume 4. Saying No

You Can Choose!: Volume 5. Doing the Right Thing

You Can Choose!: Volume 6. Dealing with Disappointment

You Can Choose!: Volume 7. Appreciating Yourself

You Can Choose!: Volume 8. Asking for Help

You Can Choose!: Volume 9. Being Friends

You Can Choose!: Volume 10. Resolving Conflicts

Zoobilee Zoo

Zoobilee Zoo: Blue Ribbon Zooble and Other Stories

Zoobilee Zoo: Lady Whazzat and Other Stories

Zoobilee Zoo: Laughland and Other Stories

Zoobilee Zoo: Zoobadoobas and Other Stories

Zoobilee Zoo: Zooble Hop and Other Stories

Gardening

Empty Pot, The

Look What I Grew

German Language and German American Culture

Multicultural Peoples of North America: German Americans

Sesame Street Specials: Celebrates Around the World

Spot: Spot's First Video - German

Spot: Spot's Adventure - German

Girls — Great Videos Featuring Females (SEE ALSO Women's History)

Abuela's Weave

And the Children Shall Lead

Anna Maria's Blanket

Anne of Green Gables

Annie Oakley (Rabbit Ears)

Astronomy 101: A Family Adventure

Baby-Sitters Club Videos

The Baby-Sitters Club: The Baby-Sitters Remember

The Baby-Sitters Club: The Baby-Sitters and the Boy Sitters

The Baby-Sitters Club: Christmas Special (1991)

The Baby-Sitters Club: Claudia and the Missing Jewels

The Baby-Sitters Club: Claudia and the Mystery of the Secret Passage

The Baby-Sitters Club: Dawn and the Dream Boy

The Baby-Sitters Club: Dawn and the Haunted House

The Baby-Sitters Club: Dawn Saves the Trees

The Baby-Sitters Club: Jessi and the Mystery of the Stolen Secrets

The Baby-Sitters Club: Kristy and the Great Campaign

The Baby-Sitters Club: Mary Ann and the Brunettes (1990)

The Baby-Sitters Club: Stacey's Big Break

The Baby-Sitters Club: Stacey Takes a Stand

Ballet Shoes

Berenstain Bears: No Girls Allowed and The Missing Dinosaur Bone

Bill Nye the Science Guy

Bill Nye the Science Guy: Outer Space Way Out There

Bill Nye the Science Guy: Dinosaurs Those Big Boneheads

Bill Nye the Science Guy: The Human Body The Inside Scoop

Birthday Dragon

Cherries and Cherry Pits

Chicken Sunday

Child of Mine: The Lullaby Video

Corduroy Bear

Dancing with the Indians

Free to Be...You and Me

Gift of Amazing Grace, The

Harriet Tubman (1820-1913) — Anti-Slavery Activist

Hideaways, The

Jacob Have I Loved (Bridget Fonda)

Jacob Have I Loved (Amanda Plummer)

Jazz Time Tale

Josephine's Imagination

Linnea in Monet's Garden

Lion, the Witch, and the Wardrobe, The (Animated)

Lion, the Witch, and the Wardrobe, The (live action)

Madame C.J. Walker (1867-1919) — Entrepreneur

Madeline

Madeline (Narrated by Christopher Plummer)

Madeline and the Dog Show

Madeline and the Easter Bonnet

Madeline and the Toy Factory

Madeline at Cooking School

Madeline in London

Madeline's Rescue and Other Stories About Madeline

Madeline's Christmas

Maricela

Mommy's Office

My Friend Walter

My Neighbor Totoro

National Velvet

Norman the Doorman and Other Stories

Pollyanna (BBC)

Ramona

Ramona: Goodbye, Hello

Ramona: Great Hair Argument

Ramona: New Pajamas

Ramona: The Patient

Ramona: Perfect Day and Bad Day

Ramona: Rainy Sunday

Ramona: Ramona's Bad Day

Ramona: Siblingitis

Ramona: Squeakerfoot and Goodbye, Hello

Reach for the Sky

Red Shoes, The (Animation)

Roxaboxen

Secret Garden, The (Agnieszka Holland)

Secret Garden, The (BBC)

Secret Garden, The (MGM)

Shelley Duvall Presents Mrs. Piggle-Wiggle

Shelley Duvall Presents Mrs. Piggle-Wiggle: The Not-Truthful Cure and The Radish Cure

Shelley Duvall Presents Mrs. Piggle-Wiggle: The Pet Forgetters Cure and The Never-Want-To-Go-To-Bedders Cure

Shelley Duvall Presents Mrs. Piggle-Wiggle: The Answer Backer Cure and The Chores Cure

Sojourner Truth (1797-1883) — Abolitionist Leader

Song of Sacajawea (Rabbit Ears)

Story of the Dancing Frog

Sweet 15

Tadpole and the Whale

Teddy Bear's Picnic, The

Vincent and Me

You Must Remember This

Greek American Culture and Greek Mythology

Abuela's Weave

King Midas and the Golden Touch (Rabbit Ears)

Multicultural Peoples of North America: Greek Americans

Pegasus

Growing Up

Abuela's Weave

African Story Magic

Alexander and the Terrible, Horrible, No Good, Very Bad Day

Anna Maria's Blanket

Anne of Green Gables

Baby-Sitters Club Videos

The Baby-Sitters Club: The Baby-Sitters Remember

The Baby-Sitters Club: The Baby-Sitters and the Boy Sitters

The Baby-Sitters Club: Christmas Special (1991)

The Baby-Sitters Club: Claudia and the Missing Jewels

The Baby-Sitters Club: Claudia and the Mystery of the Secret Passage

The Baby-Sitters Club: Dawn and the Dream Boy

The Baby-Sitters Club: Dawn and the Haunted House

The Baby-Sitters Club: Dawn Saves the Trees

The Baby-Sitters Club: Jessi and the Mystery of the Stolen Secrets

The Baby-Sitters Club: Kristy and the Great Campaign

The Baby-Sitters Club: Mary Ann and the Brunettes (1990)

The Baby-Sitters Club: Stacey's Big Break

The Baby-Sitters Club: Stacey Takes a Stand

Caterpillar's Wish, A

Classroom Holidays

Classroom Holidays: Bee My Valentine: A Valentine's Day Story

Classroom Holidays: Don't Eat Too Much Turkey: A Thanksgiving Story

Classroom Holidays: Liar, Liar, Pants on Fire: A Christmas/Chanukah Story

Classroom Holidays: Starring First Grade: An Anytime Celebration

First and Second Grade Feelings: How Come?

Human Race Club: A Story About Fights between Brothers and Sisters

Human Race Club: A Story About Making Friends, A Story About Prejudice and Discrimination

Human Race Club: A Story About Self-Esteem

Jacob Have I Loved (Bridget Fonda)

Jacob Have I Loved (Amanda Plummer)

Kidsongs Music Video Stories: What I Want to Be!

Mine and Yours

Mop Top

Mr. Rogers Videos

Mr. Rogers: Dinosaurs & Monsters

Mr. Rogers: Music and Feelings

Mr. Rogers: Musical Stories

Mr. Rogers: What About Love

Mr. Rogers: When Parents Are Away

Mr. Rogers' Neighborhood: Circus Fun

Mr. Rogers' Neighborhood: Kindness

Mr. Rogers' Neighborhood: Love

Mr. Rogers' Neighborhood: Making Music

My Sesame Street Home Videos

My Sesame Street Home Video: Alphabet Game, The

My Sesame Street Home Video: Bedtime Stories & Songs

My Sesame Street Home Video: Best of Ernie and Bert, The

My Sesame Street Home Video: Big Bird's Favorite Party Games

My Sesame Street Home Video: Big Bird's Story Time

My Sesame Street Home Video: Count It Higher: Great Music Videos from Sesame Street

My Sesame Street Home Video: Getting Ready for School

My Sesame Street Home Video: Getting Ready to Read

My Sesame Street Home Video: I'm Glad I'm Me

My Sesame Street Home Video: Learning About Letters

My Sesame Street Home Video: Learning About Numbers

My Sesame Street Home Video: Learning to Add and Subtract

My Sesame Street Home Video: Play-Along Games & Songs

Never Talk to Strangers

Peep and the Big Wide World

Pinocchio (Rabbit Ears)

Ramona

Ramona: Goodbye, Hello

Ramona: Great Hair Argument

Ramona: New Pajamas

Ramona: The Patient

Ramona: Perfect Day and Bad Day

Ramona: Rainy Sunday

Ramona: Ramona's Bad Day

Ramona: Siblingitis

Ramona: Squeakerfoot and Goodbye, Hello

Sammy and Other Songs from Getting to Know Myself

Sesame Songs: Dance Along!

Sesame Songs: Elmo's Sing-Along Guessing Game

Sesame Songs: Monster Hits!

Sesame Songs: Rock & Roll!

Sesame Songs: Sing Yourself Silly!

Sesame Songs: Sing, Hoot and Howl

Sesame Street Specials: Big Bird in China

Sesame Street Specials: Big Bird in Japan

Sesame Street Specials: Celebrates Around the World

Sesame Street Specials: Christmas Eve on Sesame Street

Sesame Street Specials: Don't Eat the Pictures — Sesame Street Visits the Metropolitan Museum of Art

Sesame Street Specials: Sesame Street's 25th Birthday: A Musical Celebration

Sesame Street Start to Read Videos

Sesame Street Start to Read Videos: Don't Cry, Big Bird and Other Stories

Sesame Street Start to Read Videos: Ernie's Big Mess and Other Stories

Sesame Street Start to Read Videos: Ernie's Little Lie and Other Stories

Sesame Street Start to Read Videos: I Want to Go Home! and Other Stories

Sesame Street Visits: The Firehouse

Sesame Street Visits: The Hospital

Sharon, Lois & Bram's: Elephant Show

Sharon, Lois & Bram's: Elephant Show: Back by Popular Demand

Sharon, Lois & Bram's: Elephant Show: Live in your Living Room

Sharon, Lois & Bram's: Elephant Show: Pet Fair

Sharon, Lois & Bram's: Elephant Show: Radio Show

Sharon, Lois & Bram's: Elephant Show: Sleepover

Sharon, Lois & Bram's: Elephant Show: Soap Box Derby

Sharon, Lois & Bram's: Elephant Show: Treasure Island

Sharon, Lois & Bram's: Elephant Show: Who Stole the Cookies

Sweet 15

Treasury of Children's Stories: Stories to Help Us Grow

Winnie the Pooh: Making Friends, Learning

Zoobilee Zoo: Zooble Hop and Other Stories

Guidance SEE:

Careers

Conflict Resolution and Cooperation

Dating

Death

Disabilities

Divorce

Feelings

Family Relationships

Friendship

Growing-up

Health And Safety

Manners

Moving to a New Home

Prejudice and Discrimination

Self-Image and Self-Esteem

Skills for Living

Starting School

Values

Haitian Culture (SEE Latin American/ Caribbean Culture)

Halloween

First and Second Grade Feelings: The Real-Skin Rubber Monster Mask

Holidays for Children: Halloween

Seasons and Holidays Around the World: Halloween in Britain

Health & Safety (SEE ALSO: Anorexia, Disabilities, Drug Education, Food, Hospital Stays, Smoking, Sports, Stranger Danger)

Barney and the Backyard Gang: Barney's Campfire Sing-Along

Barney and the Backyard Gang: Barney's Safety Video

Fire and Rescue

Fireman Sam: The Hero Next Door

Mose The Fireman (Rabbit Ears)

Sesame Street Visits: The Firehouse

Skating Safe for Kids

There Goes a Fire Truck

Hebrew Language

Lovely Butterfly — Pepar Nechmad

Lovely Butterfly — Pepar Nechmad: Chanukah

Lovely Butterfly — Pepar Nechmad: Flowers for the Independence Day

Lovely Butterfly — Pepar Nechmad: Passover

Lovely Butterfly — Pepar Nechmad: Purim

Lovely Butterfly — Pepar Nechmad: Tishrei Month Holidays (Rosh Hashana and Sukkot)

Lovely Butterfly — Pepar Nechmad: Tu B'Shvat

Now I Know My Aleph Bet

Shalom Sesame

Shalom Sesame: Aleph-Bet Telethon

Shalom Sesame: Chanukah

Shalom Sesame: Jerusalem

Shalom Sesame: Journey to Secret Places

Shalom Sesame: Kibbutz

Shalom Sesame: Kids Sing Israel

Shalom Sesame: Land of Israel

Shalom Sesame: Passover

Shalom Sesame: People of Israel

Shalom Sesame: Sing Around the Seasons

Shalom Sesame: Tel Aviv

Hispanic Culture (SEE Latin American, Caribbean and Hispanic Culture)

Holidays SEE:

Arbor Day

Chanukah

Christmas

Chinese New Year

Cinco de Mayo

Dr. Martin Luther King Jr.'s Birthday

Halloween

Independence Day/ Fourth of July

Kwanzaa

New Year's Eve

Passover

Purim

Rosh Hashanah

Sukkot

Thanksgiving

Tu B'Shvat

Valentine's Day

Yom Kippur

Hospital Stays

The Baby-Sitters Club: Christmas Special (1991)

Madeline

Madeline (Narrated by Christopher Plummer)

Sesame Street Visits: The Hospital

How-To Videos SEE:

Activities

Art

Construction

Dance and Creative Movement

Food and Cooking

Juggling

Music

Magic

Sports

Illustrators (SEE Authors)

Indoor Fun (SEE Activities)

Independence Day/ Fourth of July

Holidays for Children: Independence Day

India and Indian Culture

Fun in a Box Volume 2: New Friends and Other Stories (Metal Dogs of India)

National Geographic Kids Videos: Adventures in Asia

Shalom Sesame: People of Israel

Irish and Irish American Culture

Finn McCoul (Rabbit Ears)

Multicultural Peoples of North America: Irish Americans

Italian Videos, Italian and Italian American Culture, Folktales

Foolish Frog and Other Stories (Strega Nonna)

Multicultural Peoples of North America: Italian Americans

Pinocchio (Rabbit Ears)

Strega Nonna and Other Stories

Jamaican Videos (SEE Latin American/Caribbean Culture)

Japanese Videos, Japanese and Japanese American Culture, Tales

Little Duck Tale, A

Multicultural Peoples of North America: Japanese Americans

My Neighbor Totoro

Sesame Street Specials: Big Bird in Japan

Sesame Street Specials: Celebrates Around the World

Jewish Videos, Jewish and Jewish American Culture, Holidays

Bubbe's Boarding House Series: Chanuka at Bubbe's

Bubbe's Boarding House Series: Passover at Bubbe's

Holidays for Children: Hanukkah Passover

Holidays for Children: Rosh Hashanah Yom Kippur

Lights: The Miracle of Chanukah

Lovely Butterfly — Pepar Nechmad

Lovely Butterfly — Pepar Nechmad: Chanukah

Lovely Butterfly — Pepar Nechmad: Flowers for the Independence Day

Lovely Butterfly — Pepar Nechmad: Passover

Lovely Butterfly — Pepar Nechmad: Purim

Lovely Butterfly — Pepar Nechmad: Tishrei Month Holidays (Rosh Hashana and Sukkot)

Lovely Butterfly — Pepar Nechmad: Tu B'Shvat

Multicultural Peoples of North America: Jewish Americans

Now I Know My Aleph Bet

Sesame Street Specials: Celebrates Around the World

Shalom Sesame

Shalom Sesame: Aleph-Bet Telethon

Shalom Sesame: Chanukah

Shalom Sesame: Jerusalem

Shalom Sesame: Journey to Secret Places

Shalom Sesame: Kibbutz

Shalom Sesame: Kids Sing Israel

Shalom Sesame: Land of Israel

Shalom Sesame: Passover

Shalom Sesame: People of Israel

Shalom Sesame: Sing Around the Seasons

Shalom Sesame: Tel Aviv

Jobs (SEE Careers)

Juggling

Imaginaria: A Computer Animation Music Video for Children

Juggle Time

Korean American Culture

Multicultural Peoples of North America: Korean Americans

Kwanzaa

Holidays for Children: Kwanzaa

Language Arts and Grammar SEE:

Book-Based Videos

Reading/Pre-Reading, Writing and Concepts

Poetry and Rhymes

Languages SEE:

French Language

German Language

Hebrew Language

Non-Verbal (Videos Without Words)

Sign Language

Spanish Language

Latin American, Caribbean and Hispanic Culture

Abuela's Weave

Alejandro's Gift

Anansi (Rabbit Ears) (Jamaican)

Anansi Goes Fishing (Jamaican)

Caribbean Kids: English Version

Caribbean Kids: Spanish Version

Carlitos, Dani y Luis Alfredo

Cri-Cri: El Grillito Cantor

Folk Games

Gryphon

Holidays for Children: Cinco De Mayo

Joan Baez (1941-Present) — Mexican American Folksinger: English

Joan Baez (1941-Present) — Mexican American Folksinger: Spanish

Josephine's Imagination (Haitian)

Madre Tierra

Magical Coqui — Puerto Rico — Mi Tierra!

Maricela

The Monkey People (Rabbit Ears)

Multicultural Peoples of North America: Central Americans

Multicultural Peoples of North America: Mexican Americans

Multicultural Peoples of North America: Puerto Ricans

National Geographic Kids Videos: Totally Tropical Rainforest

Pepito's Dream

Red Shoes, The (Animation)

Seasons and Holidays Around the World: Christmas in Mexico

Sesame Street Specials: Celebrates Around the World

Sesame Street: Plaza Sesamo

Sesame Street: Plaza Sesamo: De Compamento Con Montoya: Big Bird Goes Camping

Sesame Street: Plaza Sesamo: El Alfabeto De Montoya: Learn the Alphabet with Bert and Ernie

Sesame Street: Plaza Sesamo: Plaza Sesamo Canta: Favorite Songs From Past Shows

Sesame Street: Plaza Sesamo: Vamos a Imaginar: Learn About Sounds and Shapes

Sesame Street: Plaza Sesamo: Viaja Con Nosotros: Big Bird and Oscar Go to Venezuela and Mexico

Sesame Street: Plaza Sesamo: The Plaza Sesamo Complete Set

Spanish Club: Fiesta!

Spanish Club: Los Animales!

Spirits of the Rainforest

Sweet 15

Where in the World Kids Explore: Volume 1. Kids Explore Mexico

Literature (SEE Book-Based Videos)

Magic

Amazing Things

Amazing Things, Volume 1

Amazing Things, Volume 2

Rainy Day Magic Show

Shari Lewis: You Can Do It!

Manners

Barney and the Backyard Gang: Barney's Best Manners

Berenstain Bears and the Messy Room

Shari Lewis: Lamb Chop in the Land of No Manners

There's a Cricket in the Library

Thomas the Tank Engine & Friends: Better Late Than Never and Other Stories

Math and Numbers

Bill Cosby's Picturepages: Who's Counting?

Clifford's Fun with Numbers

Dozen Dizzy Dogs, A

Dr. Seuss: One Fish, Two Fish, Red Fish, Blue Fish: English Version

Dr. Seuss: One Fish, Two Fish, Red Fish, Blue Fish: Spanish Version, Un Pez, Dos Peces....

Good Morning Miss Toliver

Living and Working in Space: The Countdown Has Begun

Math...Who Needs It?

Mathnet The Case of The Unnatural

Morris the Moose: Goes to School Gets a Cold

My Principal Lives Next Door

My Sesame Street Home Video: Count It Higher: Great Music Videos from Sesame Street

My Sesame Street Home Video: Learning About Numbers

My Sesame Street Home Video: Learning to Add and Subtract

Postman Pat's 123 Story

Richard Scarry's Best Counting Video

Zillions TV: A Kid's Guide to Toys and Games

Mexico and Mexican Culture (SEE Latin American/Caribbean Culture)

Money Management

Human Race Club: A Story About Self-Esteem

Madame C.J. Walker (1867-1919) — Entrepreneur

Piggy Banks to Money Markets

Zillions TV: A Kid's Guide to Toys and Games

Moving to a New Home

Ira Says Goodbye

Let's Get a Move On!

Mr. Rogers Videos

Mr. Rogers Videos

Mr. Rogers: Dinosaurs & Monsters

Mr. Rogers: Music and Feelings

Mr. Rogers: Musical Stories

Mr. Rogers: What About Love

Mr. Rogers: When Parents Are Away

Mr. Rogers' Neighborhood: Circus Fun

Mr. Rogers' Neighborhood: Kindness

Mr. Rogers' Neighborhood: Love

Mr. Rogers' Neighborhood: Making Music

Music: Sing-Alongs, Instruction, Making Music, Videos About Music

(SEE ALSO Dance)

American Women of Achievement: Marian Anderson (1902-1993) — Singer

Anansi

At the Zoo

Baby Goes...Songs to Take Along

Baby Songs 1

Baby Songs 2: More Baby Songs

Baby Songs: Even More Baby Songs

Baby Songs Christmas

Baby Songs Presents: Follow Along Songs with Hap Palmer

Baby Songs Presents: John Lithgow's Kid-Size Concert

Baby Songs: Sing Together

Baby Songs: Super Baby Songs

Baby's Bedtime

Baby's Morningtime

Barney and the Backyard Gang

Barney and the Backyard Gang: Barney Goes to School

Barney and the Backyard Gang: Barney in Concert

Barney and the Backyard Gang: Barney's Best Manners

Barney and the Backyard Gang: Barney's Birthday

Barney and the Backyard Gang: Barney's Campfire Sing-Along

Barney and the Backyard Gang: Barney's Imagination Island

Barney and the Backyard Gang: Barney's Home Sweet Homes

Barney and the Backyard Gang: Barney's Magical Musical Adventure

Barney and the Backyard Gang: Barney's Safety Video

Barney and the Backyard Gang: Rock with Barney

Barney and the Backyard Gang: Waiting for Santa

Beethoven Lives Upstairs

Bethie's Really Silly Clubhouse

Big Bird's Favorite Party Games

Candles, Snow and Mistletoe

Caribbean Kids: English Version

Caribbean Kids: Spanish Version

Child of Mine: The Lullaby Video

Clifford's Sing-A-Long Adventure

Cri-Cri: El Grillito Cantor

Dan Crow's Oops!

Don Cooper: Mother Nature's Songs

Ella Jenkins: For the Family

Ella Jenkins Live! At the Smithsonian

Foolish Frog and Other Stories

Gift of Amazing Grace, The

Good Morning Sunshine

Imaginaria: A Computer Animation Music Video for Children

It's Not Easy Being Green

Jazz Time Tale

Jessi Sings Songs from Around the World

Joan Baez (1941-Present) — Mexican American Folksinger: English

Joan Baez (1941-Present) — Mexican American Folksinger: Spanish

Joe Scruggs First Video

Joe Scruggs in Concert

Kidsongs Music Video Stories

Kidsongs Music Video Stories: Cars, Boats, Trains and Planes

Kidsongs Music Video Stories: A Day at Camp

Kidsongs Music Video Stories: A Day at the Circus

Kidsongs Music Video Stories: A Day at Old MacDonald's Farm

Kidsongs Music Video Stories: A Day with the Animals

Kidsongs Music Video Stories: Boppin' with Biggles

Kidsongs Music Video Stories: Country Sing-Along

Kidsongs Music Video Stories: Good Night, Sleep Tight

Kidsongs Music Video Stories: I'd Like to Teach the World to Sing

Kidsongs Music Video Stories: If We Could Talk to the Animals

Kidsongs Music Video Stories: Let's Play Ball!

Kidsongs Music Video Stories: Ride the Roller Coaster

Kidsongs Music Video Stories: Sing Out, America!

Kidsongs Music Video Stories: Very Silly Songs

Kidsongs Music Video Stories: We Wish You a Merry Christmas

Kidsongs Music Video Stories: What I Want to Be!

Kidsongs Music Video Stories: The Wonderful World of Sports

Let's Sing Along

Little People: Favorite Songs

Magical Coqui — Puerto Rico — Mi Tierra!

Making Music with Children

Making Music with Children, Program 1: Making Music with Children: Ages 3-7

Making Music with Children, Program 2: Making Music with Children: Ages 7-11

Making Music with Children, Program 3: Making Music in the Classroom: Ages 3-7

Making Music with Children, Program 4: Making Music in the Classroom: Ages 7-11

Mr. Rogers Videos

Mr. Rogers: Dinosaurs & Monsters

Mr. Rogers: Music and Feelings

Mr. Rogers: Musical Stories

Mr. Rogers: What About Love

Mr. Rogers: When Parents Are Away

Mr. Rogers' Neighborhood: Circus Fun

Mr. Rogers' Neighborhood: Kindness

Mr. Rogers' Neighborhood: Love

Mr. Rogers' Neighborhood: Making Music

Music Mania Professor Iris

Music and Magic

My First Activity Series: My First Music Video

My Sesame Street Home Videos

My Sesame Street Home Video: Alphabet Game, The

My Sesame Street Home Video: Bedtime Stories & Songs

My Sesame Street Home Video: Best of Elmo, The

My Sesame Street Home Video: Best of Ernie and Bert, The

My Sesame Street Home Video: Big Bird's Favorite Party Games

My Sesame Street Home Video: Big Bird's Story Time

My Sesame Street Home Video: Count It Higher: Great Music Videos from Sesame Street

My Sesame Street Home Video: Getting Ready for School

My Sesame Street Home Video: Getting Ready to Read

My Sesame Street Home Video: I'm Glad I'm Me

My Sesame Street Home Video: Learning About Letters

My Sesame Street Home Video: Learning About Numbers

My Sesame Street Home Video: Learning to Add and Subtract

My Sesame Street Home Video: Play-Along Games & Songs

Original Tales and Tunes

Pete Seeger's Family Concert

Puppy Pals

Raffi in Concert with the Rise and Shine Band

Raffi: Young People's Concert with Raffi

Rupert and the Frog Song

Sammy and Other Songs from Getting to Know Myself

Sesame Songs: Dance Along!

Sesame Songs: Elmo's Sing-Along Guessing Game

Sesame Songs: Monster Hits!

Sesame Songs: Rock & Roll!

Sesame Songs: Sing Yourself Silly!

Sesame Songs: Sing, Hoot and Howl

Sesame Songs: Sing-Along Earth Songs

Sesame Songs: We All Sing Together

Sesame Street Specials: Big Bird in China

Sesame Street Specials: Big Bird in Japan

Sesame Street Specials: Celebrates Around the World

Sesame Street Specials: Christmas Eve on Sesame Street

Sesame Street Specials: Don't Eat the Pictures — Sesame Street Visits the Metropolitan Museum of Art

Sesame Street's Specials: Sesame Street's 25th Birthday: A Musical Celebration

Sesame Street Start to Read Videos

Sesame Street Start to Read Videos: Don't Cry, Big Bird and Other Stories

Sesame Street Start to Read Videos: Ernie's Big Mess and Other Stories

Sesame Street Start to Read Videos: Ernie's Little Lie and Other Stories

Sesame Street Start to Read Videos: I Want to Go Home! and Other Stories

Sesame Street Visits: The Firehouse

Sesame Street Visits: The Hospital

Shalom Sesame

Shalom Sesame: Aleph-Bet Telethon

Shalom Sesame: Chanukah

Shalom Sesame: Jerusalem

Shalom Sesame: Journey to Secret Places

Shalom Sesame: Kibbutz

Shalom Sesame: Kids Sing Israel

Shalom Sesame: Land of Israel

Shalom Sesame: Passover

Shalom Sesame: People of Israel

Shalom Sesame: Sing Around the Seasons

Shalom Sesame: Tel Aviv

Shari Lewis: Kooky Classics

Sharon, Lois & Bram's: Elephant Show

Sharon, Lois & Bram's: Elephant Show: Back by Popular Demand

Sharon, Lois & Bram's: Elephant Show: Live in your Living Room

Sharon, Lois & Bram's: Elephant Show: Pet Fair

Sharon, Lois & Bram's: Elephant Show: Radio Show

Sharon, Lois & Bram's: Elephant Show: Sleepover

Sharon, Lois & Bram's: Elephant Show: Soap Box Derby

Sharon, Lois & Bram's: Elephant Show: Treasure Island

Sharon, Lois & Bram's: Elephant Show: Who Stole the Cookies

Sign Songs: Fun Songs to Sign and Sing

Silly Tales and Tunes

Sing-Along, Dance-Along, Do-along

Sparky's Magic Piano

Strega Nonna and Other Stories

Tall Tales: Darlin' Clementine

Teddy Bears' Jamboree

This Pretty Planet

Tickle Tune Typhoon: Let's Be Friends

Wee Sing in Sillyville

Wee Sing Together

Wee Sing Train

Wee Sing: Grandpa's Magical Toys

Wildlife Symphony

You On Kazoo!

Young People's Concert with Raffi

Zeezel the Zowie Zoon in the Color Chase

Zoobilee Zoo: Laughland and Other Stories

Mystery

The Baby-Sitters Club: Claudia and the Missing Jewels

The Baby-Sitters Club: Claudia and the Mystery of the Secret Passage

The Baby-Sitters Club: Dawn and the Haunted House

The Baby-Sitters Club: Jessi and the Mystery of the Stolen Secrets

Basil Hears a Noise

Berenstain Bears: No Girls Allowed and The Missing Dinosaur Bone

Fun in a Box Volume 1: Ben's Dream (Fish)

Jumanji

Mathnet The Case of the Unnatural

Ramona: Rainy Sunday

Shalom Sesame: Aleph-Bet Telethon

Shalom Sesame: Passover

Sharon, Lois & Bram's: Elephant Show: Treasure Island

Native American Culture

Dancing with the Indians

Gift of the Whales

Hawk, I'm Your Brother

Knots on a Counting Rope

Native Indian Folklore

Other Way to Listen, The

Princess Scargo and the Birthday Pumpkin (Rabbit Ears)

Song of Sacajawea (Rabbit Ears)

Spirits of the Rainforest

Thirteen Moons on Turtle's Back

Way to Start a Day, The

Where in the World Kids Explore: Volume 2. Kids Explore Alaska

Nature (SEE Animals, Earth Science and Science)

New Year's Eve

Sesame Street Specials: Celebrates Around the World

Non-Verbal (Videos Without Words)

Doing Things: Eating, Washing, in Motion

Good Morning, Good Night: A Day on the Farm

Language Primer

Language Primer: Adventuresome Max: Discovering the World

Language Primer: Max in Motion: Developing Language Skills

Language Primer: Max's Library: Beginning to Write

Magic of Discovery, The (Body Talking)

The Mole and the Green Star

The Mole in Town

Snowman, The

Numbers (SEE Math and Numbers)

Party Videos

Amazing Things

Amazing Things, Volume 1

Amazing Things, Volume 2

Barney and the Backyard Gang: Barney's Birthday

Berenstain Bears and Too Much Birthday and to the Rescue

Big Bird's Favorite Party Games

Birthday Dragon

Birthday! Party Professor Iris

Fun in a Box Volume 3: The Birthday Movie

Happy Birdy

Moira's Birthday (plus Blackberry Subway Jam)

My Sesame Street Home Video: Big Bird's Favorite Party Games

Real Story Videos: The Real Story of Happy Birthday to You

Sharon, Lois & Bram's: Elephant Show: Sleepover

Simply Magic: The Rainy Day Adventure

Teddy Bear's Picnic, The

Wee Sing Together

Winnie the Pooh and a Day for Eeyore

Passover (Pesach)

Bubbe's Boarding House Series: Passover at Bubbe's

Lovely Butterfly — Pepar Nechmad: Passover

Shalom Sesame: Passover

Planet Earth (SEE Earth Science, Ecology and Environment)

Poetry and Rhymes (SEE ALSO Book-Based Videos)

Baby's Nursery Rhymes

Emily Dickinson (1830-1890) — Poet

Baby's Morningtime

Child's Christmas in Wales, A

Clifford's Fun with Rhymes

Dr. Seuss Videos

Dr. Seuss' ABC

Dr. Seuss: The Butter Battle Book

Dr. Seuss' Cat in the Hat

Dr. Seuss: The Cat in the Hat Comes Back

Dr. Seuss: Green Eggs and Ham

Dr. Seuss: Hoober-Bloob Highway

Dr. Seuss: Hop on Pop

Dr. Seuss: Horton Hears a Who

Dr. Seuss: Horton Hatches the Egg

Dr. Seuss: How the Grinch Stole Christmas

Dr. Seuss: I AM NOT Going to Get Up Today!

Dr. Seuss: The Lorax

Dr. Seuss: One Fish, Two Fish, Red Fish, Blue Fish: English Version

Dr. Seuss: One Fish, Two Fish, Red Fish, Blue Fish: Spanish Version, Un Pez, Dos Peces....

Dr. Seuss: Pontoffel Pock

Dr. Seuss' Sleep Book

Dr. Seuss Video Festival

Free to Be...You and Me

I Need a Hug!

Madeline

Madeline (Christopher Plummer)

More Pre-School Power

The Night Before Christmas (Rabbit Ears)

Nonsense and Lullabyes: Poems for Children

Nonsense and Lullabyes: Nursery Rhymes

Real Story Videos: The Real Story of Baa Baa Black Sheep

Real Story Videos: The Real Story of Happy Birthday to You

Real Story Videos: The Real Story of I'm a Little Teapot

Real Story Videos: The Real Story of Itsy Bitsy Spider

Real Story Videos: The Real Story of Rain, Rain Go Away

Real Story Videos: The Real Story of Three Little Kittens

Real Story Videos: The Real Story Twinkle Twinkle Little Star

Thirteen Moons on Turtle's Back

`Twas the Night Before Christmas

Polish American Culture

Multicultural Peoples of North America: Polish Americans

Pre-Reading (SEE Reading and Poetry)

Prejudice and Discrimination

Abuela's Weave

Alice Walker (1944-Present) — Author

American Women of Achievement Video Collection

American Women of Achievement: Abigail Adams (1744-1818) — Women's Rights Advocate

American Women of Achievement: Jane Addams (1860-1935) — Social Worker

American Women of Achievement: Marian Anderson (1902-1993) — Singer

American Women of Achievement: Susan B. Anthony (1820-1906) — Woman Suffragist

American Women of Achievement: Clara Barton (1821-1912) — Founder, American Red Cross

American Women of Achievement: Emily Dickinson (1830-1890) — Poet

American Women of Achievement: Amelia Earhart (1897-Disappeared in 1937) — Aviator

American Women of Achievement: Helen Keller (1880-1968) — Humanitarian

American Women of Achievement: Sandra Day O'Connor (1930-Present) — Supreme Court Justice

American Women of Achievement: Wilma Rudolph (1940-Present) — Champion Athlete

And the Children Shall Lead

The Baby-Sitters Club: Dawn and the Haunted House

The Baby-Sitters Club: Kristy and the Great Campaign

Berenstain Bears: No Girls Allowed and The Missing Dinosaur Bone

Dancing with the Indians

Danny and the Dinosaur and Other Stories (The Island of Skog)

Dr. Seuss: The Butter Battle Book

First and Second Grade Feelings: So What?

Follow the Drinking Gourd (Rabbit Ears)

Harriet Tubman (1820-1913) — Anti-Slavery Activist

Hideaways, The

Human Race Club: A Story About Making Friends, A Story About Prejudice and Discrimination

Madeline and the Dog Show

Maricela

Picture Book of Martin Luther King, Jr., A

Simon the Lamb

Sojourner Truth (1797-1883) — Abolitionist Leader

Speeches of Martin Luther King, Jr., The

Sweet 15

Tickle Tune Typhoon: Let's Be Friends

You Must Remember This

Zoobilee Zoo: Blue Ribbon Zooble and Other Stories

Zoobilee Zoo: Zooble Hop and Other Stories

Puerto Rican Culture (SEE Latin American/ Caribbean Culture)

Purim

Lovely Butterfly — Pepar Nechmad: Purim

Quinceanera

Sweet 15

Rabbit Ears Video Series

Anansi (Rabbit Ears)

Annie Oakley (Rabbit Ears)

Brer Rabbit and the Wonderful Tar Baby (Rabbit Ears)

Emperor and Nightingale (Rabbit Ears)

Emperor's New Clothes (Rabbit Ears)

Finn McCoul (Rabbit Ears)

Follow the Drinking Gourd (Rabbit Ears)

A Gingerbread Christmas (Rabbit Ears)

The Gingham Dog and the Calico Cat (Rabbit Ears)

How the Leopard Got His Spots (Rabbit Ears)

Jack and the Beanstalk (Rabbit Ears)

John Henry (Rabbit Ears)

Johnny Appleseed (Rabbit Ears)

King Midas and the Golden Touch (Rabbit Ears)

Koi and the Kola Nuts (Rabbit Ears)

Lion and the Lamb, The (Rabbit Ears)

The Monkey People (Rabbit Ears)

Mose the Fireman (Rabbit Ears)

The Night Before Christmas (Rabbit Ears)

Noah and the Ark (Rabbit Ears)

Paul Bunyan (Rabbit Ears)

Pecos Bill (Rabbit Ears)

Pinocchio (Rabbit Ears)

Princess Scargo and the Birthday Pumpkin (Rabbit Ears)

Puss in Boots (Rabbit Ears)

Savior Is Born, The (Rabbit Ears)

Song of Sacajawea (Rabbit Ears)

Velveteen Rabbit (Rabbit Ears)

White Cat, The (Rabbit Ears)

Rainy Day Fun (SEE Activities)

Reading/Pre-Reading, Writing and Concepts (SEE ALSO Book-Based and Poetry)

All About ABC's

Alphabet Library

Alphabet City

Alphabet House

Alphabet Zoo

Animal Alphabet

Bill Cosby's Picturepages

Bill Cosby's Picturepages: What Goes Where?

Bill Cosby's Picturepages: What's Different?

Bill Cosby's Picturepages: What's That Shape?

Bill Cosby's Picturepages: What's Missing?

Bill Cosby's Picturepages: Who's Counting?

Can I Be Good?

Clifford's Fun with Letters

Clifford's Fun with Numbers

Clifford's Fun with Opposites

Clifford's Fun with Rhymes

Clifford's Fun with Shapes and Colors

Clifford's Fun with Sounds

Clifford's Sing-A-Long Adventure

Dozen Dizzy Dogs, A

Dr. Seuss' ABC

Dr. Seuss' Cat in the Hat

Dr. Seuss: The Cat in the Hat Comes Back

Dr. Seuss: Green Eggs and Ham

Dr. Seuss: Hop on Pop

Dr. Seuss: I Am NOT Going to Get Up Today!

Dr. Seuss: One Fish, Two Fish, Red Fish, Blue Fish: English Version

Dr. Seuss: One Fish, Two Fish, Red Fish, Blue Fish: Spanish Version, Un Pez, Dos Peces....

Happy Birdy

Jay O'Callahan: A Master Class in Storytelling

Jay O'Callahan: Herman & Marguerite

Language Primer

Language Primer: Adventuresome Max: Discovering the World

Language Primer: Max in Motion: Developing Language Skills

Language Primer: Max's Library: Beginning to Write

Language Stories

Language Stories: A Cache of Jewels and Other Collective Nouns

Language Stories: Kites Sail High

Language Stories: Many Luscious Lollipops

Language Stories: Merry-Go-Round

Little People: Fun with Words

Little Lou and His Strange Little Zoo

Magic of Discovery, The

Morris the Moose: Goes to School Gets a Cold

My New York

My Sesame Street Home Videos

My Sesame Street Home Video: Alphabet Game, The

My Sesame Street Home Video: Bedtime Stories & Songs

My Sesame Street Home Video: Best of Ernie and Bert, The

My Sesame Street Home Video: Big Bird's Favorite Party Games

My Sesame Street Home Video: Big Bird's Story Time

My Sesame Street Home Video: Count It Higher: Great Music Videos from Sesame Street

My Sesame Street Home Video: Getting Ready for School

My Sesame Street Home Video: Getting Ready to Read

My Sesame Street Home Video: I'm Glad I'm Me

My Sesame Street Home Video: Learning About Letters

My Sesame Street Home Video: Learning About Numbers

My Sesame Street Home Video: Learning to Add and Subtract

My Sesame Street Home Video: Play-Along Games & Songs

"Not Now!" Said the Cow

Postman Pat's ABC Story

Real Story Videos: The Real Story of Baa Baa Black Sheep

Real Story Videos: The Real Story of Happy Birthday to You

Real Story Videos: The Real Story of I'm A Little Teapot

Real Story Videos: The Real Story of Itsy Bitsy Spider

Real Story Videos: The Real Story of Rain, Rain Go Away

Real Story Videos: The Real Story of Three Little Kittens

Real Story Videos: The Real Story Twinkle Twinkle Little Star

Richard Scarry's Best Ever ABC Video

Richard Scarry's Best Learning Songs Ever

Sand Castle, The
(Alphabet)

Sesame Songs: Dance
Along!

Sesame Songs: Elmo's
Sing-Along Guessing
Game

Sesame Songs: Monster
Hits!

Sesame Songs: Rock &
Roll!

Sesame Songs: Sing
Yourself Silly!

Sesame Songs: Sing, Hoot
and Howl

Sesame Street Specials:
Big Bird in China

Sesame Street Specials:
Big Bird in Japan

Sesame Street Specials:
Celebrates Around the
World

Sesame Street Specials:
Christmas Eve on Sesame
Street

Sesame Street Specials:
Don't Eat the Pictures —
Sesame Street Visits the
Metropolitan Museum of
Art

Sesame Street Specials:
Sesame Street's 25th
Birthday: A Musical
Celebration

Sesame Street Start to
Read Videos

Sesame Street Start to
Read Videos: Don't Cry,
Big Bird and Other
Stories

Sesame Street Start to
Read Videos: Ernie's Big
Mess and Other Stories

Sesame Street Start to
Read Videos: Ernie's
Little Lie and Other
Stories

Sesame Street Start to
Read Videos: I Want to Go
Home! and Other Stories

Sesame Street Visits: The
Firehouse

Sesame Street Visits: The
Hospital

Shalom Sesame: Aleph-
Bet Telethon

Sharon, Lois & Bram's:
Elephant Show

Sharon, Lois & Bram's:
Elephant Show: Back by
Popular Demand

Sharon, Lois & Bram's:
Elephant Show: Live in
your Living Room

Sharon, Lois & Bram's:
Elephant Show: Pet Fair

Sharon, Lois & Bram's:
Elephant Show: Radio
Show

Sharon, Lois & Bram's:
Elephant Show: Sleepover

Sharon, Lois & Bram's:
Elephant Show: Soap Box
Derby

Sharon, Lois & Bram's:
Elephant Show: Treasure
Island

Sharon, Lois & Bram's:
Elephant Show: Who
Stole the Cookies

Squiggles, Dots and Lines

Three Sesame Street
Stories

To Bathe a Boa

Today Was a Terrible Day

Water Is Wet

We All Sing Together

We Learn About the
World: English Version

We Learn About the
World: Spanish Version

Zeezel the Zowie Zoon in
the Color Chase

**Rhymes (SEE
Poetry)**

Rosh Hashanah

Holidays for Children:
Rosh Hashanah Yom
Kippur

Lovely Butterfly — Pepar
Nechmad: Tishrei Month
Holidays (Rosh Hashana
and Sukkot)

**Recycling (SEE
Earth Science,
Ecology,
Environment)**

Holidays for Children:
Rosh Hashanah Yom
Kippur

Lovely Butterfly — Pepar
Nechmad: Tishrei Month
Holidays (Rosh Hashana
and Sukkot)

**Russian American
Culture**

Chicken Sunday

Folk Games

Magic of Discovery, The
(Matrioska)

Shalom Sesame: People of
Israel

**Safety (SEE Health
and Safety)**

**Science (SEE ALSO:
Archeology,
Astronomy,
Animals, Earth
Science, Space,
Seasons of the Year,
Senses)**

American Women of
Achievement: Clara
Barton (1821-1912) —
Founder, American Red
Cross

Astronomy 101: A Family
Adventure

Best of Beakman's World,
The

Bill Nye the Science Guy

Bill Nye the Science Guy:
Outer Space Way Out
There

Bill Nye the Science Guy:
Dinosaurs Those Big
Boneheads

Bill Nye the Science Guy:
The Human body The
Inside Scoop

Creepy Critters Professor
Iris

Gateway to the Mind

I Dig Fossils

Indoor Fun (A Close Look
at Volcanoes)

Look What I Grew

Look What I Found

Magic School Bus

The Magic School Bus:
For Lunch

The Magic School Bus:
Gets Eaten

The Magic School Bus:
Gets Lost in Space

The Magic School Bus:
Hops Home

The Magic School Bus:
Inside Ralphie

My First Activity Series:
My First Science Video

National Geographic Kids
Videos

National Geographic Kids
Videos: Adventures in
Asia

National Geographic Kids
Videos: Amazing North
America

National Geographic Kids
Videos: Deep Sea Dive

National Geographic Kids
Videos: Swinging Safari

National Geographic Kids
Videos: Totally Tropical
Rainforest

National Geographic Kids
Videos: Wonders Down
Under

Science Primer: Earth,
Air, Water, Fire

Science Primer: The Five
Senses

Science Primer: Habitats

Walking on Air

Woman's Place, A

Zillions TV: A Kid's Guide
to Toys and Games

**Seasons of the Year
(SEE ALSO the
names of holidays)**

Ezra Jack Keats Library

Five Sesame Street
Stories (Big Bird Brings
Spring to Sesame Street)

Follow That Bunny!

Frog and Toad Are
Friends (Spring)

Fun in a Box Volume 2:
New Friends and Other
Stories (Howard)

Jay O'Callahan: Herman
& Marguerite

Native Indian Folklore
(Summer Legend)

Sand Castle, The (The
North Wind & the Sun)

Seasons and Holidays
Around the World

Seasons and Holidays
Around the World:
Chinese New Year

Seasons and Holidays
Around the World:
Christmas in Mexico

Seasons and Holidays
Around the World:
Christmas in Sweden

Seasons and Holidays
Around the World:
Halloween in Britain

Shalom Sesame: Sing
Around the Seasons

Smile for Auntie and
Other Stories (The Snowy
Day)

Snowman, The

Thirteen Moons on
Turtle's Back

Which Way, Weather?

Self-Image and Self-Esteem

Abuela's Weave

American Women of Achievement Video Collection

American Women of Achievement: Abigail Adams (1744-1818) — Women's Rights Advocate

American Women of Achievement: Jane Addams (1860-1935) — Social Worker

American Women of Achievement: Marian Anderson (1902-1993) — Singer

American Women of Achievement: Susan B. Anthony (1820-1906) — Woman Suffragist

American Women of Achievement: Clara Barton (1821-1912) — Founder, American Red Cross

American Women of Achievement: Emily Dickinson (1830-1890) — Poet

American Women of Achievement: Amelia Earhart (1897- Disappeared in 1937) — Aviator

American Women of Achievement: Helen Keller (1880-1968) — Humanitarian

American Women of Achievement: Sandra Day O'Connor (1930-Present) — Supreme Court Justice

American Women of Achievement: Wilma Rudolph (1940-Present) — Champion Athlete

The Baby-Sitters Club: Kristy and the Great Campaign

Barney and the Backyard Gang

Barney and the Backyard Gang: Barney Goes to School

Barney and the Backyard Gang: Barney in Concert

Barney and the Backyard Gang: Barney's Best Manners

Barney and the Backyard Gang: Barney's Birthday

Barney and the Backyard Gang: Barney's Campfire Sing-Along

Barney and the Backyard Gang: Barney's Imagination Island

Barney and the Backyard Gang: Barney's Home Sweet Homes

Barney and the Backyard Gang: Barney's Magical Musical Adventure

Barney and the Backyard Gang: Barney's Safety Video

Barney and the Backyard Gang: Rock with Barney

Barney and the Backyard Gang: Waiting for Santa

Can I Be Good?

Creative Movement: A Step Towards Intelligence

Dr. Seuss: Pontoffel Pock

50 Below Zero (plus Thomas' Snowsuit) (Thomas' Snow Suit)

First and Second Grade Feelings: The Real-Skin Rubber Monster Mask

First and Second Grade Feelings: So What?

Free to Be...You and Me

Human Race Club: A Story About Self-Esteem

It's Not Always Easy Being a Kid

Land of Pleasant Dreams, The: Fence Too High, A

Learning About Me: A Is for Autonomy

Little Crooked Christmas Tree, The

Little Engine That Could, The: English Narration

Little Engine That Could, The: French Narration

Little Engine That Could, The: Spanish Narration

Mop Top

Mr. Rogers Videos

Mr. Rogers: Dinosaurs & Monsters

Mr. Rogers: Music and Feelings

Mr. Rogers: Musical Stories

Mr. Rogers: What About Love

Mr. Rogers: When Parents Are Away

Mr. Rogers' Neighborhood: Circus Fun

Mr. Rogers' Neighborhood: Kindness

Mr. Rogers' Neighborhood: Love

Mr. Rogers' Neighborhood: Making Music

My Sesame Street Home Video: I'm Glad I'm Me

National Velvet

Opus n' Bill: A Wish for Wings That Work

Shelley Duvall's Bedtime Stories: The Little Rabbit Who Wanted Red Wings

Thomas the Tank Engine & Friends

Thomas the Tank Engine & Friends: Better Late Than Never and Other Stories

Thomas the Tank Engine & Friends: Christmas Party

Thomas the Tank Engine & Friends: James Learns a Lesson & Other Stories

Thomas the Tank Engine & Friends: Percy's Ghostly & Other Stories

Thomas the Tank Engine & Friends: Tenders & Turntables & Other Stories

Thomas the Tank Engine & Friends: Thomas Breaks the Rules & Other Stories

Thomas the Tank Engine & Friends: Thomas Gets Bumped

Thomas the Tank Engine & Friends: Thomas Gets Tricked & Other Stories

Thomas the Tank Engine & Friends: Trust Thomas & Other Stories

Today Was a Terrible Day

Walking on Air

Winnie the Pooh

Winnie the Pooh and the Blustery Day

Winnie the Pooh and a Day for Eeyore

Winnie the Pooh and the Honey Tree

Winnie the Pooh and Tigger Too

Winnie the Pooh: Making Friends, Learning

Winnie the Pooh The New Adventures: Volume 1. The Great Honey Pot Robbery

Winnie the Pooh The New Adventures: Volume 2. The Wishing Bear

Winnie the Pooh The New Adventures: Volume 3. Newfound Friends

You Can Choose!: Volume 1. Cooperation

You Can Choose!: Volume 2. Being Responsible

You Can Choose!: Volume 3. Dealing with Feelings

You Can Choose!: Volume 4. Saying No

You Can Choose!: Volume 5. Doing the Right Thing

You Can Choose!: Volume 6. Dealing with Disappointment

You Can Choose!: Volume 7. Appreciating Yourself

You Can Choose!: Volume 8. Asking for Help

You Can Choose!: Volume 9. Being Friends

You Can Choose!: Volume 10. Resolving Conflicts

Zoobilee Zoo

Zoobilee Zoo: Blue Ribbon Zooble and Other Stories

Zoobilee Zoo: Lady Whazzat and Other Stories

Zoobilee Zoo: Laughland and Other Stories

Zoobilee Zoo: Zoobadoobas and Other Stories

Zoobilee Zoo: Zooble Hop and Other Stories

Senses: Sight, Hearing, Taste, Smell, Touch

Baby Vision

Baby Vision Volume 1

Baby Vision Volume 2

Gateway to the Mind

Magic of Discovery, The (A Sense of Touch)

Science Primer: The Five Senses

Water Is Wet

Sign Language

Joe Scruggs in Concert

Sign Songs: Fun Songs to Sign and Sing

Sign-Me-A-Story

Sing-Alongs (SEE Music)

Skills for Living

Baby Goes...Songs to Take Along

Bill Cosby's Picturepages

Bill Cosby's Picturepages: What Goes Where?

Bill Cosby's Picturepages: What's Different?

Bill Cosby's Picturepages: What's That Shape?

Bill Cosby's Picturepages: What's Missing?

Bill Cosby's Picturepages: Who's Counting?

Classroom Holidays

Classroom Holidays: Bee My Valentine: A Valentine's Day Story

Classroom Holidays: Don't Eat Too Much Turkey: A Thanksgiving Story

Classroom Holidays: Liar, Liar, Pants on Fire: A Christmas/Chanukah Story

Classroom Holidays: Starring First Grade: An Anytime Celebration

Doing Things: Eating, Washing, in Motion

Fingermouse, Yoffy and Friends

First and Second Grade Feelings

First and Second Grade Feelings: Jim's Dog, Muffins.

First and Second Grade Feelings: The Real-Skin Rubber Monster Mask

First and Second Grade Feelings: See You in Second Grade!

First and Second Grade Feelings: So What?

Good Morning Miss Toliver

How Come?

It's Not Always Easy Being a Kid

Jay O'Callahan: A Master Class in Storytelling

Kidsongs Music Video Stories

Kidsongs Music Video Stories: Cars, Boats, Trains and Planes

Kidsongs Music Video Stories: A Day at Camp

Kidsongs Music Video Stories: A Day at the Circus

Kidsongs Music Video Stories: A Day at Old MacDonald's Farm

Kidsongs Music Video Stories: A Day with the Animals

Kidsongs Music Video Stories: Boppin' with Biggles

Kidsongs Music Video Stories: Country Sing-Along

Kidsongs Music Video Stories: Good Night, Sleep Tight

Kidsongs Music Video Stories: I'd Like to Teach the World to Sing

Kidsongs Music Video Stories: If We Could Talk to the Animals

Kidsongs Music Video Stories: Let's Play Ball!

Kidsongs Music Video Stories: Ride the Roller Coaster

Kidsongs Music Video Stories: Sing Out, America!

Kidsongs Music Video Stories: Very Silly Songs

Kidsongs Music Video Stories: We Wish You a Merry Christmas

Kidsongs Music Video Stories: What I Want to Be!

Kidsongs Music Video Stories: The Wonderful World of Sports

Let's Do It! Professor Iris

Look What I Found

Mine and Yours

More Pre-School Power

Mr. Rogers Videos

Mr. Rogers: Dinosaurs & Monsters

Mr. Rogers: Music and Feelings

Mr. Rogers: Musical Stories

Mr. Rogers: What About Love

Mr. Rogers: When Parents Are Away

Mr. Rogers' Neighborhood: Circus Fun

Mr. Rogers' Neighborhood: Kindness

Mr. Rogers' Neighborhood: Love

Mr. Rogers' Neighborhood: Making Music

Never Talk to Strangers

Pre-School Power: Jacket Flips & Other Tips

Pre-School Power #3

Sharon, Lois & Bram's: Elephant Show

Sharon, Lois & Bram's: Elephant Show: Back by Popular Demand

Sharon, Lois & Bram's: Elephant Show: Live in your Living Room

Sharon, Lois & Bram's: Elephant Show: Pet Fair

Sharon, Lois & Bram's: Elephant Show: Radio Show

Sharon, Lois & Bram's: Elephant Show: Sleepover

Sharon, Lois & Bram's: Elephant Show: Soap Box Derby

Sharon, Lois & Bram's: Elephant Show: Treasure Island

Sharon, Lois & Bram's: Elephant Show: Who Stole the Cookies

Zillions TV: A Kid's Guide to Toys and Games

Smoking (SEE Drug Education)

South American Culture (SEE Latin American/ Caribbean Culture)

Space

Bill Nye the Science Guy: Outer Space Way Out There

Dr. Seuss: Hoober-Bloob Highway

Indoor Fun (A Short Journey into Space)

Living and Working in Space: The Countdown Has Begun

Magic of Discovery, The (The Sky Is Blue)

The Magic School Bus: Gets Lost in Space

Mike Mulligan and His Steam Shovel (Moon Man)

Space Cadets Professor Iris

Walking on Air

Spanish Language (SEE ALSO Latin American/Culture)

Are You My Mother?: Spanish Version (Eres Tu Mi Mama?)

At Home in the Coral Reef: Spanish Version

Caribbean Kids: Spanish Version

Carlitos, Dani y Luis Alfredo

Cri-Cri: El Grillito Cantor

Dr. Seuss: One Fish, Two Fish, Red Fish, Blue Fish: Spanish Version, Un Pez, Dos Peces....

Jay Jay the Jet Plane and His Flying Friends, Volume 1: Spanish Version, Tito Turbinitas Y Sus Amigos Voladores

Joan Baez (1941-Present) — Mexican American Folksinger: Spanish

Little Engine That Could, The: Spanish Narration

Magical Coqui — Puerto Rico — Mi Tierra!

Sesame Street: Plaza Sesamo

Sesame Street: Plaza Sesamo: De Compamento Con Montoya: Big Bird Goes Camping

Sesame Street: Plaza Sesamo: El Alfabeto De Montoya: Learn the Alphabet with Bert and Ernie

Sesame Street: Plaza Sesamo: Plaza Sesamo Canta: Favorite Songs From Past Shows

Sesame Street: Plaza Sesamo: Vamos a Imaginar: Learn About Sounds and Shapes

Sesame Street: Plaza Sesamo: Viaja Con Nosotros: Big Bird and Oscar Go to Venezuela and Mexico

Sesame Street: Plaza Sesamo: The Plaza Sesamo Complete Set

Spanish Club: Fiesta!

Spanish Club: Los
Animales!

Spot: Spot's First Video -
Spanish

Spot: Spot's Adventure -
Spanish

We Learn About the
World: Spanish Version

Sports

American Women of
Achievement: Wilma
Rudolph (1940-Present) —
Champion Athlete

Introducing: The Flying
Fruit Fly Circus

Kidsongs Music Video
Stories: Let's Play Ball!

Kidsongs Music Video
Stories: The Wonderful
World of Sports

Let's Do It! Professor Iris

Mathnet The Case of the
Unnatural

Mighty Pawns, The

National Velvet

Reach for the Sky

Sharon, Lois & Bram's:
Elephant Show: Soap Box
Derby

Skating Safe for Kids

Thomas the Tank Engine
& Friends: James Learns
a Lesson & Other Stories
(Thomas Goes Fishing)

Woman's Place, A

"You Can" Video Series:
You Can Ride a Horse

"You Can" Video Series:
You Can Fly a Kite

You Can Choose!: Volume
6. Dealing with
Disappointment

Starting School

Anna Maria's Blanket

Get Ready for School

Imagine That!

Junglies: First Day at
School

Morris the Moose: Goes to
School Gets a Cold

My Sesame Street Home
Video: Getting Ready for
School

On Our Way to School

Spot Goes to School

Who Will Be My Friend?

Stereotypes (SEE Prejudice)

Stories, Tales and Folk Tales (SEE ALSO Book-Based Videos and Poetry)

African Story Magic

Afro-Classic Folk Tales

Afro-Classic Folk Tales,
Volume 1

Afro-Classic Folk Tales,
Volume 2

Anansi (Rabbit Ears)

Animal Stories

Annie Oakley (Rabbit
Ears)

Baby's Nursery Rhymes

Brer Rabbit and the
Wonderful Tar Baby
(Rabbit Ears)

Bump — My First Video

Caterpillar's Wish, A

Danny and the Dinosaur
and Other Stories

Emperor and Nightingale
(Rabbit Ears)

Emperor's New Clothes
(Rabbit Ears)

Finn McCoul (Rabbit
Ears)

Follow the Drinking
Gourd (Rabbit Ears)

Fun in a Box Volume 2:
New Friends and Other
Stories

How the Leopard Got His
Spots (Rabbit Ears)

Imaginaria: A Computer
Animation Music Video
for Children

Jay O'Callahan: A Master
Class in Storytelling

Jay O'Callahan: Six
Stories About Little
Heroes

John Henry (Rabbit Ears)

King Midas and the
Golden Touch (Rabbit
Ears)

Koi and the Kola Nuts
(Rabbit Ears)

Lion and the Lamb, The
(Rabbit Ears)

Mose the Fireman (Rabbit
Ears)

My Sesame Street Home
Video: Big Bird's Story
Time

Opus n' Bill: A Wish for
Wings That Work

Original Tales and Tunes

Paul Bunyan (Rabbit
Ears)

Pecos Bill (Rabbit Ears)

Pegasus

Pigs (plus David's Father)

Princess Scargo and the
Birthday Pumpkin
(Rabbit Ears)

Puss in Boots (Rabbit
Ears)

Real Story Videos: The
Real Story of Baa Baa
Black Sheep

Real Story Videos: The
Real Story of Happy
Birthday to You

Real Story Videos: The
Real Story of I'm a Little
Teapot

Real Story Videos: The
Real Story of Itsy Bitsy
Spider

Real Story Videos: The
Real Story of Rain, Rain
Go Away

Real Story Videos: The
Real Story of Three Little
Kittens

Real Story Videos: The
Real Story Twinkle
Twinkle Little Star

Reluctant Dragon

Rupert

Rupert and the Frog Song

Rupert and the Runaway
Dragon

Sand Castle, The

Sign-Me-A-Story

Song of Sacajawea (Rabbit
Ears)

Tall Tales: Darlin'
Clementine

There's a Cricket in the
Library

White Cat, The (Rabbit
Ears)

Stranger Danger

Berenstain Bears Learn
About Strangers

Never Talk to Strangers

Sukkot

Lovely Butterfly — Pepar
Nechmad: Tishrei Month
Holidays (Rosh Hashana
and Sukkot)

Swedish Culture

Seasons and Holidays
Around the World:
Christmas in Sweden

Shalom Sesame: People of
Israel

Thanksgiving

Classroom Holidays: Don't
Eat Too Much Turkey: A
Thanksgiving Story

Hoboken Chicken
Emergency

Holidays for Children:
Thanksgiving

Transportation: Trains, Planes, Buses

American Women of
Achievement: Amelia
Earhart (1897-
Disappeared in 1937) —
Aviator

Angela's Airplane (plus
The Fire Station)

Here We Go

Here We Go — Volume 1

Here We Go — Volume 2

Here We Go Again

Jay Jay the Jet Plane and
His Flying Friends,
Volume 1: Jay Jay's First
Flight and Three Other
Stories

Jay Jay the Jet Plane and
His Flying Friends,
Volume 1: Tito Turbinitas
Y Sus Amigos Voladores

Jay Jay the Jet Plane and
His Flying Friends,
Volume 2: Old Oscar
Leads the Parade and
Three Other Stories

Kidsongs Music Video
Stories: Cars, Boats,
Trains and Planes

Little Engine That Could,
The: English Narration

Little Engine That Could,
The: French Narration

Little Engine That Could,
The: Spanish Narration

Moira's Birthday (plus
Blackberry Subway Jam)
(Blackberry Subway Jam)

Moving Machines

There Goes a Bulldozer

There Goes a Fire Truck

There Goes a Police Car

There Goes a Train

There Goes a Truck

Thomas the Tank Engine
& Friends

Thomas the Tank Engine & Friends: Better Late Than Never and Other Stories

Thomas the Tank Engine & Friends: Christmas Party

Thomas the Tank Engine & Friends: James Learns a Lesson & Other Stories

Thomas the Tank Engine & Friends: Percy's Ghostly & Other Stories

Thomas the Tank Engine & Friends: Tenders & Turntables & Other Stories

Thomas the Tank Engine & Friends: Thomas Breaks the Rules & Other Stories

Thomas the Tank Engine & Friends: Thomas Gets Bumped

Thomas the Tank Engine & Friends: Thomas Gets Tricked & Other Stories

Thomas the Tank Engine & Friends: Trust Thomas & Other Stories

Wee Sing Train

Tu B'Shvat

Lovely Butterfly — Pepar Nechmad: Tu B'Shvat

Valentine's Day

Classroom Holidays: Bee My Valentine: A Valentine's Day Story

Holidays for Children: Valentine's Day

Values

Afro-Classic Folk Tales

Afro-Classic Folk Tales, Volume 1

Afro-Classic Folk Tales, Volume 2

American Women of Achievement Video Collection

American Women of Achievement: Abigail Adams (1744-1818) — Women's Rights Advocate

American Women of Achievement: Jane Addams (1860-1935) — Social Worker

American Women of Achievement: Marian Anderson (1902-1993) — Singer

American Women of Achievement: Susan B. Anthony (1820-1906) — Woman Suffragist

American Women of Achievement: Clara Barton (1821-1912) — Founder, American Red Cross

American Women of Achievement: Emily Dickinson (1830-1890) — Poet

American Women of Achievement: Amelia Earhart (1897- Disappeared in 1937) — Aviator

American Women of Achievement: Helen Keller (1880-1968) — Humanitarian

American Women of Achievement: Sandra Day O'Connor (1930-Present) — Supreme Court Justice

American Women of Achievement: Wilma Rudolph (1940-Present) — Champion Athlete

Baby-Sitters Club Videos

The Baby-Sitters Club: The Baby-Sitters Remember

The Baby-Sitters Club: The Baby-Sitters and the Boy Sitters

The Baby-Sitters Club: Christmas Special (1991)

The Baby-Sitters Club: Claudia and the Missing Jewels

The Baby-Sitters Club: Claudia and the Mystery of the Secret Passage

The Baby-Sitters Club: Dawn and the Dream Boy

The Baby-Sitters Club: Dawn and the Haunted House

The Baby-Sitters Club: Dawn Saves the Trees

The Baby-Sitters Club: Jessi and the Mystery of the Stolen Secrets

The Baby-Sitters Club: Kristy and the Great Campaign

The Baby-Sitters Club: Mary Ann and the Brunettes (1990)

The Baby-Sitters Club: Stacey's Big Break

The Baby-Sitters Club: Stacey Takes a Stand

Barney and the Backyard Gang

Barney and the Backyard Gang: Barney Goes to School

Barney and the Backyard Gang: Barney in Concert

Barney and the Backyard Gang: Barney's Best Manners

Barney and the Backyard Gang: Barney's Birthday

Barney and the Backyard Gang: Barney's Campfire Sing-Along

Barney and the Backyard Gang: Barney's Imagination Island

Barney and the Backyard Gang: Barney's Home Sweet Homes

Barney and the Backyard Gang: Barney's Magical Musical Adventure

Barney and the Backyard Gang: Barney's Safety Video

Barney and the Backyard Gang: Rock with Barney

Barney and the Backyard Gang: Waiting for Santa

Berenstain Bears Videos

Berenstain Bears Christmas Tree

Berenstain Bears in the Dark

Berenstain Bears Easter Surprise

Berenstain Bears Learn About Strangers

Berenstain Bears and the Messy Room

Berenstain Bears: No Girls Allowed and The Missing Dinosaur Bone

Berenstain Bears and Too Much Birthday and to the Rescue

Berenstain Bears and the Trouble with Friends

Berenstain Bears and the Truth

Berenstain Bears Get in a Fight

Classroom Holidays

Classroom Holidays: Bee My Valentine: A Valentine's Day Story

Classroom Holidays: Don't Eat Too Much Turkey: A Thanksgiving Story

Classroom Holidays: Liar, Liar, Pants on Fire: A Christmas/Chanukah Story

Classroom Holidays: Starring First Grade: An Anytime Celebration

Discovery Stories

Dr. Seuss: Horton Hears a Who (Thidwick the Big-Hearted Moose)

Dr. Seuss: Horton Hatches the Egg

Dr. Seuss Video Festival (Horton Hears a Who)

First and Second Grade Feelings

First and Second Grade Feelings: Jim's Dog, Muffins.

First and Second Grade Feelings: The Real-Skin Rubber Monster Mask

First and Second Grade Feelings: See You in Second Grade!

First and Second Grade Feelings: So What?

First and Second Grade Feelings Set

Free to Be...You and Me

Gryphon

Human Race Club: A Story About Fights between Brothers and Sisters

Human Race Club: A Story About Making Friends, A Story About Prejudice and Discrimination

Human Race Club: A Story About Self-Esteem

Jay Jay the Jet Plane and His Flying Friends, Volume 1: Jay Jay's First Flight and Three Other Stories

Jay Jay the Jet Plane and His Flying Friends, Volume 1: Tito Turbinitas Y Sus Amigos Voladores

Jay Jay the Jet Plane and His Flying Friends, Volume 2: Old Oscar Leads the Parade and Three Other Stories

Jay O'Callahan: Six Stories About Little Heroes

Jay O'Callahan: Herman & Marguerite

Land of Pleasant Dreams, The

Land of Pleasant Dreams, The: Bearly There At All

Land of Pleasant Dreams, The: Fence Too High, A

Land of Pleasant Dreams, The: Is It Soup Yet?

Learning About Me

Learning About Me: A Is for Autonomy

Learning About Me: B Is for Belonging

Learning About Me: Ipsilwhich Adventures

Little Lou and His Strange Little Zoo

Madeline at Cooking School

Magic Thinking Cap, The

More Pre-School Power

Mr. Rogers Videos

Mr. Rogers: Dinosaurs & Monsters

Mr. Rogers: Music and Feelings

Mr. Rogers: Musical Stories

Mr. Rogers: What About Love

Mr. Rogers: When Parents Are Away

Mr. Rogers' Neighborhood: Circus Fun

Mr. Rogers' Neighborhood: Kindness

Mr. Rogers' Neighborhood: Love

Mr. Rogers' Neighborhood: Making Music

My Sesame Street Home Videos

My Sesame Street Home Video: Alphabet Game, The

My Sesame Street Home Video: Bedtime Stories & Songs

My Sesame Street Home Video: Best of Ernie and Bert, The

My Sesame Street Home Video: Big Bird's Favorite Party Games

My Sesame Street Home Video: Big Bird's Story Time

My Sesame Street Home Video: Count It Higher: Great Music Videos from Sesame Street

My Sesame Street Home Video: Getting Ready for School

My Sesame Street Home Video: Getting Ready to Read

My Sesame Street Home Video: I'm Glad I'm Me

My Sesame Street Home Video: Learning About Letters

My Sesame Street Home Video: Learning About Numbers

My Sesame Street Home Video: Learning to Add and Subtract

My Sesame Street Home Video: Play-Along Games & Songs

Pinocchio (Rabbit Ears)

Pre-School Power: Jacket Flips & Other Tips

Pre-School Power #3

Red Shoes, The (Animation)

Rights from the Heart Droits au Coeur

Sesame Songs: Dance Along!

Sesame Songs: Elmo's Sing-Along Guessing Game

Sesame Songs: Monster Hits!

Sesame Songs: Rock & Roll!

Sesame Songs: Sing Yourself Silly!

Sesame Songs: Sing, Hoot and Howl

Sesame Street Specials: Big Bird in China

Sesame Street Specials: Big Bird in Japan

Sesame Street Specials: Celebrates Around the World

Sesame Street Specials: Christmas Eve on Sesame Street

Sesame Street Specials: Don't Eat the Pictures — Sesame Street Visits the Metropolitan Museum of Art

Sesame Street Specials: Sesame Street's 25th Birthday: A Musical Celebration

Sesame Street Start to Read Videos

Sesame Street Start to Read Videos: Don't Cry, Big Bird and Other Stories

Sesame Street Start to Read Videos: Ernie's Big Mess and Other Stories

Sesame Street Start to Read Videos: Ernie's Little Lie and Other Stories

Sesame Street Start to Read Videos: I Want to Go Home! and Other Stories

Sesame Street Visits: The Firehouse

Sesame Street Visits: The Hospital

Shalom Sesame

Shalom Sesame: Aleph-Bet Telethon

Shalom Sesame: Chanukah

Shalom Sesame: Jerusalem

Shalom Sesame: Journey to Secret Places

Shalom Sesame: Kibbutz

Shalom Sesame: Kids Sing Israel

Shalom Sesame: Land of Israel

Shalom Sesame: Passover

Shalom Sesame: People of Israel

Shalom Sesame: Sing Around the Seasons

Shalom Sesame: Tel Aviv

Shelley Duvall Presents Mrs. Piggle-Wiggle

Shelley Duvall Presents Mrs. Piggle-Wiggle: The Not-Truthful Cure and The Radish Cure

Shelley Duvall Presents Mrs. Piggle-Wiggle: The Pet Forgetters Cure and The Never-Want-To-Go-To-Bedders Cure

Shelley Duvall Presents Mrs. Piggle-Wiggle: The Answer Backer Cure and The Chores Cure

Sparky's Magic Piano

Thomas the Tank Engine & Friends

Thomas the Tank Engine & Friends: Better Late Than Never and Other Stories

Thomas the Tank Engine & Friends: Christmas Party

Thomas the Tank Engine & Friends: James Learns a Lesson & Other Stories

Thomas the Tank Engine & Friends: Percy's Ghostly & Other Stories

Thomas the Tank Engine & Friends: Tenders & Turntables & Other Stories

Thomas the Tank Engine & Friends: Thomas Breaks the Rules & Other Stories

Thomas the Tank Engine & Friends: Thomas Gets Bumped

Thomas the Tank Engine & Friends: Thomas Gets Tricked & Other Stories

Thomas the Tank Engine & Friends: Trust Thomas & Other Stories

Tickle Tune Typhoon: Let's Be Friends

"You Can" Video Series: You Can Ride a Horse

"You Can" Video Series: You Can Fly a Kite

You Can Choose!: Volume 1. Cooperation

You Can Choose!: Volume 2. Being Responsible

You Can Choose!: Volume 3. Dealing with Feelings

You Can Choose!: Volume 4. Saying No

You Can Choose!: Volume 5. Doing the Right Thing

You Can Choose!: Volume 6. Dealing with Disappointment

You Can Choose!: Volume 7. Appreciating Yourself

You Can Choose!: Volume 8. Asking for Help

You Can Choose!: Volume 9. Being Friends

You Can Choose!: Volume 10. Resolving Conflicts

Zoobilee Zoo

Zoobilee Zoo: Blue Ribbon Zooble and Other Stories

Zoobilee Zoo: Lady Whazzat and Other Stories

Zoobilee Zoo: Laughland and Other Stories

Zoobilee Zoo: Zoobadoobas and Other Stories

Zoobilee Zoo: Zooble Hop and Other Stories

Westerns

Annie Oakley (Rabbit Ears)

Pecos Bill (Rabbit Ears)

Tall Tales: Darlin' Clementine

Women's History (SEE ALSO Girls)

Alice Walker (1944-Present) — Author

American Women of Achievement Video Collection

American Women of Achievement: Abigail Adams (1744-1818) — Women's Rights Advocate

American Women of Achievement: Jane Addams (1860-1935) — Social Worker

American Women of Achievement: Marian Anderson (1902-1993) — Singer

American Women of Achievement: Susan B. Anthony (1820-1906) — Woman Suffragist

American Women of Achievement: Clara Barton (1821-1912) — Founder, American Red Cross

American Women of Achievement: Emily Dickinson (1830-1890) — Poet

American Women of Achievement: Amelia Earhart (1897-Disappeared in 1937) — Aviator

American Women of Achievement: Helen Keller (1880-1968) — Humanitarian

American Women of Achievement: Sandra Day O'Connor (1930-Present) — Supreme Court Justice

American Women of Achievement: Wilma Rudolph (1940-Present) — Champion Athlete

Annie Oakley (Rabbit Ears)

Harriet Tubman (1820-1913) — Anti-Slavery Activist

Joan Baez (1941-Present) — Mexican American Folksinger: English

Joan Baez (1941-Present) — Mexican American Folksinger: Spanish

Madame C.J. Walker (1867-1919) — Entrepreneur

Mary McLeod Bethune (1875-1955) — Educator

Mary Poppins

Sojourner Truth (1797-1883) — Abolitionist Leader

Song of Sacajawea (Rabbit Ears)

Woman's Place, A

WonderWorks Video Series

And the Children Shall Lead

Boy Who Loved Trolls, The

Gryphon

Hoboken Chicken Emergency

Jacob Have I Loved (Bridget Fonda))

Lion, the Witch, and the Wardrobe, The (Live Action)

Maricela

Mighty Pawns, The

My Friend Walter

Sweet 15

Walking on Air

You Must Remember This

Workout Videos

Hip Hop Animal Rock Workout

Workout with Daddy & Me

Workout with Mommy & Me

Yom Ha'atz Ma'ot

Lovely Butterfly — Pepar Nechmad: Flowers for the Independence Day

Yom Kippur

Holidays for Children: Rosh Hashanah Yom Kippur

Lovely Butterfly — Pepar Nechmad: Tishrei Month Holidays (Rosh Hashana and Sukkot)

Author Index

Adler, David A.

   Picture Book of Martin Luther King, Jr., A

Ahlberg, Janet and Allan

   Max's Chocolate Chicken and Other Stories for Young Children (Each Peach\Plum)

Albert, Richard E.

   Alejandro's Gift

Andersen, Hans Christian

   Emperor and Nightingale (Rabbit Ears)

   Red Shoes, The (Animation)

Awdry, Rev. W.

   Thomas the Tank Engine & Friends: Better Late Than Never and Other Stories

   Thomas the Tank Engine & Friends: Christmas Party

   Thomas the Tank Engine & Friends: James Learns a Lesson & Other Stories

   Thomas the Tank Engine & Friends: Percy's Ghostly & Other Stories

   Thomas the Tank Engine & Friends: Tenders & Turntables & Other Stories

   Thomas the Tank Engine & Friends: Thomas Breaks the Rules & Other Stories

   Thomas the Tank Engine & Friends: Thomas Gets Bumped

   Thomas the Tank Engine & Friends: Thomas Gets Tricked & Other Stories

   Thomas the Tank Engine & Friends: Trust Thomas & Other Stories

Barrett, Judy

   Cloudy with a Chance of Meatballs

Baxter, Charles

   Gryphon

Baylor, Byrd

   Hawk, I'm Your Brother

   Way to Start a Day, The

Bemelmans, Ludwig

   Madeline

   Madeline (Christopher Plummer)

   Madeline and the Dog Show

   Madeline and the Easter Bonnet

   Madeline and the Toy Factory

   Madeline at Cooking School

   Madeline in London

   Madeline's Christmas

   Madeline's Rescue and Other Stories About Madeline

Berenstain, Jan and Stan

   Berenstain Bears Christmas Tree

   Berenstain Bears in the Dark

   Berenstain Bears Easter Surprise

   Berenstain Bears Learn About Strangers

   Berenstain Bears and the Messy Room

   Berenstain Bears: No Girls Allowed and The Missing Dinosaur Bone

   Berenstain Bears and Too Much Birthday and to the Rescue

   Berenstain Bears and the Trouble with Friends

   Berenstain Bears and the Truth

   Berenstain Bears Get in a Fight

Berken, Joanne

   Anna Maria's Blanket

Berry, Joy

   Human Race Club: A Story About Fights between Brothers and Sisters

   Human Race Club: A Story About Making Friends, A Story About Prejudice and Discrimination

   Human Race Club: A Story About Self-Esteem

Blake, Quentin

   Doctor De Soto and Other Stories (Patrick)

   Story of the Dancing Frog

Bradbury, Ray

   Walking on Air

Breathed, Berkeley

   Opus n' Bill: A Wish for Wings That Work

Brett, Jan

   Wild Christmas Reindeer, The

Briggs, Raymond

   Snowman, The

Burnett, Frances Hodgson

   Secret Garden, The (Agnieszka Holland)

   Secret Garden, The (BBC)

   Secret Garden, The (MGM)

Burningham, John

   Granpa

Casteneda, Omar S.

   Abuela's Weave

Chorao, Kay

   Baby's Nursery Rhymes

Cleary, Beverly

   Mouse and the Motorcycle, The

   Ramona: Goodbye, Hello

   Ramona: Great Hair Argument

   Ramona: New Pajamas

   Ramona: The Patient

   Ramona: Perfect Day and Bad Day

   Ramona: Rainy Sunday

   Ramona: Ramona's Bad Day

   Ramona: Siblingitis

   Ramona: Squeakerfoot and Goodbye, Hello

   Runaway Ralph

Cohen, Miriam

   First and Second Grade Feelings: Jim's Dog, Muffins

First and Second Grade Feelings: The Real-Skin Rubber Monster Mask

First and Second Grade Feelings: See You in Second Grade!

First and Second Grade Feelings: So What?

Collodi, Carlo

Pinocchio (Rabbit Ears)

Cummings, Pat

Clean Your Room, Harvey Moon!

Dayrell, Elphinstone

Why the Sun and the Moon Live in the Sky

De Paola, Tomie

Foolish Frog and Other Stories (Strega Nonna)

Shelley Duvall's Bedtime Stories: Elizabeth and Larry / Bill and Pete

Demi

Empty Pot, The

Dobrin, Arnold

Josephine's Imagination

Eastman, P.D.

Are You My Mother?

Eres Tu Mi Mama?

Emberly, Barbara & Ed

Five Stories for the Very Young (Drummer Hoff)

Freeman, Don

Beady Bear

Mop Top

Norman the Doorman and Other Stories

Rainbow of My Own, A

Giff, Patricia Reilly

Today Was a Terrible Day

Guiberson, Brenda Z.

Spoonbill Swamp

Hadithi, Mwenye

Owl Moon and Other Stories (Hot Hippo)

Haley, Gail

Strega Nonna and Other Stories (A Story—A Story)

Hill, Eric

Spot Goes to School

Where's Spot

Hru, Dakari

Joshua's Masai Mask

Hutchins, Pat

Five Stories for the Very Young (Changes)

Johnson, Crockett

Five Stories for the Very Young (Harold's Fairy Tale)

Harold and the Purple Crayon

Keats, Ezra Jack

Ezra Jack Keats Library

Five Stories for the Very Young (Whistle for Willie)

Kent, Jack

Owl Moon and Other Stories (The Caterpillar and the Polliwog)

Kimmel, Eric A.

Anansi Goes Fishing

Kindersley, Dorling

See How They Grow: Farm Animals

See How They Grow: Insects and Spiders

See How They Grow: Pets

See How They Grow: Wild Animals

Konigsburg, E.L.

Hideaways, The

Kudrna, C. Imbior

To Bathe a Boa

Lewis, C.S.

Lion, the Witch, and the Wardrobe, The (Animated)

Lion, the Witch, and the Wardrobe, The (live action)

Lionni, Leo

Five Lionni Classics

Lobel, Arnold

Frog and Toad Are Friends

Frog and Toad Together

Locker, Thomas

Family Farm

Martin, Jr., Bill and John Archambault

Knots on a Counting Rope

Mayer, Mercer

Just Grandma and Me

Just Me and My Dad

McCloskey, Robert

Norman the Doorman and Other Stories (Lentil)

Owl Moon and Other Stories (Time of Wonder)

Robert McCloskey Library

McCully, Emily Arnold

Max's Chocolate Chicken and Other Stories for Young Children (Picnic)

McLerran, Alice

Roxaboxen

Medearis, Angela Shelf

Dancing with the Indians

Milne, A.A.

Winnie the Pooh

Winnie the Pooh and a Day for Eeyore

Winnie the Pooh and the Blustery Day

Winnie the Pooh and the Honey Tree

Winnie the Pooh and Tigger Too

Winnie the Pooh: Making Friends, Learning

Winnie the Pooh / The New Adventures: Volume 1. The Great Honey Pot Robbery

Winnie the Pooh / The New Adventures: Volume 2. The Wishing Bear

Winnie the Pooh / The New Adventures: Volume 3. Newfound Friends

Montgomery, L.M.

Anne of Green Gables

Mosel, Arlene

Strega Nonna and Other Stories (Tikki Tikki Tembo)

Munsch, Robert

Angela's Airplane (plus The Fire Station)

50 Below Zero (plus Thomas' Snowsuit)

Moira's Birthday (plus Blackberry Subway Jam)

Murmel, Murmel, Murmel (plus The Boy in the Drawer)

Pigs (plus David's Father)

Something Good (plus Mortimer)

Muzik, Katy

   At Home in the Coral Reef (English Version)

   At Home in the Coral Reef (Spanish Version)

Paterson, Katherine

   Jacob Have I Loved (Bridget Fonda)

   Jacob Have I Loved (Amanda Plummer)

Petersham, Maud and Minska

   Max's Chocolate Chicken and Other Stories for Young Children (The Circus Baby)

Pinkwater, D. Manus

   Hoboken Chicken Emergency

Polacco, Patricia

   Chicken Sunday

   Thunder Cake

Porter, Eleanor

   Pollyanna (BBC)

Rey, Margaret and H.A.

   Curious George

   Curious George: Fun in the Sun

   Curious George Goes to Town

   Doctor De Soto and Other Stories (Curious George Rides a Bike)

Robertus, Polly M.

   Dog Who Had Kittens, The

Rubin, Mark

   Little Lou and His Strange Little Zoo

Sadler, Marilyn

   Shelley Duvall's Bedtime Stories: Elizabeth and Larry / Bill and Pete

Scarry, Richard

   Get Ready for School

   Richard Scarry's Best Busy People VideoRichard Scarry's Best Counting Video

   Richard Scarry's Best Ever ABC Video

   Richard Scarry's Best Learning Songs Ever

Seeger, Pete & Charles

   Foolish Frog and Other Stories

Sendak, Maurice

   Maurice Sendak Library, The

Seuss, Dr.

   Daisy-Head Mayzie

   Dr. Seuss Video Festival

   Dr. Seuss: The Butter Battle Book

   Dr. Seuss: The Cat in the Hat Comes Back

   Dr. Seuss: Green Eggs and Ham

   Dr. Seuss: Hoober-Bloob Highway

   Dr. Seuss: Hop on Pop

   Dr. Seuss: Horton Hatches the Egg

   Dr. Seuss: Horton Hears a Who

   Dr. Seuss: How the Grinch Stole Christmas

   Dr. Seuss: I Am NOT Going to Get Up Today!

   Dr. Seuss: The Lorax

   Dr. Seuss: One Fish Two Fish Red Fish Blue Fish (English Version)

   Dr. Seuss: One Fish Two Fish Red Fish Blue Fish (Spanish Version, Un Pez Dos Peces Pez Rojo Pez Azul)

   Dr. Seuss: Pontoffel Pock

   Dr. Seuss' ABC

   Dr. Seuss' Cat in the Hat

   Dr. Seuss' Sleep Book

Sharmat, Marjorie

   I'm Not Oscar's Friend Anymore and Other Stories

Shook, Barbara

   Mommy's Office

Slobodkina, Esphyr

   Five Stories for the Very Young (Caps for Sale)

Souci, Robert San

   Talking Eggs, The

Steig, William

   Amazing Bone and Other Stories, The

   Doctor De Soto and Other Stories

   Norman the Doorman and Other Stories (Brave Irene)

Stevenson, James

   New Friends and Other Stories

Streatfield, Noel

   Ballet Shoes

Stren, Patti

   I'm Not Oscar's Friend Anymore and Other Stories (Hug Me)

Taylor, M. W.

   Harriet Tubman (1820-1913) — Anti-Slavery Activist

Thomas, Dylan

   Child's Christmas in Wales, A

Travers-Moore, John and Margaret

   Pepito's Dream

Ungerer, Tomi

   Doctor De Soto and Other Stories (The Hat)

Van Allsburg, Chris

   Fun in a Box Volume 1: Ben's Dream

   Jumanji

Viorst, Judith

   Alexander and the Terrible, Horrible, No Good, Very Bad Day

Waber, Bernard

   Ira Sleeps Over

   Ira Says Goodbye

Ward, Lorraine

   A Walk in the Wild

Wells, Rosemary

   Max's Chocolate Chicken and Other Stories for Young Children

Wheatcroft, John

   Boy Who Loved Trolls, The

Williams, Margery

   Velveteen Rabbit (Christopher Plummer)

   Velveteen Rabbit (Rabbit Ears)

Williams, Vera B.

   Cherries and Cherry Pits

Wiseman, Bernard

   Morris the Moose: Goes to School / Gets a Cold

Yolen, Jane

   Owl Moon and Other Stories

Author Index   229

Resources

ABC Studios
Dan DiDio, Director of Children's
Programming
2040 Avenue of the Stars
Century City, CA 90067
310-557-7777
Call to make suggestions, lodge complaints or find out about children's programming.

American Academy of Pediatrics
Michael Copeland, Dir. of Public
Relations
141 Northwest Point Rd.
Elk Grove Village, IL 60007
708-228-5005
Call for their task force statement, and other recommendations concerning children's media.

American Center for Children's TV-
The Ollie Awards
David Kleeman, Director
1400 E. Touhy, Ste. 260
Des Plaines, IL 60018
708-390-8700
Annually awards the "Ollie's" to recognize the best in children's television programming; offers workshops and seminars on approaches for improving children's television.

American Federation of Television
and Radio Artists
National Women's Division
260 Madison Ave.
New York, NY 10016
212-532-0800
The Women's Division of this organization of professionals is concerned with improving the image of women in the media.

American Women in Radio and
Television
1101 Connecticut Ave. NW, Ste. 700
Washington, DC 20036
202-429-5102
Call for listings of resources and publications on women in media.

Annenberg School of
Communication
Attn: Robert Hornick, Associate
Professor
University of Pennsylvania
3620 Walnut St.
Philadelphia, PA 19104-6220
215- 898-7041
Good resource for academic studies on the impact of media on children.

Better Viewing Magazine
CCI/Crosby Publishing
238 Broadway, Bldg. 2
Cambridge, MA 01239
617-497-8991
Quarterly magazine with articles to help parents and children develop positive viewing habits and creative activities from television viewing.

Booklist
American Library Association
50 E. Huron
Chicago, IL 60611
800-545-2433
A good source of children's video reviews.

Cable in the Classroom
86 Elm St.
Peterborough, NH 03458
800-216-2225
Magazine for teachers and librarians to assist them in incorporating television into the learning process.

CBS Studios
Carolyn Ceslik, Director of
  Children's Programming
51 W. 52nd St., 33rd Floor
New York, NY 10019
212-975-4321
Call to make suggestions, lodge complaints or find out about children's programming.

**Center for Early Education and
  Development**
University of Minnesota
51 East River Rd.
Minneapolis, MN 55455
612-624-3567
Call or write for information about the impact of television viewing on children.

Center for Media Education
1511 K St. NW, Ste. 518
Washington, DC 20005
202-628-2620
Works with consumer groups and nonprofit organizations to improve children's television. Community Action Kit Available, together with other publications.

Center for Media Literacy and
Connect Magazine
1962 S. Shenandoah Street
Los Angeles, CA 90034
310-559-2944
Offers useful information, media literacy workshops, a hot-line and learning tools based on media literacy research. Members also receive *Connect Magazine* which includes viewing tips and articles on a wide range of child-focused media issues.

**Challenging Media Images of
  Women**
P.O. Box 902
Framingham, MA 01701
508-879-8504
An organization which critiques sexism in media and which promotes women's rights. They publish a quarterly newsletter.

**Children's Television Resource and
  Education Center**
340 Townsend St., Ste. 423
San Francisco, CA 94107
415-243-9943
Helps parents, teachers and other professionals work with issues related to children and television through services and products which promote children's social development and academic success.

Childrens' Video Report
370 Court St. #76
Brooklyn, NY 11231
718-935-0600
Reviews new children's video releases and provides articles on children's media issues.

Children's Video Review Newsletter
16765 Lena Court
Grass Valley, CA 95949-9979
916-273-7471
A good source of children's video reviews.

Citizens for Media Literacy
34 Wall St., Ste. 407
Asheville, NC 28801
704-255-0182
Helps parents, teachers and concerned citizens deal with children's issues, First Amendment rights and public access to media.

**Coalition for Quality Children's
  Video**
535 Cordova Rd., Ste. 456
Santa Fe, NM 87501
505-989-8076
The Coalition evaluates and endorses the *KIDS FIRST* program which identifies quality children's videos and CD-ROM programs.

Corporation for Public
  Broadcasting
Attn: Mary Sceiford, Dir. of
  Children's Programming
901 E St. NW
Washington, DC 20004-2037
202-879-9739/202-879-9738
Call to make suggestions, lodge com-
plaints or find out about children's pro-
gramming.

ERIC/Data Clearinghouse On
  Elementary and Early Childhood
  Education
University of Illinois
College of Education
805 W. Pennsylvania Ave.
Urbana, IL 61801-4897
1-800-583-4135
Call or write for information about the
national network of parents and teachers concerned with the impact of television viewing on children. Ask for a copy
of their "Guidelines for Family
Television Viewing," an ERIC document
published in 1990.

Facets Multimedia, Inc.
Chicago International Children's
  Film Festival
1517 W. Fullerton Ave.
Chicago, IL 60614
312-281-9075
312-929-5437/fax
Operates the largest international kids
film festival in the U.S., and offers year-
round media arts programs for children.

Family Communications, Inc.
(*Mr. Rogers Neighborhood*)
Attn: Toni Bednar, Dir. of Marketing
  Services
4802 Fifth Ave.
Pittsburgh, PA 15213
412-687-2990
Questions for Mr. Rogers? Call Family
Communications, Inc.

Girls Inc.
30 E. 33rd
New York, NY 10016
212-683-1253
The organization implements programs
to help girls overcome gender discrimination. They publish a quarterly
newsletter.

International Women's Media
  Project
2033 M St. NW, Ste. 900
Washington, DC 20036
202-233-0030
Promotes cross-cultural exchange among
women working in media. They publish
a quarterly newsletter.

KIDSNET
6856 Eastern Ave. NW, Ste. 208
Washington, DC 20012
202-291-1400
A non-profit resource service offering
information on children's programming
in all media, including print, television
and radio. Publishes the KIDSNET
monthly guide to children's programming in all media.

KQED Center for Education &
  Lifelong Learning
Milton Chen, Ph.D., Director
2601 Mariposa Street
San Francisco, CA 94110
415-553-2139
415-553-2380/fax
Media workshops, seminars and
resource materials for parents, teachers
and children.

Mediawatch
P.O. Box 618
Santa Cruz, CA 95061
408-423-6355
Newsletter concerned with improving
the image of women in media.

Media Literacy On-Line Project
University of Oregon
http://interact.uoregon.edu/MediaLit
  /HomePage
This Internet resource seeks to network
information on the national media
literacy movement.

National Council for Families and
  Television
10900 Wilshire Blvd., Ste. 700
Los Angeles, CA 90024
310-443-2022
310-208-5984
An education-focused organization,
which brings together television's creative community with other groups
interested in family life.

National Foundation for the
  Improvement of Education
Resource Center on Sex Roles in
  Education
1201 16th St. NW
Washington, DC 20036
Write for available information on gen-
der equity in education.

National Parent Teacher
  Association (PTA)
700 N. Rush St.
Chicago, IL 60611-2571
312-787-0977
Extensive resources on the appropriate
use of television in the home and school.

National Telemedia Council
120 East Wilson St.
Madison, WI 53703
608-257-7712
NTC promotes media literacy and criti-
cal television viewing skills for children
and youth.

NBC Studios
Attn: Linda Mancuso, Dir. of
  Children's Programming
3000 West Alameda Ave.
Burbank, CA 91523
818-840-4444
Call to make suggestions, lodge complaints or find out about children's programming.

Parent's Choice and
Look to Learn Newsletter
Box 185
Newton, MA 02168
617-965-5913
The Parent's Choice Foundation evaluates and presents awards for quality
videos. The newsletter reviews videos,
video games, television and other media.

Strategies for Media Literacy
1095 Market St., Ste. 617
San Francisco, CA 94103
415-621-2911
Develops and publishes educational
materials, identifies resources and conducts workshops primarily for teachers
but also for parents and community
groups.

University of Illinois at Chicago
Attn: Roxwell Huesmann, PhD,
  Leonard Eron, PhD.
727 South Morgan Ave.
Chicago, IL 60607
312-413-2622
Call for information about extensive
studies on the impact of television violence on children.

Video Librarian
P.O. Box 2725
Bremerton, WA 98310
A good source of children's video
reviews.

Video Rating Guide for Libraries
ABC-CLIO
130 Cremona Dr., Box 1911
Santa Barbara, CA 93117-3075
805-968-1911
A good source of children's video
reviews.

Women's Action Alliance, Inc.
Library and Information Services
370 Lexington Ave.
New York, NY 10017
This national organization promotes
equality for women and provides educational information on women's issues.

Yale University Family TV Research
  and Consultation Center
Psychology Dept., Yale University
P.O. Box 208205
New Haven, CT 06520-8205
203-432-4565
Conducts research on the effects of television on children; offers some publications and resource materials for parents.